Carl Dolmetsch
and the 20th-Century
Recorder Repertoire

To Anne, Elizabeth and Thomas

In memory of Carl Dolmetsch

Carl Dolmetsch and the 20th-Century Recorder Repertoire

ANDREW MAYES

Peacock Press

© Andrew Mayes 2011

All rights reserved. No part of this publication may be reproduced, stored in a retrieval system, or transmitted in any form or by any means electronic, mechanical, photocopying, recording or otherwise without the prior permission of the publisher.

Andrew Mayes has asserted his right under the Copright, Designs and Patents Act, 1988, to be indentified as Author of this Work.

ISBN 978-1-904846-71-0

Published in 2011 by
Peacock Press
Scout Bottom Farm
Mytholmroyd
Hebden Bridge HX7 5JS (UK)

Web site www.recordermail.co.uk

Contents

List of Music Examples	*vi*
List of Illustrations	*x*
Foreword	*xi*
Preface	*xiii*
Acknowledgements	*xvii*
Citations from Letters	*xx*
Abbreviations	*xxi*
Introduction	*xxiii*
Preface to the re-printed edition	*xxvii*
1 Early developments	1
2 Manuel Jacobs and the 'ten' composers	5
3 The 'Wigmore' works, 1939–89	19
4 Works not premiered at the Wigmore Hall	213
5 Works written for the Dolmetsch children	265
6 Unfulfilled invitations	277
7 Idiomatic and technical considerations	285
8 Harpsichord or piano(?)	291
9 Performance – questions of 'authenticity'	299
10 Past, present and future	307
Bibliography	*315*
List of Musical Works	*317*
Selected Discography	*323*
Index	*327*

List of Music Examples

3.1 Lennox Berkeley, Sonatina for treble recorder and piano. First movement; last five bars as they appear in an MS recorder part in the Dolmetsch archive. Reproduced by permission of Schott & Co. Ltd.   30

3.2 Lennox Berkeley, Sonatina for treble recorder and piano. Third movement, two bars before figure 22 as they appear in an MS recorder part in the Dolmetsch archive. Reproduced by permission of Schott & Co. Ltd.   30

3.3 Lennox Berkeley, Sonatina for treble recorder and piano. Third movement, two bars before figure 22 as they appear in the recorder part of the published edition. Reproduced by permission of Schott & Co. Ltd.   30

3.4 York Bowen, Sonatina for recorder and piano. Third movement, last two bars of the recorder part as they appear in the MS score. Reproduced by permission of Emerson Edition Ltd.   35

3.5 York Bowen, Sonatina for recorder and piano. Third movement, alternative ending provided in the MS recorder part. Reproduced by permission of Emerson Edition Ltd.   35

3.6 Gordon Jacob, Suite for treble recorder and strings. Second movement, recorder part seven bars after A: comparison of MS and published versions. © Oxford University Press 1959. Extract reproduced by permission.   63

3.7 Gordon Jacob, Suite for treble recorder and strings. Second movement, recorder part 15 bars after B: comparison of MS and published versions. © Oxford University Press 1959. Extract reproduced by permission.   63

3.8 Gordon Jacob, Suite for treble recorder and strings. Second movement, recorder part 19 bars after B: comparison of MS and published versions. © Oxford University Press 1959. Extract reproduced by permission.   63

3.9 Gordon Jacob, Suite for treble recorder and strings. Last movement, recorder part 15 bars before end: comparison of MS and published versions. © Oxford University Press 1959. Extract reproduced by permission.   64

List of Music Examples

3.10 Robert Simpson, Variations and Fugue. The theme shared between violin I and viola. Reproduced by permission of Angela Simpson. ... 66

3.11 Robert Simpson, Variations and Fugue. Fugue, bars 1–10. Reproduced by permission of Angela Simpson. ... 67

3.12 Robert Simpson, Variations and Fugue. Coda, final 13 bars. Reproduced by permission of Angela Simpson. ... 67

3.13 Arnold Cooke, Divertimento for treble recorder and string quartet. First movement, bars 1–6. Reproduced by permission of Julia Earnshaw. ... 72

3.14 Arnold Cooke, Divertimento for treble recorder and string quartet. Second movement, bars 1–5. Reproduced by permission of Julia Earnshaw. ... 73

3.15 Arnold Cooke, Divertimento for treble recorder and string quartet. Third movement, bars 1–12. Reproduced by permission of Julia Earnshaw. ... 74

3.16 Arnold Cooke, Divertimento for treble recorder and string quartet. First movement, notes for cadenza written in pencil in Dolmetsch's hand in the MS recorder part. ... 74

3.17 Arnold Cooke, Quartet for treble recorder, violin, cello and harpsichord. First movement, recorder part at figure 4. Reproduced by permission of Schott & Co. Ltd ... 93

3.18 Arnold Cooke, *Little Suite* No. 1 for treble recorder solo. First movement, bars 27–31. Reproduced from Pieces for Solo Recorder, 1, by permission of Forsyth Brothers Ltd. ... 93

3.19 Richard Arnell, Quintet (The Gambian), Prelude, bars 1–9. Reproduced by permission of the composer. ... 102

3.20 Arnold Cooke, Suite for three recorders with or without harpsichord. Last movement, final two bars as in the MS score of the trio version. Reproduced by permission of Moeck Verlag. ... 131

3.21 Arnold Cooke, Suite for three recorders with or without harpsichord. Last movement, final two bars as in the MS score of the version with harpsichord. Reproduced by permission of Moeck Verlag. ... 131

3.22 Arnold Cooke, Suite for three recorders with or without harpsichord. Last movement, final two bars as in the published score. Reproduced by permission of Moeck Verlag. ... 132

3.23 Gordon Jacob, *A Consort of Recorders*. Second movement, Nocturne, bars 1–4. Reproduced by permission of Emerson Edition Ltd. ... 136

3.24 *Sobre Baza estaba el Rey* (Romance), Anon. ... 140

3.25 *Tristeza, quien a mi vos dió* (Villancico), Antonio. ... 141

3.26 *Aquel caballero, madre* (Villancico), Anon. ... 141

3.27 Alan Ridout, *Sequence*, for recorder and lute. Movement 7, final eight bars. Reproduced by permission of Ampleforth Abbey Trustees. ... 155

3.28 Edmund Rubbra, *Fantasia on a Chord*, bars 1–6 of the composer's

	original version. By permission of Alfred Lengnick & Co. (a division of Complete Music Ltd). Published version available from William Elkin Music Services.	168
3.29	Edmund Rubbra, *Fantasia on a Chord*. Harpsichord part, bar 32 of the original version.	168
3.30	Alan Ridout, Chamber Concerto for recorder and string quartet. First movement, bars 1–4. Reproduced by permission of Ampleforth Abbey Trustees.	175
3.31	Alan Ridout, Chamber Concerto for recorder and string quartet. Third movement, bars 1–7. Reproduced by permission of Ampleforth Abbey Trustees.	176
3.32	Alan Ridout, Chamber Concerto for recorder and string quartet. Fourth movement, bars 1–6. Reproduced by permission of Ampleforth Abbey Trustees.	176
3.33	Michael Short, *Sinfonia* for treble recorder, harpsichord and string quartet. First movement, bars 1–8. Reproduced by permission of the composer.	191
3.34	Michael Short, *Sinfonia* for treble recorder, harpsichord and string quartet. First movement, bars 21–29. Reproduced by permission of the composer.	192–93
3.35	Arnold Cooke, Divertimento for descant and treble recorders, violin, cello and harpsichord. Three of the tone rows noted by Jeanne Dolmetsch in her MS recorder part.	197
3.36	Arnold Cooke, Divertimento for descant and treble recorders, violin, cello and harpsichord. First movement, bars 19–22 of the score. Reproduced by permission of Julia Earnshaw.	198
3.37	Arnold Cooke, Divertimento for descant and treble recorders, violin, cello and harpsichord. First movement, descant and treble recorder parts, bars 68–70. Reproduced by permission of Julia Earnshaw.	198
3.38	Arnold Cooke, Divertimento for descant and treble recorders, violin, cello and harpsichord. Third movement, violin part, bars 9–12. Reproduced by permission of Julia Earnshaw.	199
3.39	Arnold Cooke, Divertimento for descant and treble recorders, violin, cello and harpsichord. Fourth movement, bars 1–4 of the score. Reproduced by permission of Julia Earnshaw.	199
3.40	Lionel Salter, Air and Dance for treble recorder and piano. Air, bars 3 and 7, showing rhythmic variants of the D–E–F motif.	201
3.41	Herbert Howells, 'Pipe Tune' as it appears in the manuscript of Alan Ridout's *Variants on a Tune of H.H.* Reproduced by permission of the Herbert Howells Estate.	210
3.42	Alan Ridout, *Variants on a Tune of H.H.* Variation III, bars 1–4. Reproduced by permission of Ampleforth Abbey Trustees.	212

List of Music Examples

4.1	Ivor Walsworth, Sonata for recorder and harpsichord. Recurring theme/motif.	225
5.1	Herbert Murrill, *Piece for my Friends* for two treble recorders and harpsichord. Bars 9–14, containing the composer's 'one good idea'. Reproduced by kind permission of Universal Edition (London) Ltd.	268
5.2	Opening of the Matins Response for the Feast of St Andrew (from the Wolfenbüttel manuscript).	269
7.1	G.P. Telemann, Sonata in F major from *Der getreue Musikmeister*. First movement, recorder part, bars 8 and 9.	286
7.2	G.P. Telemann, Sonata in F major from *Der getreue Musikmeister*. Third movement, recorder part, bars 1–6.	286
7.3	Arnold Cooke, Quartet for treble recorder, violin, cello and harpsichord. Third movement, recorder part, bars 1–4. Reproduced by permission of Schott & Co. Ltd.	287
9.1	Cadenza for the last movement of Walter Leigh's Sonatina for treble recorder and piano, written out by Carl Dolmetsch on a portion of MS paper and inserted into his copy of the recorder part.	305

List of Illustrations

1	Joseph Saxby and Carl Dolmetsch at about the time of the re-establishment of the Wigmore Hall recitals in the late 1940s.	21
2	Herbert Murrill c. 1950.	42
3	Eleonore and Alice Schoenfeld with Joseph Saxby and Carl Dolmetsch at a rehearsal in the 1960s.	91
4	Edmund Rubbra (centre) with Joseph Saxby, Alice and Eleonore Schoenfeld and Carl Dolmetsch.	96
5	Soprano Elizabeth Harwood, who, in addition to taking part in the premiere of Walter Bergmann's *Pastorella*, was the soprano soloist in the premiere of Lennox Berkeley's *Una and the Lion*.	129
6	Lutenist Robert Spencer. His enthusiasm for Ridout's music led directly to the commissioning of *Sequence*.	153
7	Harpsichordist Ruth Dyson, who wrote out Howells's 'Pipe Tune' from memory, enabling Alan Ridout to use it as the theme for his *Variants on a Tune of H.H.*	209
8	The manuscript of Joseph Saxby's *Improvisation*.	226
9	Richard, Jeanne, François and Marguerite Dolmetsch. A photograph of the family consort taken in the mid-1950s.	266
10	Carl Dolmetsch and Joseph Saxby in a discussion during rehearsal. (The echo key fitted to Dolmetsch's instrument is clearly visible.)	297
11	Recorders from the Dolmetsch workshop: tenor, treble, descant and sopranino.	300
12	One of Carl Dolmetsch's concert instruments, a treble recorder fitted with a bell key.	302

Foreword

The remarkable story of the recorder's twentieth-century renaissance is well known and documented, but until now, the equally important history of a particularly significant portion of its twentieth-century repertoire has remained largely untold. Here Andrew Mayes explores this subject in depth for the first time, bringing to light a wealth of fascinating detail and placing this outstanding corpus of compositions in its true historical perspective.

From the earliest years Carl Dolmetsch was intimately involved in the rebirth of the recorder as designer, craftsman and performer. It was these formative experiences which shaped his vision that the recorder should not only regain the dignity and status it had once enjoyed in the eighteenth century, but also become re-established in the twentieth century musical world, exploring new realms of technique, tonal quality and expression, so that it might never again become obsolete.

This vision was the motivating force that led him to give his first solo recorder recital at London's Wigmore Hall on 1 February 1939. The programme included the premiere of a new work for descant recorder and harpsichord, his own Theme and Variations, composed the previous year at a time when there was virtually no contemporary recorder music. The overwhelming success of this recital and the audience's obvious enjoyment of the modern work encouraged our father to give a second Wigmore Hall recital on 18 November of the same year. On this occasion he featured the recently composed Sonatina for recorder and keyboard by Lennox Berkeley. The 'blue touch paper' had now been lit and the modern school of recorder composition set on a course of unstoppable momentum. From 1939 until 1989, Carl Dolmetsch and Joseph Saxby (his musical partner for over 60 years), together with other distinguished musical colleagues, gave 45 concerts at the Wigmore Hall, the highlight of each concert being the first performance of a specially commissioned work by a modern composer. London audiences were treated to a veritable feast of fine compositions by leading British composers and even to some by composers from as far afield as France, the United States and Australia. A great diversity of style and instrumentation was displayed, with the recorder proving to be a most eloquent voice as it played on equal terms with harpsichord and piano, string quartet, voice, violin, cello, oboe, bassoon, lute and guitar. Carl Dolmetsch's vision had been fulfilled – in abundance.

The Dolmetsch archive in Haslemere contains approximately 90 modern works featuring the recorder and a wealth of correspondence (in excess of 500 letters from twentieth-century composers). Andrew Mayes's exhaustive research of these resources has illuminated both the music and the creative process. The letters reveal a human story of lifelong friendships, mutual respect, infectious enthusiasm, humility and even at times, self-doubt. We sense the mounting anticipation as the day of the concert draws near and share the joy and gratitude following a successful performance.

On a personal note, we, together with our brothers François and Richard, were privileged to meet many of these eminent composers and were often present at rehearsals, providing a captive audience as composer and musicians worked together to forge an interpretation and communicate a message. We watched and listened as chords were tuned, dynamics added, harpsichord registration fixed, pauses inserted, tempi adjusted, ornamentation suggested and text altered. Now, many years later, we fully appreciate our good fortune in receiving such a rare and invaluable musical education.

The Dolmetsch family is greatly indebted to Andrew Mayes for telling a unique musical story with rare clarity and understanding. Fitting tribute is paid to the artists and composers who created this important chapter in twentieth-century music. Their work will continue to be an inspirational and life-enhancing force for musicians and music lovers far into the future. What better way than this to achieve immortality?

Jeanne and Marguerite Dolmetsch

March 2002

Preface

The recorder's non-avant-garde twentieth-century repertoire has always fascinated me, but two events in particular were to have a profound effect on my growing interest in this music. The first was interviewing Piers Adams for *The Recorder Magazine* in 1994 (I had become editor of the magazine the previous year), at about the time his *Shine and Shade* CD was to be released. This included the well-known Sonatina by Sir Lennox Berkeley, the haunting *Meditazioni sopra 'Cœurs désolés'* by Edmund Rubbra and the less frequently played but exhilarating *Scottish Suite* by Norman Fulton. In addition to these works so closely associated with Carl Dolmetsch (the Rubbra and Fulton were dedicated to him and he had premiered all three), the disc contained two further works from the Dolmetsch canon, both at that time unpublished: York Bowen's lyrical and substantial Sonata and the idiosyncratic but charming *Rhapsody from Within* by Donald Swann.

I was fascinated that such pieces had hitherto remained unpublished and virtually unperformed and, although not aware at that time just how much music had been composed for Carl Dolmetsch, could not help wondering if further pieces remained similarly neglected. The extent of this became apparent at the second of the above-mentioned seminal events – a paper by Ross Winters entitled 'The Dolmetsch Legacy', given at the end of May 1997 at the Conference of the European Recorder Teachers' Association in the UK. In the course of his research Ross had contacted Carl Dolmetsch and been furnished with a list of all the works first performed by him at his annual recitals given in London's Wigmore Hall. This contained no fewer than 50 pieces and, although some of them are established in the repertoire in their published editions, there were a number that remained unpublished and hence virtually unknown. To this list Ross had added some other works from among those that, though dedicated to Carl Dolmetsch, had not received their premieres at the Wigmore Hall. Yet, as I was later to discover, even this did not give the full picture of just how much new music for recorder had come into existence as a result of his initiative and enthusiasm.

Quite naturally, in my capacity as editor of *The Recorder Magazine*, I approached Ross to enquire if he would be prepared to write something about his findings for a future edition. He noted that there was sufficient material on the subject not just to write an article but an entire book, at which I suggested that he should perhaps consider setting about such a task. Ross felt, however, this was not something he could undertake at that time. The more I thought about it, the more it became an obsession, perhaps even a conceit, that I should research and write such a book myself, and eventually I contacted not only Ross but also John Turner to seek their opinions and advice on my embarking on such a project. Encouragingly, they were both very positive about my proposal and with such support I wrote to Dr Brian Blood, the husband of Carl Dolmetsch's daughter Marguerite, to ask if I would be permitted to research and write a book on the recorder music written for Carl Dolmetsch (who was far from well by that time).

On the morning of Saturday 12 July 1997 I received a telephone call from Brian Blood with the sad news that Carl Dolmetsch had died on the previous day. However, it was encouraging to learn that the family welcomed my proposal to write a book. Quite naturally they required time and space in the months immediately following, and I busied myself with filling the gaps in my own music library by obtaining copies of as many of the published works as I could and making initial studies of them.

It was my hope that, in addition to manuscripts of both published and particularly unpublished works, correspondence between Carl Dolmetsch and the composers who had written works for him would also have survived. In telephone conversations with both Carl Dolmetsch's other twin daughter Jeanne and his widow Greta,[1] I was assured that many letters had indeed been preserved (Greta had been Dr Carl's secretary for many years and dealt with much of this correspondence), and as soon as these had been sorted would be made available to me. Eventually Jeanne contacted me again and invited me to visit 'Jesses' in Haslemere to make a first examination of the archive. This I did in June 1998.

Although I had hoped there would be a significant amount of correspondence in the archive, nothing could have prepared me for what it contained. In a huge pile of manila envelopes were almost 400 letters to and from many of the composers with whom Carl Dolmetsch had been associated. At a glance it was obvious just what unique and important information was contained in them, but my primary task on that occasion was to examine the music itself.

Yet even more surprises awaited me, and I was shown upstairs to the office with its lining of shelves that contained the printed editions and manuscripts of this remarkable collection of twentieth-century recorder music. 'This was Dr Carl's desk and this is where you must sit and do your work', I was told encouragingly. One could not be anything other than inspired, and there and then I made a start on examining the works for recorder and keyboard. There were published editions signed by the composers themselves, and some very important manuscripts. In particular I remember my feelings as I opened those of Edmund Rubbra's Sonatina and Gordon Jacob's Variations for recorder and harpsichord. Here were the very notes of these much loved pieces set down by the composers themselves in their own handwriting. Nothing brings you quite so close to the music as this! The hope that I would find manuscripts of some of the unpublished works among the

---

[1] Greta Matthews married Carl Dolmetsch only a few months before his death. She had been his secretary since the mid-1950s.

collection soon became a reality: I was able to locate manuscripts of pieces by Alan Ridout, Stephen Dodgson and Lionel Salter along with that of Donald Swann's *Rhapsody from Within*, all performed at the Wigmore Hall. In addition there were the manuscripts of other works all inviting inspection, even a short *Improvisation* for solo recorder by Joseph Saxby. Carefully I made notes of each item for future reference, but the time available did not permit me to inspect the works for recorder with strings; this would have to wait for another visit.

Over the ensuing weeks I was able to read through all the letters and, as I had hoped, these contained in many cases the complete history of a work from Carl Dolmetsch's initial invitation to the composer to the first performance and sometimes beyond. Certain aspects of some works were especially intriguing: York Bowen's concern regarding the pianistic character of the keyboard part of his Sonatina (the original scoring was to have been for harpsichord with recorder), the gradual development (from Carl Dolmetsch's own improvisation) of the little cadenza near the end of the second movement of Herbert Murrill's Sonata, how Rubbra's *Fantasia on a Theme of Machaut* was very nearly with string trio rather than quartet, or Gordon Jacob's delight and surprise at the success of his Suite for Recorder and Strings. What was most evident throughout were Carl Dolmetsch's commitment, enthusiasm and determination to enhance the contemporary recorder repertoire with good music. He was convinced that without this the recorder would be in serious danger of suffering the eventual neglect into which it had fallen towards the end of the eighteenth century.

During my next visit I was able to begin investigating the works for recorder and strings and these revealed yet more manuscript treasures: two divertimentos by Arnold Cooke, the manuscript parts of Robert Simpson's Variations and Fugue for recorder and string quartet and another suite by Gordon Jacob, this one entitled *Trifles* and scored for recorder, violin, cello and harpsichord.

'Jesses' is a house with a remarkable atmosphere, derived not only from the family that has lived within its walls for so many years but also, perhaps, from the many other personalities who have visited it. It has only gently given up its secrets and often the investigation of an unpromising pile of music eventually resulted in the discovery (usually at the very bottom) of what had been sought over a considerable period of time. The manuscripts of Walter Bergmann's *Pastorella* for soprano voice and sopranino recorder and Carl Dolmetsch's own Theme and Variations for descant recorder and harpsichord were particular examples.

In all, just over 90 works written for or first performed by Carl Dolmetsch and his musical colleagues have been identified, featuring many different musical forms and instrumentation. Some are already established in the repertoire, but many others are worthy of attention.

Throughout the research for and writing of this book I have received inspirational support from the Dolmetsch family, generous access to the archives and the kindest hospitality, especially from Greta, who has also been a mine of first-hand information. Her personal accounts of so many of Carl Dolmetsch's encounters with the composers who wrote music for him have proved invaluable.

The influence of much of this music has, I believe, yet to make itself entirely felt, and that is why a comprehensive catalogue and description of it is of considerable importance. Future generations of recorder players will, in addition, find the fascinating details of how and why it came to be written indispensable to their understanding and interpretation of the music, especially as we move gradually further away from the life and times of Carl Dolmetsch himself.

Andrew Mayes

Cheadle Hulme, June 2002

Acknowledgements

A great many people have provided assistance of all kinds with the writing of this book and my grateful thanks is accorded to them all.

Nothing would have been possible without the total support of the Dolmetsch family: Greta, Jeanne, Marguerite, François and Brian Blood. From the time I received permission to write the book I have been provided with generous access to the archives, unstinting help, encouragement, hospitality and friendship. I am also especially grateful to Jeanne and Marguerite for writing the Foreword.

Initial inspiration and encouragement was given by Ross Winters and John Turner. Their subsequent support, advice and assistance have been invaluable.

In particular I have very much appreciated the assistance of Edgar Hunt, Evelyn Nallen, David Gordon, Dr Colin Hand, Zana Clarke, Anselm Cramer OSB (Ampleforth Abbey), Peter Dickinson, Dr Jenny Doctor (the Britten-Pears Library) David Dorward, June Emerson, Lewis Foreman, Simon Fox Gál, Matthew Greenall (the British Music Information Centre), Madeline Hunter, John LeGrove, Judith LeGrove (the Britten-Pears Library), Arthur Loeb, Alec Loretto, Andrew Millinger (the Herbert Howells Society), Alistair Pettinger (the Scottish Music Information Centre), Andrew Pledge, Tony Scotland (the Lennox Berkeley Estate), Robert Scott, Colin Scott-Sutherland, Andrew Short (the Society of Recorder Players), John Tyson, Rodney Waterman and all who took time to answer my questions, were prepared to discuss the many aspects of this repertoire and provide information of any kind.

Additionally, I am grateful to Valerie Langfield for setting the music examples and for her advice and support, to Claire Leech for translation of the texts of correspondence in French and Spanish and to Christine Stanton, Susan Marshall and Brenda Buckley for their enthusiastic sharing in my exploration of the repertoire.

A book such as this contains much material that remains the copyright of the authors or their estates, and for kind permission to reproduce extracts from letters, programme notes, or other writings and examples from musical manuscripts I would like to express my thanks to the following, many of whom have also provided additional and valuable information: Piers Adams, Ampleforth Abbey Trustees, Richard Arnell, Erica Bendix, Leon Berger, Lady Berkeley and the Lennox Berkeley Estate, Michael Berkeley, Donald Bousted, Nigel Butterley, Nicolas Chagrin, Elizabeth Cooper, Nicole Crossley-Holland, Martin Dalby, Stephen Dodgson, François Dolmetsch, Greta Dolmetsch, Jeanne Dolmetsch,

Julia Earnshaw, Carolyn Evans, Eva Fox-Gál, Jacques Françaix, Helen Fricker, John Gardner, Colin Hand, Alun Hoddinott, Joseph Horovitz, the Herbert Howells Estate, Edgar Hunt, Margaret Hyatt, Geoffrey Jacobs, Joan Johnson, Malcolm Lipkin, Yvonne Mathias, Nicholas Maw, Wilfrid Mellers, Alison Melville, Anthony Payne, the Pitfield Trust, Ellen Powers, Margaret Reizenstein, Geoffrey Salter, Desmond Scott, Michael Short, Angela Simpson, the Donald Swann Estate, John Turner, Ross Winters, Jonathan Wordsworth, Adrian Yardley and the Estate of Edwin York Bowen.

The quotations from the letters of Benjamin Britten are © copyright the Trustees of the Britten-Pears Foundation and may not be further reproduced without the written permission of the Trustees. Quotations from the letters of Carl Dolmetsch to Benjamin Britten are reproduced courtesy of the Britten-Pears Library. The letters from Sir Arnold Bax are reproduced by courtesy of the Bax Estate. The programme note for William Mathias's Concertino Op. 65 is © copyright Yvonne Mathias and reproduced by permission of the Oxford University Press.

Permission to include reviews, extracts from articles and other material published in newspapers and journals, is acknowledged as follows: extracts from reviews published in *The Farnham Herald* and *The Haslemere Herald* are reproduced by permission of Farnham Castle Newspapers Limited; extracts from the review by Edward Greenfield published in *The Guardian*, 7 March 1974, © The Guardian; extracts from the article by Manuel Jacobs ('Terpander') and review by Edgar Hunt of Carl Dolmetsch's first Wigmore Hall recital are reproduced by permission of the *Musical Times*; extract from the review of Carl Dolmetsch's second Wigmore Hall recital published in *The Observer*, 19 November 1939, © The Observer; extracts from reviews and articles published in *The Recorder and Music Magazine, Recorder and Music Magazine, Recorder & Music Magazine, Recorder & Music* and *The Recorder Magazine* are reproduced by permission of Peacock Press; extracts of reviews in *Recorder News* are reproduced by permission of the Society of Recorder Players; the extract from the review of Nigel Butterley's *The White-Throated Warbler* published in *The Sydney Morning Herald* is reproduced with their kind permission; extracts from reviews published in *The Times* are © Times Newspapers Limited. The original publication dates are as indicated for each extract.

Musical text contained in letters from Herbert Murrill in connection with his Sonata for Recorder and Harpsichord are © Oxford University Press 1951 and reproduced by permission. All other musical examples from published editions are reproduced by permission of Emerson Edition Ltd, Forsyth Brothers Ltd, Moeck, Oxford University Press, Alfred Lengnick & Co. Ltd, Schott & Co. Ltd and Universal Edition (London) Ltd. Individual copyright details and acknowledgements are provided with each example.

The photograph of Herbert Murrill is reproduced by kind permission of Carolyn Evans. The remaining photographs are reproduced from the Dolmetsch collection.

Acknowledgements

Every effort has been made to trace copyright owners and obtain permission for the reproduction of unpublished written texts and examples from musical manuscripts. In a small number of cases this has not been possible. I apologize to any copyright holders it has not been possible to contact and make due acknowledgement here.

Andrew Mayes

Cheadle Hulme, June 2002

Citations from Letters

The vast majority of sources cited in this book are located in the house where Carl Dolmetsch lived, 'Jesses', Haslemere, UK. They consist of letters to Carl Dolmetsch and copies of letters sent by Dolmetsch. In the text, this collection is generally referred to as 'the archive' or 'the Dolmetsch archive'. Unless otherwise specified, all citations of letters are drawn from sources in this collection.

Abbreviations

arr	arrangement; arranged
b	bass
bn	bassoon
cl	clarinet
des	descant
fl	flute
gamba	viola da gamba
gui	guitar
hpd	harpsichord
inst	instrument
kbd	keyboard
mvt	movement
ob	oboe
orch	orchestra
org	organ
perc	percussion
pn	piano
rec	recorder
sax	saxophone
str qt	string quartet
t	tenor
tr	treble
va	viola
var	variation
vc	cello
vn	violin

Introduction

Of all the 'early' instruments that have enjoyed a revival in the twentieth century as part of the renewed interest in the recreation of the music of the past, none can have been more spectacular than that of the recorder.

Although many of the greatest composers of the seventeenth and eighteenth centuries wrote for the recorder, the gradual growth of the symphony orchestra was a major factor in its demise in the nineteenth century. The rediscovery in the early twentieth century of its playing technique, the process of its manufacture and its earlier repertoire are remarkable, and fortunately well documented.

One reason in particular for its popularity has been its increasingly widespread adoption as an instrument for the teaching of music in schools (much regretted by some in the recorder world). Literally millions of plastic recorders have been produced and have provided a first introduction to playing a musical instrument for countless children. For many people this remains their only experience of the recorder and of practical music making generally.

However, it has gradually but significantly developed both as a solo and consort instrument in its own right, and ever rising standards of performance and musical interpretation by succeeding generations of players have brought it to a more prominent, if specialised place in the world of music.

Unlike many of the other 'early' instruments that have continued to be used almost exclusively for the recreation of the music of the past, the recorder has acquired a comprehensive repertoire of contemporary music, and this too must be seen as an important factor in its twentieth-century renaissance.

This book is about a particular part of that contemporary repertoire, created largely as a result of the determination, enthusiasm and commitment of Carl Dolmetsch, who must be regarded as the first acknowledged virtuoso of the recorder in the twentieth century. His encouragement of eminent composers to write works for the instrument resulted in a series of first performances at his annual Wigmore Hall recitals that spanned a period of half a century, interrupted only by the war years and those immediately after. Most of these included his friend and musical colleague of more than 60 years, the harpsichordist Joseph Saxby. It is a collection of music that contains works in many forms and styles and which presents the recorder in a variety of instrumental ensembles. These compositions run like a thread through the years of the recorder's re-establishment, each first performance being an eagerly anticipated feature of Dolmetsch's Wigmore Hall recitals.

Many of the manuscripts of these works, or copies of them, remain in the Dolmetsch archives at 'Jesses', the family home in Haslemere. In the case of the works that remain unpublished this is indeed fortunate. It is also fortunate that much of the correspondence between Dolmetsch and the composers who wrote works for him has survived, and from this we can, in many cases, trace the creation of a work from its inception through to its first performance and, in some cases, beyond. Also extant are many of the composers' own programme notes, and in the press books in the archive it has also been possible to read the critics' reactions to the first performances of much of this new music. Each of the works premiered at the Wigmore Hall has, as a result of this information being available, been examined in detail.

There were also a significant number of works, both published and unpublished, written for Dolmetsch but not premiered at the Wigmore Hall. These also are examined, as are a handful of works composed for the Dolmetsch children, though of necessity in some cases, not at such length.

From the correspondence it has been possible to discover that a number of intended works did not, for one reason or another, come into being. It is tempting to speculate on what might have been, but it is also a salutary reminder that not only a composer's commitments could prevent them from being able to create a new piece but also fatigue or even disillusion.

To put the 'Dolmetsch' works in context, however, it has been necessary first to take another look at the early years of the recorder revival, to recognize how quickly the instrument became re-established in the world of early music and also to investigate the earliest attempts to compose new music for it. It would also be impossible to discuss the works instigated by Dolmetsch without examining the group of important new works composed in 1939 on the initiative of Manuel Jacobs, but with which Dolmetsch was practically connected through his premieres of four of them.

Having been composed over a period of 50 years during which not only the recorder but the also the harpsichord continued to develop, the works are examined from the players' points of view both in terms of idiomatic writing and technical considerations. The harpsichord/piano options for some of the earlier works are also considered. Because of these instrumental developments and gradual changes in playing style, the question of 'authenticity' when playing this repertoire is also discussed. Is it indeed a consideration?

With the rise of the recorder avant-garde in the 1960s and 1970s there was something of a reaction against the more traditional repertoire. In a world of changing musical taste much of it did not fare well and was for a while largely ignored by many players. However, a more recent rekindling of interest has become increasingly apparent and, to conclude, this and the future significance and influence of this repertoire are appraised and speculated upon.

Finally, it must be stressed that this is not a biography. I did not know Carl Dolmetsch well and it was only after becoming editor of *The Recorder Magazine* in 1993, and thus towards the end of his life, that I had contact with him. Many biographical details do, however, emerge, and we can, through the correspondence relating to the new works, learn something of the Dolmetsch year: the annual Wigmore Hall recital, the Haslemere Festival, summer schools, preparation for and embarkation on tours abroad, particularly to the United States, and many recital tours at home.

I feel that I have come to know Carl Dolmetsch more as I have investigated the music he commissioned, inspired or, in some cases, cajoled from its composers and as I have spoken with those who were close to him. But I have also learned so much more about the music itself. It remains a testament to Dolmetsch's commitment and enthusiasm, but above all his passion for the instrument that will always be associated with his name as long as it continues to be played. It would be encouraging to think that this music will also inspire future generations of recorder players. This would have meant so much to the man for whom it was composed and who was the first to performed it.

Preface to the re-printed edition

Since publication of Carl Dolmetsch and the Recorder Repertoire of the 20th Century by Ashgate Publishing in 2003 interest in the works composed for and first performed by Carl Dolmetsch has grown steadily. This and the approach of his centenary in 2011 make the present reprint very timely. The original text remains unaltered, but in providing a new preface the opportunity has been taken to extend this to cover three works not originally included, update the information on published works (a number have appeared in new editions since 2003) and update the discography. The release of new and especially premiere recordings of a number of works is indicative of the growing interest I very much hoped the original publication of the book would stimulate. It has been most rewarding to have been involved in a number of the recording projects in various ways.

During my original research, the access to Dolmetsch and Saxby's annotated performing material in the archive revealed another specific area ripe for study, and led to its detailed examination in a PhD thesis, *Aspects of performance practice in works for recorder composed for Carl Dolmetsch between 1939 and 1989*, submitted in October 2008. A copy is retained in the library of Birmingham Conservatoire, Paradise Place, Birmingham, B3 3HG, United Kingdom. In addition, anyone further interested is invited to contact the author whose email address is: andrew.mayes@tesco.net

In reprinting the book it has been necessary to provide it with a new ISBN number. To avoid any confusion that may have arisen as a result of two ISBN numbers for a book with the same title, the title of the reprint has been very slightly amended to *Carl Dolmetsch and the 20th-century Recorder Repertoire*.

I am very grateful to Peacock Press for undertaking this reprint and to Ashgate Publishing for their kind cooperation enabling the book to be available once more, especially to recorder players, but also to all those interested in this unique repertoire.

Andrew Mayes

Cheadle Hulme, November 2010

Works not included in the original edition

Christopher Wood, Fantasia, Les Oiseaux, Op.16

des rec, hpd and string octet (double quartet)

To Carl Dolmetsch and Joseph Saxby

Single movement in several sections played without a break: Andante misterioso - Poco Allegro ma con fuoco -Tempo Allegretto - Adagio maestoso - Andante.

First performance: date and location unknown

Unpublished

Knowledge of the existence of this work is as a result of the original manuscript score held in the Jerwood Library, Trinity College of Music, London (where it has the reference CW33 in the Christopher Wood collection) which was brought to my attention in November 2003. Because there was no copy of the score in the Dolmetsch archive (an authorised copy has since been placed there) nor any correspondence relating to the work it has not been possible to discover the circumstances under which it was composed, nor indeed if it received a performance. Its opus number, just two earlier than Wood's *Sonata di Camera* for treble recorder and harpsichord, places its date of composition in the late 1930s. This makes it all the more fascinating since it was not until the 1950s that Dolmetsch encouraged new works in which the recorder was included in a chamber music scoring (Rubbra's *Fantasia on a Theme of Machaut* Op. 86 composed in 1954 for treble recorder, string quartet and harpsichord, and Berkeley's *Concertino* Op. 49 composed in 1955 for treble recorder, violin, cello and harpsichord, were the first two such works performed at the Wigmore Hall).

The scoring with harpsichord and double string quartet is unique in the recorder repertoire, and it would appear to be the first in the 20th century specifically referring to the instrument's ancient association with birdsong both in its title and figuration. It is a single movement work in several clearly defined sections played without a break. Preparation of a performance would certainly be an interesting and worthwhile project.

Elizabeth Poston, Sugar Plums
(With no apologies to Peter Ilich Tchaikovsky)

rec consort (S'nino/SATB), pardessus de viole/treble viol, bass viol, perc, octavina/hpd, portative organ

Commissioned by Gerard Hoffnung for the Hoffnung Concert Repertory

1 Andante sostenuto (IV, 1). 2 Allegro con con fuoco (IV. 4). 3 Allegro molto vivace (vii. [sic] 3). Finale, 1812 Overture, Allegro Vivace.

First performance; The Royal Festival Hall (at the Hoffnung Interplanetary Music Festival), London, 21 November 1958. The Dolmetsch Consort: Carl Dolmetsch, s'nino/d/tr recs; Michael Walton, tr rec: Natalie Dolmetsch, t rec/bass viol; Layton Ring, bass rec; Cecile Dolmetsch, tr viol/pardessus de viole; James Blades, perc.; Joseph Saxby, octavina/hpd/tr rec/perc.; Elizabeth Poston, portative organ.

Unpublished at present, but publication by Campion Press (together with *Lude*) is planned for 2011.

Elizabeth Poston's idea of a piece founded on celebrated works by Tchaikovsky (his 4th and 6th symphonies as indicated by the figures in brackets after the movement tempo indications, and the 1812 Overture) but scored for 'early' instruments is a wonderfully whimsical conceit and typical of the inventive musical hilarity which characterised Gerard Hoffnung's festivals. Nevertheless, she made considerable effort to ensure the results were practical as well as entertaining, and in a letter to Dolmetsch dated 2 June [1958] she refers to arrangements for him and Joseph Saxby to visit her and demonstrate some of the instruments with which she was not familiar. In a second letter to Dolmetsch dated 9 June [1958] (the day after the visit) Elizabeth expressed her thanks for the 'practical enlightenment' for her 'comic Hoffnung task', commenting that it remained for her to 'weave the results into something suitably absurd!'

Examination of a Photostat copy of the score in the Dolmetsch archives reveals just how cleverly her task was achieved, but of necessity resorting to frequent doubling of instruments for the players. Though the first page of the score initially has staves for descant, treble, tenor and bass recorders, treble viol, percussion, octavina/harpsichord and portative organ, many changes are noted throughout. The octavina (or ottavina) is a small virginal tuned to 4-foot pitch, and as scored for in this work requires a compass of four octaves and one note (from C to d'''). The descant recorder player (Carl Dolmetsch) doubles on sopranino, and the beginning of the finale is indicated for sopranino and treble with the direction 'CD plays two recorders at once (rises)'. The treble recorder player doubles on descant, the tenor recorder player is required to double in places on bass viol, the treble viol player doubles on pardessus de viole, and the octavina/harpsichordist doubles briefly on treble recorder. Percussion includes un-snared drum, cymbal, tubular bells and there is a part for the canon, though a marking in another copy of the score identifies this for 'pop gun *ad lib*'. Further 'exotic' percussion is indicated at bar 74, where at the head of the score is the direction 'Morris Bells (on legs) Shake ... Pieds en l'air!'

The visual element of performance, enlivened by the almost frenetic changes of instruments, must indeed have been as extraordinary as the sound, culminating in actions for the keyboard player indicated by the following direction:

> The keyboard player stops playing & throws up his arms in despair, seizes the Octavina & puts it on top of the Harpsichord, and trying to play as many instruments as possible, takes up a beater & plays Drum and Tambourin beside him, with an occasional swipe at the Harpsichord/Octavina, sticks out his bottom, & ends by playing the Harpsichord with his nose.

The Tambourin is a string drum (rather like a small dulcimer) which was evidently played with the same beater used for the drum. It is mentioned in Elizabeth Poston's letter to Carl Dolmetsch of 2 June noted above, along with Rebec and Crwth, which did not find their way into the eventual scoring.

For the final two bars the score is marked 'Tutti ... joined by Orchestra on C', (the Hoffnung Symphony Orchestra conducted by Lawrence Leonard at the first performance) and thus the work is brought to a triumphantly eccentric conclusion. There was a second performance when the Hoffnung Interplanetary Music Festival was repeated on the following day, 22 November 1958, and two further performances were given on 2 February 1959.

Following Gerard Hoffnung's tragic death in September 1959 a commemorative festival was held in October 1960 at which *Sugar Plums* received another performance, and further revivals took place in 1969, 1971 and 1976. For a broadcast in 1976 the BBC commissioned another work on similar lines. The result was *Lude*, the title of which Elizabeth explained was either pre-*Lude* or post-*Lude* to *Sugar Plums*. It was played during the closing credits for the *Music Now* programme and included extracts from *Danse de la Terre* from Stravinsky's *Sacre du Printemps*, the Prelude to Act III of Wagner's *Lohengrin*, the *Grand March* from Verdi's *Aida*, Elgar's *Pomp and Circumstance, March No. 1* and Arne's *Rule Britannia*.

Though Elizabeth sought advice on some of the more unusual early instruments she was well acquainted with the recorder. In her diaries she always kept a note on the ranges of the different sizes of recorder, and composed a number of works for the instrument including her *Concertino da Camera* for treble recorder, oboe d'amore, viola da gamba and harpsichord, a fine work very representative of her compositional style.

(Extracts from Elizabeth Poston's letters and performing instructions from the manuscript score of *Sugar Plums* are included with the kind permission of Simon Campion. The author's thanks are also accorded to John Alabaster for providing a copy of his draft note to accompany the forthcoming publication of *Sugar Plums*, from which some of the above information is taken.)

Christopher Wood, Fantasy for Treble recorder and Harpsichord - 'In Memoriam' Richard Dolmetsch

To Carl Dolmetsch

Single movement, Andante

First performance: date and location unknown

Unpublished

The tragic death of Carl's younger son Richard in May 1966 at the age of just 21 was certainly felt beyond the immediate family. In the archive is the manuscript of *Fantasy for Treble recorder and Harpsichord – 'In Memoriam' Richard Dolmetsch* by the harpsichordist Christopher Wood, a long-time Dolmetsch family friend. It is a very personal tribute to a young man who showed considerable musical talent, and as such remains a private work rather different in style from Wood's other compositions for recorder.

Update of the details of published works

The following works identified as unpublished in the original edition have since been published:

Robert Simpson: Variations and Fugue (in memoriam Horace Dann) for recorder (treble and sopranino) and string quartet. Published: Hebden Bridge, Peacock Press, 2010 (PJT 154)

Richard Arnell: Quintet (The Gambian) for treble recorder and string quartet. Published: Hebden Bridge, Peacock Press, 2004 (PJT 024)

Alan Ridout: Chamber Concerto for treble recorder and string quartet. Published: Hebden Bridge, Peacock Press, 2007 (PD 13 – full score and parts; PD 12 – keyboard reduction)

Christopher Wood: Sonata di Camera for treble recorder and harpsichord. Published: Hebden Bridge, Peacock Press, 2004 (PD 10)

Ivor Walsworth: Sonata for treble recorder and harpsichord. Published: Hebden Bridge, Peacock Press, 2008 (PD 14)

Arthur Milner: Suite for treble recorder and piano. Published: Hebden Bridge, Peacock Press, 2005 (PD 11) (the complete work; last movement only previously published by Novello)

The following works were identified as being published, but full details are as follows:

Stephen Dodgson: Warbeck Dances for recorder (treble and sopranino) and harpsichord.
Published: Hebden Bridge, Peacock Press, 2003 (PD 09)

Alan Ridout: Sequence for treble recorder and lute (or harpsichord).
Published: Hebden Bridge, Peacock Press, 2003 (PD 07)

Alan Ridout: Variations on a Tune of H(erbert) H(owells) for descant recorder and harpsichord.
Published: Hebden Bridge, Peacock Press, 2003 (PD 08)

The following works were identified as published by Oxford University Press, but are now published under licence by Peacock Press:

Herbert Murrill: Sonata for treble recorder and harpsichord (PD 06)

Gordon Jacob: Suite for treble recorder and strings (or piano) (PD 05 – piano reduction only). The full score and parts of the version with string quartet or string orchestra may be hired from Oxford University Press.

Update of Selected Discography

The following CDs have been released since 2003

Rubbra & Britten – The complete recorder works. Includes: Rubbra, *Meditazioni sopra 'Cœurs Désolés'* op. 67; *Air & Variations for Pipes* op. 70; *Fantasia on a Theme of Machaut* Op. 86; *Cantata pastorale* op. 92; *Notturno* op. 106; *Passacaglia sopra 'Plusieurs regrets'* op. 113; *Sonatina* op. 128; *Fantasia on a Chord* op. 154. Catherine Fleming, rec; Ian Wilson, rec; The Flautadors Recorder Ensemble; Laurence Cummimgs, hpd; Patricia Rozario, soprano; Susanna Pell, va da gamba; The Dante String Quartet. Dutton CDLX 7142 (2004).

Walter Leigh – Complete chamber works. Includes: Leigh, *Air* for treble recorder and piano; *Sonatina* for treble recorder and piano. Martin Feinstein, rec; Sophia Rahman, pn. Dutton CDLX 7143 (2004)

Le tombeau d'une tipula. Includes: Butterley, *The White-throated Warbler*; Murrill, *Sonata*; Rubbra, *Passacaglia sopra 'Plusieurs regrets'* op. 113; Shaw, *Air and Variations* (from Sonata in E-flat). Evelyn Nallen, r ec; David Gordon, hpd. Mister Sam Records, SAMCD002 (2004).

Jigs, Airs and Reels. Includes: Reizenstein, *Partita* op. 13a (version for recorder and string trio). John Turner, rec; The Camerata Ensemble. Campion Cameo CAMEO 2034 (2004).

Fantasising - chamber music from Wales. Includes: Mathias, *Concertino*, op. 65, for recorder, oboe, bassoon and harpsichord. John Turner, rec; Richard Simpson, ob; Graham Salvage, bn; Janet Simpson, hpd. Campion Cameo CAMEO 2038 (2004).

British Recorder Concertos. Includes: Gál, *Concertino* op. 82 (version for recorder and string orchestra). John Turner, rec; Camerata Ensemble, conducted by Philip McKenzie. Dutton CDLX 7154 (2005).

Over the Water. Includes: Reizenstein, *Partita* op. 13b (version for recorder and string orchestra); Cooke *Divertimento* (1959) (version for recorder and string orchestra); Hopkins, *Suite* (version for recorder, string orchestra and harp). John Turner, rec; Manchester Camerata Ensemble, conducted by Philip McKenzie. Dutton CDLX 7191 (2007).

Modern Music for Recorder & Piano. Includes: Gál, *Three Intermezzi* op. 103. Leora Vinik, rec; Liora Ziv-Li, pn. ACUM 12885 (2010). (Private release obtainable via vinik@Netvision.net.il).

Gordon Jacob – Chamber Music with Recorder. Includes: *Suite* for recorder and string quartet; *A Consort of Recorders* for recorder quartet; *Variations* for recorder and harpsichord (or piano); *Trifles* for recorder, violin, cello and harpsichord. Annabel Knight, rec; Robin Bigwood, hpd/pn; The Maggini String Quartet; Fontanella recorder ensemble. Naxos 8.572364 (2010).
Songs of Yesterday. Berkeley, *Sonatina* op. 13; Leigh, *Sonatina*; York Bowen, *Sonatina* op. 121; Murrill, *Sonata*; Scott, *Aubade*; Rubbra, *Passacagila sopra 'Plusieurs regrets'* op. 113; Rubbra, *Sonatina* op. 128; Dan Laurin, rec; Anna Paradiso, hpd/pn. BIS- CD-1785 (2010).

The Rose Tree. Includes: Lennox Berkeley, *Una and the Lion* for soprano voice, recorder, viola da gamba and harpsichord. Lesley-Jane Rogers, soprano; John Turner, rec; Richard Tunnicliffe, va da gamba; Ian Thompson, hpd. Prima Facie PFCD 005 (2011).

A CD including Berkeley's *Sonatina*, Bowen's *Sonatina*, Rubbra's *Meditazioni sopra 'Cœurs Désolés'* and Jacob's *Suite* (version for recorder and string quartet) has been recorded by Jill Kemp with the Brodowski Quartet for release in 2011, but for which full details were not available at the time of preparing this revised discography.

Chapter 1

Early developments

Recent research, most notably that by Nikolaj Tarasov,[1] has established that recorder-related instruments never entirely disappeared during what is normally considered to be the period of the recorder's obsolescence, the nineteenth century and earlier years of the twentieth. Nevertheless, there is a specific point in time, around 1900, when the revival of the high-baroque instrument with which we are now so familiar can be said to have originated.

Christopher Welch's paper of 1898,[2] and (perhaps of greater practical influence) Dr Joseph Bridge's lecture on the 'Chester' recorders in 1901,[3] laid the foundations of a renewed interest in the instrument. To illustrate Bridge's lecture, these historic recorders (a total of six recorders by Pierre Bressan housed to this day in the Grosvenor Museum in Chester) were used to play the Gavotte by Henri le Jeune from Mersenne's *Harmonie universelle*, and a quartet specially composed by Bridge himself.[4] As the composer later related to Edgar Hunt, the fingering of the instruments had not been fully understood and stamp paper had been stuck over the thumb holes,[5] Bridge having considered at the time that the instruments had a range of only one octave. Examination of the piece (for ATTB with the first tenor part intended for voice flute in D) reveals that all the parts indeed remain within the compass of just one octave above the lowest note of each instrument. Bridge's Quartet is nevertheless almost certainly the first piece of music specifically composed for recorders in the twentieth century.[6]

The purchase of a Bressan recorder by Arnold Dolmetsch in 1905, its loss by the young Carl Dolmetsch in 1918, Arnold's reconstruction of it from his own notes and the subsequent retrieval of the original, remain among the well documented and fundamental events in the recorder's revival. By the time of the first Haslemere Festival in 1925 the recorder made its appearance in a

---

[1] Nikolaj Tarasov, lecture recital 'The development of the recorder from 1750 until the present', Holy Trinity Church, South Kensington, London, 28 October 2000.

[2] Welch, 'Literature relating to the recorder'.

[3] Bridge, 'The Chester recorders', quoted in Kinsell, 'J.C. Bridge and the recorder' p. 159.

[4] Ibid. This includes the score of Bridge's Quartet for Recorders.

[5] Hunt, *The Recorder and its Music*, 1977 edn, p. 129.

[6] Kinsell, 'The Chester recorders', mentions that Bridge's manuscript books contain a number of his arrangements including a set of variations on *Carman's Whistle* for four recorders and keyboard.

performance of J.S. Bach's Harpsichord Concerto No. 6 in F (his own arrangement of Brandenburg Concerto No. 4, replacing the solo violin with harpsichord but retaining the pair of recorders). The 1926 Haslemere Festival included a performance of Brandenburg Concerto No. 4 itself, in which the recorders were played by Rudolph Dolmetsch and his younger brother Carl (who had celebrated his fifteenth birthday the day before the concert).

From stamp paper over thumb holes to Bach's Brandenburg Concerto No. 4 in the space of just 25 years is a clear indication of the rapid progress made in the playing of the recorder, but it remained an instrument for the recreation of the music of the past and little if any new music was being composed for it.

In January 1928 Rudolph Dolmetsch completed an Air and Minuet for three recorders (SAT),[7] and just four months later Arnold Dolmetsch composed his *Fantasie, Ayre and Jigg* for the same trio combination.[8] Arnold Dolmetsch also wrote three Duos for descant and treble recorders in 1933. Below the title in the manuscript is the note 'Joués par une seule personne: (Carl!)', for indeed the notes used in each part require the fingers of one hand only and can thus be played by one person using two instruments simultaneously.[9] Though among the earliest pieces to be composed for the recorder in the twentieth century, all three of the above compositions are founded on idioms of music of the past.

Robin Milford's oratorio *A Prophet in the Land*, composed in 1929, contains an interlude for recorder and keyboard that displays a much more contemporary harmonic language in its folk modality.[10] It is very probably the earliest composition in a contemporary idiom for the recorder in British music.

The most significant composition for recorders from these early years is the *Trio für Blockflöten* by Paul Hindemith, written for a music festival in Plön, Germany, in 1932. The manuscript is marked 'einzeln oder chorisch besetzt', indicating the possibility of performance with one or several instruments per part. At Plön it was performed by the composer with Oskar Sala and Harald Genzmer in its original version for recorders in A and D, but with the composer's authority it was later transposed by Walter Bergmann for recorders in C and F.[11]

Hindemith's trio stands out as one of the seminal works in the recorder's repertoire, all the more remarkable for its exploration at that time of specific recorder textures and sonorities within a genuine contemporary harmonic language. This no doubt stemmed from Hindemith's intimate knowledge and often

---

[7] Albany, California: PRB Productions (Contemporary Consort Series no. 29), 1992.

[8] London: Schott & Co. Ltd, 1948.

[9] Published in facsimile in *A Birthday Album for the Society of Recorder Players*, Manchester: Forsyth Brothers, 1987.

[10] Milford extracted this piece from the oratorio and added two further movements that were published as *Three Airs* for treble recorder and harpsichord, Oxford: Oxford University Press, 1958. The original air is the second of the three.

[11] London: Schott & Co. Ltd, 1952.

displayed practical understanding of the nature of musical instruments and of their individual characteristics.

Mention should also be made of a Fantasia for solo treble recorder composed in the mid-1930s by Dr Ernst Meyer. He came to England from Germany around 1934–35 and was soon befriended by Edgar Hunt. The Fantasia was specially composed by Meyer for Hunt to play between groups of madrigals sung by Bristol University Madrigal Choir during an outside broadcast from the grounds of the Royal Fort in Bristol. Hunt noted that Meyer's Fantasia might have been the first such piece in the modern revival.[12]

The above-mentioned works certainly do not represent the entire compositional output for the recorder during the late 1920s and early 1930s, but one is hard pressed to find much else of substance from these years. With the exception of Hindemith's Trio, little contemporary music was coming from Germany, although amateur playing was being encouraged by such publications as *Der Blockflöten-Spiegel* and *Zeitschrift für Spielmusik*. However, the use of the recorder for massed playing in pre-war German youth rallies was not a development likely to enhance ensemble playing or the solo repertoire.

In Britain during the same period, the recorder was gathering an enthusiastic amateur following, further strengthened by the founding in 1937 of the Society of Recorder Players. This certainly encouraged the playing of consort music, and from among its ranks began to emerge those who, inspired by such players as Rudolph and Carl Dolmetsch, Miles Tomalin and Edgar Hunt, aspired to play the baroque solo and trio sonata repertoire themselves. Of an equivalent contemporary repertoire however, there was as yet nothing.

This then was the situation of the recorder in the late 1930s, one in which a handful of players felt increasingly that the time for the establishment of a significant contemporary repertoire for the instrument was long overdue. As is frequently the case, such ideas occurred individually and separately, but the amalgamation of enthusiasm, persistence and advancing playing technique was very soon to bring about a series of new compositions that were to be the foundation of a genuine contemporary recorder repertoire.

---

[12] This information is contained in a letter dated 22 November 1999 from Edgar Hunt to the author. The piece remains unpublished, but as a result of John Turner's interest in it Hunt sent him his playing copy and the author was thus able to inspect it. Typical of the detail included in Edgar Hunt's letters, he noted that, following Meyer's arrival in England, 'I saw a lot of Meyer – we often lunched together at a Lyons teashop near the British Museum.'

Chapter 2

Manuel Jacobs and the 'ten' composers

As discussed in the previous chapter, although rapid progress was made in the revival of the recorder during the first quarter of the twentieth century, this was almost entirely in the context of its being a historical instrument. A number of shorter pieces were written for it, either with keyboard or in consort, but these remained somewhat tentative ventures into the medium, and by the mid-1930s few works of substance had been written for it.

In an article about the recorder's twentieth-century repertoire, Carl Dolmetsch commented that, although the recorder had been presented in early-music recitals, '[i]t soon became obvious, however, that the instrument's compass, chromatic completeness, range of expression and technical flexibility would enable it to emerge from its remarkably effective role in early music to serve the modern composer equally effectively.'[1]

In the same article (p. 247) Dolmetsch writes that after a visit to the Haslemere Festival in 1938, Jack Westrup had noted: 'These winning instruments are unjustly neglected today. A composer who would write for them instead of wringing painful novelty from trumpet or violin, would earn no small gratitude.'

Another musician who also advocated the use of the recorder in contemporary music at this time was Manuel Jacobs (1910–93). Among Edgar Hunt's first recorder pupils, he wrote at length in the *Musical Times* under the pen name 'Terpander', encouraging the use of the recorder in contemporary composition. In an article in the *Musical Times* of September 1938 Jacobs wrote:

> It cannot be too much insisted that if the health and strength of the present recorder revival is to be maintained, the revival itself must be recognised as essentially a contemporary phenomenon and contemporary music must be written for it. Seen and treated purely as an object of antiquarian interest, it will die the speedy death that all movements which rely too exclusively and too morbidly on the past and its associations deserve to die. Actually the recorder is less remarkable for its 'antiquity' than for the accommodating way it fits into its 20th century surroundings.[2]

Later in the same article Jacobs noted almost prophetically:

> It would not, by the way, be an unrewarding prospect if modern composers were to

---

[1] Dolmetsch, 'The recorder's 20th century repertoire', p. 247.
[2] Jacobs, Manuel ('Terpander'), 'The recorders'.

include parts for recorders in their orchestral and chamber works, and would use them occasionally in, or as, accompaniment to songs. The small orchestra, for instance, would gain immensely in tonal interest by the introduction of recorders, with their peculiarly attractive 'colour' into the woodwind section.

The modern composer, usually so enterprising, has surely lagged behind in failing to explore the fascinating possibilities of combining the old instruments with the new.

He concluded with the exhortation:

> ... but it is a fact that if the recorders are to establish themselves permanently in England as they have already done in Germany, and similarly enrich our musical life, modern composers must be made to realise their potentialities (if not their existence!) and to write regularly for them. It is up to players themselves to attract to their instruments the notice which they deserve, and to make known the merits of what may be regarded, in spite of its antiquity, as a new branch of chamber music.

The lack of repertoire was also apparent to Carl Dolmetsch who, in the absence of suitable pieces at the time of his first Wigmore Hall recital on 1 February 1939, composed his Theme and Variations in A minor for descant recorder and harpsichord.[3] In so doing he aimed to set an example that others would follow. He was as convinced as Manuel Jacobs, who in the programme for the Wigmore Hall recital of November 1939 he acknowledged as an ally in this cause, that without a contemporary repertoire the recorder was in danger of suffering the same demise as it had encountered in the 18th century.

Edgar Hunt, reviewing the recital for the *Musical Times*, reported: 'After the interval Mr. Dolmetsch's phenomenal virtuosity was displayed in his own Theme and Variations in A minor for descant recorder.' The review concluded:

> We hope that the next recorder recital may be devoted to the treble instrument, and that we may have some pieces by contemporary composers, as well as by masters of the 17th and 18th centuries. Variety could be gained by including an aria with recorder obbligato or a trio for recorder, violin and harpsichord.[4]

Dolmetsch's example was indeed soon to be emulated, and Edgar Hunt, following the comments in his review, and being aware of Manuel Jacobs's increasing frustration at the lack of contemporary recorder repertoire, suggested to him that with his involvement in music journalism he was in an excellent position to approach composers himself (as he had indeed advised in his *Musical Times* article quoted above). This Jacobs did, and a handful of composers of the then younger British school were approached directly and invited to write sonatinas or suites for

---

[3] The manuscript of this previously unpublished work was located by Jeanne Dolmetsch in the Dolmetsch archive during a research visit to Haslemere by the author on 3 October 1999 (see Chapter 3).

[4] March 1939, **80**, p. 222.

treble recorder and keyboard. It was almost certainly in the knowledge that in Carl Dolmetsch and Edgar Hunt were recorder players with the technique to perform these new compositions that the composers set about the task of producing these ground-breaking works.

By 17 June 1939 there were sufficient new compositions for Carl Dolmetsch and Edgar Hunt (with Joseph Saxby at the keyboard) to perform four of them in a recital at a studio meeting of the London Contemporary Music Centre at the home of Robert Mayer in St John's Wood. This recital also contained a performance of Hindemith's *Plöner Musiktag* trio for three recorders, perhaps the most significant composition for recorders written up to that time, and which remains a seminal work in the recorder repertoire.

Of the new sonatinas, Carl Dolmetsch played those by Lennox Berkeley and Stanley Bate. Edgar Hunt played those by Peter Pope and Christian Darnton.

In the previously mentioned article on the recorder's twentieth century repertoire[5] Dolmetsch noted that Jack Westrup had enthusiastically reported:

> The recorder has hitherto been associated with the revival of music of the 17th and 18th centuries. At the London Contemporary Music Centre's studio meeting on Saturday afternoon, we learnt how it could serve the composer today. The result was encouraging. Provided that an instrument is mechanically perfect – as the modern recorder is – there is clearly no reason why it should be confined to the music of the past. The concert as a whole proved a serious intention to establish and justify the relationship between the seductive instrument and the music of our time.

Following the private performance of the Berkeley Sonatina, Carl Dolmetsch gave the first public performance of the work in his second Wigmore Hall recital on 18 November 1939 (see Chapter 3, p. 26). The programme for the Wigmore Hall performance contained the following note:

> Acknowledgements and thanks are due to Mr. Manuel Jacobs, himself a recorder player and composer for that instrument, for his enterprise in personally bringing to the notice of ten composers of the younger British school the tempting resources offered by the recorder in a new field of operation. As a result of his efforts ten new sonatinas have been written and this collection is shortly to be published under the editorship of Mr. Jacobs.
>
> The foregoing will substantiate the view that an instrument like the recorder, which can live on its own merits irrespective of age, will surely be given a future besides its distinguished past and present. Other living composers who have already succumbed to its charms and possibilities include Hindemith, Benjamin Britten, Stanley Bate and Alan Rawsthorne.
>
> The recorder enthusiast now has something new to turn to, and may well be assured of more to come.

---

[5] See note 1.

Of significance is the mention of ten composers and the inclusion of Benjamin Britten's name among those who had already composed for the instrument.

Of the other works composed, that by Eve Kisch was withdrawn by the composer and no trace of it has been found. The Suite by Christian Darnton was likewise withdrawn. In a conversation with the author in September 1997 Edgar Hunt explained that there had been nothing wrong with the piece musically, but it had not been suited idiomatically and technically to the recorder. Hunt recalled that it had made frequent use of double tonguing in the lower register of the instrument and would perhaps have been more suited to the clarinet. As with Eve Kisch's work, no manuscript appears to have survived.

Starting with the Berkeley Sonatina in 1940, Schott & Co. in London very enterprisingly planned to publish the remainder of the works, although the onset of World War II severely interrupted the project. The prefatory note in the Berkeley mentioned the series of works written at the instigation of Manuel Jacobs but announced: 'The publishers are reluctantly obliged to delay publication of the complete series owing to the present emergency.' It was not until 1950 that the last of Schott's series found its way into print.

The second work to be published was the Sonatina by Peggy Glanville-Hicks, which was published by Schott in 1941. Glanville-Hicks (1912–90) was born in Melbourne, Australia, and studied with Fritz Hart at the Melbourne Conservatorium before winning a scholarship to the Royal College of Music in London, where she studied composition with Vaughan Williams, piano with Arthur Benjamin and conducting with Constant Lambert and Malcolm Sargent. At the time of the composition of her Sonatina, she was married to Stanley Bate.

The Glanville-Hicks Sonatina is in three movements: a lively *Animato assai* in 2/4, a reflective and lyrical *Lento recitativo* that varies between 3/4 and 4/4, and a final *Vivace*, initially in 4/8, but with a syncopated theme that leads to bars of 3/8 and 2/8 and a certain rhythmic fluidity. The musical language of Vaughan Williams is evident and never far away.

Though published in 1941, it appears the work did not receive its first performance until 1945, in a recital given by Carl Dolmetsch and Joseph Saxby. This information is to be found in a letter from Manuel Jacobs to Carl Dolmetsch dating from 1945, which will be examined in more detail below.

Walter Leigh's Sonatina was the next to be published, in 1944. Sadly its publication was posthumous, as Leigh had been killed in action near Tobruk, Libya, in 1942. Born in 1905, Leigh had studied with Hindemith in Berlin from 1927 to 1929. As will be seen, a number of the composers who studied with Hindemith wrote for the recorder and acknowledged his influence in so doing. However, another influence in the case of Leigh is likely to have been his former Cambridge colleague Dr Bland, who played the recorder. In 1998 Leigh's daughter, Veronica Leigh Jacobs, discovered a remarkable photograph showing Leigh himself at the piano and Bland playing the recorder. It was taken in Cairo shortly before the composer's death and it is thought highly likely that Leigh's last work, significantly for recorder and piano, his brief but haunting Air, was being played at the time.⁶

Leigh's Sonatina is also in three movements. The first is an *Allegretto* in 4/4 in which the recorder's wonderfully expressive stream of melody unfolds over a flowing piano accompaniment. A central *Larghetto, molto tranquillo* inhabits much the same emotional musical world as the later Air, although there is a more urgent cadenza-like four-bar solo for the recorder shortly before the close. The finale is a fleet *Allegro leggiero* mainly in 2/4 but with some effective passages in 5/8. There is a calmer middle section over piano arpeggios and a brief *Più lento* reflection before the piano heads for the ending in 5/8 figures while the recorder holds a high A. An entirely effective and satisfying work beautifully written for the recorder.

According to the letter from Manuel Jacobs noted above, it was Carl Dolmetsch who gave the first performance of this work also, although no date or venue is given.

At this point, with three of the new works published, it is worth examining the contents of Manuel Jacobs's fascinating letter in more detail. Dated 17 June 1945 (six years to the day after the seminal London Contemporary Music Centre studio recital, although almost certainly rather by coincidence than design), it is quoted here in full. It contains not only much important information about the early recorder works, but also something of Jacobs's own creative musical activity, his thoughts on an important contemporary work and his encouragement for the continued development of the recorder repertoire.

My dear Carl,

Many thanks for the advance notice of your concert. I shall certainly be there. The programme is a most alluring one. Is there any possibility of seeing you and Joseph after the concert? It would be heavenly.

I must tell you that the Glanville-Hicks will not only be the first public performance of the work, but the first performance ever, as Mrs Schragenheim had to leave it out of her programme owing to the last-minute inclusion of some Fauré celebration music. As a result she was able to concentrate all her attention on the Rawsthorne suite, of which she gave a truly magnificent performance – I wish you had been there to hear it. Your generous loan of the recorder was, let me assure you at first hand, most amply repaid by the honour done to it that evening.

I did a brief but comprehensive biographical note (on the Glanville-Hicks) for the concert, which of course was not used. If I can possibly get hold of it again from the organiser of the concert I will send it on to you. I don't imagine I shall be able to get it to you in time for printing in the programme, but you may like to say a word about the work in your inimitable way, and so the note would be useful for that purpose.

Do you realise, Carl, that on Saturday you will have "premiered" no less than four out

---

⁶ The photograph was published in *The Recorder Magazine*, Winter 1999, **19**, p. 154.

of my seven Schott recorder works (the Bate, Berkeley, Leigh and Glanville-Hicks)? If you don't, I do, and I want to tell you how grateful I am to you for your superb work on behalf of this series, and of course to Joseph too for his perfect co-operation at the piano. But you must admit that the works themselves are more than just pleasant; they really are fine, mature, positive specimens of music by composers whom time has justified. I imagine that the next to be published will be either the Bate or the Rawsthorne – I have recommended the latter as it is within the scope of the good amateur. As I wrote to Schott's, I think one can now safely state (a) that the series is well-known, and (b) that it has a long life before it; especially when all the people who are wanting recorders can get hold of them. I get a yearly return of the copies sold, and really, considering the wartime atmosphere, with all its restrictions, in which these plants flourished, I consider the sales to be amazingly good, and I think you would too.

How are you keeping, and your family? I hope all your troubles are over at last, and you are really settling down to a restful period. It's about time you did some more important London concerts, isn't it, Carl? What about another Wigmore Hall one?

I am at present at work on a suite of four songs on poems by 15th and 16th century French writers. It is all but finished and it is the most considerable thing I have done so far – poles removed both in style and conception from my earlier 1942–3 songs. The actual title is *Quatre Mouvements pour Voix & Piano.* There is a quick movement (Allegro da teatro) on a poem by Clément Marot, then a slow movement (Andante quasi adagio) on one by Louise Labé; this is followed by a scherzo-like setting (Presto) of an anonymous Children's Song, and finally another allegro movement (Vivo e giusti) on an absolute gem of a rondeau by Charles d'Orléans. All four are linked together by modulatory passages and slight thematic resemblances, and at the end of the last song there is a piano codetta (Largamente) to round the whole work off. Margaret Field-Hyde and Norman Franklin are going to perform it in the early autumn.

Have you seen 'Peter Grimes'? If you can find the slightest excuse of any kind for not seeing this epochal British art-work by hook or crook, tell me about it on Saturday! My affectionate regards to you and yours (including Joseph), Yours very minutely, Manuel.

Jacobs's comments on the Rawsthorne Suite are of particular interest in the light of its subsequent history, and although he had recommended its publication as the next in the series it was in fact the Reizenstein Partita that Schotts published in 1946.

Franz Reizenstein was born in Nuremberg in 1911 and went to the Berlin State Academy in 1930, where he studied composition with Hindemith. Amid rising Nazi power he left Germany in 1934 and came to London, where he continued his compositional studies with Vaughan Williams and took private piano lessons with Solomon. He was interned at the beginning of the war, but eventually adopted British nationality. He died at the early age of 57 in 1968.

Reizenstein was near to completing his Partita at the time he attended the premiere of the Berkeley Sonatina at the London Contemporary Music Centre studio recital in June 1939. Dolmetsch had no doubt advised Reizenstein about the difficulty of the treble recorder's high F#, which Berkeley had nevertheless included in his work. As Dolmetsch recounted later, Reizenstein (who had perfect pitch) approached him after the performance and observed: 'I distinctly heard you play high F-sharps.'⁷ Dolmetsch assured him that all things were possible on the modern recorder – within its compass – if one knew how, but it was agreed that this note was best avoided if the work were to be published. Reizenstein duly completed his Partita without resorting to high F#s.

In their underlying rhythmic structures, the work's four movements recall forms from the past. The first is a spacious Intrada (*Allegro ma non troppo*) in *alla breve* time, the second a Sarabande (*Andante con moto*) that, though beginning and ending in the usual 3/4 time associated with this dance, has passages in 2/4. A lively Bourrée (*Allegretto con spirito*) follows, containing some quite testing passage-work for the recorder, and the work concludes with a Jig (*Presto*) covering the full compass of the instrument up to high A flat. This contains a number of interesting enharmonic changes, as its catchy opening theme (founded on the nursery rhyme *Cock-a-doodle-doo*) is subject to frequent Hindemith-like modulations.

The earlier printed edition provided separate recorder and flute parts that contained many quite different articulations for the two instruments. The melody instrument line in the score of both the earlier and later editions reflects the flute version, and, though self-explanatory in the earlier edition, it is a little confusing in the later one, with which only a recorder part is provided.

Dolmetsch recorded the Partita with Joseph Saxby at the piano for Oiseau-Lyre in 1975 and his own note written for the recording is quoted in the sleevenote by Reizenstein's widow Margaret:

> His splendid sophisticated Partita reveals the composer's intuitive gift of writing with a fluency of style ideally suited to its chosen medium. The Partita is scholarly and immediately attractive; it is rhythmically strong, embodying characteristic passages of compound time and cross-accents in the quick movements, yet the Sarabande is lyrical and expressive.

In a telephone conversation with the author, Margaret Reizenstein recalled how her enthusiasm for the Bourrée led the composer to make it their signature tune. He would whistle the first bars of the melody as he approached a pre-arranged meeting place, or on his way to the front door of their home to announce his arrival.

Margaret Reizenstein wrote to Dolmetsch on 15 October 1982 enclosing two copies of the recording. Her letter notes:

> I also have pleasure in enclosing one of the new list of works. Regretfully I was too late to put in 'Composed for C[arl] D[Dolmetsch]' and I am very sorry because I looked thoroughly for first performances, and specially composed works and could trace nothing in the case of the Partita. However I have the information now, and can pass it on in individual cases and to the BIRS and BMIC[8] and Schott's. And at the next printing of the list it can be added.

---

7 Quoted in Dolmetsch, 'The recorder in evolution', p. 55.

8 The British Institute of Recorded Sound (now the National Sound Archive) and the British Music Information Centre.

On 23 October Margaret Reizenstein wrote again with good news:

> I am delighted to tell you that the printers are going to put beneath the Partita in the new brochure – 'Composed in 1939 for Carl Dolmetsch'. It luckily is the last work to be on that page, and there is just enough space to add one line – not two – without them re-setting the whole page!

Although Dolmetsch recorded the work, it seems he may not have given its first performance. He had considered including the Partita in his 1953 Wigmore Hall recital but in the event played Antony Hopkins's Suite (see Chapter 3, p. 46). Shortly after the death of Dutch recorder player Joannes Collette in May 1995 Edgar Hunt wrote to inform the author. In his letter Hunt recalled the 'Recorder in Education' Summer School held at Roehampton in 1954, at which Collette had wished to play the Reizenstein Partita, which at that time does not appear to have received a performance by Dolmetsch himself.[9] Hunt continued:

> Walter Bergmann would have liked to play the piano but did not think he would have time to study the piano part in the midst of the course: so I suggested we should ask the composer – Franz Reizenstein was delighted so we all enjoyed what was probably the first performance.

Reizenstein arranged the work for flute and string trio in 1953–54, but in this form it remains unpublished. In its original form it is among the more frequently performed of this important group of works.

It was another three years before the fifth of the new works was published. This was the Sonatina by Peter Pope,[10] first performed at the London Contemporary Music Centre studio recital in June 1939 by Edgar Hunt and dedicated to him.

Peter Pope was born in 1917 and educated at Uppingham School. At the Royal College of Music in London he studied composition with John Ireland and R.O. Morris, and piano with Freda Swain and Cyril Smith. He also won a travel scholarship that enabled him to visit Paris and study with Nadia Boulanger. His works include a quantity of songs and chamber music. He died in Herefordshire in 1991.

Pope's Sonatina is, like its companion pieces, in three movements. The first, *Allegro molto moderato*, is noteworthy for being in 7/8 time throughout and founded on a rising theme that is briefly given quasi-fugal treatment 20 bars from the beginning. The brief but intense middle movement *Lento molto* is without doubt the emotional centre of the work, while the final *Allegro molto, alla danza*

---

[9] Edgar Hunt's letter, dated 27 June 1995, suggested that Carl Dolmetsch had not played the work because he thought it was too difficult. However, it is hard to imagine, even though it does present technical difficulties, that a player who had premiered the Berkeley and York Bowen Sonatinas would have found anything technically over-demanding in the Reizenstein Partita.

[10] London: Schott & Co. Ltd, 1949.

brings the work to a whirlwind conclusion but with a will-o'-the-wisp ending on the recorder's top F.

The printed edition gives the year of composition as 1939 but notes: 'revised 1948'. The author has not been able to examine a manuscript and is thus not able to comment on the extent of the revisions. It is among the most annotated of this collection of works, especially with regard to dynamics, some of which are difficult to achieve in practice (for example, the diminuendo to a top F seven bars after letter B in the first movement). It is nevertheless an engaging work, and the remarkably rich harmonic effect of its middle movement is impressive.

The last of this series of works to be published by Schott appeared in 1950 and was the Sonatina by Stanley Bate (1913–59), first performed by Carl Dolmetsch at the studio recital of the London Contemporary Music Centre in 1939.

Bate attended the Royal College of Music, studying composition with Vaughan Williams, R.O. Morris and Gordon Jacob. He also had piano lessons with Arthur Benjamin and studied privately with Nadia Boulanger in Paris and Hindemith in Berlin (an important factor when considering these earliest works for the recorder). The performance of Bate's Concertino for piano and string orchestra at the 1937 Eastbourne Festival was an important point in his composing career, and the work was enthusiastically reviewed by Manuel Jacobs in the *Musical Times*,[11] no doubt an influence on Jacobs in requesting a work from him for recorder. It is also significant that Bate dedicated his Sonatina to Jacobs.

The Sonatina's outer movements have a particularly extrovert feel. The first, *Allegro*, has the direction 'percussively' in the piano part and the recorder is kept busy with many semiquaver passages (at ♩ = 132). The movement ends on a very top A on the recorder followed by unison A's on the piano. The central *Largo* is much calmer, and the recorder's melody unfolds over an atmospheric arpeggio figure on the piano that returns only at the end of the movement as the opening theme is briefly recapitulated. The movement ends with the recorder alone on a low A. Though headed *Presto*, the final movement has the same metronome marking as the first and shares much of its character (it is also basically in 2/4). Here, however, the opening semiquaver piano accompaniment is remarkably concentrated, covering just a tone. The recorder is again given short semiquaver motives high on the instrument. The ending is strangely subdued after all this activity, but a unity is achieved with the endings of the first two movements as the recorder plays a held low A followed by octave A's in the pianist's left hand, underlining the work's tonal centre. It is a work of energy and brittleness that, despite its technical challenges, deserves to be played more often.

The earliest edition of the Berkeley mentioned the Rawsthorne Suite as being among the works to be included in the series, but it was not to be published by them and indeed did not appear in print until published by Forsyth in an edition dated 1994. In the intervening years the work was thought to have been withdrawn

---

[11] October 1938, **79**, p. 738.

and/or lost. It is clear from Manuel Jacobs's letter of 17 June 1945 to Carl Dolmetsch that the Suite had received its first (private?) performance in that year by Mrs Schragenheim. Edgar Hunt thought that Mrs Shragenheim was a member of Walter Bergmann's recorder group during the 1930s. In a letter to the author, Hunt recalled:

> I remember the name 'Mrs. Schragenheim'. She was probably a cut above most of Walter's recorder playing group – more of a soloist who would not have been interested in the S[ociety of] R[ecorder] P[layers]. I remember there were various music circles operating in Hampstead from 1934 until 1939 but they did not always mix.[12]

The work's apparent disappearance is accounted for by its adaptation by the composer as a work for viola d'amore and piano, referred to in a letter from Rawsthorne to the BBC in 1942, and it was only after Rawsthorne's death in 1971 that a photostat copy of the manuscript of the work in this form (which remained unpublished) was found. On examination of the copy it was clear that this was indeed the Suite for recorder, as the instrumental indication of 'viola d'amore' had replaced the roughly erased but still discernible 'treble recorder' and a number of double stops added to the solo part, which otherwise suited the treble recorder perfectly.[13] The discovery of Manuel Jacobs's letter to Carl Dolmetsch in 1999 fills a gap in the unusual history of the piece, as it would appear to have received its first performance in its original form even after its reworking for viola d'amore.

Alan Rawsthorne (1905–71) was among the most distinguished British composers of his generation. The discovery of his Suite for recorder not only restores one of the earliest works for the instrument to its place among the others composed at Manuel Jacobs's instigation, but also provides the repertoire with a significant and characteristic work from its composer.

The Suite opens with a broad and sonorous Sarabande marked *Maestoso* that leads directly into a gentle Fantasia, *Andante con moto*, based on a fragment of the Elizabethan tune *Wooddy-Cock*. An elegant, smoothly flowing but quite brief Air, *Andante grazioso*, forms the third movement and a lively Jig headed *Allegro*, making use of insistent rhythmic figures, brings the work to an energetic and almost *moto perpetuo* conclusion.

The composer John McCabe was commissioned by the Rawsthorne Trust to orchestrate the piano part for strings. In this form (in which it has been recorded by John Turner, in addition to that with original piano accompaniment) it is particularly effective and takes on a character that the piano version can only hint at.

---

[12] Edgar Hunt's letter dated 22 November 1999 later notes: 'Mrs Schragenheim would be a little old lady now if she still exists. I remember her name well and must have met her, but I can't remember what she looked like.'

[13] A full account of this is given in John Turner's article on the Suite in *The Recorder Magazine* of March 1993, **13**, pp. 13–14 and his postscript to it published in *The Recorder Magazine* of March 1997, **17**, p. 36.

Although the group of composers from which Manuel Jacobs requested works is sometimes referred to as being ten in number, lists of them will frequently be found to contain only nine names. This leads to the inevitable question, who was the tenth composer?

Carl Dolmetsch maintained that Benjamin Britten was not only the tenth composer but also that he may indeed have begun sketches for a work that were lost at the beginning of the war. (Rawsthorne's Bristol flat was destroyed in an air raid in November 1940, once thought to have been a possible fate of the Suite before its rediscovery.) In a conversation between the author and Greta Dolmetsch in 1998 she also recounted Carl Dolmetsch's assertion that Britten may have begun sketches of a work for recorder.

This is mentioned in Dolmetsch's note written for his recording of the Reizenstein Partita. It was not included on the record sleeve in full, but a copy of the complete text[14] contains the following sentences:

> The original list included Lennox Berkeley, Walter Leigh, Rawsthorne, Britten, Stanley Bate, Glanville Hicks, Peter Pope and Christian Darnton. The project was interrupted by the war years and some of the works were lost in air raids – Britten's Sonata and Rawsthorne's Theme and Variations [sic] among them – or remained uncompleted.

Intriguing as even the briefest sketches of a sonatina or suite for recorder and keyboard by Britten would be, later correspondence between Dolmetsch and Britten himself confirms that whatever thoughts may have been in the composer's mind must have been at best very preliminary, and may not have been committed to paper at all. Besides, Britten left for the United States on 29 April 1939 and would have had little if any time to commit to such a work.

In January 1954 Britten wrote to Dolmetsch to thank him for the gift of a pair of recorders recently received. Britten mentions his efforts to play these recorders and being spurred on by the local music club and its 'energetic consort'. Towards the end of the letter is a sentence of particular significance that reads: 'I am also discovering for myself some of the possibilities of the instrument which will be *invaluable when I start to write for them, as I hope to soon.*' (My italics.)

A further letter from Britten to Dolmetsch dated 7 October 1954 regrets that it would not be possible, owing to his other commitments, to compose a work for Dolmetsch's 1955 Wigmore Hall recital. The letter continues: 'I am planning at the moment a rather unsophisticated work for mixed recorders, and another reason for the delay is that *I want to see how successful I am in writing for the instrument before I tackle a more elaborate piece.*' (Again, my italics.)

These statements would not seem to reflect those of a composer who had previously investigated the possibilities of writing for recorder and keyboard in any detail. Britten additionally notes in this letter: '... but quite sincerely, I must

---

[14] Held in the Dolmetsch archive.

say that it will give me great pleasure to write a serious piece for recorder and harpsichord.'

Following Britten's death in 1976 Walter Bergmann wrote a tribute 'Recollections of Benjamin Britten' in *Recorder & Music*.[15] In this, Bergmann noted: 'Britten has died before he had written a major work for the recorder which we all hoped he would write, though he never promised it.'

In 2001 the question of Britten and the recorder was again raised as a result of the publication by Boosey and Hawkes of a volume of Britten's folksong settings entitled *Tom Bowling and Other Song Arrangements*. This includes, *I Wonder as I Wander*, one of the first (if not actually the first) of Britten's folksong settings. The earliest manuscript of the setting is on paper that Britten used in America, and according to the Preface to the volume could date from as early as 1940. In this manuscript the accompaniment is indicated for piano, but consists of just a single melodic line.

John Turner's keen eyes and ears immediately recognized that this single melodic line seemed ideally suited to the treble recorder. His conviction that this was the case led him to record the piece, and as he wrote in the notes accompanying the recording:

> The accompaniment ... [is] without any octave doublings, pedal markings or other pianistic devices. The range is exactly the two-octave span of the treble recorder, which it fits entirely idiomatically, without any adjustment whatsoever. Indeed on the internal evidence of the part itself, including phrasing, the recorder seems the obvious accompanying instrument. Moreover, with its traditional pastoral connections, the treble recorder seems ideally suited to the character of the song. Peter Pears' notes on the piece, compiled for the Britten-Pears Library, allude to the possibility of performance with flute or violin. Up to that time Britten had in fact written no solo music for the flute, and it is very tempting to think that the sound of the recorder, for which some of his colleagues had so recently written, might just have been what was in his mind when he made this haunting setting.[16]

Does this simple folksong setting contain Britten's earliest writing for the recorder? And if so, does it relate to an invitation from Manuel Jacobs, the idea of which remained with Britten during his early months in America?[17] (Jacobs's comment in his *Musical Times* article advocating the use of the recorder 'in, or as, accompaniment to songs' also comes to mind.) It is unlikely that the answers will ever be known for certain. Individually, Dolmetsch's assertion that Britten was among the composers invited by Manuel Jacobs to compose for the recorder, and

---

[15] March 1977, **5**, p. 286.

[16] Turner, notes for CD *Aspects of Nature*.

[17] In November 1939 Lennox Berkeley mentioned the success of the premiere of his Sonatina in a letter written to Britten, who had by that time been in the United States for about seven months (information in a letter from Tony Scotland to the author dated 4 May 2002).

the possibility that the *I Wonder as I Wander* setting was conceived for recorder, are fascinating – together they seem to lend a certain credence one to the other.[18]

The seven works that resulted from Manuel Jacobs's initiative occupy a unique place in the recorder's repertoire ('fine, mature, positive specimens of music' as Jacobs had himself referred to them) and were the musical springboard to the remarkable flourishing of compositions for recorder that occurred in the second half of the twentieth century.

However, the repertoire grew only slowly at first. Christopher Edmunds wrote his single movement Sonatina for descant recorder and piano dedicated to Edgar Hunt, published by Schott in 1941 and in that same year Martin Shaw composed his sonata in E flat and Anthony Bernard his Prelude and Scherzo, both for Carl Dolmetsch. Also in that same year in Germany Harald Genzmer was composing the first of his two sonatas for treble recorder and piano. This was not, however, published by Schott until 1948 and at the same time as the posthumous publication of the Sonata for recorder and piano by Wilhelm Bender following his death in 1944. These earliest sonatas were soon to be followed by an increasing number of works in similar form by composers both in England and on the continent as interest in the recorder became more widespread and playing technique was consolidated.

The hope that a genuine contemporary repertoire for the recorder expressed only ten years earlier now had, in these earliest works, a remarkable beginning. By the time Schott published the Bate Sonatina in 1950, three new works had already been performed by Carl Dolmetsch in his re-established series of Wigmore Hall recitals, and by the time Forsyth published Rawsthorne's Suite in 1998 it is likely that more original music for recorder had been composed and published in the twentieth century than had been produced in its entire history hitherto.

---

[18] It would be unwise, even if there is a possibility that the accompaniment to *I Wonder as I Wander* was conceived for recorder, to trawl through Britten's song accompaniments in the hope of discovering others that may display some recorder idiomatic characteristics. However, John Turner drew the author's attention to Britten's B-flat setting for voice and piano of William Shield's *The Plough Boy* made around 1945. In this the *octava* sections for the piano right hand fit the sopranino recorder exactly and idiomatically and the piece can be played in this way without any alteration whatsoever. Additionally, a setting with piccolo and strings (without double bass) was made by Britten in 1946, indicating that the high-lying melodic interludes were intended for a solo instrument. The key and the idiom certainly make the sopranino recorder a contender.

Chapter 3

The 'Wigmore' works, 1939–89

Carl Dolmetsch's recital with Joseph Saxby at London's Wigmore Hall on 1 February 1939 was almost certainly the first of its kind devoted entirely to the recorder as a solo virtuoso instrument. Interrupted only by the war years and those immediately after, Dolmetsch's series of annual Wigmore Hall recitals continued for the next 50 years, his last being given on 27 October 1989.

The twentieth-century renaissance of the recorder had grown out of the early music revival, in which Dolmetsch's father Arnold had been pre-eminent. Quite naturally the programmes of the Wigmore Hall recitals were founded on baroque and pre-baroque repertoire, but Dolmetsch was convinced that the recorder also required a contemporary repertoire if it was ultimately to re-establish itself and indeed survive. His involvement in the performance of the handful of new works for recorder composed in 1939 as a result of Manuel Jacobs's initiative (see Chapter 2) was no doubt a fundamental influence on Dolmetsch's own unwavering efforts to encourage composers to write new works for the instrument.

Thus the place occupied by the Wigmore recitals in establishing the recorder's twentieth-century role is unique. On every occasion, with the exceptions of 1948, in which no new work was premiered, and 1951, when Berkeley's Sonatina (publicly premiered at Dolmetsch's second Wigmore Hall recital in November 1939) was given a repeat performance, the programme included the premiere of a new work. On six occasions two new works were premiered (1961, 1962, 1965, 1966, 1972 and 1974) and at the recital of 1973 no less than three.

In addition to Berkeley's Sonatina a number of the new works received repeat performances at subsequent recitals. Dolmetsch was at pains to demonstrate that this was repertoire of musical quality and not simply a collection of occasional pieces to be performed once and then forgotten. New works, having been premiered, were also frequently taken on later recital tours, often to the United States, but also elsewhere.

As Dolmetsch began to re-establish the Wigmore Hall recital series after the war, he followed Manuel Jacobs's lead and made a direct approach to composers to invite them to write works for the recorder. The first of these was York Bowen, soon to be followed by Edmund Rubbra and Herbert Murrill. Dolmetsch returned to Rubbra on two further occasions during these early years and to Lennox Berkeley also, but was naturally keen for more composers to be involved. Murrill worked at the BBC and it is likely that Dolmetsch's contacts there led to the composition of works by Norman Fulton and Robert Simpson, who also held positions at the BBC. Once the recital series had become more established, Dolmetsch must have felt sufficiently confident to make a similar invitation to a number of other composers, and Gordon Jacob, Arnold Cooke and John Gardner all wrote new pieces over the next ten years. Dolmetsch continued his direct invitations to composers throughout the remainder of the recital series, but the individual circumstances in which he made contact were many and varied and are described, where possible, in the individual sections on the works following this introduction.

From the outset Dolmetsch sought to enhance the quality of the repertoire by engaging eminent and established composers. Over the 50-year period, 32 composers provided new works, seven of them contributing more than one (John Gardner two, Lennox Berkeley, Hans Gál and Alan Ridout three each, Arnold Cooke and Gordon Jacob four each and Edmund Rubbra six). Although most of the composers were British, we also find a handful from other countries: Georges Migot and Jean Françaix from France, Nigel Butterley from Australia and Alan Hovhaness from the United States. With the exception of Françaix, who had known Dolmetsch's father, the others were met while on foreign recital tours.

A gradual assimilation of the recorder into increasingly varied instrumental scorings is significant and interesting to follow in detail. Up to 1954 all the new works had been for recorder and keyboard, but in 1955 Rubbra's *Fantasia on a Theme of Machaut* for recorder, string quartet and harpsichord represented a turning point. Dolmetsch was obviously keen to enhance further the stature of the recorder in contemporary music by integrating it into chamber sonorities similar to those of the baroque. Indeed the scoring of the new works increasingly reflected the forces assembled for the remainder of each recital programme. Thus between 1955 and 1975, of the 29 new works performed, only ten were for recorder and keyboard, and during the remaining years, solo recorder and keyboard featured in just three out of 14.

For the 1955 recital Dolmetsch engaged the Martin String Quartet, who were to take part in the recitals from 1958 to 1962 inclusive, performing in works for recorder and string quartet by Jacob, Simpson, Cooke and Gál. In 1966 the quartet performed a work for the same scoring by Arnell. Hovhaness's Sextet of 1961 made additional use of the harpsichord. For the 1956 recital Dolmetsch and Saxby were joined by the violinist Jean Pognet and the cellist Arnold Ashby for the premiere of Lennox Berkeley's *Concertino*. In 1957 the soprano Joan Alexander performed in the first new Wigmore work to include a vocal part, Rubbra's *Cantata pastorale*.

During the early 1960s Dolmetsch tutored at courses held at the Idyllwild Arts Foundation in California. Also on the faculty there were the Schoenfeld sisters, violinist Alice and cellist Eleonor. During their first tour of Great Britain they joined Dolmetsch and Saxby for the 1965 recital and subsequently in the recitals of 1967 to 1971 inclusive. They proved to be a musically inspirational quartet for which Cooke, Gardner, Horovitz and Chagrin all composed new pieces. Alice and

1   Joseph Saxby and Carl Dolmetsch at about the time of the re-establishment of the Wigmore Hall recitals in the late 1940s.

Eleonor Schoenfeld also gave the UK premiere of Gál's *Trio Serenade* with Dolmetsch at the 1967 recital.

If the new works of the later 1950s and all of the 1960s saw the addition of strings in ensemble with recorder, those of the 1970s produced a number with more varied and unusual scorings. In 1973 Dolmetsch's twin daughters Jeanne and Marguerite joined their father and Joseph Saxby for the London premiere of Arnold Cooke's Suite for three recorders and harpsichord.

Among other scorings employed in the new works at this period were: recorder and soprano voice (Bergmann's *Pastorella*), recorder, oboe, bassoon and harpsichord (Mathias's *Concertino*), recorder and lute (Ridout's *Sequence*), recorder, percussion, viola da gamba and harpsichord (Lipkin's *Interplay*), recorder and guitar (Hoddinott's *Italian Suite*), recorder, viola da gamba and harpsichord (Rubbra's *Fantasia on a Chord*) and soprano voice, recorder viola da gamba and harpsichord (Lennox Berkeley's cantata *Una and the Lion*).

The 1980s began with Michael Berkeley's *American Suite* for recorder and bassoon, but thereafter there was a return to scorings with string ensembles: recorder and string quartet (Ridout's Chamber Concerto and Hand's *Concerto cantico*), recorder, violin, cello and harpsichord (Jacob's Suite – originally composed under the title of *Trifles*), recorder, string quartet and harpsichord (Short's *Sinfonia*), two recorders, violin, cello and harpsichord (Cooke's

Divertimento) and recorder, two violins, cello and harpsichord (Jean Françaix's *Quintette*).

The variety of scorings used in the 'Wigmore' works is indicated in the following list:

Recorder and harpsichord (or piano)	21
Recorder and soprano voice	1
Recorder and lute	1
Recorder and guitar	1
Recorder and bassoon	1
Recorder, violin and cello	1
Recorder and string quartet	7
Recorder, viola da gamba and harpsichord	1
Recorder, violin, cello and harpsichord	6
Recorder, 2 violins, cello and harpsichord	1
Recorder, string quartet and harpsichord	3
Recorder, percussion, viola da gamba and harpsichord	1
Recorder, oboe, bassoon and harpsichord	1
Recorder, soprano voice, viola da gamba and harpsichord	1
Recorder, soprano voice, cello and harpsichord	1
2 recorders, violin, cello and harpsichord	1
3 recorders and harpsichord	1
Recorder quartet	1

In addition to the variety of scorings, attention should be drawn to the many different forms employed in the new works. Sonata, suite, variations and concerto are among the more orthodox, but reference to the individual sections on the works will reveal other more unusual structures. Rubbra's single-movement works in particular show an original approach to form, and Scott's *Aubade* is also cast in a single multi-sectioned movement. Simpson's Variations and Fugue link the two forms thematically. Chagrin's *Preludes for Four* are something in the nature of a suite but set out to give prominence to the individual instruments in successive movements. Lipkin favoured a two-movement plan in his *Interplay*, as did Salter in his Air and Dance, in which the two movements are linked thematically. In his two divertimentos Cooke used the same title for two very contrasted works.

In his invitations to composers Dolmetsch was rarely prescriptive with regard to form, although he did on occasions request the inclusion, if possible, of a movement or section in a lively tempo playable on its own. Dolmetsch and Saxby gave frequent recitals to schools, and the Tarantella from Gordon Jacob's Suite in the composer's keyboard reduction had proved very popular. Dolmetsch could see the practical potential of further pieces of this nature to bring the recorder to an even wider audience, and in his invitations to Nicholas Maw, Martin Dalby and Michael Short he made a specific request for a just such a quick movement.

A total of 40 musicians were involved in the 51 first performances.[1] Included among these were the composers York Bowen, Herbert Murrill and Lionel Salter, who accompanied Dolmetsch in the premieres of their own works.

For the special fiftieth-anniversary recital in 1989 Dolmetsch was joined by the Chamber Orchestra of the Royal Academy (three each of first and second violins, two violas, two cellos and double-bass) led by Martin Burgess with Sir David Lumsden at the harpsichord. The programme included one of the most celebrated works from the Dolmetsch-inspired repertoire, Gordon Jacob's Suite for Recorder and Strings of 1958 in the version for recorder and string orchestra.

At the very heart of the entire Wigmore Hall recital series, however, was the remarkable musical partnership of Carl Dolmetsch and Joseph Saxby. They were first introduced in 1932, when both had been invited to provide music for a production of Shakespeare's *Twelfth Night* at the Oxford Playhouse, Dolmetsch playing the recorder and Saxby the virginals. Very soon after, Dolmetsch, having recognized Saxby's talents, invited him to take part in the Haslemere Festival, and their musical partnership continued from then on. Their musical activities were seriously affected during the war, in which Saxby served as an ARP warden, though not entirely brought to a halt. (On occasions it had been necessary for Saxby to appear on the concert platform in uniform.) In all, their musical collaboration, which Greta Dolmetsch described to me in a conversation as being 'the only one of its kind', endured for 60 years. Examination of the numerous new works they premiered together reveals that many were dedicated to them both, for they were indeed a musical entity. It is poignant that just 17 days separated their deaths in 1997.

A separate section is devoted to each of the 'Wigmore' works and these are presented in chronological order of performance. First-hand information has been sought from a number of the composers themselves, and I am grateful to Jeanne and Marguerite Dolmetsch for their recollections of attendance at many of the recitals and participation in some of the later ones. Greta Dolmetsch, who was so closely involved with the arrangements for most of the Wigmore recitals and thus came into contact with the composers and performers involved in the new works, has likewise been a mine of information.

---

[1] Dolmetsch's own list of works premiered at the Wigmore Hall presents something of a puzzle in connection with the 1963 recital. In addition to the first performance of Gordon Jacob's Variations, the *Variations on an Air by Couperin* for alto recorder and harpsichord by Ingolf Dahl are also noted as having been premiered. The reviews of the recital did not mention the work, and inspection of a copy of the original programme confirmed that it was not included. Although Dolmetsch is likely to have given the premiere of Dahl's work (at least in the UK), it seems this did not take place at the Wigmore Hall. Composed in 1956, it was published by Joseph Boonin in the USA in 1973.

Carl Dolmetsch: Theme and Variations

des rec, hpd

First performance: Wigmore Hall, London, 1 February 1939. Carl Dolmetsch, rec; Joseph Saxby, hpd.

Published: Hebden Bridge: Peacock Press, 2001 (PD 01).

'One of my aims will be to demonstrate the possibilities of the recorder as a virtuoso instrument on a par with the already accepted violin, flute or pianoforte, and to present masterpieces of music which form part of its literature.'

So wrote Carl Dolmetsch, in the very first issue of *Recorder News* in 1939, of his plans for recorder recitals at London's Wigmore Hall, the first given in February that year. It is evident that by 'masterpieces of music' Dolmetsch did not simply mean works from the recorder's past but was also keen to present contemporary pieces for the instrument. But as Dolmetsch later wrote:

> Up to this time however, no modern solo music had yet appeared, nor had earlier composers exploited the instrument's technical resources to the extent Paganini had done for the violin, for instance. This prompted me to write a Paganini-style theme and variations for performance at the first ever recorder recital at the Wigmore Hall, on 1st February 1939.[2]

As noted in the chapter on the 'ten' composers, this recital was reviewed in the *Musical Times* by Edgar Hunt, who noted: 'After the interval Mr. Dolmetsch's phenomenal virtuosity was displayed in his own Theme and Variations in A minor for descant recorder.' Of this first performance Jack Westrup wrote:

> Here there was both an expert reconstruction of the manner of the past, and also a challenge to virtuosity which few besides the composer would care to accept. Mr Dolmetsch made it all sound like child's play, so that it was easy to revel with him in the skips and scamperings.

Dolmetsch was, by his own admission, neither a particularly accomplished nor acknowledged composer, and it was a brave move, as Edgar Hunt later commented in a conversation with the author, to include the Theme and Variations in the programme of this particular recital. However, the example the work was intended to set was perhaps more important and significant than its compositional merits.

At the time my research began the Theme and Variations had not been published and it was my hope that the manuscript would be located during one of my visits to Haslemere. After several visits, however, no manuscript had come to light, at least not among those where it might have been expected to be found. Greta Dolmetsch remained faithfully convinced of its existence but, alas, her

---

[2] Dolmetsch, 'The recorder's 20th century repertoire', p. 247.

failing eyesight prevented her from joining in the search. Eventually, on a Sunday afternoon in October 1999, not long before it was time for me to leave at the end of my visit, Jeanne Dolmetsch finally discovered the manuscript (dated 1938), unexpectedly at the very bottom of a collection of baroque pieces that had obviously been copied out for performance, possibly from originals in the Dolmetsch library. (It is easy to forget that very little recorder music of any kind, even from the seventeenth and eighteenth centuries, had been published in modern editions at the time of the earliest Wigmore Hall recitals.) The copied-out piece immediately next to Dolmetsch's work was, significantly, a set of divisions on a ground by Godfrey Finger; significantly, for Dolmetsch's Theme and Variations are also structured as a set of divisions on a ground. Jeanne noted that her father had always acknowledged a debt to Daniel Purcell and also to the virtuoso violin repertoire. (It was as a violinist that his earliest musical training had begun.)

The eight-bar theme[3] over its simple bass could almost be taken for an extract from *The Division Flute* (1706) or a similar late seventeenth- or early eighteenth-century collection, except that the solo instrument is a descant rather than treble recorder.

For the first few variations we might also be excused for believing that we are listening to a work from the baroque, as quaver, then semiquaver figuration and syncopated and dotted formulas unfold in quite familiar rhythmic patterns.

In variation 6, however, some taxing written-out ornamentation appears and by variation 7 we are left in no doubt that the work is from a later era as the semiquaver and triplet figures are invaded by chromaticism. In variation 8 the triplet figures are taken up by the harpsichord, which for the remaining four variations is increasingly involved in the rhythmic activity, especially the arpeggios in the second half of the ninth variation.

The recorder writing makes particular demands on the player's technique in the very upper reaches of the instrument. In variation 5 the note e'''' is found, and again in variations 7 and 9, where it is approached from $d\#''''$.[4] In variation 11 the recorder has sextuplet figures from beginning to end and features even more intense chromaticism, making demands hardly, if ever, encountered in seventeenth- and eighteenth-century recorder music. The twelfth and final variation returns to a more eighteenth-century style, but the work concludes with a somewhat unusually extended final bar, underlining its virtuoso intent.

The score is full of the markings so characteristically entered by Joseph Saxby, as indications both of harpsichord registration and fingering. What is of interest is that there does not appear to be a fully written-out recorder part and on two sides

---

[3] In the manuscript Dolmetsch headed the theme 1 and numbered the variations from 2 to 12. The published edition leaves the theme unnumbered and numbers the variations 1 to 11.

[4] Dolmetsch had clearly mastered the technique of obtaining these high notes and was to encourage their use in the finale of York Bowen's Sonatina, composed nine years later.

of a final separate sheet are the beginnings only of each variation. On one side is a shortened version of the work that omits variations 3, 5, 9 and 10 and on which is noted '2½ Ms.' to indicate the duration. On the other are the beginnings of the full set of variations in its entirety. It would appear from this that the part served only as a reminder for Dolmetsch, who presumably played the work mostly from memory.

Though not a work of deep musical content, it does display a recorder virtuosity hitherto largely unexplored. There can be little doubt as to the signal Dolmetsch wished it to send out – that the recorder had all the flexibility necessary for it to serve a contemporary repertoire it now so urgently deserved. Just how much influence the Theme and Variations had at the time is hard to tell, but only four months later (as described in Chapter 2) a number of new works, fully in a contemporary idiom, were complete and given their first performances. The seeds of the recorder's twentieth-century repertoire had been sown.

Lennox Berkeley: Sonatina

tr rec (or fl), pn

To Sybil Jackson

1 Moderato. 2 Adagio. 3 Allegro moderato.

First public performance: Wigmore Hall, London, 18 November 1939. Carl Dolmetsch, rec; Christopher Wood, hpd.

Published: London, Schott & Co. Ltd, 1940 (Edition 10015; later OFB 1040).

Though a work by one of the 'ten' composers and dedicated to Sybil Jackson (Berkeley's godmother and a fine amateur pianist and singer), it was Carl Dolmetsch who was destined to give this work both its first private and public performances. It is likely also that Dolmetsch's early performances were responsible for the work's being associated as much if not more with the recorder than with the flute.

As noted in a previous chapter, the first private performance of the work (with Joseph Saxby at the keyboard) was given at the seminal recital at a meeting of the London Contemporary Music Centre on 17 June 1939, and it is in connection with this that Berkeley wrote to Dolmetsch on 11 June 1939:

> Dear Mr. Dolmetsch,
>
> Unfortunately it won't be possible for me to come to the concert on June 17th. I'm very sick about it, as I so much want to hear you play my Sonatina. I was wondering whether it would be possible for me to run through it with you before – I shall be in London on Thurs. & Friday, but if you're not coming to London either of those days, I could come down to Haslemere on Friday afternoon if you could spare the time just to

play it through with me. It's not that I have any misgivings about the performance – I'm sure you'll do it marvellously, but I do want to hear it, and in that case it might be just as well for me to hear it before.

Will you let me know about this?

Yrs. Sincerely

Lennox Berkeley

In a very important postscript, Berkeley noted:

I forgot to put metronome marks. They should be –

I   ♪ = about 168
II very slow – ♪ = about 50
III ♩ = 116

I think these are right but my metronome seems to me to be a little out of order.

Whether Berkeley's metronome was out of order or not, these markings are not as in the published edition which, for the first movement gives the quicker indication of ♩. = 60 (i.e. ♪ = 180); for the second, the slightly quicker tempo of ♪ = 56, but for the last movement the fractionally slower ♩ = 112.

Reports of the 17 June performance must have been received by Berkeley, who, in a letter to Dolmetsch dated 8 August 1939, wrote:

I must congratulate you on your performance of my Sonatina which I gather was in every way excellent. Having heard you play, I had no qualms! I hope that you will play it again sometime – it seems to have been appreciated, and I think it has the advantage of being easily understood.

The success of the first private performance encouraged Dolmetsch to include the work in his Wigmore Hall recital on 18 November 1939. The programme note mentioned the performance at the London Contemporary Music Centre and continued: 'It was the general appreciation, coupled with Mr. Carl Dolmetsch's personal enjoyment and esteem of Mr. Berkeley's Sonatina at this private performance which decided him to give the work its first public performance at the Wigmore Hall today.'

The review in the *Observer* of 19 November 1939 noted: 'Lennox Berkeley has in this sonatina been extremely successful in exploiting the instruments' qualities and the work is without suggestion of pastiche.' That in *The Times* of 20 November 1939 went into more detail:

The work is a success both for the instrument and the composer. Mr. Berkeley has taken some time to find himself stylistically, but in this sonatina his characteristic use of figuration sounds well on the crisp tones of the harpsichord and the melodic material for the wind instrument is happily conceived so that the whole effect is neat, piquant and gay without seeming feather-brained. Here then is something intrinsically charming in a modern idiom that neither imitates nor parodies the 18th century but picks up from it a tradition that had lapsed but can now go forward.

What is of particular interest is the use in this performance of the harpsichord, of which no mention is made in the published score. In view of the smaller number of harpsichords to be found at that time, this is entirely practical and a feature of a number of the earliest published works for recorder and keyboard. However, as the work is so often heard on the piano, and the keyboard writing reminiscent in places of that in Berkeley's Six Preludes for piano, it is perhaps difficult to imagine the work played on the harpsichord. It would nevertheless, be of interest to hear it played this way.[5] The copy of the published score in the archive contains, among Joseph Saxby's characteristic markings, his indications for harpsichord registration, and it is clear he played the work on that instrument.

On 29 November 1939 Berkeley wrote to Dolmetsch: 'I was delighted to get your letter, and it is a great encouragement to me that your fine performance of my Sonatina was so successful. I was very pleased with your playing of it.'

It is worthy of mention that the original date and time for the recital were to have been 8 November at 8.15 p.m., as indicated by a handbill in the archive, overstamped with the rearranged date and time (3.15 p.m.). It should also be mentioned that Christopher Wood deputized at the harpsichord for Joseph Saxby who, a note in the programme states, was on civil defence duties. Both these changes were symptomatic of the onset of the war, which had an obvious and serious affect on the commissioning, performing and publishing of new works for the recorder.

Dolmetsch performed the Sonatina again in August 1941 in a radio broadcast and wrote to Berkeley to inform him. Berkeley replied on 11 August 1941, and the letter, in addition to continued enthusiasm for the work, gives some indication of his preferences regarding performance of the last movement:

> It was very kind of you to write and tell me that you were playing my Sonatina, and I am delighted that you still like it.
>
> I listened to it, and it was a joy to hear again the lovely sound that you make. I enjoyed the performance, the first movement was particularly good. My only criticism (you know that composers are never satisfied) is that I think the last movement is better without any variation of tempo at all. It sounded to me that you took the introductory

---

[5] During conversations with Evelyn Nallen and David Gordon in August 2001 I mentioned the earliest performances with harpsichord. This clearly intrigued them and they included a performance with harpsichord in a recital in Holy Trinity Church, Prince Consort Road, South Kensington, on 27 October 2001. As was to be expected, the work took on an entirely different character, somehow leaner and more brittle in the outer movements, while David's use of the harp stop and spread chords maintained the atmosphere of the slow movement. Despite the initially apparent pianistic nature of the keyboard part, performance with harpsichord is entirely practical.

bars slower than the rest, and I think that the coda must be in very strict time too. Some of the passages must be appallingly difficult on the recorder – I can't think how you do it!

It would be so nice to see you. When you are in London do let me know, and come and see me.

I hope you'll be able to play my Sonatina often. Your interest in it is very encouraging.

Berkeley mentioned the difficulty of the work on the recorder again in a letter dated 6 May 1957 with reference to another performance to be given by Dolmetsch: 'I quite often hear it played on the flute – it appears that nobody but you can manage it on the recorder.'

Of course it is now firmly established in the recorder repertoire, and students tackle it confidently, although it does present a number of technical difficulties.

The opening is as arresting as any in the repertoire: a *fortissimo* chord of A minor on the keyboard leads immediately to a quiet rustling semiquaver accompaniment in 6/8 over which the recorder enters with a slightly uneasy melody. The second subject is smoother and in semiquavers over a rhythmic pedal C. Both are developed extensively before the movement concludes with a quiet coda based on the first subject.

The second movement is a quiet reverie based almost entirely on elements of the opening melody. Its mood of quiet resignation (even in C major) seems to anticipate that of the finale of Berkeley's Serenade for strings Op. 12, completed between September and November 1939, shortly after the Sonatina.

Unlike the serenade however, in which the slow movement is placed last (of four), the Sonatina ends in a much more lively mood. After a brief introductory flourish the recorder re-enters with the rondo theme, a melody of both wit and elegance showing a distinctly French influence. The first interlude is based on a march-like motif that cunningly returns to the rondo theme, the first phrase of which is played on the piano and the second on the recorder. The second interlude develops with bustling semiquaver figuration, sometimes exchanged between the players, and leads to a final restatement of the opening rondo theme with the recorder at the octave. With increasingly transparent textures, the movement ends like the first, quietly, with octave As on the piano.

While examining the structure and character of the work, it is of considerable interest to compare the published edition of the recorder part with that in a manuscript in the Dolmetsch archive. Professor Peter Dickinson kindly examined a copy of the first page and concluded that it had been copied from Berkeley's own manuscript with a tendency to imitate some of his mannerisms in the lettering of expression marks. It is not, however, in Berkeley's hand, and it seems likely that the copy was made by Dolmetsch himself while he had the score for the first performance. There are a number of minor differences of articulation, and what are almost certainly some accidentally missed slurs, but of particular significance are the closing bars of the first movement (Ex. 3.1).

Ex. 3.1. Lennox Berkeley, Sonatina for treble recorder and piano. First movement; last five bars as they appear in an MS recorder part in the Dolmetsch archive. Reproduced by permission of Schott & Co. Ltd.

A pencil note above the stave over the group of three semiquavers in the penultimate bar indicates '8ve', and the appoggiatura in the final bar is crossed out, thus reading as the published edition. An unaltered change appears in the third movement four bars before figure 22 (Ex. 3.2).

Ex. 3.2. Lennox Berkeley, Sonatina for treble recorder and piano. Third movement, two bars before figure 22 as they appear in an MS recorder part in the Dolmetsch archive. Reproduced by permission of Schott & Co. Ltd.

Compare this with the published edition (Ex. 3.3).

Ex. 3.3. Lennox Berkeley, Sonatina for treble recorder and piano. Third movement, two bars before figure 22 as they appear in the recorder part of the published edition. Reproduced by permission of Schott & Co. Ltd.

If the manuscript part was copied from Berkeley's manuscript, then the different readings it contains must be considered as first thoughts. Whether the pencil alterations to the end of the first movement were by the composer or suggestions by Dolmetsch it is not possible to tell. This manuscript part does not contain the alternatives in the first movement provided to avoid the recorder's problematic high F#.

In conclusion, it is significant that Berkeley noted the work had the advantage of being easily understood. It is this, and the work's musical refinement and technical challenges, that have no doubt earned it an enduring place in the recorder repertoire enjoyed by few other pieces from the period.

York Bowen: Sonatina, Op. 121

rec, pn

To Carl Dolmetsch

1 Moderato e semplice (tr rec). 2 Andante tranquillo (tr rec). 3 Allegro giocoso (des rec).

First performance: Wigmore Hall, London, 28 May 1947. Carl Dolmetsch, rec; York Bowen, pn.

Published: Ampleforth: Emerson Edition Ltd, 1994 (Emerson Edition 113).

After the war, Dolmetsch was keen to continue with the commissioning of new works for recorder and, as Manuel Jacobs had done previously, made a direct approach to various composers.[6] The first was York Bowen, whom Dolmetsch visited at his home in Worthing in the late summer of 1946, taking his recorders with him to give the composer a practical demonstration of the instrument's capabilities.

Dolmetsch approached Bowen for a work for recorder at the suggestion of Clinton Gray-Fisk,[7] though there are other possible links. Perhaps the most direct is that Bowen was Joseph Saxby's godfather. Greta Dolmetsch identified another link in the person of Miss Keyte-Perry, the headmistress of Oak Hall School in Haslemere. She was a good friend of Bowen's wife Sylvia, and an enthusiastic supporter of the Dolmetsch cause. Greta further noted that an early performance of the Sonatina took place at Oak Hall School.

Dolmetsch's visit created just the stimulation necessary, and in a letter dated 4 September 1946 Bowen wrote:

> ... I thought you would be interested to hear that your visit and enthusiasm has borne immediate response and I have been engaged in writing you a short Sonata (or Sonatina) in three movements. In fact the rough sketch is already finished and I feel quite delighted with it – finding the greatest interest in it.

The composer's reference to a short sonata or sonatina seemed to cause him continued uncertainty, as the work's title is given sometimes as Sonata, and at others as Sonatina in subsequent correspondence. Indeed the uncertainty remains even in the manuscript score, which is titled 'Sonata' while the recorder part is headed 'Sonatina'. Bowen's enthusiasm for the piece is clearly apparent, as his letter continues:

> When you have returned [from Holland] I hope we may arrange a meeting to try it over and I will have a clear recorder part in copy, although I shall not make a proper piano score until any details are discussed – in case of alteration. I am leaving out certain indications of legato or staccato until you advise as to the most effective way.

---

[6] Dolmetsch, 'The recorder's 20th century repertoire', p. 247.

[7] Id., 'An introduction to the recorder', p. 50.

It was also in this letter that Bowen confirmed his intention to score the finale for descant recorder: 'I have decided on the descant (C) recorder as I suggested for the finale and it will be fun to have the change of register and character.' This was the first instance in modern times of the use of more than one size of recorder in the same solo work.

It would appear that Dolmetsch had requested a work for recorder and harpsichord, as the piece was to be included in a recital made up almost entirely of early music. This seemed to be causing the composer some difficulty and his letter concludes:

> The only thing is that I can't somehow feel the keyboard part is quite suited to the harpsichord! It seems like piano colour to me – however this can be decided on after you have seen the work.
> I feel it is going to be a success and shall be eager to show you presently.

This uncertainty regarding the keyboard writing was to continue to occupy the composer's thoughts, as will be seen from later letters.

In a letter dated 10 September 1946 Bowen invited Dolmetsch to try through the work at the Royal Academy of Music on 27 September. The composer was keen to involve Dolmetsch in details of articulation noting: 'I have omitted to indicate legato or tonguing where I feel in doubt, and you can help me over that.'

Further concern regarding the use of the harpsichord is expressed in a letter dated 18 September 1946: 'I hope the Sonata will suit harpsichord all right but shall be anxious to try that at first opportunity!' The letter concluded with the positive news: 'I have finished the work (in rough copy) and your part is copied neatly!'

The play through duly took place, and it is clear that the composer learned much from it, as in a letter to Dolmetsch dated 28 September 1946 he notes:

> Thank you so much for coming along to try over the Sonatina and I must say I felt quite pleased with the effect of it! You certainly can deal with any kind of passage with great ease and I am glad to find that I have not been writing absurd difficulties.

The letter continues regarding the question of the suitability of the harpsichord for the keyboard part, and concludes that perhaps the piano will be the more appropriate instrument. It is interesting to note, however, that Bowen's keen composer's ear could detect that problems of balance were likely to occur when the recorder was set against a modern grand piano:

> I cannot get away from the feeling that probably owing to habit and instinct I have written in a pianistic way and in hardly suitable compass and passages for harpsichord in this case, and I would suggest that in the event of any performance in a hall such as Wigmore for instance, they should provide a *small* sized grand instead of a concert grand. In this case there should not be the massive depth of *bass* as is so prevalent with these monsters!

I have in fact heard two pianos of approx 6 feet size used at a recital there and the effect was quite perfect.

I give this suggestion for what it is worth and if handled gently (as some of us *can*!) I think the balance could be made perfect.

Looking forward to playing it again with you and now I will see about making a decent copy of the score.

Dolmetsch was obviously equally pleased with the new work and wrote to Bowen to express this and to invite him to play the piano for the first performance due to take place on 28 May 1947. The composer was delighted and replied to Dolmetsch in a letter dated 6 October 1946:

Dear Mr. Dolmetsch

Thank you for your kind letter of 30th Sept.

Next May has been filling up rapidly for me and I am delighted to find that so far May 28th is free. So I shall *keep* it free and will be most happy to play the Sonatina with you at its 1st performance!

Our best wishes to you,

Yours very sincerely,

York Bowen

At its first performance, the Sonatina was well received by the critics. Dolmetsch's article on the recorder's twentieth-century repertoire mentioned above quotes a review from *The Times*: 'Its first two movements (for treble recorder) are lyrical, but the brilliance of the finale (for descant recorder) will put the work beyond the reach of many players, which is a pity, since it is agreeable music and preserves a happy balance between the two unequal instruments.'

Bowen's comment regarding this is contained in a letter written to Dolmetsch soon after: 'Of *course* the Finale is beyond most players but it was written to suit you!' In this respect the work shares similarities with the Violin Concerto by Samuel Barber, with its first two lyrical and technically straightforward movements and dazzling and virtuoso finale.

Dolmetsch's above-mentioned article also quotes from a *Daily Telegraph* review that comments in particular on the gentle effect of the lower register of the recorder in the second movement.

Although there was discussion between Bowen and Dolmetsch regarding publication of the work, it remained unpublished at the time it received its second performance on 8 February 1960 at the Wigmore Hall. As at the first performance, Bowen played the piano, and at the request of Dolmetsch produced a short programme note:

This work is in three movements, the first of which is in conventional sonata form with two themes and a short section of development. The music moves gently and leans to the lyrical in style. The second and slower movement remains tranquil in mood and is in very free form. The last movement demands a quick change of recorder from the previous treble in F to the smaller descant in C which like the piccolo to the flute sounds an octave higher than actually written. In this Finale the music is completely different to the preceding and shows the more brilliant and agile possibilities of this very effective instrument. This movement might well be termed 'Scherzo – Finale.'

The composer achieves an overall unity by using the same melodic formula for the initial theme of all three movements. The first three notes rise by tones or semitones, followed by the next two rising by the interval of a third. In the 6/8 time of the first two movements, and at moderate tempos, this is immediately apparent. In the last movement, however, the change to common time and the regrouping of note values, converts the languorous melodies of the first two into one which, in its lively and extrovert character, at once suits the descant recorder in a manner that initially disguises this subtle metamorphosis.

It was not until the work was in a sense 'rediscovered' in 1993 and championed and recorded by Piers Adams that the Sonata finally appeared in a published edition. Some very high notes exceeding the usual upward compass of the descant recorder are retained and the Emerson edition provides some fingerings for these notes suggested by Carl Dolmetsch as follows:

High E 0-2-/----   High F# 0-2-/45--

This fingering for high E is frequently flat, and Piers Adams prefers the alternative indicated below that makes use of stopping the bell of the instrument with the knee, a practice of which Carl Dolmetsch did not entirely approve, preferring to use a specially fitted bell key.[8]

High E 0-23/-56-/8 (8 = stopping the bell with the knee)

However, at the time of the first performance in 1947 a bell key had not yet been fitted to a recorder and some practical method of playing the problematic high F# in the second movement would have had to be found. This was usually achieved by the use of a special fingering and slurring up from the E immediately below.

On examination of the manuscript in the Dolmetsch archive, the flourish in bar 69 of the final movement is something of a puzzle. This ascends to a top F in the recorder part and this is also the reading in the published edition. However, in the manuscript score the top F appears to have had a ledger line drawn through it and 'E' written above in pencil. A tie has been marked between the preceding top E and

---

[8] In what was almost certainly his last article on the recorder Dolmetsch described the use of the knee to stop the bell of the instrument as looking 'amateurish beyond belief': see 'The recorder in evolution', p. 55.

this altered note. The first broadcast performance given by Dolmetsch and Bowen is preserved in a recording in the archives and was drawn to my attention by Jeanne Dolmetsch. In this, the top Es are indeed played tied, as rather cryptically indicated in the manuscript.

Comparison of the manuscript score with the recorder part is required to determine which alterations were initiated by Dolmetsch, and what was originally notated by the composer. The published edition does not make this distinction, and it is therefore interesting to compare Piers Adams's recording of the work with the published edition in this respect. In particular, in the upward moving flourish concluding the finale Adams plays only up to a top C as in the manuscript (Ex. 3.4). The extension up to high E is in pencil in Dolmetsch's hand and is as he played it in the first broadcast performance.

Ex. 3.4. York Bowen, Sonatina for recorder and piano. Third movement, last two bars of the recorder part as they appear in the MS score. Reproduced by permission of Emerson Edition Ltd.

Not included in the published edition is an alternative ending that Bowen supplied in the manuscript recorder part and which contains a very high G, which Dolmetsch has marked down an octave in pencil. It is not clear how the keyboard part is to be adapted to match this extended ending (Ex. 3.5).

Ex. 3.5. York Bowen, Sonatina for recorder and piano. Third movement, alternative ending provided in the MS recorder part. Reproduced by permission of Emerson Edition Ltd.

At the end of the recorder part the timings of the movements have been written in pencil as 3.10 for the first, 3.30 for the second and 3.15 for the finale. These are appreciably quicker for the first two movements than in Piers Adams's recording and would indicate that Dolmetsch, and presumably the composer, understood faster speeds for the tempo indications (for which no metronome markings are given) than they might otherwise suggest.

Why such an immediately attractive work should remain for so long unpublished and largely unperformed may seem at first sight difficult to explain. The technical demands of the finale movement in comparison with the other two are almost certainly the reason why it was not published at the time of its composition and indeed subsequently. Fashions in music also change, and the years following Bowen's death in 1961 saw his music largely neglected. However, more recent interest in the Sonatina coincides with a revival in that of his music generally and in his piano and chamber music in particular, some of which has been recorded. This has enabled the Sonatina also to enjoy something of the attention it deserves.

Edmund Rubbra: Meditazioni sopra 'Cœurs désolés', Op. 67

rec (or fl), hpd (or pn)

For Carl Dolmetsch and Joseph Saxby

First performance: Wigmore Hall, London, 10 May 1949. Carl Dolmetsch, tr rec; Joseph Saxby, hpd.

Published: Croydon: Alfred Lengnick & Co. Ltd, 1949 (3689).

Carl Dolmetsch's awareness of Edmund Rubbra dated back to the 1930s, when Rubbra was a student at the Royal College of Music and a contemporary of Dolmetsch's brother Rudolf.[9] It was at this time that Rubbra's interest in and love of early music was first aroused.[10] Edgar Hunt had first met Rubbra in 1935 at the Casa d'Arte Studio in St John's Wood, where he led a group of madrigal singers. The Casa d'Arte Circle had been formed by Madame Matton-Painparé (who played the viola da gamba) to promote interest in early music. Thus, when Dolmetsch was seeking a composer for a new work for recorder, Edgar Hunt suggested that Rubbra might be sympathetic to the idea.

It has not been possible to discover any letters from Dolmetsch to Rubbra regarding the genesis of the work, but a letter from Rubbra to Dolmetsch dated 12 March 1949 reads:

Dear Mr. Dolmetsch,

I will write a little recorder work for you. Kindly give full particulars of the concert, and the latest date you would like to have the work. Please remind me of the compass of the recorder for which you would like the work written.

Best wishes,

Yours sincerely,

Edmund Rubbra

This short letter was the beginning not only of what Edgar Hunt considers to be

---

[9] Letter dated 11 January 1994 from Carl Dolmetsch to the author.
[10] Ibid.

among the greatest works written for recorder in the twentieth century, but also of a musical relationship with Dolmetsch that was to result in a long friendship and a series of fine works for the instrument.

The date of this letter is significant, as below the closing bar in the published score is printed 'Easter Monday 1949' (18 April). The work was thus completed in barely five weeks.

Only one other letter relating directly to *Meditazioni* has come to light and is again from Rubbra. It is dated 11 May 1949, the day after the first performance, which Rubbra obviously attended. It reads as follows:

Dear Mr. Dolmetsch,

It was, I felt, all a great success last night, and I do congratulate you on your playing, which was first rate throughout. Please do also thank Mr. Saxby from me. When you know the piece better I think you will feel that it should move a little more leisurely, especially in the transitions from one meditation to another.

Kindly send the score back to me as soon as possible so that the printing can be done: and would you please indicate in your part all the ornaments that you made (and which I liked). Please also ask Mr. Saxby if the harpsichord part is alright: I am a little doubtful about the low bass octaves. I shall dedicate the work to you both.

With all best wishes,

Yours sincerely,

Edmund Rubbra

This letter reveals much: first, that the composer's slow tempo indications should be carefully observed (see later comments by Edgar Hunt); second, that the ornamentation included in the published edition stems from Dolmetsch's own interpretation; and finally, that Rubbra had certain doubts about the harpsichord part. It is thus interesting to note the bracketed octaves in the bass seven bars after figure 4 in the published keyboard score.

Edgar Hunt performed the piece with Rubbra himself at the piano at a concert given at the Royal Opera House in 1957 to mark the seventy-fifth anniversary of the formation of the Incorporated Society of Musicians. (Dolmetsch had been invited to perform the piece, but he and Joseph Saxby were to be on tour in the United States at the time.) From the rehearsals for this performance Hunt noted that Rubbra really did mean the very slow metronome speeds marked, and that he preferred the piano to the harpsichord for the keyboard part.[11]

The work seems to have been well received from the outset. In an article in *Recorder and Music Magazine*[12] Dolmetsch quoted the critic in *The Times* who wrote: 'This piece is built on the theme of the chanson "Cœurs désolés" by Josquin

---

[11] Obituary of Edmund Rubbra by Edgar Hunt in *The Recorder and Music Magazine*, March 1986, p. 279.

[12] Dolmetsch, 'The recorder's 20th century repertoire', p. 247.

des Prés ... noble music which was nonetheless original and striking for having its roots in the past.'

In an article on Rubbra's chamber music (*The Listener*, 15 May 1952)[13] Wilfred Mellers describes the *Meditazioni* in these terms: '... though small in size and scope [it] is not little in effect. Evolutionary variation, flowing lyricism, new melodic derivations in contrasting rhythms, warm spacing of the harmony – all the features of the mature Rubbra symphony occur, as it were in microcosm.'

In a letter to Rubbra dated 11 October 1954 Dolmetsch commented:

> ... I have just heard from a firm which sells many modern recorder works and acts as an agent for Lengnick that your 'Meditazioni' is still the best seller of them all. As you know, I have occasion to play it constantly during my tours here and abroad – it was particularly well received in New Zealand last year.

The *Meditazioni* received a repeat performance in Dolmetsch's Wigmore Hall recital on 6 February 1963, for which Rubbra wrote the following programme note:

> This work is based on a fragment from the chanson *Cœurs Désolés*, used by Josquin des Prés. Although this fragment develops variation-wise through a series of eight contrasted sections, it is not to be construed as a set of variations in any rigid sense. The title *Meditazioni sopra 'Cœurs Désolés'* was deliberately chosen, for the composer uses a process akin to the psychological law of 'free association', whereby links in the subconscious come to the surface. Here, then, any melodic or rhythmic resemblances that may be found between the chanson fragment and any of the eight sections are, in a sense, fortuitous. The sections are continuous, and each one derives its particular pattern-formation from hints thrown out by its predecessor: No. 1 from the mordent of the tune; No. 2 from the chain of quavers at the end of (1); No. 3 (A major) from isolations of a pattern found more continuously in (2); the accompaniment of No. 4 (C sharp minor) takes over this pattern, the recorder adding a long independent tune; No. 5 uses the melodic interval of a second prominent at the end of (4) and which is also in the tune; No. 6 (*grazioso*) develops the recorder ending of (5) in the harpsichord part, the recorder making a playful addition to it; No. 7 develops the triplet pattern ending (6); and No. 8 makes of this a mirror canon (in D major). A *fortissimo* return is then made to the opening.

Following this performance, the reviewer in *The Times* of 7 February 1963 wrote that the work was, 'music of heart-easing noble beauty somehow transcending the expressive limitations of both these instruments.'

Although Dolmetsch advised composers to avoid the treble recorder's high F#, the *Meditazioni*, like York Bowen's and Lennox Berkeley's Sonatinas, includes this problematic note. It is, however, placed so as to be able to be slurred from the E below, and the fingering is given in the score. At seven bars after figure 5 an

---

[13] 'Rubbra's recent chamber music'. A cutting of the article is preserved in the Dolmetsch archive.

alternative held minim F# is given for recorder, crotchets being provided for the flute which, together with the oboe is indicated as an alternative solo instrument in the printed edition. This was no doubt as much a practical or commercial as it was an artistic consideration.

Edgar Hunt informed me in a conversation I had with him regarding the work in September 1997 that he had been concerned, not having a bell key, about the high F# seven bars after figure 5 when preparing for the performance for the ISM 75th anniversary. Rubbra had thus provided a modification to the passage avoiding the problematic note, which has not however survived.

Dolmetsch himself included a performance of the *Meditazioni* at his Wigmore Hall recital on 3 April 1986 as a tribute to Rubbra, who had died on 14 February that year.

The popularity of this piece with players and audiences alike is not difficult to appreciate. From its opening bars it creates a remarkable and unique atmosphere. I attended a recital given by Ross Winters in Aylsham, Norfolk, in July 1998. The audience, made up mostly of non-recorder players and probably hearing the work for the first time, was, at the conclusion of the piece, visibly moved by what they had just heard. Edgar Hunt's claims for the piece remain as valid now as when he first made them.

Herbert Murrill: Sonata

tr rec (or fl), hpd (or pn)

To Carl Dolmetsch

1 Largo. 2 Presto. 3 Recitativo (Andante a piacere). 4 Finale (Allegro non troppo).

First performance: Wigmore Hall, London, 10 May 1950. Carl Dolmetsch, rec; Herbert Murrill, hpd.

Published: Oxford: Oxford University Press, 1951.

There is correspondence in the Dolmetsch archive between Carl Dolmetsch and Herbert Murrill dating back to 1942, when Murrill was music programme organizer at the BBC. The earliest letters are in connection with broadcasts of early music by the Dolmetsch Consort, but those from 1947 and 1949 relate to broadcasts of the new works for recorder by York Bowen and Edmund Rubbra then recently premiered. It is likely that the idea of requesting Murrill to write a new piece for recorder came to Dolmetsch at this time. It is evident that Dolmetsch had sent a recorder as a gift for Murrill's daughter with the suggestion of a work for the instrument, as a letter from Murrill dated 17 May 1949 reads:

> It is so extremely kind of you to write, and I am bidden by Carolyn Jane to reply immediately to thank you for the lovely surprise she received. Actually, we both will be

competing for the instrument, and there will be rivalry until she flies off to school again. Then I don't know which of us will have the recorder!

Seriously, thank you so very much for a charming and unexpected gift. My own piece, in return, will be a poor thing in comparison, but when it is done I hope it will give you pleasure.

Work on the new piece seems not to have got under way for a while, as on 1 January 1950, in a letter of greeting for the New Year, Murrill wrote:

> It is time for me to think seriously about this recorder piece of mine. I have the recorder you gave me and I know the compass, but before I begin I would like to ask if any particular *sort* of piece suits your purpose best. A sort of slow (pastoral) thing – a Pavan & Galliard (truly English form) – a miniature 3 movement Sonatina. Have you any ideas? If you have, I'll be glad to hear them, as it always helps me to see more clearly the finished product.

We cannot determine if it was Dolmetsch who suggested a sonata-type work, as no copy of a reply to the above letter is to be found in the archive. However, work must have progressed rapidly over the next few weeks, as on 20 February 1950 Murrill wrote to Dolmetsch in connection with a play-through of the new piece that had obviously recently taken place.

> It was grand to see you last week and especially kind of you to give such pleasure to those dear friends of ours, who were thrilled to hear you at close quarters and to be 'in' on the birth of a new piece – however small (like the housemaid's baby – 'only a very *small* one'!)[14]

The letter continued with discussion of more technical and practical considerations. Dolmetsch had obviously suggested that the recorder play an octave higher at the beginning of the second movement:

> I've been thinking about that 8ve opening of the Presto movement. Honestly I'd prefer to keep it at written pitch, *if* you think it will effectively 'get through' in the lower register. If you really want to put it up, I will (a little sadly) agree, but I don't think this should extend beyond the first note of the third bar. Then a drop of a 10th to the low G. If you don't start on this low G, I think the line up to the high B is spoiled. But I'll leave it to you to decide when you begin to work on the piece. The low register is nice, and the keyboard part *very* light.

From the published edition it is clear that Murrill's wishes were, in the end, adopted. The letter concludes with considerations regarding the flourish near the end of the same movement:

---

[14] In view of the title *Piece for my Friends* that Murrill gave to the little work he wrote soon afterwards for Dolmetsch's twin daughters Jeanne and Marguerite, it is likely they to whom the composer is referring here.

As to the tiny cadenza at the end of this movement, I like the one you improvised immensely. But if there is any arpeggio figure in it, you will want to know the basic chord. So here it is:

I have wondered whether a simple up-and-down scamper might not be as effective as anything:

Again I'm content to leave this to your good judgement. But do you think we should print a cadenza when the piece is published?

And now – do you want a keyboard part? I have only one as yet, but could make another fairly soon if you like.

I apologise for so many questions!

The little cadenza was to come under further consideration in later correspondence before the work was published.

The day after the first performance (10 May 1950) Murrill, who had obviously enjoyed taking part in it, wrote to Dolmetsch: '... I must thank you for launching this very small ship of mine – of ours – so happily and delightfully on the troubled waters of the musical world! It was a great joy to have a part in your recital and I spent a fine evening in every way.'

A review in the *Daily Telegraph* of 11 May 1950 commented on the work's brevity and unpretentiousness.

Three months later, on 11 July, Dolmetsch and Murrill gave the first broadcast performance of the Sonata on the BBC Third Programme in a recital that also included first performances of works by Croft Jackson and Richard Arnell.

The work was then still in manuscript, but was soon being prepared for publication. On 10 September Murrill wrote to Dolmetsch requesting his assistance:

I'd be most grateful if you could cast your eye over the proof of the recorder part. It is fairly clean I think – I've added a correction or two.

1) Is the second movement best left entirely unslurred? It looks a little curious to me, but if you think it best tongued throughout, of course it will be left.

2   Herbert Murrill c. 1950.

2) Your little cadenza – is the notation right as it stands? I wondered if the final D were better indicated as a small quaver or semi quaver, so –

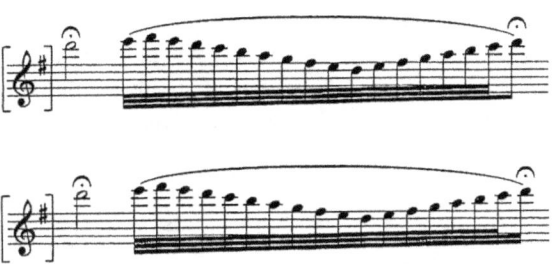

Let me know what you think. If it's clear as it stands in proof, let's leave it.

Interestingly, although the final note was included as a quaver, the published version of the cadenza differs from both the versions indicated in Murrill's letter. A manuscript recorder part in Murrill's hand is in the archive and contains Dolmetsch's pencil markings showing his articulation and ornamentation suggestions. These are quite close to the published version, but in the third movement a number of quaver groups have been slurred below the longer phrase marks. Also in the third movement, three quaver pairs (in the sixth, seventh and eleventh bars from the end) have been pencilled in as dotted quaver – semiquaver. In the last movement staccato dots have been placed over the unslurred notes in the first bar, but no slurs have been indicated in bars 2 to 6. These were no doubt added by analogy. The Finale contains three high F#s: one is indicated as slurred up from E, but the remaining two are more hazardously slurred up from D. The F sharp fingering and need for slurring are noted at the foot of the page in Dolmetsch's hand. Yet another version of the second-movement cadenza is written in ink and is not yet as that finally published, descending only to an F#.

Dolmetsch considered that the work clearly reflected the composer's love of French music. The critic in *The Times* of 11 May 1950 reported it as 'an admirably poised new sonata for treble recorder and harpsichord in four concise movements by Herbert Murrill, who with customary skill, combines piquant harmony with much rhythmic ingenuity ...'

The *Largo* has, from the outset, a delicate expressiveness and the Presto revels in the rhythmic ambiguity provided by the 6/8 – 3/4 time signature, with 9/8 and 5/8 bars adding further subtlety. In the *Recitativo*, the recorder's melody, in a mixture of 3/4 and 2/4 bars, is accompanied with impressive economy by transparent, arpeggiated chords. The Finale is gigue-like, with an imitative opening, a calmer middle section and a flourish in a concluding coda.

There is a signed copy of the published score in the archive inscribed: 'To Carl, with gratitude for his performance. Herbert Murrill 1951.' In the front cover is taped a letter from Herbert Murrill to Marie Dolmetsch dated 17 February 1951.

The final paragraph reads: 'Here, for Carl, is an advance copy of *our* Sonata, to be published on 1st March. It looks very well in print, and although they print alternatives for both instruments, I do hope the recorder players won't be put off by the flautists or the pianists by the harpsichordists!'

As with a number of the earlier new works, Murrill's Sonata has retained a place in the repertoire, possibly because of its inclusion in grade examination syllabuses, but certainly because it is an attractive work of only modest technical difficulty.

Cyril Scott: Aubade

tr rec (or fl/vn), pn

To Carl Dolmetsch

First performance: Wigmore Hall, London, 10 May 1952. Carl Dolmetsch, rec; Joseph Saxby, hpd.

Published: London: Schott & Co. Ltd, 1953 (Edition 10330 (R.M.S. 512)).

Unfortunately only one letter regarding this work has come to light at Haslemere, and all that is to be found in the archive in addition to this is a copy of the published score containing a note which reads 'From Mr. Cyril Scott and Schotts'. This score also contains a manuscript of the recorder part, which is possibly in Scott's hand, and contains only a few very minor differences from the published edition.

For the reasons why Dolmetsch requested a work for recorder from Scott, we should turn, perhaps, to Edmund Rubbra. In his early teens Rubbra had discovered the music of Scott, and at the age of 16 given a concert in Northampton (his home town) devoted entirely to Scott's music. As a result Rubbra became a pupil of Scott both for piano and composition, even before winning a composition scholarship to Reading University at the age of 19 and an open scholarship to the Royal College of Music a year later.

Following the success of Rubbra's *Meditazioni sopra 'Cœurs désolés'* in 1949, Dolmetsch made several requests to the composer in the early 1950s for a further new work for recorder. A letter from Rubbra to Dolmetsch dated 9 December 1950 apologizes that it will not be possible to get a new work ready in time for the 1951 Wigmore Hall recital and suggests Wilfrid Mellers be approached. In the event, Dolmetsch did not perform a new work at the 1951 recital, instead giving a repeat performance of the Berkeley Sonatina. This was the only occasion between 1949 and 1989 on which a new work was not performed.

It is possible that in subsequent communication (perhaps not written) Rubbra suggested to Dolmetsch his former teacher Cyril Scott, or perhaps knowing Rubbra's early enthusiasm for Scott's music, Dolmetsch approached the composer himself. (Scott had abandoned composition in 1940 but renewed his activities in 1946 with some large-scale works and also, significantly, chamber music.) However, in the absence of any firm evidence, this remains conjecture.

Scott was very appreciative of the first performance, as his letter of 14 May 1952 makes clear:

> Dear Mr. Dolmetsch and Mr. Saxby,
>
> May I express my thanks for the trouble you took over my work and for giving it such a fine performance? I was very pleased to see what a full and appreciative house you got, though it was only what you deserved. The notice in THE TIMES was very gratifying, and that in the D.T. also good by implication. I didn't see any others.
>
> Mrs. Carl suggested that I should one day write you a Concerto – well, with luck, who knows ...
>
> With warm greetings to you both and again many thanks.
>
> Sincerely,
>
> Cyril Scott

The review in *The Times* of 12 May 1952 was indeed encouraging: 'In his new 'Aubade' Cyril Scott does not overload the medium emotionally, yet nevertheless treats it with sufficient respect to produce a piece of solid musical substance (with a particularly interesting and harmonically stimulating harpsichord part) instead of a mere sweet nothing.'

The published edition makes no mention of the harpsichord for the keyboard part, no doubt, as with the Rubbra *Meditazioni*, for practical and commercial considerations. If indeed Scott did make a conscious effort to write idiomatically for the harpsichord, the result is certainly as effective when played on the piano.

The popularity and performance of much of Scott's music between the wars was due, to an extent, to its novelty and at times its exoticism. The *Aubade* exhibits some of these characteristics. Constructed in one continuous movement, it nevertheless contains many changes of tempo and mood (and time signature). The harmonies are rich and unusual, and the melodic line embraces a number of phrases making use of the whole tone scale.

From the very first entry of the recorder at bar 9 there is a seemingly inexhaustible flow of melodic invention that gives a feeling of improvisation. It is not until bar 127 that the opening theme is effectively re-introduced, but the recorder's melody is given a somewhat different harmonic accompaniment. Much the same treatment is given to the recorder melody moving in quavers played in parallel with the piano right hand between bars 38 and 45. This reappears, again in varied form, between bars 134 and 137. The final page maintains the rhapsodic atmosphere with long recorder trills and a last reference to the recorder's quaver theme before the music finally comes to rest on a G major chord, even then with C# and E♭ appoggiaturas.

The given alternative scorings for flute or violin might lead to the assumption that the writing is not totally idiomatic for the recorder. Perhaps at times it is not, but the recorder's sound certainly adds to the colour of the work.

Since much of the recorder repertoire of this period had its roots in the music of the past, Scott's piece stands out for its originality. Indeed the brief programme note for the first performance notes, 'The composer's style is in no way influenced by the earlier literature for the instrument, but, in unashamed fashion, treats their resources on their own merits without compromise.' For this, if no other reason, it deserves to be better known, and players who do get to know it will discover a work of considerable originality in a harmonic language rarely to be found elsewhere in the repertoire.

Antony Hopkins: Suite

des rec, pn

To Walter Bergmann

1 Prelude (Allegretto, quasi pastorale). 2 Scherzo (Prestissimo). 3 Canon (Andante tranquillo). 4 Jig (Vivace).

First performance: Wigmore Hall, London, 8 May 1953. Carl Dolmetsch, rec; Joseph Saxby, hpd.

Published: London: Schott & Co. Ltd, 1953 (Edition 10339).

Dolmetsch seemed to have had some difficulty in obtaining a work for his 1953 Wigmore Hall recital. Rubbra was busy with other compositional commitments and Arnold Bax had unfortunately not found the inspiration to compose a work as had been hoped. There had also been mention of performing the Reizenstein Partita.

Fortunately, the young Antony Hopkins had recently completed a new work dedicated to Walter Bergmann. As Dolmetsch recounted, Schott generously held up publication to allow the first performance from the composer's manuscript at the Wigmore Hall.

This was not Hopkins's first composition for recorder as he had written four short pieces for treble recorder and spinet as incidental music for the Arts Theatre Club 1946 Production of Bernard Shaw's *Back to Methusalah*. These had been published by Schott (Edition 11719) as *Four Dances* for treble recorder and piano in 1949. They are delicate miniatures, each just a page of music, and in two movements, 'Sarabande' and 'Wilman's Ground', early dance forms are recalled.

Hopkins's new Suite owed little to these previously composed dances, but the brief programme note for the first performance made more mention in particular of the scoring rather than the form:

> This work receives its first performance today and is a welcome addition to the

recorder's fast-growing modern repertoire. The majority of contemporary recorder compositions have so far been written for the treble. In this lively and playful suite, however, the composer breaks precedent by employing the brilliance of the descant recorder.

Although the critic writing in the *Daily Telegraph* of 9 May 1953 obviously enjoyed the Suite, a review in *The Times* of 9 May 1953 found the work rather more lightweight but was nevertheless positive:

> ... a new suite for descant recorder and harpsichord by Antony Hopkins, a young composer who apparently considers the instrument incapable of profundities of expression though well able to entertain. Its four movements were as brief as the movements in an early seventeenth century suite, but each was based on a motif of character and charm.

If Hopkins set out to write a light-hearted work for descant recorder, he was certainly successful. The Prelude is gently evocative of its *quasi pastorale* indication and opens with a swaying figure on the keyboard that is to pervade the entire movement. The fleet Scherzo is extraordinarily punctuated by held piano chords, over which are placed pauses. A footnote directs that each pause should be *longer* than four bars at the *prestissimo* tempo.

Even a work as light as this requires an emotional centre or moment of reflection, and this is provided in the calm Canon. The recorder enters first, the keyboard entering a bar later with the canon in the right hand an octave lower. In a modulatory middle section the canon moves down to the keyboard bass before the original theme returns, this time with the keyboard leading and the theme an octave higher in the same register as the recorder.

A return to high spirits is made with the rollicking Jig, which concludes with rising scale passages up to top C on the recorder and plummeting *brillante* chords on the keyboard.

Although first performed on harpsichord, frequent pedalling indications in the last movement of the published score show that the piano was the composer's first and most effective choice.

Writing in 1968, Dolmetsch noted that the Suite had since become a great favourite in concert programmes and at recorder courses.[15] On the other hand it displays, perhaps, those characteristics that the advocates of the recorder avant-garde most readily found to criticize in the mainstream recorder repertoire of this period. However, if the work is approached in the spirit in which I believe it was composed, then there is no reason why it cannot continue to be enjoyed as much for its unpretentious light-heartedness as for its moments of genuine originality.

---

[15] Dolmetsch: 'The recorder's 20th century repertoire', p. 248.

Norman Fulton: Scottish Suite

tr rec (or fl), pn (or hpd)

For Carl Dolmetsch

1 Prelude (Moderato, piacevole). 2 Air (Andantino tranquillo). 3 Musette (Moderato). 4 Nocturne (Molto lento). 5 Reel (Allegro giusto).

First performance: Wigmore Hall, London, 7 May 1954. Carl Dolmetsch, rec; Joseph Saxby, hpd.

Published: London: Schott & Co. Ltd, 1955 (edition 10466)

Sadly, there is no correspondence between Fulton and Dolmetsch in the archive, and it is necessary, as previously, to search for clues as to how player and composer came into contact. The answer may well lie once more with the BBC, which Fulton joined in 1936. After holding various appointments, he became head of west regional music in 1953, about the time of the composition of the *Scottish Suite*. Dolmetsch had a number of contacts at the BBC and it seems very possible this is what led to his requesting (or possibly Fulton offering) a composition for recorder.

If no letters are to be found in the archive, this is made up for by a very neatly written score, which appears to be a photostat copy of the composer's manuscript, and a manuscript recorder part. On the front of the score is written in Dolmetsch's hand: 'This copy was played from for the first performance at Wigmore Hall recital 7th May 1954'. This is evident from the pencil fingerings and other markings made by Joseph Saxby. Such markings, often quite copious, are to be found in many of the scores in the archive, and bear witness not only to their use but also to the thoroughness of Saxby's approach. In a letter to John Gardner some years later Dolmetsch refers to 'Joe's need for scattering self-expression marks all over the place!'

For the first performance there is nothing much of a programme note, which simply refers to the work as making a welcome addition to the recorder's fast-growing modern repertoire. It does, however, mention Fulton as being a native of Ayrshire, whereas other sources give his birthplace as London. Whichever is correct, there are, in addition to the Scottish Suite, other 'Scottish' works among his compositions; an Introduction, Air and Reel, for viola and piano and his Symphony No. 3 subtitled 'Mary Stuart'.

The critics welcomed the work. *The Times* of 10 May 1954 noted: 'For the occasion Norman Fulton had written a Scottish Suite for recorder and harpsichord, a pleasantly unpretentious affair, with bagpipe imitations, some modalism gingered up with traces of Hindemithian harmony (which suits a Scottish musical palette), and a charming Nocturne – as it were, Nights in the Gardens of Balmoral.'

The *Daily Telegraph* of 8 May 1954 noted the open-air quality of the music and that the final Reel received an encore.

Considering the work in more detail, we find the opening Prelude appropriately featuring 'Scotch snaps' in the recorder part, and bustling semiquavers on the keyboard. Later, the 'Scotch snaps' move down onto the keyboard while the recorder has a much smoother melody with notes tied over the bar lines.

The Air opens with an ascending figure in semiquavers on the keyboard, and smooth semiquavers continue in the accompaniment almost uninterrupted throughout the movement, above which the recorder plays a beautiful melody in which there are hints of the pentatonic scale. The entire movement does have a fine spaciousness about it, which perhaps gave rise to the comment of the *Daily Telegraph* critic.

In a musette we expect to find drones, but not perhaps to the extent Fulton uses one here. The keyboard player's left hand plays octave D's for all but the last four bars, which, with the thinning textures, reduces to a single note. The keyboard right hand and the recorder are kept much busier with passages requiring very accurate synchronization. There are smoother moments, but it is the combination of the static drone with an almost *moto perpetuo* feel above that gives this movement its appeal.

A return to the mood of the Air is made in the Nocturne, although achieved by rather different musical means. Over spacious keyboard chords, the recorder enters with a melody of rhythmic freedom marked *alla recitativo*. After these initial musings the score is marked *a tempo* and, above a chordal accompaniment, the recorder has a melody characterized by a falling phrase, which seems not unlike one to be heard in Delius's *Song of the High Hills*. After a slightly lengthened restatement of the *alla recitativo*, the main melody returns in an ABAB structure, but it is with hints of A, and a sort of lingering semiquaver passage for the recorder over long held keyboard chords, that the movement ends.

The final Reel has the most overtly Scottish feel of any of the movements. The recorder's pentatonic melody enters over grace noted open fifths in imitation of bagpipes on the keyboard. After just eight bars however the keyboard has the tune while it is the recorder's turn to imitate the bagpiper. When the tune returns to the recorder, the keyboard continues with figuration similar to that found in the first movement, but in both hands, and looking almost Bachian on the page. There follows a cunningly crafted development in which the keyboard has the opening melody over a drone, above which the recorder plays a lively countermelody. Further on, the Bach-like figurations accompany a section in which the recorder alternates between long held notes and upward moving phrases based on the rhythm of the opening melody. All the material is recapitulated before the movement ends in a flourish that characterizes the energy of the entire movement.

I have purposely referred to the keyboard part without instrumental indication, as it seems to avoid extremes of compass and is entirely practical on either harpsichord or piano but with very different overall effect.

Comparison of the manuscript score with the printed edition shows no changes. Dolmetsch added slightly slower metronome rates for the first and third movements, and many slurs to the first two semiquavers of the frequently occurring groups of four, especially in the third and last movements. However, none of these suggestions, which reflect Dolmetsch's own performance, found their way into the published score. There is also a pencilled suggestion that the recorder's bottom F# at the beginning of the fourth bar from the end of the Reel be raised an octave. This was no doubt due to fears it would not be heard against the keyboard, but the note as it stands in context is more elegant, and was duly retained.

In Piers Adams's memorable recording of the work (played on a sopranino recorder) the close of the Musette has the final recorder A held for two bars. When questioned about this, Piers felt that the final drop to an F in the last bar was possibly an error. However, as the score and manuscript part contain the same reading as the published edition, we must conclude that this was the composer's intention.

Movements from the work have found their way into the syllabus of the Associated Board grade examinations in recent years. This is a good thing if it encourages young players to get to know the piece, but it should not create the impression that this is music simply for study. It remains a very individual and characteristic work, which, in its slow movements, creates moments of great beauty in an unusual idiom. The work as a whole is very satisfying to play for both performers.

Edmund Rubbra: Fantasia on a Theme of Machaut, Op. 86

rec, str qt, hpd

For Carl Dolmetsch

First performance: Wigmore Hall, London, 11 February 1955. Carl Dolmetsch, tr rec; Martin String Quartet: David Martin, Marjorie Lavers, Eileen Grainger, Bernard Richards; Joseph Saxby, hpd.

Published: Croydon: Alfred Lengnick & Co. Ltd, 1956 (3869).

Following the considerable success of *Meditazioni sopra 'Cœurs désolés'*, Dolmetsch was keen for Rubbra to write another work for recorder. However, in correspondence dating from 1950 and 1952 Rubbra regretfully had to decline Dolmetsch's requests owing to busy composing commitments (a 'choral and orchestral' work was noted together with scoring his new Viola Concerto).

Dolmetsch did not give up, however, and on 11 October 1954 wrote to Rubbra following a telephone conversation:

> During our telephone conversation the other day, when I asked you whether you would be able to write a short work for recorder and strings (quartet or chamber orchestra plus harpsichord), you kindly said you would let me know if you could do this in time for my next recital at the Wigmore Hall on 11th February.

The letter continues: 'I believe I mentioned to you how welcome I know such a work would be, not only among people directly concerned with recorders, but among the musical public generally.'

Dolmetsch's persistence was duly rewarded, and on 12 October Rubbra replied:

Dear Carl,

Many thanks for your letter. Forgive me for not writing sooner but I've been immersed in proof-reading of my new symphony [No.6].

Yes, I'd like to do a work for your February concert, & have in mind a Fantasia for the instruments you mention. It's only my enthusiasm to say "Yes" that metaphorically pushes on one side all the volumes of work that lie ahead of me!

Kindest regards

Edmund

Knowing that Dolmetsch would require details for publicity for the Wigmore concert, Rubbra followed this with a letter dated 26 October 1954: 'I thought you'd like to know the exact title of my new piece ... It is "Fantasia on a theme by Machaut" for recorder, string quartet & harpsichord, Op. 86. I hope it will be ready for you by the end of the year.'

On 13 November 1954 Dolmetsch wrote to Rubbra with enthusiastic congratulations on his sixth symphony, the broadcast of which Dolmetsch had listened to from his sickbed, having contracted chickenpox. The letter continued with thoughts regarding the new work for recorder string quartet and harpsichord:

... I am very anxious to do it fullest justice. With this end in mind, also the hope that the B.B.C. will be interested in broadcasting the work, do you think I would be well advised to engage one of the recognised quartets, either the Martin or the MacNaughten with whom I have very good relations, rather than the individual players whom I usually assemble for the occasion? Please let me know what you think about this.

Rubbra replied on 27 November 1954 noting his appreciation of Dolmetch's comments on the sixth symphony, and in answer to the query regarding a string quartet continued: 'Yes, I *would* engage a recognised quartet, particularly if it's broadcast (And I think it will from what I hear).'

Dolmetsch replied on 1 December:

Very many thanks for your letter and for confirming what I had already thought would be the best thing to do on this occasion.

I have been speaking to David Martin by phone about it and he is delighted to have the opportunity of playing the Fantasia with us. So it will definitely be the Martin Quartet and I am writing to the B.B.C. to this effect by the same post.

We are now going ahead with the printing of our publicity and then we shall try to curb our impatience to see the new work until it arrives.

The letter concluded with the news that Joseph Saxby had been 'stricken with the fashionable malady [chickenpox]!'

This letter must have crossed in the post with one of the same date from Rubbra indicating that he was having second thoughts regarding the scoring:

> My dear Carl,
>
> Having now started the Fantasia it seems to be working out better with a string *trio*! Do you mind? I hasten to write to you in case you are making arrangements for a quartet (unless of course you're needing a quartet in another part of the programme).
>
> In haste,
>
> As ever
>
> Edmund

On receipt of Dolmetch's letter Rubbra had to change his plans, and on 14 December sent a postcard that read: 'R.I.P. It shall be a quartet! Will do my best to get it to you by the end of the month: but I also have been laid up & am only really now getting down to it.'

Rubbra was as good as his word and on 29 December wrote to Dolmetsch enclosing the score:

> Here's the 'Fantasia' & I do hope you'll all like it. There won't be time for my publisher to get all the parts out, so may I leave them to you? – but perhaps this is as well, as there may be a few adjustments to make. I'd very much like to come to the first run-through if I may. Kindly let me know when that will be.
>
> Shall you use a larger harpsichord than the one you used for the first performance of the 'Meditazioni'? It seems to me this new work needs a bigger sonority and greater variety of registration.
>
> All best wishes for 1955 & may this work be a success!

Only a brief programme note was written for the first performance, but Rubbra wrote about the piece in more detail for a subsequent performance at the Wigmore Hall in 1964:

> The form of this work, from the opening *Grave* statement of the medieval theme to the climax preceding the coda, is characterised by a slow building-up of movement. The theme itself is a very long one (thirty bars), and, to preserve its continuity and at the same time avoid monotony of colour, irregular sections of it are given to all performers excluding the 'cello. At the conclusion of the theme (recorder) a modulatory extension of the cadence leads to the "*Doppio movimento*" section (C major as against the prevailing D minor of the theme), which can be considered as a development growing out of the above mentioned cadence. The time changes from slow three to a quicker four, and the music now flows in more continuous quavers, increasing in contrapuntal complexity (there is a counter-subject of repeated notes on the recorder) until an *Allargando* brings a forte statement of the first four bars of the theme embedded in the middle of the texture. After a tonal change to G major the mood of the third section is

more dance-like, there is a plucked accompaniment, and semi-quavers prevail. The repeated notes of the previous section take a big part in the build-up to a strongly rhythmic climax, above which the recorder has a fortissimo statement of part of the main theme. The seven-bar *Adagio* coda, quiet and sustained, uses the main thematic material from Section 2, the recorder playing a chromatic counter-subject above it.

After the Wigmore Hall premiere a review in the *Daily Telegraph* of 12 February 1955 made note of Rubbra's ability to make convincing use of the music of a past age. The reviewer in *The Times* of 14 February 1955 described the piece as 'music of grace and noble contrapuntal beauty, with the bright tone of the recorder imparting a radiant halo of light to the darker strings.'

Rubbra's letter of 29 December 1954 mentions leaving the writing of parts to Dolmetsch. A set of parts remains in the archive that are not in Rubbra's hand, and are presumably those which Dolmetsch prepared for performance, as they contain bowing and other markings. There are some ornaments marked in pencil in the recorder part: a mordent on the last crotchet of the bar after figure 4, a trill on the last crotchet of the next bar, and a trill on the last crotchet three bars after figure 6. These were included in the published edition together with a number of others that do not appear in the manuscript part.

Another change to the recorder part included in the published edition occurs at the end of the bar after the two bar rest after figure 11. In the manuscript the demisemiquaver group is an octave lower and leads to a crotchet G at the beginning of the next bar. Notes an octave higher are written above in pencil, as are the quavers dropping an octave to replace the crotchet G. At the end of the recorder part is written 6.30, indicating the approximate duration of the piece.

In the string parts, the pizzicato indication four bars after figure 9 and *arco* immediately after figure 10 (omitted in error from the violin part of the published edition but present in the score) have been pencilled in, as have the group of two semiquavers and a quaver on the last beat of the bar before figure 10, which replace a crotchet in the manuscript parts. This too has been included in the published edition.

In requesting this work from Rubbra, Dolmetsch departed from usual recorder and keyboard scoring. The string quartet were taking part in the recital for the performance of eighteenth-century concerted works for the recorder, but Dolmetsch could clearly see the potential of integrating the recorder into a chamber music context in contemporary works. Although works for recorder and keyboard continued to be included in the Wigmore Hall recitals, there was an increasing number featuring the recorder as part of a chamber ensemble from this time onwards. This integration of the recorder with other instruments remained an important feature of the establishment of the recorder in twentieth-century music. Rubbra's *Fantasia* remains however, among the first and most accomplished.

Lennox Berkeley: Concertino, Op. 49

tr rec (or fl) vn, vc, hpd (or pn)

1 Allegro moderato. 2 Aria I (Lento) (rec, vc). 3 Aria II (Andantino) (vn, hpd). 4 Vivace.

First performance: Wigmore Hall, London, 1 February 1956. Carl Dolmetsch, rec; Jean Pognet, vn; Arnold Ashby, vc; Joseph Saxby, hpd.

Published: London: J & W Chester/Edition Wilhelm Hansen, 1961 (J.W.C. 279).

Having premiered a work for recorder with strings and harpsichord at his Wigmore Hall recital in 1955, Dolmetsch was obviously intent on increasing the modern repertoire for recorder with chamber ensemble. The recorder, violin, cello and harpsichord combination was employed quite frequently in high-baroque trio sonatas by composers such as Telemann and Handel, but with the cello liberated from its continuo role, the same ensemble forms an effective instrumental grouping for chamber music in a contemporary idiom.

Berkeley's Sonatina had remained very much in Dolmetsch's repertoire since its first performance in 1939, and it was from Berkeley that the work for the 1956 Wigmore Hall recital came. There is only one letter regarding the work in the archive, and this dates from after the first performance, so it is not possible to determine precisely the circumstances in which the new work came to be written.

The programme note for the first performance gives a brief outline of the work:

> This work, dedicated to Carl Dolmetsch, was written in July and August 1955. It is in four movements, the first is a slightly modified version of the traditional sonata first movement. In place of the usual slow movement are two very short pieces entitled Aria I and Aria II. As the title implies, they are melodic in style, and the ensemble is broken up into recorder and 'cello alone for the first and violin and harpsichord alone for the second. The last movement is a Rondo, somewhat lighter in feeling than the other two.

Stravinsky also used the titles Aria I and II for the lyrical inner movements of his D major violin concerto.

Berkeley's keyboard writing here falls very happily onto the harpsichord, and the published edition gives it as the preferred instrument ahead of the piano.[16] However, the version with flute and piano is effective, if very different in musical colour.

The critics in two of the broadsheets seemed to dwell both on the work's modern idiom and its technical difficulties. *The Times* of 3 February 1956 noted: '... a piece in which no concession was made to the eighteenth century was a

---

[16] Berkeley's discovery of the harpsichord seems to have been through his friendship with Vere Pilkington, an amateur musician with whom he shared rooms during his early years at Oxford. Pilkington had himself come to the harpsichord after attending a recital by Violet Gordon-Woodhouse, and he eventually became the first of her only two pupils (letter from Tony Scotland to the author, 4 May 2002).

concerto for recorder, violin, 'cello and harpsichord by Lennox Berkeley. This was frankly modern music of delicate texture and ingenious, but not too ingenious ideas. Its first performance was warmly received as it deserved to be.'

The Star of 2 February 1956 commented almost entirely on the work's virtuosity, whereas the critic in the *Daily Telegraph* of 2 February 1956 gave a more general view of the work's structure and musical qualities, noting that the finale had received an encore.

In the archive are a manuscript recorder part and a score, and it is in connection with this that the single letter from Berkeley, previously mentioned, is concerned. It is dated 1 August 1957:

> Here at last are your score and parts. The only actual alterations are in the harpsichord part at the end of the first movement on pages 18 and 19. I have carried on the semi-quaver passage on the harpsichord instead of transferring it to the violin. On page 37 (figure 12). I found that the purely harmonic accompaniment gives greater solidarity than what I had before. I hope you will have an opportunity to do it again before long.

It is possible that Dolmetsch required the performing material for his next US tour, and the *Concertino* was recorded in the United States a few years later with Alice and Eleonore Schoenfeld and Joseph Saxby. An inspection of the manuscript score reveals the alterations noted in Berkeley's letter, and also two passages in the last movement, present in the recording, but which have been cut from the published edition.

The first of these passages occurs after figure 2, in which the recorder enters on a long-held note above cello figuration before the entries at figure 3 in the published score. Observant players will discover that no figure 10 is to be found in the rehearsal numbers in the score and it is here that the second cut has been made. A modified second half of the bar four-and-a-half bars after figure 9 leads directly into figure 11. A total of 12 bars, including a descending passage in dotted crotchets for the recorder and a seven-bar passage for cello and harpsichord, have been omitted. Also in the recording, Dolmetsch alters the final descending scale passage so that the recorder does not end on a low G, as in the published edition.

As with Berkeley's Sonatina, the *Concertino*'s technical demands are quite modest by present standards, but a performance that achieves the required balance between its emotional and intellectual aspects while satisfying its technical demands, remains a challenge.

Edmund Rubbra: Cantata pastorale, Op. 92

high voice, tr rec (or fl), hpd (or pn), vc

For Carl Dolmetsch

1 'Silence Dryads leafy keep' (Plato, trans. Walter Leaf). 2 'Softly the west wind blows' (MS of St Augustine at Canterbury, trans. Helen Waddell). 3 'Now the fields are laughing' (MS from Benedictbeuern Monastery, trans. Helen Waddell).

First performance: Wigmore Hall, London, 1 February 1957. Joan Alexander, soprano; Carl Dolmetsch, tr rec; Arnold Ashby, vc; Joseph Saxby, hpd.

Published: Croydon: Alfred Lengnick & Co. Ltd, 1962 (3980).

Rubbra's plans for a work for recorder, voice, cello and harpsichord had been made known to Dolmetsch when they met at the BBC during the summer of 1956, and this is discussed in a letter from Dolmetsch to Rubbra dated 17 August 1956:

> Ever since our last happy meeting at the BBC on 28th June last, I have had in the back of my mind the joyful thought of the work you are planning to write for recorder, voice, cello and harpsichord.
>
> You will perhaps remember my mentioning that the date for our next recital at the Wigmore Hall is 1st February 1957, and that it would be nice if the work could be conceived for a soprano voice, because I had in mind someone like Joan Alexander, or perhaps Ilse Wolf.
>
> As I shall need to engage my personnel well in advance, may I mention the proposed work to those concerned quite soon?

Rubbra replied on 22 August: 'Many thanks for your letter. Yes, do please mention the work (for soprano, recorder, cello and harpsichord) as soon as ever you wish.' This was just the news Dolmetsch wanted to hear, and especially welcome as it arrived on his birthday (23 August) He replied by return:

> Your letter came as a delightful birthday present! I am so glad to hear that I have carte blanche to mention the new work and you may be sure that I shall do so on every possible occasion!
>
> Now, of course, I shall start counting the days until 1st February, but I mustn't be impatient. I can at last nail my singer and Arnold Ashby and the incorrigible Joseph.

In an exchange of correspondence at the end of August and the beginning of September, Dolmetsch reported that Arnold Ashby and Joan Alexander were delighted at the news of the new work and had reserved the date. However, Joan Alexander wished to know the vocal range of the piece and be sure it would suit her voice before definitely accepting. Dolmetsch asked if Rubbra could let him know what the range would be, or whether he would prefer to write to suit Joan Alexander's voice. Rubbra replied that he thought it would be best for Joan Alexander to let him know her vocal range, and asked if she could write to him direct. Dolmetsch confirmed that he had written to Joan Alexander asking her to get in touch with Rubbra in the knowledge she would be happy with this arrangement.

On 8 October Dolmetsch wrote to Rubbra advising him that he was about to leave for a series of tours which would keep him on the go until December. He was keen to deal with the publicity for the recital on 1 February next and in connection with the new work asked: 'Can you give me an idea of what form it will take, or better still, the title itself, if it has one yet?'

Rubbra was able to reply on 10 October: 'The work will be called "Cantata Pastorale" and will be settings of two poems by Plato and one early medieval (both in English translations).'

In the completed work Rubbra set only one Plato poem. Apart from Dolmetsch's letter of thanks for the details of the new work, which also gave the dates fixed for rehearsals, there is no further correspondence about the work, so just how the final texts came to be chosen is not certain.

The programme note for the first performance mentions Rubbra's use of a characteristic five-note scale:

> This work, completed in December 1956, consists of linked settings of three poems. The first by Plato (translated by Walter Leaf) and the second and third are anonymous lyrics from Helen Waddell's 'Medieval Latin Lyrics' (one from a Canterbury manuscript and the other from a Benedictbeuern Monastery manuscript). All the sections are linked by transitional material. The pervasive scale used is the five-note E – G – A flat – B – C; the obsessional use of this in an item in a concert of Indian music heard just before the Cantata was started so impressed itself on the composer's mind that he decided to use it as an appropriate melodic basis for the work.[17]

If there is no correspondence to inform us of Dolmetsch's reaction to the work, the critic in *The Times* of 4 February 1957 was in no doubt of its qualities:

> Rubbra admits to having been deeply influenced in the work by a five-note scale heard in a concert of Indian music; this together with the exotic sonorities he draws from the accompanying instruments (particularly in the first poem) gives the music a strange and arresting piquancy. The beautiful, slow central section of the work is strongly reminiscent of Britten in its harmonic shifts and the shape of the vocal line, but the rest is quintessential Rubbra, a work of real substance and compulsion, not just an 'occasional' piece including the recorder.
>
> In the final section, the slow tempi and rich textures of the first two give way to music that is lighter and which moves at a quicker pace, albeit a lilting *Allegretto moderato*.

Having based his previous two works with recorder on themes by two masters of early music, Rubbra's use of a scale derived from the music of India is an innovative departure. This is combined with an instrumental and vocal ensemble often employed by composers of the baroque in pastoral cantatas. Pepusch comes immediately to mind, and the use of the recorder in works with pastoral and amorous texts is among its traditional associations. Rubbra's work is entirely within this tradition, but its exoticism brings something fresh to the medium in a

---

[17] Rubbra, together with Peter Crossley-Holland, attended a performance in London by the celebrated Indian musician Ali Akbar Khan. This is almost certainly to have been the source of the five-note scale used in *Cantata pastorale* and was also the main influence on his work for solo harp *Pezzo ostinato*, Op. 102, of 1958, similarly founded on a four-note ascending pattern. The piece is dedicated to Peter Crossley-Holland, and Rubbra's Piano Concerto of 1955 is dedicated to Ali Akbar Khan.

very individual and characteristic way that takes us far away from the world of the baroque.

Gordon Jacob: Suite

tr rec (or fl; 7th mvt: optional sopranino rec), str qt (or small str orch)

For Carl Dolmetsch

1 Prelude (Adagio ma poco con moto). 2 English Dance (Allegro molto). 3 Lament (Adagio). 4 Burlesca alla rumba (Allegro giocoso). 5 Pavan (Lento). 6 Introduction and cadenza (Andante sostenuto). 7 Tarantella (Presto con fuoco).

First performance: Wigmore Hall, London, 31 January 1958. Carl Dolmetsch, rec; Martin String Quartet: David Martin, Marjorie Lavers, Eileen Grainger, Bernard Richards.

Piano reduction published Oxford: Oxford University Press, 1959. Full score and parts available for hire only. Republished under licence, Hebden Bridge: Peacock Press, 2002 (PD 05).

There is more correspondence in the archive in connection with this work than any other, but unfortunately nothing to indicate how Dolmetsch first came to contact Gordon Jacob about a work for recorder. Jacob's musical craftsmanship, and in particular his skill in writing for wind instruments, was well known, and no doubt the prospect that a work for recorder from his pen would be a significant addition to the now growing repertoire appealed to Dolmetsch greatly.

What is clear, however, is that Dolmetsch had arranged to visit Jacob to discuss a work at first hand, for a postcard from Jacob dated 21 May 1957 reads: 'Looking forward very much to meeting you on Thurs. Please bring your recorder and some music to play. I shall want to see how it works at close quarters!'

As far back as 1929 Dolmetsch had discovered, almost by accident, that covering the end of the recorder enabled a 'firm, pure and reliable' top F# to be produced. Sometime in 1957 therefore he perfected a bell key and fitted it to a treble recorder. Whether or not he had this facility at the time of his visit to Jacob is also not clear, but the finished work includes top F#s in the second and final movements, and a bell key was certainly used at the first performance the following year.

Dolmetsch wrote to Jacob the day following his visit to say how much he had enjoyed their meeting and talk. It can be deduced from this letter that the scoring of the proposed work had been discussed, as Dolmetsch notes: 'In accordance with your suggestion I am getting into touch with David Martin and I hope very much that his quartet will be available to launch our new work.'

By August, Dolmetsch was preparing to leave for a tour of the United States and would not be returning until December. He was understandably keen to be able to have details of the new work, if possible, for publicity for the Wigmore

Hall recital due to take place on 31 January 1958. On 20 August he wrote to Jacob:

> I wonder if you could let me know at this stage the form and title of the work which you are writing for the occasion? As a result of our very pleasant meeting and discussion at your home, I have engaged the Martin Quartet and they, like myself, are much looking to performing your composition for recorder and string quartet.

Jacob replied the very next day:

> You won't believe it, but I was going to write to you today to make sure of the date of your recital and report that I have started work on your piece.
> It will just be called 'Suite for Treble Recorder and String Quartet', and will consist of a (as yet unspecified) number of short pieces, rather in the style of the Divertimento I wrote for Harmonica & IVtet for Larry Adler. I have sketched out 3 numbers so far, an English Dance (not 'folky'), an Adagio 'Lament' and a Latin-American dance in Rumba style which will I hope prove to be an amusing parody! Other pieces will probably include a Prelude and a Pavane and there may also be an Eclogue, a Minuet & Trio & perhaps a Jig. The whole thing will be quite short – 20–25 minutes in all, probably.
> I am very glad that you are having the Martin Quartet. They are very good friends of mine and I am very glad that you and they are looking forward to the work. I know it will have a splendid performance anyway.

Jacob concluded: 'I am enjoying working at the Suite very much and I hope you will be pleased with the result.'

Dolmetsch was able to acknowledge this letter before his departure to the United States. By his return in December, the Suite was all but complete, and arrangements being made for it to be tried through with Jacob at the piano, as noted in a letter from Jacob dated 28 December 1957: 'Here is the part. I do hope it is all right (or at any rate most of it!) ... We are looking forward immensely to Sunday, 5th, at 11 a.m.'

Dolmetsch expressed his thanks and anticipation in a letter of 31 December:

> Very many thanks for sending me the recorder part of your new Suite so promptly – I do appreciate this.
> I too am very much looking forward to seeing you both again on Sunday morning and to our going through the work together; a glance at the recorder part has made me all the keener to hear the work entire.

The visit, and especially the play-through, seem to have been a great success, prompting Dolmetsch to write to Jacob on 7 January 1958:

> I so much enjoyed my visit to Pine Cottage on Sunday and playing through the new Suite with you – I was telling David Martin about it that evening and now he is dying to get his hands on it! Could you and your wife join us all for lunch and a subsequent rehearsal on Saturday, 25th January?

On the same day Jacob wrote to Dolmetsch enclosing a programme note and reported: 'I heard from Alan F. [Frank] today that OUP will publish an arrangement for Recorder & Piano. So that's good.' There were also plans being made for a performance of the Suite with string orchestra in Newcastle on 15 February and obtaining the necessary extra parts. The letter concludes: 'We greatly enjoyed your visit and your playing. I am so delighted that you like the Suite.'

A rapid exchange of letters continued regarding the forthcoming rehearsal with the Martin Quartet, and the piano arrangement, about which Jacob in a letter of 17 January notes: 'Yesterday I sent Alan Frank a piano score of the Suite which he is going to print. I have made the piano part quite playable and the work should go quite well in that form.' The letter concludes: 'I enclose a few bars of the [score of the] "Rumba" movement (No. 4) as the rhythm is a bit tricky unless you can see it on paper.' Dolmetsch wrote to thank Jacob for the fragment of the Rumba movement, and there is no further correspondence until after the first performance.

The programme note Jacob sent to Dolmetsch reads as follows:

> This Suite, which was written towards the end of 1957, is dedicated to Carl Dolmetsch in whose hands the recorder has become an instrument possessing a great range of colour and expressiveness and also brilliant technical virtuosity.
>
> A number of contemporary British composers have written works for the recorder which have shown that it is by no means restricted to the interpretation of old music but can also respond to the exacting demands of the present day.
>
> The Prelude, Lament and Pavane in this Suite are quiet and contemplative in mood in contrast with the other movements which are brisk and rhythmical. The Burlesca alla Rumba belongs, as its name suggests, to the category of parody but it is written affectionately rather than satirically. The Cadenza is a kind of improvisatory rumination on the themes of the pieces which precede it. In the introduction to this movement the cello plays a prominent part. In the final movement (Tarantella) the composer recommends the alternative use of the sopranino recorder which bears the same relation to the treble recorder as the piccolo does to the flute, i.e. it has the same fingering but sounds an octave higher than the written notes.
>
> The composer has provided an ad libitum Double Bass part so that the Suite can be played with a small string orchestra if so desired.

Following the first performance, the critics were unanimous in their praise. The *Daily Telegraph* of 1 February 1958 made particular mention of the composer's craftsmanship in combining old and new musical forms. *The Times* of 3 February 1958 was similarly enthusiastic:

> It is music abounding in felicitous details – intriguing rhythms, cunning counterpoint and, needless to say with this composer, the most telling scoring for recorder and strings alike; its main virtue nevertheless, was that while remaining a work of fundamentally serious (though also diverting) intent, it is not overloaded with more 'feeling' than the recorder can summon from its little body.

As would be expected, the reviewer in *Recorder News*[18] was also aware of the work's special qualities:

> Gordon Jacob showed himself master of his craft: the string writing was vivid, varied in tone colour and expression, tremendously rhythmic and vital in the quick movements, and lyrical in the more contemplative ones; the recorder part had great tonal and expressive range, and there was delightful wit and humour in the Burlesca alla Rumba and the Tarantella (played on the optional Sopranino recorder). This was a notable performance.

Happily, Dolmetsch's enthusiasm and Jacob's gratitude are fully expressed in the letters they exchanged after the first performance, the texts of which are given here in full. Dolmetsch's is dated 3 February 1958.

> My dear Gordon,
>
> After what everyone felt to be one of the happiest and most successful of all our recitals at the Wigmore Hall, I am writing to tell you again of my great gratitude for and admiration of the latest and very welcome addition to the recorder's repertoire – I really feel I cannot thank you enough. You have set a new standard for 20th century writing and it gave us all tremendous pleasure to collaborate with you.
>
> The Times and Telegraph have justly praised the Suite and how heartily I agree with all they say. We too felt inspired by the work of a master craftsman and our audience made it abundantly evident that they shared this feeling. Kenneth Skeaping writes this morning – 'Congratulations on another new chamber work which keeps up the standard already established by its predecessors over quite a few years now. You are building up a repertoire of modern English works which should certainly amount to something in our national musical literature'. From Edgar Hunt, a well-known recorder player outside the Haslemere circle, comes this generous tribute – 'I thought your technique and the recorder emerged with flying colours from the Gordon Jacob. A work of real craftsmanship demanding the best from both recorder and strings – and you could not have chosen a finer quartet as your partners. How nice the continuo sounded on Bernard Richard's 'cello.'
>
> Yesterday we made what we all felt to be a very successful recording of the Suite for the B.B.C. and I earnestly hope it will not be long before it is broadcast. Tomorrow and during the next seven days we shall have the delight of playing the Tarantella to audiences in Dorset and Devon. And on 15th February we look forward to the fresh experience of playing the Suite in Newcastle with orchestra.
>
> Once again, my sincere thanks for a very happy partnership and my warmest greetings to you both,
>
> As ever,
>
> Carl

Jacob's reply is dated 7 February 1958:

---

[18] April 1958, New Series, no. 21, p. 1.

My dear Carl,

Thank you very much for your nice letter of Feb. 3rd. I am delighted that you are so pleased with the Suite. It must always be rather an anxiety for a player when he asks a composer to write something for him, especially in these days when musical monstrosities sometimes result from such requests! It is a relief to know how well the work has been received. This was largely due to your really astonishing performance and the very sympathetic attitude of my good friends of the Martin Quartet.

I had a nice letter from the Headmaster of the County Modern School at Blandford. He was very pleased with the Tarantella, which seems to have gone down very well in its piano arrangement.

I am so glad to have the comments of Kenneth Skeaping and Edgar Hunt and also to know that you were pleased with the B.B.C. recording.

I shall be most interested to hear how it goes with String Orch. at Newcastle. Alan Frank is most enthusiastic about it and thinks it is one of my best works. He is particularly pleased to have it to coincide with the launching of a new O.U.P. series of recorder publications to which he wants me to contribute some more pieces (solo & concerted) for less exalted performers than you! I hope to do so some time.

It has been a very great pleasure to collaborate with you and to be admitted into the distinguished Dolmetsch circle.

I very much hope that your X ray examination has been reassuring and that you will not run any risk of impairing your health by incessant activity and travel. You must remember that you are unique and look after yourself properly.

Sidney joins me in sending love to you all. As you know she takes a great and intelligent interest in my work & is very pleased about all this.

Yrs. ever Gordon

Just four days later Jacob wrote again to say he had received several enthusiastic letters from schools and recorder clubs where Dolmetsch and Saxby had performed the Tarantella, noting it had been well worth while getting Alan Frank to rush through the piano arrangement of this movement.

On 26 February Dolmetsch wrote to Jacob about the performance in Newcastle with string orchestra: 'I am sure you will be pleased to hear that your Suite was an enormous success in Newcastle. It sounded very well indeed with orchestra, and gained from the (at times) independent double bass part.' The letter concludes: 'If Alan Frank would let us have copies of the entire Suite in piano score sometime, Joseph and I would love to come and play it over to you one day, and also the delightful harpsichord piece you have just written for Joseph.'

A reply from Jacob dated 2 March 1958 is the last of the many letters exchanged in connection with the Suite. In it, Jacob expresses his delight at the reception of the work in Newcastle with string orchestra, but also his surprise at the reception the Suite had received generally:

I never imagined for a moment that this work would arouse enthusiasm like this. I think it must be your persuasive playing of it that is chiefly responsible, also perhaps that I treated the recorder as a perfectly normal musical instrument, which it is, and not in any way as a museum piece. Any way, there it is!

This very happy collaboration was the beginning of a long friendship between Dolmetsch and Jacob and was to result in three further compositions including recorder.

In the archive are photostat copies of Jacob's full score of the work and parts, but what is of particular interest is a manuscript of the recorder part in Jacob's hand. It has obviously seen much use and must have been played from many times. It contains a number of differences from the published version. Typical of those in the second movement are Ex. 3.6, 3.7 and 3.8:

Ex. 3.6. Gordon Jacob, Suite for treble recorder and strings. Second movement, recorder part seven bars after A: comparison of MS and published versions. © Oxford University Press 1959. Extract reproduced by permission.

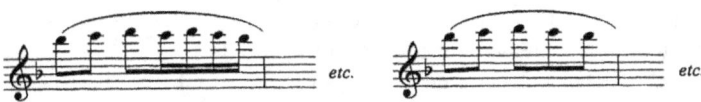

Ex. 3.7. Gordon Jacob, Suite for treble recorder and strings. Second movement, recorder part 15 bars after B: comparison of MS and published versions. © Oxford University Press 1959. Extract reproduced by permission.

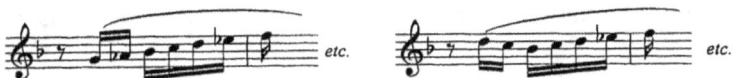

Ex. 3.8. Gordon Jacob, Suite for treble recorder and strings. Second movement, recorder part 19 bars after B: comparison of MS and published versions. © Oxford University Press 1959. Extract reproduced by permission.

One of the most interesting variants is to the repeated motive beginning 15 bars from the end of the final movement (Ex. 3.9). The figuration in equivalent later bars is similarly notated.

Following the publication of the Suite in the piano reduction, Anthony Rowland-Jones reviewed the work in the *Recorder News*. He noted that although the piano version was the composer's own, it 'was but a shadow of the original'.[19]

---

[19] October 1959, New Series, no. 26, p. 12.

Ex. 3.9. Gordon Jacob, Suite for treble recorder and strings. Last movement, recorder part 15 bars before end: comparison of MS and published versions. © Oxford University Press 1959. Extract reproduced by permission.

Anyone who has heard Jacob's string writing in the piece would probably agree, but Rowland-Jones's review continues with nothing but enthusiasm:

> Technically the Suite is difficult but does not verge on the impossible and is superbly well written for the recorder. It is a masterly achievement and a most gratifying addition to the recorder's repertoire, bearing comparison only with Berkeley's Sonatina and Rubbra's two sets of variations on old French themes. Let us hope that recorder players will respond to its existence by aspiring to perform it.

Gordon Jacob's Suite remains an important work and a landmark in the recorder's repertoire. He did indeed treat the recorder as 'a perfectly normal instrument', but, although it has received far more advanced treatment from many composers since, Jacob's work is worthy of the attention of all recorder players who indeed aspire to perform it.

Robert Simpson: Variations and Fugue

rec, str

In memoriam Horace Dann

First performance: Wigmore Hall, London, 9 February 1959. Carl Dolmetsch, recs; Martin String Quartet: David Martin, Marjorie Lavers, Eileen Grainger, Bernard Richards.

Unpublished.

As with a number of the earlier works written for Dolmetsch, although there are letters from the composer in the archive, there are no copies of those from Dolmetsch, so again it is necessary to make assumptions as to the work's origins based on what other clues are available. Among the letters from Simpson are two on BBC notepaper. Simpson joined the BBC in 1950 and it is almost certainly this link, as with a number of other composers around this time, that led to the composition of the present work.

Correspondence in the archive from earlier in 1958 reveals Dolmetsch's efforts to obtain a work, first from Peter Racine Fricker and then from Sir Malcolm Arnold, but neither had been able to fulfil the commission.

It is not clear at what date Dolmetsch had first contacted Simpson, but from Simpson's earliest letter in the archive, dated 23 December 1958, we can deduce that Dolmetsch, having obtained Simpson's agreement to write a new work, had sent him a copy of the advanced notice announcing this. Simpson's uncertainty about writing for recorder is immediately apparent, but the mood in which he was composing the piece, and progress on it are clear:

> Many thanks for your letter and the leaflet. Those red letters scared the life out of me – almost. I hope it will be good enough. As so often with me, I find the work is turning out a bit different (in character), more serious than originally intended, with a fugue to end with. For the performance, could you have it described as follows: –
> Variations and fugue (In memoriam Horace Dann), for recorder and string quartet.
> The dedication will be to you, but the music at the end is (or will be) a tribute to one of my dearest friends, who has just died very tragically. But don't worry, it won't be funeral music, or anything like it! I'm now about two-thirds through the whole thing and I hope to finish it over Xmas. It should be about 12 mins – or maybe a bit longer, even 15. I'm full of trepidation that it shouldn't be good enough for you, but you have moved me at least to take the recorder very seriously as an expressive instrument, even though my invention should fail to match your artistry
> Looking forward to seeing you again.

Simpson was a little delayed by illness in his completion of the work, but was able to write to Dolmetsch on 8 January 1959:

> My apologies for having been so long with the enclosed. An attack of 'flu put me right back. I hope the parts are all right and totally legible – I haven't had time to do a proper decent score, and perhaps the pencil one will do for a rough guide. The parts are more accurate and up-to-date than the score, as I made little changes while doing them. I do hope it's all right! Some of it may be pretty difficult, especially the very fast pianissimo fugue that should go like the wind, but at a whisper. Please let me know if there's anything downright impossible, then perhaps we could meet over it when you're next in town.
> I'm afraid it's turned out as a real quintet – how it would come over with string orchestra I'm not sure. You'd need a pretty good orchestra to do it, I think. However ... We shall see. I almost dread hearing it, having done it in such a rush & with so many things buzzing around my head. I hope it isn't too bad.

This letter continues to show Simpson's real anxieties about writing for the recorder, but there are certain aspects, not least about the dynamics and texture of the fugue, that seemed to have formed very firmly in his mind.

Although no copy of the letter is to be found, it is clear that Dolmetsch wrote to Simpson putting his mind at rest about the practicalities of the recorder writing, as a letter from Simpson dated 14 January 1959 shows:

Many thanks for your letter. I'm greatly relieved to hear that that the recorder part works – it was that I was worried about. I'm sure the string parts will be playable, though there are difficulties here and there. Here is the programme note, which I hope will be suitable. I'd suggest *not* putting my name or initials at the end of it – it seems to read anonymously all right, I think. Now you say your part is playable I'm much looking forward to hearing it at a rehearsal.

When the tickets are ready, could you let me have a few – among others I would like to ask are Horace Dann's widow and his daughter to come. Did you know him? He retired from here about 18 months ago – no finer gentleman ever breathed.

Looking forward to seeing you again.

Horace Dann, in addition to being a colleague of Simpson at the BBC, was also a composer.

Simpson's programme note for the first performance is given here in full:

This work composed specially for Carl Dolmetsch, is also intended as a tribute to the composer's friend Horace Dann, whose recent sudden death was grievously felt by all who new him in the BBC and elsewhere. The music, though serious and even elegiac in parts, is by no means funereal, and the Fugue is light in texture, swift in pace. The recorder player is asked to use treble and sopranino instruments; at first the recorder plays a subsidiary part, the theme being given to violin and viola (the latter taking the middle lower-pitched section of it). This theme moves tonally from a D-flat majorish – B-flat minorish region into that of E minor – G major and back again. Each of the seven variations follows the same trend, and throughout the set there is a gradual increase in tension of feeling. The last variation is turbulent and the sopranino recorder is pitted against the strings. After this crisis the music is pulled definitely into the key of E and the fugue follows, *vivacissimo grazioso*, nearly all *pianissimo* and never rising above *piano*, the sopranino recorder now showing its fleetness and delicacy. At the end the music floats into a slow, gentle, rather sad coda that settles at last in E major.

Although not immediately apparent, because of the way in which it is divided between the first violin and viola, the theme is a perfect palindrome (Ex. 3.10). Each variation also forms a palindrome.

Ex. 3.10. Robert Simpson, Variations and Fugue. The theme shared between violin I and viola. Reproduced by permission of Angela Simpson.

The fugue subject begins with a falling and ascending two-note figure that recalls the theme of the variations, but which scampers off into semiquavers four bars later (Ex. 3.11).

Ex. 3.11. Robert Simpson, Variations and Fugue. Fugue, bars 1–10. Reproduced by permission of Angela Simpson.

At the end of the coda the recorder solo seems to take a final glance backwards at the fugue subject before coming to rest on a G♮. For two bars this clashes with the viola's G# of the strings' final E major chord, but when the recorder falls silent for the final bar the E major chord seems all the warmer (Ex. 3.12).

Ex. 3.12. Robert Simpson, Variations and Fugue. Coda, final 13 bars. Reproduced by permission of Angela Simpson.

The day after the first performance Simpson wrote to Dolmetsch:

Dear Carl,

Just to say, once more, how grateful I was for that admirable performance last night. It went beautifully and I was more than satisfied. The whole concert was very enjoyable and I thought it a considerable feat on your part to keep going with such vitality for so long!

Yours as ever,

Bob

The reviews in the dailies were full of praise for the work, *The Times* of 10 February 1959 noting:

> The music was written as a memorial to Horace Dann, Simpson's friend at the BBC, who died last year. The circumstances of its composition inevitably conditioned its character, which though never heavily funereal, is nevertheless shot through with a sharpness, and sometimes a bleakness of sorrow. Much of this sharp poignancy was cleverly conveyed by the use of the sopranino recorder (alternating with the treble) in a piercingly high register. All the scoring is piquant, the harmonic writing is arrestingly fresh without being aggressively dissonant, and the working out of the material is done with Simpson's characteristic logic. It was well played by Mr. Dolmetsch and the Martin String Quartet, but we would have liked to hear it a second time.

The *Daily Telegraph* of 10 February 1959 was similarly positive, but the review in the *Recorder News*,[20] though generally enthusiastic about the work, made an interesting comment about the approach of modern composers when writing for the recorder that nevertheless appeared not to apply to Simpson's work:

> ... I am most grateful to Mr. Simpson and Mr. Dolmetsch for this work. It fascinated me throughout by its emotional warmth intensity and sincerity. As a composition it is original and well balanced in its structure, and has moments of great beauty. Whether it would have been better not to make the recorder one of five parts, but to oppose it to the string quartet (as Mozart did with his Clarinet Quintet) is a question only the composer can answer. But I wonder why modern composers do not learn from each other in the treatment of the recorder, choice of key, sonority etc. instead of picking the best from the best – I am speaking here only about the craft of writing for the instrument – they start all on their own from scratch as though they have never heard a recorder. I am probably too impatient and it may be thirty years until we have a wonderful literature of new recorder music, to which Mr. Simpson's Quintet will certainly be one of the important contributions.
>
> W[alter] B[ergmann]

Among Simpson's works, the *Variations and Fugue* come after the first two of his 11 symphonies, and after the first three of his 15 string quartets. The work thus occupies a significant position in his compositional output.

---

[20] March 1959, New Series, no. 25, p. 16.

Since the publication of York Bowen's Sonatina in 1994, Simpson's Variations and Fugue remains the earliest of the new works first performed at the Wigmore Hall not to have been published. Despite Simpson's apparent satisfaction with the piece expressed in his letter to Dolmetsch, it is possible that elements of the work in performance remained to trouble him and prevented him from preparing or presenting it for publication.

During the course of research for his talk at the 1997 ERTA (UK) conference and subsequent article,[21] Ross Winters contacted Mrs Angela Simpson (Robert Simpson was by this time far from well, and died in November 1997). From this conversation it seemed that the work may have been withdrawn, and it is described as such in the list of works published in Ross Winters's previously mentioned article. However, as it remained in the selective list of Simpson's works in *New Grove I*,[22] and indeed in a booklet published as a 50th birthday tribute to Simpson in 1971, there was at least some evidence that it had not.

Having read Simpson's own description in his letters following my first visit to the Dolmetsch archive in June 1998, I was naturally curious about the piece, so it was with considerable excitement, but also some trepidation, that on my second visit I located the autograph manuscript parts. Of the pencil, or any other score, no trace has been found. At the end of the recorder part the durations of the various sections of the work are noted in pencil, and these are totalled up to 14 minutes 18 seconds, close to Simpson's original estimate.

This discovery led to considerable interest from John Turner. From earlier enquiries he had gathered that the score and parts rather than having been withdrawn, had simply been mislaid. Now that the parts had been located, a performance was possible, and the composer John McCabe, a friend of Simpson and first president of the Robert Simpson Society, sought permission for this to take place. With the additional assistance of composer David Ellis, also a friend of Simpson, a performance was arranged and given by John Turner with the Camerata Ensemble at a concert in the Royal Northern College of Music on 5 December 2000.[23]

An examination of the recorder part showed that in a number of places Dolmetsch had pencilled in some suggested octave transpositions. John Turner also considered some judicious octave transposition to make the part more practical and included these in his performance. Another fascinating feature that Mr Turner brought to the author's attention was a passage that bears a close thematic resemblance to an ascending phrase in Rubbra's *Meditazioni sopra 'Cœurs désolés'*. Whether it is a deliberate reference cannot be determined with certainty, but Simpson was a close friend of Rubbra and the theme of the 'desolate heart' is in keeping with the mood in which the work was composed.

---

21 Winters, 'The Dolmetsch legacy'.

22 Cole, 'Simpson, Robert', *New Grove Dictionary* (1980), 17, 331.

23 The work was recorded by the same performers on the CD *Thirteen Ways of Looking at a Blackbird*, Olympia (OCD 170).

The work is full of musical palindromes and other intellectual compositional devices typical of Simpson, yet it is also a deeply felt and moving piece, certainly among the finest composed for Dolmetsch and in the twentieth-century recorder repertoire.

Arnold Cooke: Divertimento

tr rec, str qt (or str orch)

For Carl Dolmetsch

1 Vivace. 2 Andante. 3 Allegro giocoso.

First performance: Wigmore Hall, London, 8 February 1960. Carl Dolmetsch, rec; Martin String Quartet: David Martin, Marjorie Lavers, Eileen Grainger, Bernard Richards.

Unpublished.

It is a constant source of regret to recorder players that, apart from his early and significant *Plöner Musiktag* trio of 1932, Hindemith left no other works for recorder. How a recorder sonata or chamber concerto from his pen might have sounded we can only imagine. However, a number of the composers who studied with Hindemith wrote for recorder and were no doubt influenced to do so by his enthusiasm for it. One such, who acknowledges his own interest in the recorder directly to Hindemith, is Arnold Cooke.

Cooke's first work for recorder, a concerto for recorder and strings, dates from 1956.[24] It is possible that Dolmetsch knew of this (a copy of the published edition of the keyboard reduction is in the archive), and was the reason Cooke was requested for a new work for the instrument. A number of letters from Cooke regarding this new work have survived, but alas, none from Dolmetsch, though these are referred to in those from Cooke. From the first letter, dated 17 August 1959, we can deduce that Dolmetsch had requested a piece, probably for recorder and string quartet, and was keen to know details of it for advance publicity for the 1960 Wigmore Hall recital before leaving for a tour of the United States:

> Thank you very much for your letter. I have not actually started on the work yet, as I have been away on my summer holiday recently and have had one or two other things to finish first, but I should be starting on it very soon now. In the meantime however I have decided more or less what form the work will take, and I think the term *Divertimento* best meets the kind of thing I have in mind. It will probably be in three movements.

---

[24] Cooke's recorder concerto is in four movements, of which the last is a set of variations on Prince Rupert's March. It is dedicated to the recorder player Philip Rodgers and was published by Schott & Co. in 1957.

Dolmetsch clearly acknowledged this, as Cooke wrote again on 25 September, not only reporting on progress, but also giving an indication of the duration of the new piece:

> Many thanks for your letter. I am glad to be able to tell you that I have just finished two movements of the Divertimento, the first and slow movement, and there only remains the third to complete the work. It will not be a long piece of course; about 10 to 12 minutes as you originally suggested. I shall have it all ready for you with score and parts when you return from your tour in the States.

The new work must indeed have been ready on Dolmetsch's return, as on 16 January 1960 Cooke acknowledged receiving, with a letter, a copy of the programme and two tickets for the Wigmore Hall recital. We can also deduce that Dolmetsch found the recorder part very satisfactory and invited Cooke to attend a rehearsal as the letter continues:

> I am very glad to hear that you find the recorder part lies well. I am not an expert player of the instrument! I did play a bit once (with one of your own make of recorders) but that is a long time ago. But I think I learned quite a lot about recorder writing when I wrote my concerto a few years ago.
>
> I shall be free to join you at your rehearsal on Friday the 22nd at Dinelys, and look forward to seeing you there. I will do a programme note and give it to you there, if that will be soon enough.

Cooke's programme note is quite detailed and is given here in full:

> This is the second work in which the composer has employed the treble recorder as a solo instrument. The first was a concerto with string orchestra in 1956. The title 'Divertimento' usually denotes a light and cheerful type of music, but does not necessarily preclude seriousness.
>
> The first movement of this work reveals its character immediately with a lively tune on the recorder accompanied by a dancing figure in repeated notes on the strings. A subsidiary staccato figure and a second tune for the recorder complete the thematic material, and the movement is in a straightforward sonata form.
>
> The second movement is more serious in feeling, although it is light and simple in texture and construction. It begins with a quiet song-like melody on the recorder. The form is in two parts, the second being a varied repeat of the first.
>
> The last movement is a rondo, with the main theme given out by the recorder after four bars introduction by the quartet. There is also a sprightly second subject, which, when it returns in the latter part of the movement, gives the soloist the opportunity to change his instrument for the sopranino recorder.

Ex. 3.13, 3.14 and 3.15 show the openings of all three movements and are taken from the manuscript score in the archive. This is of a version with string orchestra that is headed:

DIVERTIMENTO
for
Treble Recorder and
String Orchestra (arr. from S.Q.)
Arnold Cooke
Written for Carl Dolmetsch
Duration 10½ min

Ex. 3.13. Arnold Cooke, Divertimento for treble recorder and string quartet. First movement, bars 1–6. Reproduced by permission of Julia Earnshaw.

In addition there are parts for recorder and strings that are titled Divertimento for recorder and string quartet. These are not in Cooke's hand but in those of two separate copyists.

Ex. 3.14. Arnold Cooke, Divertimento for treble recorder and string quartet. Second movement, bars 1–5. Reproduced by permission of Julia Earnshaw.

Although the manuscript score is marked 'arr. from S.Q.', the double-bass part does not have any independent material and, where it appears, simply doubles the cello part. It is very possible that this version was arranged for Dolmetsch's 1964 American tour. (Dolmetsch liked to have the added option of a string orchestral version of the works with quartet, as Gordon Jacob had supplied for his Suite in 1958.) The string orchestral arrangement is referred to in the early correspondence relating to Cooke's Quartet (Sonata) that Dolmetsch requested in 1964 for the 1965 Wigmore Hall recital. The archive does not contain a manuscript of the original quartet version, but this is clearly the orchestral arrangement minus the double-bass, and the parts thus provide the performing material for either version.

In the separate recorder part, the bar before figure 13 in the first movement has a pause marked over the recorder's top B♭, and seems to indicate that a short cadenza should be inserted at this point. The tutti that follows is also marked *a tempo*. That a cadenza belongs here is confirmed in the score, as the bar in question intentionally takes up an entire line and has a brief flourish written in Cooke's hand. Strangely, however, this has been crossed out in ink and apparently by Cooke himself. In the recorder part, at the foot of the opposite page from the proposed location of the cadenza, a piece of manuscript paper, on which is written a short cadenza in Dolmetsch's hand, has been taped in. It is only slightly different

Ex. 3.15. Arnold Cooke, Divertimento for treble recorder and string quartet. Third movement, bars 1–12. Reproduced by permission of Julia Earnshaw.

from and based on the same arpeggio figures as that in the manuscript score.[25] Below in pencil are the basic notes on which this short flourish is founded (Ex. 3.16).

Ex. 3.16. Arnold Cooke, Divertimento for treble recorder and string quartet. First movement, notes for cadenza written in pencil in Dolmetsch's hand in the MS recorder part.

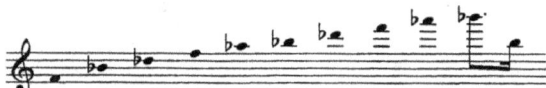

---

[25] Both Cooke's and Dolmetsch's versions of the cadenza conclude with trills separated by arpeggios reminiscent of those in the recorder cadenza in Cooke's Quartet for recorder, violin, cello and harpsichord of 1964.

It is not clear precisely what has taken place here, or the chronology of events. Did Cooke leave the long bar in the score to contain a written out version of what Dolmetsch was intended to improvise, and filled in his impression of it later? Jeanne Dolmetsch noted that Cooke was keen to attend rehearsals and that the cadenza is very likely to have resulted from a Dolmetsch improvisation. Why then has that in the score been crossed out, especially as it is so similar to that in Dolmetsch's hand in the recorder part? Were either Cooke or Dolmetsch not entirely satisfied with the result? At present it is not possible to provide answers with any certainty.

No letters in connection with the first performance are to be found in the archive, but the *Daily Telegraph* of 9 February 1960, though commenting favourably on the middle movement's ability to make use of the recorder's limitations, considered the outer movements as occasional music.

Walter Bergmann, writing in the *Recorder News*,[26] was much more enthusiastic, obviously hearing in the work a craftsmanship in the recorder writing not appreciated by the *Daily Telegraph* critic:

> Cooke's Divertimento came like fresh air from the world of Hindemith; two sprightly movements enclose a profound slow middle movement; the work was so heartily applauded that the last movement was repeated. It seems to be a miracle that Mr. Cooke, who does not play the recorder himself, could write so unfailingly well for this instrument. He seems to be a composer who knows his craft and who wants to write for and not against the instrument (and audience).

Because this work is unpublished, it remains virtually unknown. Walter Bergmann's enthusiasm for it was well founded, and long overdue publication would no doubt enable it to establish a place along side Cooke's already substantial number of works including the recorder.

Georges Migot: Sonatine

des rec, pn

à Carl Dolmetsch

1 Prélude (Allant – souple et chantant). 2 Andante (Comme une berceuse). 3 Final (Bien allant).

First UK performance: Wigmore Hall, London, 7 February 1961. Carl Dolmetsch, rec; Joseph Saxby, pn.

Published: Kassel: Bärenreiter-Verlag, 1958 (Edition 3224).

At his 1961 recital Dolmetsch presented two new works, both receiving their UK

---

[26] March 1960, New Series, no. 28, p. 1.

premiere. There is just one letter from Migot in the archive that dates from after the Wigmore Hall premiere of his *Sonatine*, and we have to turn to the programme note for this performance to learn that the work had its genesis in a tour of France Dolmetsch made in 1956.

The programme note also tells us that George Migot was a leading French composer whose works frequently displayed an affinity with the great contrapuntal and polyphonic music of the past, and that his output numbered well over 200 works often scored for unusual vocal and instrumental combinations.

Of the *Sonatine*, the programme note informs us:

> It is in three short movements; the Prélude (sub-titled 'Allant – souple et chantant') begins with 79 bars for the recorder unaccompanied; the Andante ('Comme une berceuse') has alternating forte and piano passages where the repetition of two bar phrases is marked 'en echo'. The Final ('bien allant') is a brisk allegro, this time begun by the piano alone, the recorder weaving independent figuration above the florid contrapuntal keyboard part.

The single brief letter from Migot is dated 12 February 1961 and appears to be in response to a letter from Dolmetsch. It notes that he had heard from Edgar Hunt that the *Sonatine* had been a success thanks to the Dolmetsch-Saxby partnership. In a postscript he further comments that it is also thanks to Dolmetsch that his name appeared in the programme.

Despite Edgar Hunt's positive report to the composer, the work was not enthusiastically received by the critics (neither was Hovhaness's Sextet, the other new piece in the recital). *The Times* of 9 February 1961 declared: 'Unfortunately neither of them made more than the slightest of impacts nor even created any impression of genial note-spinning.' Walter Bergmann writing in the *Recorder News* was even more unequivocal, stating that: 'The Sonatine is dull ...'[27]

Is this lack of enthusiasm justified? The music has an evasive character and can seem strangely unrewarding even for the performers. However, I would not wish to be unduly prejudicial, and players (and listeners) interested in the work should have an opportunity to make up their own minds.

A *Sonatine* No. 2 was to appear a few years later.[28]

Alan Hovhaness: Sextet, Op. 164

tr rec, str qt, hpd (or pn/org)

To Carl Dolmetsch and Joseph Saxby

1 Andante. 2 Pastoral. 3 Allegro vivo. 4 Landscape.

---

[27] January–March 1961, New Series, no. 32, p. 7.
[28] Schott & Co. Ltd, 1965; recorder part ed. Hans-Martin Linde.

First UK performance: Wigmore Hall, London, 7 February 1961. Carl Dolmetsch, rec; Martin String Quartet: David Martin, Marjorie Lavers, Eileen Grainger, Bernard Richards; Joseph Saxby, hpd.

Published: New York: C.F. Peters, 1958. Copyright later assigned to Fujihara Music Co., Inc.

Hovhaness's Sextet was the second of two new works (the other being Migot's *Sonatine*) that received their UK premieres at Dolmetsch's 1961 Wigmore Hall recital. As with the Migot, it was also a foreign tour, this time to the United States, that was the origin of this work.

The programme note by Ellen Powers gives brief biographical notes on Hovhaness and details of the work's origins. It is quoted here in full, as there is no correspondence in the Dolmetsch archive to provide such details:

> Alan Hovhaness, born in Summerville, Mass., is of Armenian descent. For several years he taught at the Boston Conservatory of Music, later moving to New York to devote his full time to composition. He received two Guggenheim awards, in 1953 and 1955, in addition to major commissions from leading American orchestras. His Sextet for treble recorder, string quartet and harpsichord Op. 164, dedicated to Carl Dolmetsch and Joseph Saxby, was commissioned by the Boston branch of the American Recorder Society in association with the Longy School of Music, subsequent to the first recorder study course conducted by Carl Dolmetsch and Joseph Saxby in 1957. The complete score was presented to them in Boston during another study conducted by them in 1959. The Sextet displays the composer's originality of style and tends towards the Asiatic in its tranquillity and contemplative moods.

A photostat copy of the composer's manuscript score dated 19 October 1958 (with a note marked 'copyright C.F. Peters 1958') and parts are in the archive, presumably those presented to Dolmetsch in 1959.

After I had contacted Ellen Powers to seek her permission to publish her programme note, she suggested I should write to Arthur Loeb, who had been president of the Boston Recorder Chapter of the ARS at the time of the commission. She felt sure he would be able to provide further information on Hovhaness's work and indeed he was. In a telephone call from the United States on receipt of my letter, Arthur Loeb informed me that he had played the recorder in the first performance, with Melville Smith playing the harpsichord together with an unnamed string quartet.

He also explained that the Hovhaness Sextet was the second commission by the Boston Recorder Chapter, the first being Daniel Pinkham's *Dithyramb*, for recorder and harpsichord or strings, of which the composer also made a version for oboe and harpsichord or strings.

Like Migot's *Sonatine*, Hovhaness's Sextet was not well received by the critic of *The Times* (see the section on Migot's *Sonatine*) and Walter Bergmann in the

Recorder News[29] was once again less than enthusiastic, describing the work as 'a succession of instrumental sounds but not a composition ... one had for long stretches the feeling that the composer had forgotten to score for recorder and harpsichord. When he remembered, the result was poor.'

Hovhaness was a very prolific composer of symphonies in particular. Many of his works show non-western influence and some have also included microtonality and aleatoric procedures. Short examples of the latter are to be found in the present work at the conclusion of the first and last movements.

In recent years there has been increasing interest in Hovhaness's work and a growth in what has become known as world music. The Sextet, tending 'towards the Asiatic in its tranquillity and contemplative moods', may now enjoy a more sympathetic reception, and American recorder player John Tyson has recorded the work. As with Migot's *Sonatine*, it is up to players and listeners to explore and make up their own minds. It would be unfair to judge the Sextet entirely on its initial reception.

Edmund Rubbra: Passacaglia sopra 'Plusieurs regrets', Op. 113

rec (or fl), hpd (or pn)

For Carl Dolmetsch

First performance: Wigmore Hall, London, 6 February 1962. Carl Dolmetsch, tr rec; Joseph Saxby, hpd.

Published: Croydon: Alfred Lengnick & Co. Ltd, 1964 (4144).

It would appear that, although Dolmetsch already had a new piece from Hans Gál for his 1962 Wigmore Hall recital, he was keen, having already received three fine works from Rubbra, to encourage him to add further to the repertoire. Dolmetsch must have contacted Rubbra sometime in late October or early November 1961 regarding a new work. The recital was due to take place on 6 February, so time was quite short. Whether contact was by letter or by telephone is not known as no letters from this time from Dolmetsch to Rubbra are in the Dolmetsch archive. Rubbra's response, in a letter dated 4 November 1961, was very positive, and after expressing pleasure at hearing from Dolmetsch again and in his own new house in Buckinghamshire, continued:

> ... Now about your request: there's not really very much time & I'm *frenetically* busy: but I'd *like* to do it & all I can say is 'D.V.'! I won't try to compete with the 'Meditazioni' – but I'll do my best. It's so nice to know that the 'Meditazioni' *is* such a favourite.

---

[29] January–March 1961, New Series, no. 32, p. 7.

A little over a month later, in a letter dated 16 December 1961, Rubbra wrote to report on the progress of the new work: 'I've got started on the new work: & it's a "Passacaglia sopra Plusieurs regrets". Hope this appeals to you as an idea. The chanson is a most wonderful tune.'

It is interesting that, having gone away from the inspiration of early music in his *Cantata pastorale*, Rubbra once more returned, not only to a theme from the music of the past, but to another by Josquin des Prez.

Work must have continued rapidly, for on 2 January 1962 Rubbra wrote: 'The "Passacaglia sopra Plusieurs regrets" is finished and *I* think it is my best yet. Hope you agree when you see it! I'm busy writing it out & I wonder how we could meet over it. Are you ever this way, or in London?' Rubbra's assessment may surprise those who hold the *Meditazioni* as a favourite.

On 6 January Rubbra forwarded the manuscript and a programme note, and confirmed he would like tickets for the recital. Three days later he wrote again in answer to a letter from Dolmetsch (a copy of which has not been found), to ask him if, when he felt like going through the work, he would telephone to arrange a time.

Although no record exists, there can be no doubt that a run-through took place, as a letter dated 11 January 1994 from Dolmetsch to the author notes that 'the composer ... rehearsed every one of his recorder works with me and was present at every one of the first performances.'

As usual, Rubbra's programme note for the recital is comprehensive:

This Passacaglia, completed on the first of January this year, is based on a fragment from the first twelve bars of Josquin des Prés's five-part setting of the chanson *Plusieurs Regrets*. Contrapuntal hints have been taken from this setting, but they have been modified freely in order to adapt them to a purely instrumental conception. The theme, D minor – A minor, in 2/2 time and eight bars long, is not in its opening statement confined to the harpsichord but completed by the recorder. It is in these last bars of the theme that the most characteristic cross-rhythms are found, and in development it is these that give the most dominant impulse to the music. The work is in three continuous sections. Six tonic entries of the subject in the first section suffice to change the smooth counterpoint of the opening to something much more forcefully rhythmic, although everything remains related to elements in the basic subject-matter. Enharmonically, the music now moves to a C–G minor statement of the theme in canonic imitation. This is the beginning of the second section, and it is soon characterised by a 3/4 counter-rhythm in the recorder that is sustained over a climax in the original key. The Fortissimo chordal ending of this section slows down to introduce (*adagio*) a free chromatic line on the recorder. This chromaticism continues as a descant to the recapitulation of the theme (third section). The next entry is an augmentation (in 3/2) accompanied by quaver patterns derived from the cadence of the theme. An *allargando* leads to the coda, a slower version of the theme with its original note-values. The new element here is a free and expressive line in compound time, given to the recorder as an accompaniment to the final statement of the theme.

The critic of the *Daily Telegraph* of 7 February 1962 was brief but enthusiastic about the new piece, commenting on the richness of the counterpoint and use of cross-rhythms.

Edgar Hunt, writing in the *Recorder News*, noted that the work 'has a unity – quite different from *Meditazioni*' and added: '... we shall look forward to the music's publication in order to study its intricacies.'[30]

The review in *The Times* of 7 February 1962 noted:

> Rubbra's 'Passacaglia sopra Plusieurs regrets' is his second piece for recorder and harpsichord and the immediate reaction to it last night was that it is too short. The players gave an encore but there were at least some regrets that Rubbra had not pursued further the rich possibilities he found in des Prés' theme and the two instruments. Modal implications and free chromatic melody; the recorder as a working polyphonic line or as an embroidery; cross-rhythms developing their own way in each instrument – the brief, distinguished work sets up any number of ideas.

The suggestion that the piece was too short seemed to worry Rubbra and writing to Dolmetsch on 12 February 1962 he noted:

> It was very nice to hear from you & am grateful that you all like the work so much. I certainly enjoyed the evening greatly. *Is* the work (vide The Times) too short? I don't feel it is when it is known, but would like to know what you honestly feel. I suppose you will be broadcasting it? As soon as the ornaments & other details have been set & incorporated in the m.s. Lengnicks would like to have it to engrave.

Dolmetsch wrote back the next day:

> Many thanks for your letter – I am *so* glad you enjoyed the recital last week. I have had several letters from people saying how much they had liked the Passacaglia, among them Julian Herbage and Alec Robertson – the Daily Telegraph gave it a good notice too, as I expect you saw. I do not find it at all too short, since in playing it I get a sense of completeness and fulfilment from the work just as it stands. But looking again at the score, it has occurred to me that where the harpsichord reaches the first chord of the bar before the coda (i.e. 10 bars from the end), it might be possible to return to the beginning to make a da capo and reserve the final 10 bars for the second time through. What do you think of this? Don't hesitate to toss the idea aside if it makes nonsense to you.

And later on: '... of course I shall be glad to give you all the help I can with ornaments when you reach the stage of sending the work to Lengnicks.'

There is no response from Rubbra regarding Dolmetsch's suggestion for extending the work and the published score stands as first conceived. The Passacaglia requires a similar length of time for performance as *Meditazioni*, a work which has never been criticized for its brevity, and I tend to share

---

[30] *Recorder News*, February–May 1962, New Series, no. 36, p. 8.

Dolmetsch's view that the work is perfectly satisfactory and fulfilling to play (and to listen to) just as Rubbra wrote it.

On 31 January 1964 Rubbra sent Dolmetsch a copy of the published edition of the Passacaglia with a note saying: 'Here at last is the Passacaglia, and I hope it will have as long a life as the Meditazioni!'

There is a quite natural tendency to consider the Passacaglia as something of a companion piece to the *Meditazioni*: it is, after all, based on another Josquin fragment. Yet it is worth remembering that Rubbra himself considered it his 'best yet', and Edgar Hunt's comment regarding its quite different unity is an astute observation. It is simply another example of Rubbra's unfailing ability to compose very fine music for the recorder while integrating a theme from the past with contemporary idioms. It remains one of the very special works in the recorder repertoire.

Hans Gál: Concertino, Op. 82

tr rec, str qt

To Carl Dolmetsch

1 Preludio (Poco andante). 2 Scherzo lirico (Allegro grazioso). 3 Notturno (Allegretto tranquillo). 4 Rondo capriccioso (Vivace).

First performance: Wigmore Hall, London, 6 February 1962. Carl Dolmetsch, rec; Martin String Quartet: David Martin, Marjorie Lavers, Eileen Grainger, Bernard Richards.

Published: London: Universal Edition, 1963 (UE 12644).

As in Dolmetsch's 1961 Wigmore Hall recital, that for 1962 contained two new works. There can scarcely have been a greater contrast than between Rubbra's Passacaglia and Hans Gál's *Concertino*.

Hans Gál was born in Vienna in 1890 and from an early age showed considerable musical talent, an early symphony being awarded the newly created Austrian State Prize for composition in 1915. Orchestral and chamber music and operas brought him international success (his Symphony in D, Op. 30, was awarded a Colombia Prize on the occasion of the Schubert centenary in 1928), and in 1929 he was appointed director of the conservatory in Mainz. A flow of compositions continued during the next four years, but the coming to power of the Nazis brought, as with other Jewish composers, a ban on the performance and publication of his music, and in 1933 he was dismissed from his directorship. Gál returned to Vienna, but on the annexation of Austria in 1938 he fled with his family to England, eventually making his home in Edinburgh. From 1945 he was lecturer in music at Edinburgh University, where he continued to work until and beyond his retirement.

Dolmetsch was a fairly frequent visitor to the city, to the Society of Recorder

Players branch there, and in connection with adjudication and other musical activities. It was almost certainly on such a visit that Dolmetsch first met Hans Gál. Their friendship lasted for the remainder of Gál's life, during which they frequently corresponded.

Despite this, it has not been possible to trace the precise origins of the *Concertino*. The earliest letter from Gál regarding the work to be found in the archive dates from 13 August 1961. From this it is evident that Dolmetsch had, by that date, received a copy of the score and expressed his approval, as Gál's letter notes: '... I am delighted with your generous approval. Well, I am looking forward to hearing that Quintet on the 6th of February, and I'll certainly not miss that occasion. Meanwhile, I'll have everything properly done by my copyist and you will get it in due course.' Some discussion must have taken place regarding proposals for performance of the *Concertino* in Edinburgh, as the letter continues: 'As to Edinburgh, I hope to find an occasion for it sooner or later, with quartet or with string orchestra. Kindly let me know in any case if you have any Scottish plans during the 2nd half of the coming season.'

The letter concludes by suggesting Kenneth Leighton, Geoffrey Bush and Edmund Rubbra as composers who might write a work for the recorder. Gál was perhaps not aware of the works Rubbra had already composed for Dolmetsch. He also mentions having heard Franz Reizenstein's Suite [*sic*] for recorder played on the flute, and suggests that he too 'might write something new for you, and I am sure he would do it well.'

On 14 December 1961 Gál sent Dolmetsch the performing material for the *Concertino* with a letter that begins: 'Well, here is a score and the string parts, everything carefully revised and, I hope, without mistake.' The letter concludes: 'Could you let me know in due course when and where you will rehearse with the Martins? I would love to hear the piece at least once before the performance, there are always little bits to be adjusted.'

Soon after, Gál found that he would be in London shortly before the premiere, and on 31 December he wrote to Dolmetsch:

> Well, it turns out that I should be able to be in London during the weekend preceding the 6th of February. Would there be a chance of having a good running through if I could come to Haslemere during that weekend? This would simplify matters for me, especially with the respect to the possibility of one or another little change appearing to be necessary.

Interestingly, as he had already composed at least two works including recorder, Gál continued by expressing reservations about his writing for the instrument, much as Robert Simpson had done a number of years earlier: 'I am quite certain of my string quartet writing, but not half as certain with the recorder, and at a final rehearsal with the strings there is so little time to do anything beyond the most essential problems of balance.'

There is no further correspondence in the archive, so it is not possible to discover whether the work required any 'little changes' of any kind. Gál, however, wrote a comprehensive programme note for the first performance:

> As is obvious in a quintet for a wind instrument and strings, the recorder plays the part of a *primus inter pares*, of a distinguished soloist in a chamber music ensemble. With a certain preponderance of contrapuntal writing, the formal design of the four movements remains simple and symmetric.
> The first movement, in ternary form, starts with an ostinato motif, alternating between the two violins, as an accompaniment of a continuous flowing arioso of the recorder, to which the 'cello corresponds as a duet partner. In the middle section a more rhythmically articulative motif takes over, with a lively interplay of the instruments. In the following recapitulation the arioso melody, starting a fifth higher, rises to an extensive climax.
> The scherzo, a graceful dance movement, presents the recorder as a solo ballerina, the accompaniment of muted strings being reduced to a minimum weight. In the Trio section, the first violin joins the recorder in a dialogue, with the second violin and the viola as another couple of melodically alternating partners.
> The third movement, Notturno, is in the character of a serenade in which the 'cello occasionally plays the part of a guitar. The serenade tune, shared between the first violin and the recorder, is followed by an energetic second motif, inclined to contrapuntal entanglements that later spread into a thematic development. Shaped as a concise sonata form, with a shortened and transposed recapitulation, the movement is concluded by an expressive and lyrical coda.
> The Finale, a 'sonata rondo' with frequent, ever changing entries of a burlesque, clown-like main idea, confronts this with various contrasting episodes among which a kind of pastoral tune claims its rights as a 'second subject' reappearing in a recapitulation. In the end, the clown makes his entry in a pacified mood, changing from 3/4 to 4/4 and from a burlesque to a lyrical character, leading to a soft wistful conclusion.

Both *The Times* and the *Daily Telegraph* of 7 February 1962 carried reviews that, though appreciative of the music, were less enthusiastic about the performance. *The Times* noted that the *Concertino* 'was sociable music of easy charm, which asked for a less dogged performance than it got.' Likewise the *Daily Telegraph* felt more sophistication from the strings had been required.

In his review in the *Recorder News*,[31] Edgar Hunt was more generous, and made an interesting comparison with Gál's musical language: 'Dr. Gál's Concertino has a more direct appeal [than Rubbra's Passacaglia] and the Martin String Quartet joined in giving a finished performance. The music breathed the same air as Richard Strauss, and it was interesting to speculate what that composer might have written for the recorder.'

Gál's music does show an affinity with Strauss and certainly the influence of Brahms, but the very personal compositional style that he had forged by his late twenties also had its roots in the counterpoint of J.S. Bach and the delicacy and

---

[31] Ibid.

precision of Haydn and Mozart (important to understand when interpreting his music). While Gál resisted following more fashionable directions taken by some of his contemporaries, he nevertheless constantly explored new forms and instrumental combinations. His works are marked by a natural lyricism and a consistent craftsmanship that delights in the making of good music.

The friendship between Gál and Dolmetsch resulted in a number of further works including recorders. These represent only a small part of Gál's compositional output, which runs to 110 published works, but among the recorder pieces the *Concertino* is the most substantial and certainly representative of his very characteristic style.

Gordon Jacob: Variations

tr rec, hpd (or pn)

For Carl Dolmetsch and Joseph Saxby in honour of 30 years' collaboration

Theme: Andante semplice. 1 Allegro. 2 Andante espressivo. 3 Alla marcia. 4 Andante espressivo. 5 Molto vivace (hpd only). 6 Poco adagio, espressivo. 7 Molto vivace (inversion of var. 5; rec and hpd). 8 Andante con moto. 9 Lento. 10 Finale. Presto.

First performance: Wigmore Hall, London, 6 February 1963. Carl Dolmetsch, rec; Joseph Sazby, hpd.

Published: London: Musica Rara, 1967 (MR 1110).

It was a significant celebration that brought about Gordon Jacob's second work for recorder written for Dolmetsch. Unfortunately, because there is no letter from Dolmetsch to Jacob in the archive to indicate exactly how or when an invitation to write the work was made, this cannot be deduced with any certainty. However, in a letter from Jacob to Dolmetsch dated 26 September 1962 we read: 'Thank you too for asking me to write something for your thirty years partnership with Joseph Saxby. I will certainly try to think up something for you.' Dolmetsch must have responded positively to the news, as two days later Jacob wrote to Dolmetsch again:

> My dear Carl,
>
> Thank you so much for being so pleased about my promise to write something for you and your good wishes.
>
> I would like to call it 'Variations for Treble Recorder and Harpsichord', as I have a little theme I could use for that purpose.
>
> Yrs ever
>
> Gordon

A letter from Jacob dated 31 October 1962 starts by clarifying a misunderstanding as to where the first performance was to take place, but continues concerning the scoring. It would seem that after the work was under way Dolmetsch had asked if it would be possible to add parts for violin and cello. This is no doubt because violinist David Martin and cellist Bernard Richards would be taking part in the recital which also included another performance or the Berkeley *Concertino* for recorder, violin, cello and harpsichord first performed in 1956. Dolmetsch would also have seen the potential for performance of the work with Alice and Eleonor Schoenfeld while on tour in the United States the following autumn. Jacob however reported: 'The rough draft is nearing completion, so I'm afraid it won't be possible to add violin & cello to it. In any case as it is being written in honour of your 30 years partnership with Joseph it is suitable that only you & he should be in it!'

On the 22 November 1962 Jacob sent Dolmetsch the new work with the accompanying letter:

My dear Carl,

Here is your piece at last! I hope you will both enjoy playing it, though when I've finished something I always wish it was better than it is!

Yrs

Gordon

Obvious signs of the self-criticism to which, on occasions, many creative artists subject themselves.

There is only one further letter from Jacob from the time between composition and the first performance that is dated 4 January 1963. It thanks Dolmetsch for his letter (of which there is unfortunately no trace), for tickets for the recital and 'for billing the Variations so conspicuously.' Dolmetsch had clearly expressed his and Joseph Saxby's satisfaction with the work as the letter continues: 'I am glad you are both enjoying them and we both look forward to hearing them very much.'

This letter also enclosed Jacob's detailed programme note, given here in full:

Written in the autumn of last year and dedicated to Carl Dolmetsch and Joseph Saxby specially for this occasion, the work consists of an air and ten variations.

There is no introduction, the Air (Andante semplice) being played by the recorder with a chordal accompaniment on the harpsichord.

The variations are as follows:

1. A quick, scherzo-like movement featuring the repeated triplet notes of the Air.
2. A slow piece in somewhat elegiac mood in which the repeated triplet notes are again prominent.
3. Alla marcia. The triplets are here replaced by a dactylic metre. Short sharp chords accompany, with some degree of dissonance a satirical version of the Air. This leads into:

4. Andante espressivo. The harpsichord has arpeggio figuration based on the open-string intervals of the treble viol, an acknowledgement of the Dolmetsch family's interest in other old instruments besides the recorder and keyboard group.
5. Vivace – For harpsichord alone. Robust and vigorous, recalling in some of its cadences idioms of sixteenth-century origin though by no means a pastiche.
6. Poco adagio, espressivo. Quiet and lyrical.
7. An inversion of Var. 5, but with recorder this time.
8. Andante con moto. In the style of a Siciliano. The melodic line is divided between the two instruments.
9. Lento – A ground bass over which recorder and harpsichord discuss in free canonical style a somewhat oriental version of the Air.
10. Finale – Presto. This provides a short concluding flourish to the piece in the nature of a tarantella.

Among the special manuscripts at Haslemere is the composer's autograph score of the Variations dated 15 November 1962. This contains Joseph Saxby's fingering and registration marks in pencil and was no doubt used for the first and subsequent early performances.

The Times of 7 February 1963 described the Variations as being: 'on a simple air artfully evoking the recorder's rightful period without resorting to archaic figures of speech. The ensuing variations are too extrovert in style to carry highly charged emotion, yet all are marked by this composer's sterling resourcefulness of invention, and they provide stimulating contrasts.'

Edgar Hunt found himself making quite natural comparisons with Jacob's highly acclaimed Suite for Recorder and Strings of which he had heard the first performance just five years earlier. Writing in the first issue of the newly launched *The Recorder and Music Magazine*[32] which incorporated the former *Recorder News*, Hunt noted:

> It is difficult to assess a work of this calibre at a first hearing, but it did not make an immediate impact on the writer comparable to that of the Suite for Recorder and Strings. It was of course competent music competently played, and the composer was present to share the well-merited applause.

In 1967 Jacob's Variations were published, and Ates Orga, reviewing the new edition in *Recorder & Music Magazine*,[33] noted more ungenerously: '... during the last twenty years I feel he doesn't have the necessary creative imagination to mould his material into something more memorable than a mere succession of notes.' Later, however, it is a little more complimentary: 'But if Jacob lacks their [Britten's, Tippett's, Rubbra's] concentration, he helps to compensate by writing music which is effective, well balanced and enjoyable to perform.'

---

[32] May 1963, **1**, p. 31.
[33] February 1968, **2**, p. 265.

The archive also contains a signed copy of the published edition dated 9 January 1967.³⁴ This was sent to Dolmetsch with a letter that reads:

Dear Carl,

At last this has come out! I send it to you in token of my profound admiration for your work.

By the way, Musica Rara is also bringing out my new Sonata for Treble Recorder & Piano, but publication is a slow business these days.

With kind regards & affection from us both,

Gordon

Jacob's work is not simply a series of variants of the air, but more a set of individual responses, not just to the melody as it stands, but to various aspects of its character. A particular rhythmic fragment, especially the triplet figure with which the Air opens, or a characteristic interval from its melody is often made to infuse an entire variation. Jacob also makes use of other musical devices: inversion in variations 5 and 7 and ground bass and free canon in variation 9. His use of the intervals of the open strings of the viol in the accompaniment of variation 4 is also inventively introduced. Although it is not necessary to know of this, or of the other musical devices, to enjoy the work, it makes it all the more satisfying if one does.

The Variations do not perhaps have the immediate impact of the Suite for Recorder and Strings, but being in a different form and for more modest forces, a comparison is somewhat invidious.

John Gardner: Little Suite in C, Op. 60

tr rec, hpd (or pn)

For Carl Dolmetsch and Joseph Saxby

1 Overture (Slow). 2 Scherzo (Moderately fast). 3 Saraband. 4 Finale (Fast).

First performance: Wigmore Hall, London, 12 February 1964. Carl Dolmetsch, rec; Joseph Saxby, hpd.

Published: Oxford: Oxford University Press, 1965. Copyright assigned to Anglo-American Music Publishers 1984.

---

[34] The keyboard score of this copy contains some written-in alterations to the right hand of the harpsichord part at the beginning of variation 3. The fifth note (semiquaver G) in bar 1 and the third note (semiquaver G#) in bar 2, have both been marked as F#. A check against Jacob's manuscript shows these alterations to be correct (and the phrase is repeated an octave lower in the next two bars with the F#s in place). However, it is easy to understand how the reading could have been misinterpreted, as in Jacob's musical handwriting, until one gets to know it, it is sometimes difficult to distinguish between the notes F and G at the top of the treble stave.

There is only one letter in the archive in connection with this work (see later) but it does not give any indication of the work's origins. However, enquiries of John Gardner revealed that Dolmetsch contacted him directly with the request for a work for recorder and keyboard for the 1964 Wigmore Hall recital. The archive does contain a copy of the published edition signed by the composer and dated May 1965.

The programme note for the first performance is very brief. Apart from noting that the work 'was written earlier this year', it informs us: 'It is the composer's first piece for this combination of instruments.'

Following the first performance Edgar Hunt noted in *The Recorder and Music Magazine*[35] that the four movements were 'alternatively slow and quick – as might have fitted something from the eighteenth century; but there is nothing "period" about their content.'

The review in *The Times* of 14 February 1964 was of greater length and noted:

> This is a virtuoso work with a most individual flavour in which both instruments were kept busy, the recorder having many sustained phrases in the Overture and Saraband and needing agility in the Scherzo and Finale. Each of the four compact movements was well defined. The Overture had considerable complexity in its harmonic texture, but it was not until the Scherzo that the composer's wit began to take over. The Saraband was a thing of dignity and the Finale contained the germs of traditional jazz.

The *Daily Telegraph* of 13 February 1963 also commented on the influence of jazz on the Finale and the wit and virtuosity of the Scherzo.

The Overture, despite Edgar Hunt's assertion that the work has nothing 'period' about it, does have a baroque feel. It even looks a little Bachian on the printed page, with the individual parts taking over one from another as the music moves forward.

A brisk syncopated exchange between the recorder and the keyboard right hand open the fleet Scherzo, which generates considerable energy in the minute taken for its performance. Two bars after figure 10 the recorder introduces a new repeated note figure that is to appear twice more and create the rhythmic formula that propels the movement onward. The basic 2/4 pulse is spiced with occasional bars of 2/8 and 3/8 and the semiquaver movement becomes more involved. However, this reverts to the hocket-like exchanges of the opening, the movement closing with a bar of silence.

Although of considerable elegance, the Saraband has much rhythmic sophistication. The usual accentuation of the second beat of the 3/4 bars to be found in eighteenthcentury sarabands is achieved here by a sort of Scotch snap, at first confined to the recorder, but transferring with telling effect to the keyboard left hand towards the end.

Whereas the Scherzo is mostly in 2/4 with 3/8 interruptions, the Finale has a

---

[35] May 1964, **1**, p. 137.

reversal of this formula, being basically in 3/8 with the occasional bar of 2/8 again providing further interest to the already lively rhythmic structure. The movement opens with the keyboard alone, its right-hand melody repeated at the octave at the recorder's entry. Later the music does in places take on a jazzy feel, but there is also a hint in the recorder part of an inversion of fragments of the opening theme. Even smaller fragments bring the movement to a cheeky conclusion, punctuated most effectively by two bars of silence.

In his review of the published edition, Edgar Gordon writes: 'The idiom is essentially modern without striving desperately to be so and should present no problems. Technically there are many challenges to the players, both individually and in ensemble, but the effort should be found well worth while.'[36]

The one letter in connection with the work was found in the signed copy of the printed edition. It is dated 24 May 1965 and reads as follows:

Dear Carl,

At last this has come out. Slightly amended since you did it – improved, I hope.

Yours ever

John Gardner

However, no details of the amendments are given.

Recorder technique has developed in such a way that the challenges of this piece are not now considered so demanding. However, the effort remains worthwhile, not least for those who might be put off by the diminutive in the title, which I learned from a conversation with Greta Dolmetsch, Dr Carl himself would have preferred left out. The composer nevertheless retained it, no doubt with reference to the work's brevity and conciseness rather than to any slightness of content that may, incorrectly in this case, be implied.

Arnold Cooke: Quartet (Sonata)

tr rec, vn, vc, hpd (or pn)

Written for Carl Dolmetsch (1964)

1 Moderato poco maestoso – Allegro – Moderato poco maestoso. 2 Andante. 3 Allegro vivace.

First performance: Wigmore Hall, London, 3 February 1965. Carl Dolmetsch, rec; Alice Schoenfeld, vn; Eleonore Schoenfeld, vc; Joseph Saxby, hpd.

Published: London: Schott & Co. Ltd, 1968 (Edition 10938; R.M.S. 1228).

---

[36] *Recorder and Music Magazine*, March 1966, 2, p. 29.

In July 1964 Dolmetsch was making plans for his visit later that year to the Idyllwild Arts Festival at which he was planning to play Arnold Cooke's Divertimento (first performed at the Wigmore Hall in 1960). In a letter to Cooke dated 10 July, Dolmetsch asked if it would be possible for copies of the string parts of the orchestral version to be sent to Dr Max Krone, the Director of the Idyllwild Arts Foundation in California. The letter continued:

> And now I am wondering whether I can persuade you to do something else for me? Working on the Faculty at these courses have been two charming and brilliantly talented sisters, one a violinist, and the other a 'cellist – Alice and Eleonore Schoenfeld. They are well known in the States and on the Continent, but have not yet toured this country. Hearing that they hope to remedy this omission during the coming season, I have invited them to appear at my next Wigmore Hall recital, on 3rd February 1965. Which brings me to the point. Would you consider writing a work for recorder, violin, 'cello and harpsichord – the same combination as the Lennox Berkeley Concertino – for next year? I believe we might have the makings of a pretty irresistible first performance, coupling a work from you with the Schoenfeld sisters. What do you think?

Cooke replied on 14 July, and after confirming that he would send a score and parts of the Divertimento to Idyllwild, reported: 'I would be delighted to write a work for recorder, violin, 'cello & harpsichord for your next Wigmore Hall recital. I think this will be a very attractive combination.'

Before leaving for California Dolmetsch wrote to Cooke:

> I ought to have written to you at once to tell you how *very* delighted I was to hear that you are going to write another work for me, for recorder, violin, 'cello and harpsichord. This is indeed splendid news and I am already looking forward enormously to seeing the new work when it is ready.

With the need for arranging advance publicity soon after his return, Dolmetsch concluded: '... if you could let me know what form the work is going to take, i.e. suite, trio-sonata or what have you, this will be very helpful when the time comes.'

Cooke responded in a letter dated 12 August 1964 and noted:

> I am certainly looking forward to writing a new work for you, but as I am at present occupied with another work which has to be ready for the autumn, I have not yet had time to think about your work.
>
> However, by the time you return from California in October, I shall have had time to think about what sort of form the work will take, and I will let you know then.

Cooke duly contacted Dolmetsch again in October with a proposed title: 'As I suspect you will be back by now, or else very soon from California, I am writing to let you know about the work you have asked me to write ...' Cooke continued:

> I find it difficult to decide in advance just what form a work like this will take, but I think it would be best to call it simply Quartet for Recorder, Violin, 'cello and Harpsichord.

3 Eleonore and Alice Schoenfeld with Joseph Saxby and Carl Dolmetsch at a rehearsal in the 1960s.

> Probably it will be in three movements but anyway the title would be enough for any announcements.

Cooke's referral to the work's title as 'Quartet' will become significant later.

Dolmetsch replied on 16 October, and his letter opens by informing Cooke of the enthusiastic reception the Divertimento had received at Idyllwild. It continues:

> It is splendid to have such encouraging news of the new Quartet for 3 February and I am greatly looking forward to seeing it when it is ready. We are filling in forms and pulling strings for the Schoenfeld sisters – what a palaver one has to go through to obtain permission to give a concert with one's friends if they happen to come from abroad!

About a month later, Dolmetsch wrote to Cooke again, as it was clear time for rehearsals with the Schoenfelds was going to be limited, to inform of plans to tape the recorder and harpsichord parts, once ready, to send to the Schoenfelds, noting however that this was not a 'prod'.

On 12 November Cooke replied: '... I have actually not been working on it for very long, and so far have completed only the first movement.' He continued by explaining about a request also received in July for a work for the MacNaughton

Concerts, which was to receive its first performance the following day, and about a talk on Hindemith being written for a BBC Third Programme broadcast early the next year. However, Cooke concludes by noting: 'But I reckoned there would be enough time to do your work after these, and I am now going ahead with it.'

Cooke must have worked quickly on the remaining two movements, as on 12 December he wrote to Dolmetsch enclosing the completed work:

> I am now sending you my new work for your concert soon enough, I hope, to give you and your colleagues adequate time for rehearsal. I have decided after all to call it a Sonata rather than a quartet, because it is related to the old type of sonata, Bach & pre-Bach, and to call it Quartet would suggest more the type of chamber composition of the later classical period.
>
> Sonata is therefore. I feel, more appropriate. Sorry I didn't think of this before, as by now you have probably had your advance notices printed, but so often I can't be sure in advance what form my pieces are going to take. However it won't matter and the programmes will be correct.
>
> I hope you will find the writing satisfactory, but if there are any awkward or ineffective bits, please let me know. I have made another copy of the work, so I can refer to it.
>
> Shall look forward to hearing you play it in due course, and meanwhile all good wishes for Christmas and the New Year.

The manuscript score and recorder part remain in the archive at Haslemere together with a note that states that 'violin and 'cello parts [are] with Alice and Eleonor'. The score contains the often found pencil markings made by Joseph Saxby.

A little over a week later Cooke wrote again enclosing a programme note and in a PS added: 'Just received your card. Am so pleased you like the work, and think it will be successful.'

The programme note is of interest, not only because of the succinct description of the work, but also for Cooke's continued explanation of the use of the title 'Sonata'.

> The title 'Sonata' is used because the work is more closely related to the old type of sonatas for various instruments with harpsichord (duo and trio sonatas etc.), rather than to the forms of instrumental ensembles of the later classical period. It begins with a rather slow introduction leading into an allegro in a semi-fugal style, the main theme of which is first presented by the violin and 'cello. There is also a subsidiary theme first heard on the recorder. The movement ends with a reference to the introduction. The Andante is also fairly contrapuntal in texture, but is lyrical and quietly flowing. There is a short cadenza for the recorder just before the end. The last movement is a simple rondo, the main theme being heard at the beginning on the recorder. Whereas the first two movements are for treble recorder, here the higher instrument (sopranino or descant) is used, as being more suited to the sprightly character of the music.

The subsidiary theme of the fugal section in the first movement bears a close resemblance to a theme in Cooke's *Little Suite* No. 1 for treble recorder solo, written some years later for John Turner, and published by Forsyth Brothers (Ex. 3.17 and 3.18).

Ex. 3.17. Arnold Cooke, Quartet for treble recorder, violin, cello and harpsichord. First movement, recorder part at figure 4. Reproduced by permission of Schott & Co. Ltd.

Ex. 3.18. Arnold Cooke, *Little Suite* No. 1 for treble recorder solo. First movement, bars 27–31. Reproduced from Pieces for Solo Recorder, 1, by permission of Forsyth Brothers Ltd.

Whether it is a deliberate quotation or a chance thematic resemblance cannot be determined with any certainty.

The reviews in the broadsheets were enthusiastic about the work, *The Times* of 4 February 1965 noting: 'The Sonata, a deftly written essay in the neo-classical manner, has three movements, in the last of which Mr Dolmetsch exchanged his treble recorder for a sopranino, this higher instrument being (in the words of the composer) "more suited to the sprightly character of the music."'

The *Daily Telegraph* of 4 February 1965 commented on the work's combination of seriousness and wit and on the lyricism of the slow movement.

Edgar Hunt's review in *The Recorder and Music Magazine*[37] made the most accurate observation of the origins of the first movement style, but was less sure about the effect of the change to sopranino for the last movement.

> [the Sonata] may be described as a modern trio sonata – in fact the first movement with all its dotted rhythms suggests that it might be descended from the French overture. In the final Rondo, as in some other works, the treble recorder is exchanged for a sopranino, giving extra brilliance but detracting somewhat from the work's unity as chamber music.

Dolmetsch must have written to Cooke after the first performance, but a copy of the letter has not survived. Cooke wrote on the 11 February:

> Thank you very much for your letter. I am indeed encouraged that you all appreciated

---

[37] May 1965, **1**, p. 263.

my Sonata so much. The notices were favourable and for my part I was delighted with the splendid performance you gave the work. It is seldom that one gets a first performance on this level.

When the work came to be published the following year, Cooke noted in a letter to Dolmetsch dated 17 February 1966:

Schotts ... have accepted the work for publication and it is in process of publication. They want to change the title of the work from Sonata to Quartet. [Walter] Bergmann agrees with me in preferring Sonata for this work, but says that it is better for their catalogue to describe it more precisely. So rather reluctantly I have agreed.

What is in a title, one might ask. Cooke obviously felt quite strongly about it, and in a way he was probably right. This is a work that in its form owes more to the early eighteenth century than to later models, and this needs to be recognised if the work is to be fully understood. The musical world of Hindemith is also never far away, but although these influences are strong, Cooke's own musical personality shines through what is one of his most successful works including recorder.

Edmund Rubbra: Sonatina, Op. 128

rec, hpd

1 Allegretto comodo. 2 Adagio mesto. 3 Variations on *En la fuente del Rosel*[38] (Moderato scherzando).

First performance: Wigmore Hall, London, 3 February 1965. Carl Dolmetsch, tr rec; Joseph Saxby, hpd.

Published: Croydon: Alfred Lengnick & Co. Ltd, 1965 (4200).

It is not difficult to imagine the excitement this letter from Edmund Rubbra, dated 10 September 1964, must have created:

My dear Carl,

I am writing a 3-movement Sonatina for treble recorder and harpsichord (the 1st movement is well on). Would you like it for your next Wigmore recital?

All good wishes

Yours sincerely

Edmund Rubbra

Dolmetsch was away on tour in the United States and did not receive the news

---

[38] Melody by the sixteenth-century composer Juan Vazquez.

immediately. Greta Matthews appreciated the significance of Rubbra's offer, and anticipating Dolmetsch's reaction wrote to Rubbra the next day:

> In Dr. Dolmetsch's absence on tour in California, I am writing on his behalf to thank you for your letter of 10th September.
> I am quite sure he will be overjoyed by the news that you are writing a Sonatina for treble recorder and harpsichord and that he will – metaphorically speaking – grab it with both hands for his next Wigmore Hall recital, on Wednesday, 3rd February. I am writing to him today and will send your letter on to him, just in case his morale needs a boost!

Towards the end of October Rubbra wrote with further news:

> How did Carl re-act to the news of the Sonatina? It is now quite finished and written out, and the three movements last 15 minutes exactly.
> When he comes back – but perhaps he is back already? – would he like (also Joseph) to come over here one day so that I can play it over to them?

Dolmetsch was indeed back from California and wrote to Rubbra immediately:

> You really cannot imagine how very delighted I was to receive the news of your Sonata [*sic*] while I was in California. My time there was so heavily 'skeduled' that I simply couldn't write then and there to tell you of my joy and to assure you of a warm welcome for the new work in our next Wigmore Hall programme.

The letter continued with the news that the Schoenfeld sisters would be taking part in the recital and that Arnold Cooke was writing a new work for recorder, violin, cello and harpsichord to mark their debut in this country. Dolmetsch's letter later noted:

> With your Sonatina too, we shall have a beautifully balanced programme – ancient and modern, solo and ensemble, and just the right amount of each.
> Joseph and I would love a get-together with you, though it occurs to me that it is really our turn to be hosts. We are very soon moving into Jesses, my late parents' home, which has been modernised and re-decorated for the family and myself; so we would love to welcome you here when we have moved in and tidied up! But please Edmund, could I have a look at the recorder part before we meet to try it over, just to familiarise myself with the notes?

It is evident that Dolmetsch received a copy of the Sonatina and played it through. He must also have requested a programme note as a letter from Rubbra dated 1 January 1965 reads: '*So* glad you like the Sonatina. Here's my programme note (the typewriter broke down halfway through!)' The letter continues about arrangements for a visit to Haslemere on 10 January to try the work through and to attend a party at 'Jesses' that evening.

Dolmetsch replied on 4 January commenting: 'Joe and I like the new work more and more as we get to know it, and we are greatly looking forward to playing it to you on Sunday.'

4 Edmund Rubbra (centre) with Joseph Saxby, Alice and Eleonore Schoenfeld and Carl Dolmetsch.

Rubbra's programme note, the original of which does indeed begin typed and finish handwritten, is as comprehensive as usual. The text is given here in full:

> This Sonatina was written at the beginning of October last year. The first movement takes its origin from an idea I noted down sometime before, but which had not then been given any particular instrumental colouring. Taking it up again, I was suddenly aware of its relevance for recorder and harpsichord. The idea in question is built round a succession of fourths. This is heard first as an accompanimental figuration, and only afterwards are the fourths incorporated in the solo line. The second subject is also built round the interval, but is given freshness by a key change that leads more to the major. The form is classical, even including a repeat of the exposition. In the more dance-like development the metre changes from three-four to three-two (with an occasional seven-four), but the fourth still persists as a dynamic part of the texture. The second movement (Adagio mesto) consists of a long winding tune over a chordal accompaniment that gains expression from a persistent use of a slow dissonant appoggiatura. There follows a free cadenza for the recorder, the appogiatura chords breaking in on it to form the brief coda. The third movement (Moderato scherzando) is a set of variations and coda on a sixteenth century Spanish tune *En la fuente del rosel* by Juan Vazquez, found in a collection published in Mexico. The theme is played on the solo harpsichord.
>
> Var. I: (L'istesso tempo, four-eight) exploits the three note final cadence of the tune, and goes into the minor (C).

Var. II: (L'istesso tempo, three-eight): a brief return to part of the tune given to solo harpsichord leads to a development of the reiterated semiquavers in it.

Var. III: (L'istesso tempo, three-four): expansive with trills, and melodically stemming from a pattern (F-E-D) found in the body of the tune.

Var. IV: Prefixed by part of the theme (harpsichord) this variation (two-four, C minor) takes over and exploits ornamentally its two final notes.

Var. V: Largo. A free canon that takes its cue from the mordent that ends the previous Variation.

The Coda is brief and quick.

The reviews in the dailies were very brief, *The Times* of 4 February 1965 noting: 'Rubbra's Sonata [*sic*], which ends with a set of variations on a sixteenth century Spanish tune, is somewhat monotonous in texture but contains much happy invention.' The *Daily Telegraph* of 4 February 1965, however, commented on the richness of the textures and the exploitation of dissonance in the slow movement.

The recorder world reacted favourably, but understandably made comparisons with the *Meditazioni*. Edgar Hunt in *The Recorder and Music Magazine*[39] commented that the work: 'approaches near to the "Meditazioni ..." in quality.'

Rubbra himself was delighted with the premiere, and on 4 February 1965 wrote to Dolmetsch:

> It was a *wonderful* send off for my work last night. Thank you both for a magnificent performance. When you have finished with the score after the Newcastle performance, would you be kind enough to send it direct, registered, to my publisher, as he is anxious to get it engraved as soon as possible. Please indicate on the score any 'editorial' markings you think are apt.

The autograph manuscript score remains in the Dolmetsch archive, as does a copy of the published edition inscribed 'To Carl & Joseph from Edmund 21.4.66'.

Study of the manuscript reveals that the opening two phrases of the last movement theme were originally an octave lower. The '8ve' indication in pencil (adopted in the published version) appears to be in Dolmetsch's hand and was presumably his suggestion. Further suggestions for upward octave transpositions are marked in pencil in bars 15 and 16 of variation 3 (to avoid low F#) and are indicated as ossias in the published edition. Another passage is similarly marked in variation 5 from halfway through bar 4 to immediately after the first note of bar 8 (avoiding low E# and F#), but was presumably not adopted by the composer and does not appear in the published edition.

The published work was reviewed by Garth Kay in *Recorder and Music Magazine*,[40] in which the comparisons with *Meditazioni* continued, but which was enthusiastic and encouraged players to try the work for themselves:

---

[39] May 1965, **1**, p. 263.
[40] November 1966, **2**, p. 91.

> Here is a worthy companion to 'Coeurs désolés', perhaps less intense but cogent and sinewy in musical thought ... There is much more to understand in this music, particularly in the variations, and every reasonably good recorder player should get a copy to work away at. For encouragement, I don't think it is quite so hard for either player as 'Coeurs désolés'.

However, in a book of essays on Rubbra's music, Lewis Foreman noted that the Sonatina is the least likely to be attempted by the average amateur, being the most difficult of Rubbra's works in the medium.[41]

This is the only recorder work of Rubbra's that does not include metronome marks, so it is of particular interest to note his statement that the three movements 'last 15 minutes exactly'. To achieve a performance of this length will require much broader tempos than the indications at the beginnings of the movement would perhaps indicate, or than we are used to hearing.

The first two movements show Rubbra in an introspective mood; even in what he described as the 'dance-like' development of the first movement, the music is quite restrained. The melody of the *mesto* middle movement has a particular poignancy as it unfolds over brittle arpeggiated keyboard chords. Only in the third movement do we find more ebullient music, due to the lively nature of the Spanish theme on which the very free and creative variations are constructed. Once again Rubbra turned most effectively to early music for inspiration. Recorder players should indeed get a copy to work away at. Their efforts will be amply rewarded as they get to know one of Rubbra's most personal compositions.

Richard Arnell: Quintet (The Gambian), Op. 107

tr rec, str qt

To Carl Dolmetsch

First performance: Wigmore Hall, London, 10 February 1966. Carl Dolmetsch, rec; Martin String Quartet: David Martin, David Stone, Brian Hawkins, Bernard Richards.

Unpublished.

From correspondence in the archive it is evident that Dolmetsch met Richard Arnell in early November 1965,[42] as in a letter to Arnell dated 13 November Dolmetsch writes:

---

[41] Foreman, 'Recorder music', in id. (ed.), *Edmund Rubbra, Composer*, p. 73.

[42] I contacted Richard Arnell to seek further information about this meeting. He was unable to recall the exact details of the occasion, but thought it must have been an official function, as he remembered that Dolmetsch was wearing a chain of office. Arnell also noted that he had previously contacted Dolmetsch in connection with a harpsichord concerto he (Arnell) had written in 1946 for an American harpsichordist. Dolmetsch's reputation in the field of early music was well known and hence also his connection with the harpsichord,

> It was a great pleasure to meet you last week and I so much enjoyed our talk together. I am delighted to think that you are writing a work for the recorder and I am anxious now to press forward with printing publicity etc.
>
> Would you be able soon to let me have a line about the form of the work is likely to take, i.e. sonata, suite, concerto or what-have-you?

In a letter in reply to the above dated 26 November 1965 Arnell described the unusual source of the theme upon which he was planning to write variations:

> It was indeed a pleasure to meet you and to learn more of the possibilities of the recorder. I would like to call my piece "Variations on a tune by a Gambian."
>
> Two years ago, I was involved with arranging a tune composed by the Reverend John Faye from Gambia. He hoped that this would become the National Anthem, but unfortunately it did not win the prize. However, it is a delightful tune.

This is surely among the most unusual inspirations for any of the works written for Dolmetsch, and as he noted in his reply to Arnell's letter: '... nothing could be more topical than the title you have chosen for the new work and I think it will intrigue a lot of people!' Dolmetsch also requested a programme note. This gave a little more detail of the work's origins:

> A melody composed by the Rev. John Faye – High Commissioner for Gambia in London, before that country's independence – has been used as the basis for this set of variations for recorder and string quartet by Richard Arnell. He first arranged the theme for voice and piano and in this form the work was runner-up in a contest to choose Gambia's national anthem. Using the same theme, Mr. Arnell has since written a free prelude which is followed by his variations on Rev. Faye's melody.

By 6 January 1966 Arnell was able to report in a letter to Dolmetsch: 'The work is coming along quite well and I hope to have it ready early next week. I am sorry to be a little behind, but I suddenly had to go to Lisbon adjudicating.'

Progress on the piece must not have gone entirely according to Arnell's plans noted above, as by 21 January Dolmetsch wrote to him to request if it would be possible to forward the string parts directly to David Martin. Everything must have come together soon afterwards however, and although Arnell had been able to attend the rehearsal he had not been present at the first performance, about which Dolmetsch wrote to the composer on 17 February 1966:

> I am delighted to say that your Prelude and Variations was very warmly appreciated by a packed house last Thursday, as it fully deserved to be. In fact, its message reached all but the critics, who do not appear to have made much attempt to hear what was happening!

---

through which a UK performance of the piece could possibly have been arranged (telephone conversation with the author, 27 January 2001).

> The performance itself went without a hitch, even more smoothly than when you heard it at Dinely's. Audiences being what they are, the only suggestion that I would like to make is that the work does really call for a fifth and lively variation or coda, though I personally found your slow finale *very* satisfying.

Dolmetsch continued with news of the possibilities of a broadcast of the work and noted that he was looking forward to further performances with quartet or chamber orchestra. He further suggested:

> It has occurred to me that a piano/harpsichord reduction, if you think this is a feasible proposition, could be very useful for Joseph Saxby and me to perform when on tour as a duo.
>
> Once again my very warm thanks for a work which gave a large number of people tremendous pleasure. My only regret was that you yourself were not there to share the ovation with us.

Arnell replied on 24 February: 'I hear that your concert was a great success, and I much appreciated being a part of it.' In a postscript Arnell added: '... and I agree about another variation.' However, the work was never to receive this.

It also would appear to have been the composer's intention to follow Dolmetsch's suggestion and produce an arrangement of the work for recorder and keyboard, as in a letter written to Dolmetsch in August 1966 Arnell enquired about the score's whereabouts noting: 'I want to get on with the keyboard arrangement.' However, this was not made.

What had been the response of the critics with which Dolmetsch disagreed? The *Daily Telegraph* of 11 February 1966, though considering that the prelude demonstrated skilful writing, noted a certain monotony in the variations. *The Times* of 12 February 1966 was less generous, describing the work as: 'an apparently careless piece of composition in which no idea was allowed to expand even if it possessed the potential.' The *Recorder and Music Magazine*[43] similarly did not express much enthusiasm: 'The theme ... was then followed by a set of variations rather too short to maintain interest.'

Neither the manuscript score nor parts, or a copy of either is to be found in the Dolmetsch archive, but John Turner kindly allowed me to inspect a numbered photocopy of the manuscript score in his possession. This gives the composer's preferred title for the work rather than that under which it received its first performance.

Having had an opportunity to hear a recorded performance of the work I would tend to agree with Dolmetsch rather than the critics in finding it an effective composition (the atmospheric Prelude in particular), certainly unusual in its inspiration.

---

[43] March 1966, **2**, p. 21.

The *andante* Prelude of 48 bars in 4/4 time opens with muted strings. The recorder enters after four bars, quietly and on its lowest note, with a melody featuring triplets that rises steadily in tessitura and dynamic towards a top F (Ex. 3.19). At this point the strings enter, unmuted, with a descending figure similar to the opening.

The recorder part bears the frequent direction *espr*, and use is made of a falling phrase. Another short falling phrase for the recorder alone, marked *molto espr*, leads to the statement of the G major theme in 2/4 time on the recorder above mainly pizzicato strings.

Variation 1 (4/4, *Allegro*) opens with a double-stopped ostinato figure on the cello and short interjections on the upper strings before the entry of the recorder with the theme now transposed up a fourth. The characteristic rhythm from the theme's first full bar is repeated and eventually the recorder scampers off in semiquavers while the strings are left with the theme's rhythmic figure. The entire variation is over in just 15 bars.

Variation 2 (6/8, *Andantino*) starts with the recorder, which is soon joined by muted strings. The melodic outline remains clearly discernible in the recorder's figuration.

Variation 3 (2/4, *Allegro molto*) loses the sharp from the key signature. Almost the entire variation is based on the figure to be found in bars 9–12 of the theme.

Variation 4 (4/4, *Largo*) begins very quietly, the three lower strings muted and double-stopped above which the first violin weaves semiquaver figuration. The recorder's melody, marked '[Chorale]', moves in crotchets, but seems to owe little to the original theme. The first violin's figuration moves down to the second violin, then to both, and finally alternates between them before moving down to the cello in the quiet concluding bars.

Although the Quintet remains unpublished at the time of writing, it has been recorded in the United States, and another recording by John Turner and the Camerata Ensemble was released in 2001.[44] The opportunity these will provide to appreciate the work's qualities will, it is hoped, lead to publication.

---

44 CD *Thirteen Ways of Looking at a Blackbird*, released by Olympia (OCD 710).

Ex. 3.19. Richard Arnell, Quintet (The Gambian), Prelude, bars 1–9. Reproduced by permission of the composer.

Nigel Butterley: The White-Throated Warbler

sopranino rec, hpd

For Carl Dolmetsch and Joseph Saxby

First performance: New South Wales Conservatorium, Australia, 27 February 1965. First UK performance: Wigmore Hall, London, 10 February 1966. Carl Dolmetsch, rec; Joseph Saxby, hpd.

Published: Sydney: Albert and Son, 1965; Armidale, Australia: Orpheus Music, 2001.

There is no correspondence in the archive between Dolmetsch and Butterley in connection with this work, but it does contain an autograph manuscript inscribed 'Sydney 22.2.65'. It was clearly as a result of the Dolmetsch/Saxby tour of Australia early in 1965 that the work came to be composed.

The circumstances of the composition are described in a letter written to the author by Nigel Butterley in September 2001. At the time of the tour he was a producer in the ABC Music Department in Sydney and was assigned to look after the recording of the Dolmetsch/Saxby recitals, recalling there were at least two. He was also in the control room for a half-hour television recital they gave, met them briefly and heard them play Couperin's *Le rossignol en amour* several times.

Butterley based his composition on the call of a bird he had often heard near his home in Beecroft, but being uncertain of its identity telephoned the naturalist and authority on Australian birds, Alec H. Chisholm, who was a regular contributor to the *Sydney Morning Herald*. Not having been able to see the bird, Butterley could not describe its appearance, but whistled the song over the telephone. Chisholm identified it at once as the white-throated warbler, and thus the piece, drafted on a Sunday afternoon and completed in fair copy the following morning, received its title.

To Butterley's delighted Dolmetsch and Saxby liked the piece and premiered it as an encore after their final Sydney recital. Albert had just undertaken to publish some of Butterley's music and had the work engraved and produced so that it would be ready to present to the dedicatees on their return from New Zealand, also visited on the tour.[45]

From the outset the originality of the piece created critical enthusiasm. The reviewer of the *Sydney Morning Herald* of 1 March 1965 writes:

> In its own unpretentious right it was a completely successful response to a challenge likely to assay any composer's tact: the task of incorporating a naturally occurring sound in a design of some musical coherence while remaining true to its original flavour.

Butterley's 'Warbler' partially mimics on the sopranino recorder the timbre and the

---

[45] In a letter to the author dated 2 September 2001 Butterley commented in connection with the speed with which the edition was published: 'That's why the printed score had a couple of mistakes and was sold with a typed errata slip!'

apparently characteristic intervals of the call of its eponym and provides it with a wholly appropriate echo in the spidery lacing of the harpsichord part'

If anyone still doubts that the textures of the post Webern serial composers have become one of the permanent acquisitions of music, he should listen to this work. Fresh and engaging, not at all insistent in its modernity as such, it is a piece which could not have been as successful as it is without the discoveries of the newer composers or the avuncular example of Messiaen.[46]

The note included in the programme at the first UK performance gives further indications of the work's inspiration:

> This brief evocation of the fine, clear throb of the white-throated warbler's song was written for Carl Dolmetsch and Joseph Saxby by the Sydney composer Nigel Butterley during their tour of Australia last spring. It was inspired by their performance of Couperin's 'Le Rossignol en Amour' though in no respect is it an imitation of the 18th century work. Within a framework of serial technique, the piece mimics the characteristic intervals and timbre of the bird's call and evokes the arid atmosphere of the Australian bush, where the air is full of the sounds of bell birds, kookaburras and a multitude of others. Although of miniature proportions, the work is nonetheless important, demonstrating as it does that the idiom employed can successfully convey a message to be comprehended and enjoyed at first hearing, without in any sense resorting to pastiche.[47]

The English critics were as enthusiastic if briefer than their Australian counterpart. The *Daily Telegraph* of 11 February 1966 noted the originality of the style, the use of serial technique and the virtuoso writing for the sopranino recorder. Likewise *The Times* of 11 February 1966 commented that the work: 'achieves within a serial framework a neat and attractive impressionistic sketch.'

Although the work is founded on a 12-tone row, it does not proceed along strict serial lines, taking a more Alban Berg-like approach. The opening bar (marked 'Rather slowly – ♩ = c. 48) contains all 12 notes of the chromatic scale, which are divided between the recorder and the harpsichord. The same note sequence is immediately repeated in the second and third bars, but with the intervals modified. (The harpsichord arpeggio figure now moves downwards.) There is a distinctive rhythmic identity in which the harpsichord's arpeggiated figure plays an important part.

---

[46] Ibid. Butterley commented in connection with this final sentence: 'I should mention that at the time my knowledge of Messiaen's music and techniques was quite perfunctory, so his influence on the piece was minimal.'

[47] Ibid. This note was not Butterley's own, and in connection with the description of the piece capturing 'the arid atmosphere of the Australian bush' he observed: 'of course "the bush" is often loosely used to refer to anywhere that isn't city, but if used more specifically to refer to wooded areas, "arid" is hardly appropriate – it's often quite lush, and ranges from sub-tropical rainforest to snowfields!' He further added '... my warbler was a suburban one, long since gone from the Sydney area I should think.'

These elements appear again in the middle and towards the end of the work, but there are interludes that begin with a descending figure on the recorder leading to further birdsong motives above trills and tremolos on the harpsichord. All three elements in quick succession, ending with quiet birdsong, bring the work to an atmospheric conclusion.

This was among the earliest pieces to use serial techniques in a recorder composition, Americans Ervin Henning and Roslyn Brogue having pioneered recorder serialism in the 1950s. Butterley's work is as effective as it is concentrated (it occupies just 27 bars), and by its subtle manipulation of 12-tone procedures and synthesis of baroque sonorities and birdsong achieves originality within one of the most traditional of recorder associations.

A note in the 2001 Orpheus Music edition advises that since it is essentially a serial work, the composer does not encourage elaborations and improvisations during performance. This perhaps underlines how far removed Butterley's warbler is from the nightingale of Couperin, the works' original inspiration.

In addition to the recording made by Dolmetsch and Saxby during their seventeenth American tour, David Munrow also included it in his memorable recorded survey of music for recorder *The Art of the Recorder* made at much the same time.

Greta Dolmetsch informed me that because of its brevity (about one and a halfminutes) Carl Dolmetsch and Joseph Saxby frequently played the piece through twice in performance.

Although Butterley has not composed another piece for solo recorder, his first orchestral work, *Meditations of Thomas Traherne*, written in 1968, includes a children's recorder group of 22 players. His catalogue of works also includes among his music for young people *Music for Sunrise*, for recorders and percussion, composed in 1967.

Hans Gál: Trio Serenade, Op. 88

tr rec (or fl), vn, vc

1 Allegro moderato. 2 Andante. 3 Intermezzo scherzoso (Vivace leggiero). 4 Rondo (Allegretto piacevole).

First performance: Los Angeles, California, United States, 23 October 1966. First UK performance: Wigmore Hall, London, 6 February 1967. Carl Dolmetsch, rec; Alice Schoenfeld, vn; Éleonore Schoenfeld, vc.

Published: London: N. Simrock, 1967 (Edition no. 3123).

Only one letter in connection with this piece (dated 18 June 1966) is to be found in the archive, and it is thus not possible to establish precisely the circumstances under which the *Trio Serenade* was composed. It is likely that Dolmetsch requested, or Gál offered it for Dolmetsch's autumn tour of the United States where it would receive its first performance with the Schoenfeld sisters. Before this, however, Gál had sent Dolmetsch the score and parts (noting that his copyist had kept him waiting) with the above-mentioned letter. Also with this letter was a tape recording of the piece played by Fabienne Smith (recorder), Eva, Gál's daughter (violin), and Moray Welsh (cello). Gál commented that: 'the speeds are correct but the third movement could be a little faster.'

The archive contains a photocopy of the copyist's manuscript score together with a recorder part. A note contained in the score in Dolmetsch's hand reads: 'violin and 'cello parts left with Schoenfelds after broadcast recording on 27.2.69.'

Having given the first performance in the United States, Dolmetsch included the *Trio Serenade* as the new work in his 1967 Wigmore Hall recital, in which he was again joined by Alice and Eleonore Schoenfeld.

For the UK premiere Gál wrote the following programme note:

> The Trio, written in the spring of 1966 is, so to speak, open air music in the sense of genuine Serenade; music as an amiable homage, a lively conversation of the three individuals whose opinions vary but never clash. The diverse characters of the three instruments constitutes a challenge to the noblest techniques of music – three-part writing – each offering its own particular stimulation. The formal layout follows a freely treated classical pattern: the first movement is a sonata form; the second a song form with a varied contrasting section: the third a brief lively interlude – vivace e leggiero; the finale a rondo – allegretto piacevole.

The note concludes with the information that the piece was specially written for Carl Dolmetsch and Alice and Eleonore Schoenfeld.

The review in *The Times* of 8 February 1967 was quite brief but generally positive: 'Cast in four movements, it is skilfully devised and full of pleasing invention, though the first two movements seemed a little too protracted.'

The *Recorder & Music Magazine*, not usually disposed to controversial criticism contained a review[48] that was certainly among the most critically outspoken the journal has ever published. It displays a misunderstanding of Gál's musical language inexplicable in its apparent prejudice, and to reproduce it here would not provide a fair appraisal of the work.

The *Trio Serenade* possesses the lightness of a 'genuine serenade' and is totally characteristic of Gál's craftsmanship. It is nevertheless a technically demanding work, for the recorder certainly, but especially for the cello. It thus needs a special commitment on the part of the players, who require a particular virtuosity to convey its lightness but at the same time its vigour. Approached in the spirit and understanding of the 'noblest techniques of music' it will reveal one of Gál's finest trios, a form he particularly cherished.

---

[48] May 1967, **2**, p. 163.

John Gardner: Concerto da camera, Op. 91

tr rec, vn, vc, hpd

1 Rondo. 2 Ground (rec, vn, vc). 3 Gavotte (vn, vc, hpd). 4 Soliloquy (rec, hpd). 5 Final rondo.

First performance: Wigmore Hall, London, 2 February 1968. Carl Dolmetsch, rec; Alice Schoenfeld, vn; Eleonore Schoenfeld, vc; Joseph Saxby, hpd.

Published by the composer.

A number of letters in connection with this work are in the Dolmetsch archive. The earliest of these is from Dolmetsch to Gardner and dated 4 September 1967. Its second paragraph reads:

> I am so very pleased that you have agreed to write another work for the recorder – and so are Jeanne and Marguerite. They absolutely rejoiced when I told them the news. Alice and Eleonore Schoenfeld will be equally delighted, since it was Alice herself who so admired the Little Suite when Joseph and I played it in Palo Alto and she remarked then how nice it would be if you could write something for the four of us one day.

The *Little Suite* in C having proved of such appeal, it appears Dolmetsch responded to Alice Schoenfeld's enthusiasm and requested Gardner for a suitably scored work for the quartet to play.

I attended a concert given on 27 September 1997 in the concert hall at Manchester University music department to celebrate John Gardner's eightieth birthday. This included what was perhaps only the second UK performance of the work (with recorder rather than flute), given by John Turner, recorder; Ben Holland, violin; Jonathan Price, cello; and Keith Elcombe, harpsichord. In my review of the concert for *The Recorder Magazine*[49] I commented that, as in the similarly scored *Concertino* by Lennox Berkeley, the inner movements made use of smaller groupings of instruments than the quartet. It was thus of interest to read in the previously quoted letter Dolmetsch suggesting to Gardner: 'After our telephone conversation yesterday evening, it occurred to me that I could send you my own printed copy of Lennox Berkeley's Concertino to look at.'

I was intrigued to know if Berkeley's use of reduced scoring in the inner movements had influenced Gardner, but on enquiring of the composer I learnt that he had not in the event seen a copy of the Berkeley *Concertino*. The idea of framing three movements containing smaller instrumental groupings with outer movements for the entire quartet simply appealed to Gardner and was thus the form he adopted.[50]

Dolmetsch's letter further informs us that on the handbills for the Wigmore Hall

---

[49] December 1997, **17**, p. 153.
[50] Letter dated 24 January 2001 from John Gardner to the author.

recital the work would be announced as a concerto for recorder, violin, cello and harpsichord, and also noted that its duration would be about 12 minutes.

Early in November Dolmetsch was still away on his US tour when the handbills for the forthcoming Wigmore Hall recital arrived, and in his absence Greta Matthews sent Gardner a copy. About a month later, Greta contacted Gardner again, as the Wigmore Hall were requesting details of Dolmetsch's programme for their concert list, to ask if there was anything she could 'add to the bare facts that you are writing a concerto for recorder, violin, cello and harpsichord'. Gardner replied on 17 December:

> Title of my piece, which looks like being ready in the first week of January (with God's grace and a bit of luck), is *Concerto da Camera*. If the Wigmore Hall have billed it as a mere Concerto, however, it doesn't matter.
>
> I shall be in touch with Dr. Dolmetsch immediately upon completion or just before it.

On 17 January 1968 Gardner sent the work to Dolmetsch and in the accompanying letter wrote:

> Herewith Recorder and Harpsichord parts of Concerto da Camera. The score, which is both illegible and, in many places downright incorrect, I have kept as an insurance against the loss of the parts in transit: a spectre which has always haunted me on these occasions without ever, as it were, materialising.
>
> The Violin and Cello parts went to the Schoenfelds some days ago, though I haven't yet had a note of their safe arrival.
>
> See you on Sunday 28 January. Hope you like the piece. It takes, at a rough guess, about seventeen minutes to play. The M.M.s are about right and should give the correct tempo within a point or two.

Although there is a letter from Gardner confirming that the Schoenfelds had received their copies of the parts and confirming his attendance at a rehearsal at Haslemere, there is no further correspondence relating to the first performance. However, in August, Gardner sent Dolmetsch a copy of the score and parts in readiness for his autumn tour of the United States, during which it was intended that there should be further performances of the *Concerto da camera* with the Schoenfelds.

There is little by way of a programme note for the first performance, but it is of particular interest to read what the critics thought of the piece. The reviewer in *The Times* of 3 February 1968 wrote:

> John Gardner's music has often been characterised by a strong vein of wit, and a heretic might be excused for detecting the faintest trace of parody in the *Concerto da Camera* he had composed for last night's Dolmetsch concert at Wigmore Hall.
>
> The recorder is an instrument of limited expressive range, so that when Gardner writes an impassioned soliloquy we can take it as a sign either of incompetence or gentle mockery; and the former judgement was patently invalidated by the skilful pastiche of the rest of the work. As a whole the music proved pleasantly inconsequential, with a

delicious Gavotte for violin and cello (with harpsichord interpolations) and a drone Rondo far too obsessed with its key note to be taken quite seriously.

Gardner's lucid instrumental style was appreciated by the players.

The critic in the *Daily Telegraph* of 3 February 1968 seems to have taken the piece altogether more seriously, noting the composer's exploitation of the capabilities of all the instruments and briefly describing the character of the individual movements.

A photostat copy of the composer's manuscript (inscribed after the final bar 'New Malden Sept. 1967 to Jan. 1968') is in the archive at Haslemere, and the British Music Information Centre catalogue of recorder music lists the work as being published by the composer.

The substantial rondo first movement opens with a very brief flourish for the recorder, violin and cello, but it is over held notes for the string instruments that the harpsichord introduces the initial musical idea in two-part counterpoint, immediately after which the roles are reversed. Musical ideas come thick and fast and the entire effect is kaleidoscopic, in terms of both instrumental colour, with various combinations from the quartet following one another in quick succession, but also rhythmically, bars of 2/8, 3/16, 2/4 and 3/4 infiltrating the opening and underlying 3/8 time signature.

In the following Ground, the recorder is accompanied by pizzicato violin and cello (the harpsichord is *tacet*) and their opening quaver motion gradually takes on the more intricate textures of the recorder line as the movement progresses.

There is certainly something of the Bach of the solo suites in the Gavotte's lively opening theme, first heard as a violin solo then taken over by the cello. The rhythms become more detailed as the two instruments play in duet, but at the entry of the harpsichord the cello falls silent and the violin takes on the role of a rustic drone while the dance is played by the harpsichord. There is a recapitulation of the string duet before all three instruments finally combine to bring the movement to a close.

Rich harpsichord chords accompany the recorder in a Soliloquy of expressively shifting tempo full of accelerandos and rubatos. The effect is almost improvisatory.

The Rondo finale is a jig of unremitting rhythmic energy and instrumental virtuosity. As in the first movement, various groupings from the quartet provide colour to the imitative textures. At the very end the harpsichord falls silent, leaving the violin and recorder to recall the opening theme over a held cello B♭, the cello having the final word with a hushed and staccato answering phrase.

My impression of the *Concert da camera* when hearing it for the first time at John Gardner's eightieth birthday concert was not one of pastiche, but of a work in which any baroque inflections or sonorities grew out of the composer's response to the very form and instrumentation. It most certainly takes its place among the handful of works for this scoring composed at Dolmetsch's invitation, which, in

Joseph Horovitz: Quartetto concertante

tr rec, vn, vc, hpd

For Carl Dolmetsch, Jan. 1969

1 Allegro. 2 Andante. 3 Vivace.

First performance: Wigmore Hall, London, 28 February 1969. Carl Dolmetsch, rec; Alice Schoenfeld, vn; Eleonore Schoenfeld, vc; Joseph Saxby, hpd.

Unpublished: withdrawn by the composer.

The earliest letter in the archive in connection with this piece is from Dolmetsch to Horovitz and is dated 30 September 1968. It is not clear from this how contact had first been made, but it is evident that Horovitz had agreed to write a piece for Dolmetsch, the Schoenfeld sisters and Joseph Saxby for their 1969 Wigmore Hall recital. The letter also indicates that the work's title had already been decided upon: '... and let me say again how thrilled we all are that you will be writing the Quartetto Concertante for recorder, violin, cello and harpsichord, for our Wigmore Hall recital on 28th February next.'

Dolmetsch advised that he would be sending, under separate cover, recordings of Hans Gál's *Trio Serenade* and Gordon Jacob's Suite, which he thought would give an idea of 'what can be done with the recorder.' Dolmetsch also gave brief advice on the more suitable keys for the instrument: 'Extremes of key are not ideal for fast passage work, although the instrument can play in any key. In terms of the treble recorder, some of the most comfortable are – major and minor – F, G, B flat, C, E flat; A minor is happier than A major.'

Dolmetsch made his by now customary autumn tour of the United States, but on his return sent Horovitz a copy of the handbill for the Wigmore Hall recital, noting in a letter dated 26 November 1968:

> The Schoenfeld sisters are very interested in your Quartetto Concertante; they asked me to tell you that they would be most grateful to have their string parts as soon as they are available, since they have a great deal of concert work in the States before they arrive here in mid February.

Dolmetsch suggested that the parts be sent directly to the Schoenfelds in the United States. On 1 February 1969 Horovitz wrote to Dolmetsch confirming that the parts for the Schoenfelds had been dispatched, and that the score and recorder part had been sent by recorded delivery to Dolmetsch's address. The letter, which also enclosed a programme note for the new work concluded: '... I am most willing to come and meet you all when the Schoenfelds arrive, to perfect the little work with one or two personal suggestions for performance, or indeed, to "weed" out some notes and change tempi.'

Dolmetsch was on tour in Dorset, so Greta Matthews acknowledged receipt of the score, recorder part and programme note, adding that the Schoenfelds would be arriving on 18 February and that the work would be ready to hear by 24 or 25 February. Two tickets for the Wigmore Hall recital were also enclosed.

Horovitz wrote back immediately to thank Greta for the tickets and to confirm that he would be able to travel down to Haslemere on 25 February to attend a rehearsal of the new work. He would in any case be meeting the performers at the Royal College of Music four days before.

The composer's programme note reads:

> This work was commissioned by Carl Dolmetsch and completed in January this year. As a traditionalist, I have not tried to convert the general ambience of such an ensemble from its 18th century heritage, and have therefore left the instruments to speak more or less in their traditional language. However, most pieces written for this combination in former times have used contemporary dance forms as a framework e.g. Allemande, Bourrée, Gigue, Sarabande etc. I have continued in this manner by basing the whole work on our own contemporary dance patterns, which will be obvious on hearing. The themes are taken rather loosely from several of my previous ballet scores, for this rather convenient reason. A further similarity to old procedures will be noticed in the more intellectualised treatment of the first movement, and in this way the character of the movements follows the old pattern of appealing first to the head, then to the heart and lastly to the toes.

It is interesting to speculate whether, having been sent a recording of Gordon Jacob's Suite for Recorder and Strings, Horovitz was influenced by the *Burlesca alla rumba* movement in that work to adopt contemporary dance idioms in his own.

The manuscript score and recorder part remain in the Dolmetsch archive with a note in Dolmtesch's hand that reads: 'violin & 'cello parts left with Alice and Eleonore.'

The work was well received by the critics. The review in the *Daily Telegraph* of 1 March 1969, though noting a conservatism of idiom, praised the work for its sprightliness and syncopated rhythms, also commenting on its appeal to the large proportion of young people in the audience, presuming them to be recorder players. *The Times* of 3 March 1969 described the work as being 'in three brightly rhythmical movements, the first astringent and cool, the second quizzical, the third witty. Perhaps this is too relentlessly light-weight music, but there are few composers about so willing and able to cheer us up as Mr. Horovitz.'

Writing in *Recorder & Music Magazine*[51] Freda Dinn referred to the composer's programme note, in which he stated that the movements appealed in turn to the

---

[51] June 1969, **3**, p. 69.

head, the heart and the toes, noting: 'It certainly fills these roles, as was obvious from the applause, and the last movement is a performers' "lollipop" in its immediate appeal.'

We can gauge even more of the audience reaction from a letter dated 6 March 1969 that Dolmetsch wrote to Horovitz following the Wigmore Hall premiere:

> Although nearly a week has passed since last Friday's concert, our enthusiasm has remained at a very high level, shared by audience and artists alike, for your highly successful Quartetto. All four of us rejoiced when we heard the shouts for an encore and had time permitted we would gladly have played the entire work again.
>
> I am glad that the press – Times and Telegraph – appreciated the work, the Telegraph being particularly enthusiastic I thought. I still hear the glorious sound of the violin and cello solos in the slow movement.
>
> We are now looking forward to playing the work to our American audiences in the 'fall'. I fancy their love of the jazz idiom will make them all the more alive to your refinements of syncopation and off-beat accents, all of which (though I sez as shouldn't) had truly become a part of us.
>
> You have added another dimension to the recorder in music and I am immensely grateful; and, not least, we all thoroughly enjoyed working with you. Thank you again Joseph.

A letter from Horovitz to Dolmetsch dated the same as that above was found in the manuscript score. It reads:

> Dear Carl,
>
> I have taken a copy of the enclosed part, which I return for your safe keeping. All the parts and the original score are naturally yours for future use.
>
> I wish to express in writing my complete delight with your performance of Quartetto Concertante, and I am sure that when the ensemble has played it several times, it will be even more 'nuanced', which I'm sure you agree.
>
> I am particularly happy that I have made your acquaintance in such a nice way, by writing a work for you.
>
> When the broadcast takes place we shall have a good tape of the piece into the bargain!
>
> Yours most cordially,
>   with kind regards to your family and Joseph S.
>
>   Joseph

Despite favourable reviews, Dolmetsch's obvious enthusiasm for the piece and the views expressed in the above letter, Horovitz withdrew the work. His wishes must of course be respected, but in so doing, a work for recorder in Horovitz's characteristic idiom is unfortunately lost to the instrument's repertoire.[52]

---

[52] In a letter to the author dated 1 December 2001 Joseph Horovitz confirmed that he had withdrawn the work, adding: 'this has nothing to do with Carl D. nor his delightful and talented family.'

Francis Chagrin: Preludes for Four

tr rec (or fl) vn, vc, hpd (or pn)

To Dr Carl Dolmetsch and his ensemble

Prelude 1: Vivace (Tempo I°) – Andantino (Tempo II°). Prelude 2: Lento pensieroso – Andante. Prelude 3: Lento. Prelude 4: Presto (Tempo I°) – Andantino (Tempo II°). Prelude 5: Moderato (Tempo I°).

First performance: Wigmore Hall, London, 6 February 1970. Carl Dolmetsch, rec; Alice Schoenfeld, vn; Eleonore Schoenfeld, vc; Joseph Saxby, hpd.

Published: London: Novello & Co. Ltd, 1972.

In the archive may be found the following letter from Francis Chagrin dated 2 December 1965:

> Dear Mr. Dolmetsch,
>
> Last week I heard a recording of the Handel C Major Sonata for Treble Recorder and Harpsichord which you performed with Joseph Saxby.
> I do not think I have ever heard the Recorder played with such consummate skill and artistry and producing a sound that was not only homogeneous but quite beautiful. If this sounds presumptuous, please forgive me, but as you know, in other people's hands, Recorders can sound like instruments of torture.
> I was particularly interested because in recent years I wrote a number of pieces for various combinations of Recorders, some of which are published by Schotts and one piece, (Album for Nicolas), by Chappells. However, I can hardly hope ever to hear these pieces performed as beautifully unless by yourself.
>
> Again, many congratulations.
>
> Kind regards, also to Mr. Saxby.
>
> Yours sincerely,
>
> F. Chagrin

Dolmetsch replied to Chagrin's letter to thank him for his kind comments and to invite him to the 1966 Wigmore Hall recital, an invitation that Chagrin accepted in a letter dated 20 January 1966.

This contact must have remained in Dolmetsch's mind, as when the time came to seek a composer to write a new work for the 1970 Wigmore Hall recital he wrote to Chagrin. The letter, dated 6 September 1968 reads:

> Dear Mr. Chagrin,
>
> Two or three years ago, you were so kind as to write to me after hearing my recording of the Handel C major Sonata for treble recorder and harpsichord with Joseph Saxby.
> I am wondering now whether I could prevail upon *you* to write something for me, for

a first performance at the Wigmore Hall? I have in mind a work of between ten and twenty minutes in length.

If you are agreeable to this proposal, what I would particularly like is a work for recorder, violin, 'cello and harpsichord, which I could play with Alice and Eleonore Schoenfeld on tour in the United States as well as at the Wigmore Hall.

With kind regards and hoping to have the pleasure of hearing from you soon.

Yours sincerely,

Carl Dolmetsch

Chagrin was in the United States himself at the time, but on his return wrote to Dolmetsch immediately:

Thank you so much for your letter of the 6th Sept. which I found on my return from New York. Hence the delay, for which I do apologise.

Yes I would love to write a work for treble(?) recorder, violin, 'cello and harpsichord, for you to play with Alice and Eleonore Schoenfeld and Joseph Saxby on tour in the United States as well as at the Wigmore Hall. When would you want it for?

I am at present working on my 2nd Symphony – but perhaps the two works may not be mutually exclusive.

Thank you for asking me. I am looking forward to hearing further from you.

Dolmetsch was delighted and, before leaving for his autumn tour of the United States, wrote to Chagrin on 1 October 1968:

I am *delighted* to hear that you would like to write a work for us for performance next year and if possible, could we have it by August or September please? We will take it on tour next Autumn in the United States and give the first London performance at the Wigmore Hall the following February. Joseph Horovitz is writing us a work for February 1969.

Finally, yes please, treble recorder. If there should be any queries in my absence, my secretary will be able to deal with them.

Dolmetsch was thus intending to reverse the usual arrangement and give the first performance of the new work during his autumn tour of the United States. However, from later correspondence it would seem that there were problems in forwarding the performing material to the United States and as a result, the first performance did indeed take place at the Wigmore Hall.

From a letter to Chagrin dated 23 April 1969 we learn that Dolmetsch had met him at a recent Hoffnung concert. No doubt discussion about the new work took place, and we find two rather interesting paragraphs about the style in which Dolmetsch considered it might be composed:

I just wanted to emphasise at this point that the work can be as sophisticated and avant garde as you like. I say this because I am aware of your noted versatility and the possibility that you might expect me to prefer something in 'early music' style.

I can assure you that provided the notes are all obtainable within the compass of the treble recorder and the work maintains lines of communication from composer to performer and from performer to audience, I do not mind how modern your chosen idiom may be. Forgive me for taking the liberty of 'influencing the composer' – I just thought it might be helpful to you to know this at this stage.

Chagrin had been away conducting and busy writing, and did not reply to Dolmetsch until 20 June. Of the new work his letter notes:

> I do not think that it is going to be avant garde, nor will it, in any case, be in the 'early music' style.
> I have thought of writing a number of preludes in varying moods giving prominence in turn to the various instruments and forming at the same time a complete work, although more on the lines of a suite than a sonata. One of the advantages of a series of preludes may be that each could also be played separately. I am working on this idea and in fact, I have finished the first of these preludes yesterday. I hope you will like them.

Work on the preludes had progressed sufficiently for Chagrin to write to Dolmetsch on 7 August:

> I have taken yesterday to Mr. Basil Ramsey of Novellos, the first three of the short Preludes I am writing for your ensemble. I have the fourth piece finished in draft form which I hope to finalise, if at all possible, before I go away. If so I will send it also to Mr. Ramsey who has kindly offered to have them all photographed and sent to you. Would you think that your colleagues might prefer to have extra parts written out or would they like each to have a full score? I hope you like the pieces and am looking forward to hearing you all performing them.

Chagrin concluded the letter by noting that he would be away from London from 10 August until 7 September and asking for Dolmetsch's forwarding address in America so that any additional preludes could be sent there.

Because he would be away at the end of August and leaving for America himself on 9 September, Dolmetsch wrote to Chagrin on 15 August: 'I think your idea of writing short Preludes for us is an extremely happy one and I like it more and more; it will offer the greatest flexibility in programming, though at the Wigmore Hall we shall of course play them all.'

Later in the letter Dolmetsch noted that the Schoenfeld sisters would probably prefer separate parts and gave the address in the United States to which further preludes could be sent. From this letter we also learn something of the tour itinerary, which was to start with the Schoenfelds in California in September. The second half of September and the whole of October was to be spent in Alaska and Canada, returning to California and the Schoenfelds from 7 to 25 November. Dolmetsch concluded by noting that his secretary would deal with any correspondence in his absence and that she would be glad to know how Chagrin would like the Preludes billed in the publicity for the Wigmore Hall.

In a letter dated 18 September Chagrin wrote:

The separate parts will be copied and sent to you as soon as they are finished and corrected by me. If I should decide to write further Preludes they will also be sent to you as soon as they are composed. Meanwhile, the 5 Preludes written so far represent a playing time of approx. 12½ minutes and are probably a long enough work – in any case something to get on with.

I have decided on the following title:

'PRELUDES FOR 4'

and hope Dr. Dolmetsch and the Ensemble will like it.

It is clear from other details in the above letter and the correspondence that followed that, due to various misunderstandings, the parts for all the preludes had not arrived in America by 10 November. A letter of that date from Greta Matthews to Chagrin urged that, as rehearsal time would be limited during the final part of the tour, these be sent to California as soon as possible.

There is no further correspondence in the archive until a telegram to the Dolmetsch Schoenfeld Ensemble at the Wigmore Hall sent on the day of their recital there (6 February 1970): 'My thanks for your endeavours[,] my congratulations for your excellent playing and my warmest wishes of success for tonight = Francis Chagrin.' From this telegram and references in a later letter, it would appear that Chagrin had attended at least one rehearsal for the Wigmore Hall premiere.

There is no programme note for the work in the Wigmore Hall recital programme, and the brief analysis that follows is based on the published edition and a photocopy of the manuscript score in the archive, which is inscribed 'To Dr. Carl Dolmetsch and his ensemble'. This contains Joseph Saxby's pencil markings in the harpsichord part.

Prelude No. 1 is constructed on two basic elements that are alternated: a figure that rises or falls through the melody instruments (accompanied at its second appearance by sustained chords on the harpsichord) and passages of melodic fragments over broken chords, first on the harpsichord and then on the cello. The movement ends with a rising arpeggio, *meno mosso*, through all the instruments, starting with the harpsichord and finishing with a recorder top C. Some of the very high recorder notes are marked with an asterisk and a footnote indicates that these may be played an octave lower if not obtainable on the instrument. The manuscript is marked '1 min 15s', indicating the duration.

Early on, Chagrin mentioned his idea of giving prominence to the instruments in turn. This becomes immediately apparent in Prelude No. 2, in which the recorder part is marked 'solo' and introduces arpeggiated and scalic fragments of ever decreasing note values above sustained broken chords on the other three instruments. After 13 bars there is an increase in tempo and the recorder takes on a subsidiary role, while a right-hand harpsichord descending melodic fragment is now marked 'solo'. The movement ends with a six-bar coda marked *molto tranquillo*, the harpsichord's final broken chord marked 'sonore'. The duration is noted as two minutes.

In Prelude No. 3 no single instrument is to the fore, and it is almost entirely founded on two short phrases. The first is introduced in bar 1 by violin and cello, and taken up by the recorder in bar 2. The second and longer phrase occurs first at bar eight and is for recorder, violin and cello. From the beginning the harpsichord is mainly accompanimental, but takes up the opening motive at bar 12. These two phrases are exchanged and developed as the movement unfolds and, although the closing bars are marked *tranquillo*, the final chord is indicated *ff*. The tempo is slow throughout and the duration is given as three minutes.

Prelude No. 4 opens with a *presto* harpsichord solo marked 'with amplification' in the manuscript score (and the published edition).[53] The upper stave is marked with a large natural sign and 'all notes natural', while the lower stave has a large flat sign and 'all notes flat'. The right hand moves mainly in quaver and semiquaver arpeggios above left-hand crotchets. A gradual crescendo is indicated up to bar 16, after which there is a slight diminuendo to the end of this solo on a chord marked *lunga* with the additional direction 'hold until sound vanishes'. Recorder, violin and cello enter with a complete contrast of tempo (*andantino*) and atmosphere. The recorder melody is marked 'solo' and constructed of falling phrases that, together with the violin and cello accompaniment, have carefully marked dynamic and tempo fluctuations. There is a short *presto* harpsichord interjection based on the opening material before a return of the contrasted material on the three other instruments. This exchange of ideas continues, but at the fourth entry of the recorder, violin and cello, the harpsichord right hand adds a fourth voice. Eventually the violin is given the melody in the final two episodes and the harpsichord a chordal accompaniment, before a last harpsichord interjection and a two-bar *lento* for the entire quartet, with the recorder again marked solo, bring the movement to a close. The published score gives the duration of performance as three and a half to four minutes.

At the opening of the final Prelude No. 5 the harpsichord enters with a rippling figure (marked *fluido*) above which the other three instruments, each marked solo, enter in turn with an upward moving rhythmic phrase. The tempo slows very slightly to a contrasted central section in which, after two bars of shimmering arpeggios exchanged between all the instruments, the cello has a bold solo with double-stopped appoggiaturas while the accompanying arpeggios continue. Returning to an accompanimental role, the cello gives way to the harpsichord, which now takes up the solo to bring this middle section to a close, after which the opening material follows without a break. The final three bars, marked *andante*, echo the rhythmic character of the central section solos, and come to rest on a

---

[53] No mention is made in the review (or in any correspondence) of what might be considered this rather unusual device. Neither Jeanne nor Marguerite Dolmetsch were able to recall if harpsichord amplification was actually used at the first performance.

chord of D major. This finale is given an approximate duration of two and a half minutes in the manuscript score.

Of the national newspapers only the *Daily Telegraph* of 7 February 1970 appears to have carried a review. This makes brief but constructive comment on the work, noting the unusual combination of the instrumental forces and the neo-impressionism of the style.

Enclosing a copy of the review and thanking Chagrin for the 'encouraging and heart-warming' telegram, Dolmetsch wrote to the composer on 13 February 1970:

> May I say again, on behalf also of Alice, Eleonore and Joseph, how greatly we all enjoyed every moment of our happy collaboration with you in launching 'Preludes for 4'. We all felt that by the time of the concert the Preludes had become a part of ourselves which, in my opinion, is an essential to transmitting the spirit and meaning of a work to an audience. This is something which is frequently lacking when good sight-reading and technicians have given insufficient rehearsal to a work to get beyond the mere notes, and may well constitute a barrier to the ready acceptance of many a new work.
>
> We were delighted with the obvious success of the Preludes, and now we look forward to touring them in California next Autumn.

It is this final sentence, and a lack of any details of a performance during the previous autumn tour of the United States, that would appear to indicate that the performance at the Wigmore Hall was indeed the first. This seems to be further endorsed by Chagrin's comment at the end of the second paragraph of the letter dated 21 February he wrote in reply to the above:

> Thank you so much for your lovely letter of the 13th February. May I once again thank you most warmly for all the trouble you have, all four, taken in preparing my PRELUDES FOR FOUR. I was delighted with the performance, and I was very happy to hear the spontaneous applause which followed your excellent performance.
>
> The day after the concert, Alice and Eleonore phoned me up from their London Hotel, to my greatest delight, and confirmed the feeling I had had myself, that we had established a great friendship. I am hoping to write a work for the two of them, at their suggestion. The two girls, Joseph and you, really did me proud, and I feel greatly tempted to try and arrange to be in California next autumn, when you perform it in the States. If this is at all possible, I should indeed be very happy.
>
> May I also thank you, and your delightful daughters, and last, but by no means least, Miss Greta Matthews, for having made me so warmly welcome when I came to visit you and work with you.

Chagrin included a list of his published works for recorders that he was arranging to have sent by the publishers to Dolmetsch, adding: 'I shall be looking forward with the greatest pleasure to hearing you play one or the other of these pieces, and I am having them sent mainly to have an excuse for coming to visit you under the pretext of a rehearsal.'

Whether Chagrin was able to visit California in the autumn of 1971 it has not been possible to establish. Sadly, however, he died in November 1972, and was thus unable to fulfil his wish to hear Dolmetsch play 'one or other' of his recorder pieces, or collaborate further, as it is evident from his letters he would very much have enjoyed doing.

Chagrin's noted versatility, to which Dolmetsch referred in earlier correspondence, was demonstrated in his film scores (of which he wrote over 200) and his tireless promotion of contemporary composition through his founding and running of the Committee (later Society) for the Promotion of New Music. *Preludes for Four* was his most ambitious and accomplished work involving recorder.

Stephen Dodgson: Warbeck Dances

rec, hpd

1 Processional: The Uneasy Crown (Proud, steady and unyielding). 2 The Earl of Huntley (Graceful, courteous, tempo of minuet). 3 Edinburgh Revels (Very fast and lively). 4 Whitsand Bay to Tyburn (Expressive, rather intense and very free).

First performance: Wigmore Hall, London, 19 February 1971. Carl Dolmetsch, recs; Joseph Saxby, hpd.

Published: Hebden Bridge: Peacock Press, 2003.

By the early 1970s Dolmetsch had been responsible for encouraging a number of leading composers of the time to contribute works to the growing recorder repertoire over a period of some 30 years. It was thus with an understandable confidence that he entered a fourth decade of his quest for new works by continuing to make direct contact with established composers.

On 28 January 1970 Dolmetsch wrote to Stephen Dodgson enclosing a leaflet giving the details of and complimentary tickets for the Wigmore Hall recital to be given on 6 February, together with a copy of the programme for the previous year's recital. The letter concluded:

> I am wondering whether you would be interested in joining the series of distinguished composers who have written works specially for us? We would premier such a work at the Wigmore Hall and subsequently take it to the United States in our annual tour with the Schoenfeld sisters.
>
> I look forward to the pleasure of hearing from you.

There are no further letters in the archive until one dated 8 October 1970, in which Greta Matthews, in Dolmetsch's absence on tour in the United States, requested details of the title of Dodgson's new work for inclusion on the handbills for the 1971 Wigmore Hall recital. Dodgson replied the very next day:

> As I have, during the past week, settled on a scheme for my work for recorder and harpsichord, I am happily able to answer your letter by return! In fact I've not only settled on a scheme but am at work on it.

> About a year ago I wrote music for B.B.C. production of *Perkin Warbeck* by the Tudor playwright, John Ford, which included several dance scenes and I had a recorder in addition to other wind instruments. My scheme is for a work, probably in four movements, which makes free use of these pieces, which I felt at the time had much more potential for development than the framework of a drama production permitted.
>
> I contacted the B.B.C. and my proposed adaptation has their approval. I am not under obligation to show an acknowledgement, but I think it would be nice to indicate the origin in the eventual programme, space etc permitting so, I think the short title for your present purposes is simply *WARBECK DANCES*.
>
> I fancy the individual movements will also have titles, and I should know this for certain in plenty of time for your later wares of publicity!
>
> In fact I hope to have completed the whole work, in rough at least, by the time Dr. Dolmetsch returns at the end of November.

Although Dolmetsch's original invitation to write a work mentioned the Schoenfeld sisters and the intention to take the new work on tour to the United States, it does not specifically request a piece for recorder, violin, cello and harpsichord. What subsequent correspondence exists does not give any idea of why Dodgson seems from the outset to have conceived the work for recorder and harpsichord without additional strings. In July 1999 I was pleased to be present at the premiere in Manchester of Dodgson's *High Barbaree*, a work for recorder, guitar and harpsichord. After the recital I spoke to the composer and mentioned to him the implication of Dolmetsch's request for a work for performance with the Schoenfelds; however, he had no recollection of this.[54] Dodgson was able to confirm that David Munrow played the recorder in the original incidental music recorded for the BBC.

The only other letter in the archive in connection with the work is a brief note from Dodgson dated 19 November. It confirmed that the composer had indeed completed the work by the time he had intended:

> Have quite completed the *Warbeck Dances*.
>
> Am taking score and recorder part for duplication today – a copy of each to be forwarded to you direct; intended to coincide (more or less) with your return from USA.
>
> If nothing received by end of first week in December, please let me know.

These copies of the score and recorder part remain in the Dolmetsch archive; the score contains an important composer's note: 'These four pieces derive from the incidental music composed for the BBC production (1969) of John Ford's

---

[54] On receiving the final draft of this section on the *Warbeck Dances*, Stephen Dodgson was reminded of the circumstances surrounding the invitation for the new work. In a letter to the author dated 31 May 2001 he noted that Dolmetsch's original letter had not made clear what instruments the Schoenfeld sisters played, or what sort of programme the new piece might be a part of. As Dolmetsch was going to be away, Dodgson thought it wiser to proceed with a composition for the forces he knew would be available.

historical play PERKIN WARBECK. In the case of pieces nos. 2 & 3 the derivation is close, the other two are very much freer.'

For the first performance the composer also wrote a programme note:

> This four movement work was inspired by dance scenes in 'Perkin Warbeck', a historical play by the Tudor playwright John Ford. The composer has here developed some of his themes used originally for the B.B.C. production of the play in 1969. The first movement, for treble recorder, is by the composer's direction 'proud, steady and unyielding'; the second movement, again for treble recorder, is marked 'graceful, courteous, tempo of minuet'. Edinburgh Revels, in 'very fast and lively' tempo, is written for sopranino recorder; the last movement – 'expressive, rather intense and very free' – specifies treble recorder, changing to sopranino in the alternating quick sections, with a final flourish on the sopranino.

Of the daily papers, only the *Daily Telegraph* of 20 February 1971 appears to have contained a review of the piece, noting the acclaim for the work among the many young people in the audience, the different moods of the individual movements and admiring their compactness.

The review by M.J. Kemp in *Recorder and Music Magazine*[55] seemed less certain: 'The forms and phrasing were derived from early dances, but the harmony was a mixture of twentieth century and modal and the whole effect was distinctly uneasy.'

Whatever the harmonic foundations, there is generally more rhythmic flexibility than found in early dance music, and the slower sections in the finale provide contrast with the overall early character by introducing an even greater rhythmic freedom.

Dodgson's writing for the recorder in *Warbeck Dances* is entirely idiomatic, but he attains a greater refinement and character in his later works for the instrument that include a fine concerto for treble recorder and strings.

There is a postscript that should be added to complete the history of this work. In June 2001 the author wrote to the composer to ask if he would be amenable to the inclusion of *Warbeck Dances* in the series of works from the Dolmetsch archives to be published by Peacock Press. His interest was rekindled, and on looking at the work again Dodgson felt that before publication some revisions would be appropriate. In a letter to the author dated 11 December 2001 Dodgson noted that he had sketched out amendments to the first movement and also to the second where they were 'a bit more extensive'. He considered that the third movement was in least need of adjustment, but envisaged 'a complete dismantling and re-assembly' of the fourth.

By the end of December 2001 the revisions were complete, and it is in this revised version that it is now published.[56]

---

[55] June 1971, **3**, p. 379.

[56] The composer has subsequently made an arrangement for recorder, bassoon and harpsichord, which he has entitled *Warbeck Trio*.

Nicholas Maw: Discourse

rec, hpd

1 Theme (hpd), Nine Variations and Coda (Grave and sostenuto). 2 Vivo.

First performance: Wigmore Hall, London, 3 March 1972. Carl Dolmetsch, rec; Joseph Saxby, hpd.

Unpublished.

On the same day that Dolmetsch had written to Stephen Dodgson (28 January 1970) an almost identically worded letter was sent to Nicholas Maw inviting him to write a work for recorder.

On the copy of this letter held in the archive is a telephone number (presumably Maw's) written in Dolmetsch's handwriting. From later correspondence it is clear that he did have further contact by telephone with Maw about the possibility of writing a work for recorder and harpsichord (not recorder, violin, cello and harpsichord as may be implied by the original letter), and it was not until 22 September 1971 that Maw wrote: 'I think I might be able to write a little work for recorder and harpsichord lasting about ten minutes in time for your Wigmore Hall recital in March of next year.' Maw concluded by suggesting a fee for writing the work.

Dolmetsch replied immediately, agreeing to the fee, and noting that in his impending absence on tour in America, Jeanne Dolmetsch would be able to answer any queries the composer may have regarding compass, dynamics etc. The letter continues:

> As mentioned in our telephone conversation, I would like one of the movements to be lively and of immediate appeal to young audiences, without any sacrifice in quality or musical substance. This movement is the one to be scored for optional sopranino recorder, the work as a whole being for the treble.

In conclusion Dolmetsch asked whether it would be possible to have a title for the piece by 15 October for the advance publicity leaflets, and in a postscript requested a programme note.

Dolmetsch was rarely quite so prescriptive about the form of a work (see also the section on Martin Dalby's *Páginas*) but had no doubt found individual lively movements, such as the 'Tarantella' from Gordon Jacob's Suite, useful and effective during his recitals in schools. However, it might have been better with these later commissions to allow such things to happen more naturally, and indeed, after a similar request to Martin Dalby, Dolmetsch reverted to a much less specific approach (although he also suggested a lively finale that could be played on its own in his request for a new piece from Michael Short in 1984).

On 11 October Maw wrote to Greta Matthews in Dolmetsch's absence:

Mr Dolmetsch will have informed you before leaving that I am to write a work for recorder and harpsichord to be given its first performance in his Wigmore Hall recital next March. He asked me to get in touch with you before the 15th of this month and let you know the title of the work as you had to have some leaflets etc. printed. I'm afraid at the moment I can't give you a title, as I have not begun to write the work and shall not be able to for several weeks yet. So you will just have to say that there will be a 'New work for recorder and Harpsichord by Nicholas Maw'. Sorry that I can't be a little more specific, but I'm not at-all sure at present what kind of piece it will turn out to be.

Maw wrote to Dolmetsch again on 17 January 1972, but no copy is to be found in the archive. However, from Greta Matthew's reply, written in Dolmetsch's absence, it can be deduced that Maw had asked a number of questions regarding the work, as her reply, after making Dolmetsch's apologies continues: 'As you will see, he gave me points for a letter of reply, but I really think his annotations will be clearer as they stand, complete with question and answer.' (Perhaps the annotations referred to were made on Maw's original letter, hence the reason for there being no copy in the archive.)

The letter concludes by noting the printer's deadline for the programme as 4 February, requests the title of the new work and a programme note and confirms the enclosure of two tickets for the Wigmore Hall concert.

It is unfortunate that Maw's questions and Dolmetsch's answers are not to hand, as they would be of undoubted interest in learning more of how the work developed.

Maw was apparently still experiencing difficulties with completing the work, as a note in Greta's handwriting at the top of the copy of the above letter reads: 'Telegram 5/2/72 prog. notes & music urgently required.'

On 14 February Maw wrote from an address in Dorset rather than that of his London home: 'Herewith a movement (the second) of your *Discourse*. Most of it was copied out by candlelight during various power cuts so I hope it is legible. I shall hope to send you the first movement early next week.'

It would seem, from conversations I have had with members of the Dolmetsch family that the piece continued to be sent in a rather fragmentary way up to a time not long before the first performance (see later letter from Dolmetsch). The title itself was also changed quite late in the day. There is no score of the work in the archive, but in addition to a recorder part in Dolmetsch's hand bearing the title 'Theme and Variations' is Maw's elegantly written manuscript recorder part with the revised title of *Discourse*. This has a few annotations in Dolmetsch's hand, but it appears he probably did not play from it, preferring to use the part he had written out himself.

A programme note for the first performance (probably not Maw's) reads as follows:

In the summer of 1971, Carl Dolmetsch invited Nicholas Maw to join the distinguished company of modern composers who have, at his instigation, built up an impressive 20th century repertoire for the recorder. It was necessary only to give the range of the instrument and ask for no concessions with it. Consequently, Nicholas Maw has written the present work for recorder with the same freedom as for any other completely sophisticated instrument. In 'Discourse' he speaks in his own idiom as characteristically as have the many other composers for the instrument in a vivid diversity of individual styles, over the past four decades.

Unfortunately Maw became ill and sent a telegram to Haslemere the day before the Wigmore Hall premiere. It simply reads: 'Regret indisposed best wishes for concert = Maw.'

Three days after the premiere Dolmetsch wrote to Maw:

> We were so sorry to learn from your telegram that you were ill and unable to come to the Wigmore Hall on Friday. We hope you are fit again now. There was a wave of sympathy from the audience when I announced the reason for your absence, while also telling them of the change of name of the first movement of 'Discourse'.
>
> Taking into account the very short time we had to prepare the work, Joseph and I felt we had given a good account of it in the circumstances. But of course we know that given another opportunity in the future, we could do it greater justice.

Dolmetsch's letter continues by noting that, while he was glad a review by Anthony Payne had been mostly devoted to *Discourse*, he did not feel it had given a true picture of the recital as a whole, failing to mention important pieces of early music or the presence of soprano Elizabeth Harwood. Anthony Payne's review did, however, seem to detect some of the problems that had arisen from the short time available for rehearsal:

> Recorder and harpsichord is not a combination we would normally associate with Nicholas Maw's luxurious style, yet these are the instruments for which he composed 'Discourse' performed for the first time at the Wigmore Hall last night by Carl Dolmetsch and Joseph Saxby.
>
> It was interesting to see what substitutes he would find for the elaborately figured textures and romantic sweep of his most characteristic work, and in the event the piece relied much on neo-classical gestures and, in the finale, achieved a vivacious humour which was not too well served by the performers. The sparseness of the first of its two movements, a theme with variations, seemed less characteristic, but again, continuity was lacking in the interpretation.

Lorna Lewis reviewed the recital in *Recorder and Music Magazine*[57] and in the case of *Discourse* took a more recorder-orientated point of view:

> The Discourse for treble recorder and harpsichord written by Nicholas Maw at the invitation of Carl Dolmetsch, begins with a lovely air and set of variations, followed by a rather restless Vivo, which makes demands demonstrably within the resources of the

---

[57] June 1972, **4**, p. 63.

instrument and substantiates the recorder repertoire of works in current idiom with little reference to those tranquil passages more characteristic of its pedigree.

On the same date as Dolmetsch's above letter (6 March 1972) Maw wrote to Dolmetsch, (their letters crossing in the post):

> I am very sorry to have missed the Wigmore on Friday but the day before I went down with a nasty attack of gastric flu and had to go to bed, where I have remained until this morning. I do hope things went well with my piece, and I am sure the concert as a whole was a great success. Unfortunately, I have not been able to see any press notices, as the paper we get did not review the concert, but I would be interested to hear what they had to say if you have any spare copies available.
>
> Now that the concert is over I would be grateful if you could return me the music (I only need the score, not the separate part I copied out for you), as it is the only fair copy of the work and I will have it photo-copied by my publishers. I would also like to have another look at the last movement and see if I can do anything about making it a little easier to play.
>
> It was a great pleasure to meet yourself and Joseph and the members of your family and household last weekend, and I much enjoyed the tea and conversation after our rehearsal.

It is evident from this letter (and confirmed in a conversation between Greta Dolmetsch and the author) that, despite the short time available for rehearsal, Maw had been able to hear the work in preparation, and it is likely that it was as a result of this he felt it necessary to make revisions to the last movement. Dolmetsch replied on 16 March:

> Many thanks for your letter which crossed with mine to you.
>
> Since then I have been away 'concertizing' and before I could return the score to you I heard from the BBC that they want to re-record 'Discourse'. The recording session has been arranged on Tuesday, 9th May.
>
> I see that you want to make some amendments to the last movement, but as you are not a recorder player, don't you think it would be a good idea if we met to discuss the various passages which do not lie comfortably on the instrument?
>
> In the meantime, Joseph and I do not want to be without the score for any length of time, since we must use our advantage to learn the work more thoroughly than was possible in the short time we had it before the recital.

Maw continued to express his concern regarding the last movement in his reply to Dolmetsch of 5 April:

> I note what you say regarding keeping the score of the 'Discourse' for the moment until you have done the BBC recording on May 9th – of course, do please hang on to it. I confess though, that I am very worried about the last movement; I wonder whether it can really be made to work properly for the recorder. As you say, I am not a recorder player, so I feel I shall largely have to take your advice about this. If it really does not work I think we ought to drop it and just leave the first movement which would probably make

a substantial enough work on its own. I think also that one or two of the Variations would benefit from being played on a descant or sopranino. When you have it all a little more under the fingers perhaps I could come over again and see you, say in the next ten days or fortnight?

It is not clear whether any further meetings between Maw and Dolmetsch regarding the work were held before a re-recording took place.

During the course of my research, I contacted the BBC to enquire whether any recordings made of the 'Wigmore' works remained in the sound archives. From their reply and my subsequent enquiries, I learned that most of the recordings had been transferred to the National Sound Archive. However, the list of Dolmetsch recordings sent to me included details of the first broadcast performance of Discourse which, interestingly, is timed at 14' 55". I have not had an opportunity to hear this recording, but the timing would indicate that the work was played in its entirety.

There is but one further item of correspondence in the archive, which is a post card from Maw dated 13 June 1972 making a further request for the return of the score: 'May I please have the score of *Discourse* back? It is the only copy I made, and my publishers need it for publication, and I need it for revision. As soon as they have made a photocopy of it I will return it if you want it back again.'

Whether Maw made any revisions is not certain and the work remains unpublished. It seems that all-in-all *Discourse* did not enjoy an easy birth, and that, in addition, neither Dolmetsch nor Saxby were apparently entirely at home with its musical language. Dolmetsch's reservations and comments are expressed in correspondence with Martin Dalby the following year (see the section on Dalby's *Páginas*). Dolmetsch was always keen to become well acquainted with a work before performance to establish, as he noted, a direct line of communication between composer and performer, and performer and audience. In the case of *Discourse* it would appear that the limited time available for rehearsal prevented this and indeed may have coloured his view of the piece thereafter.

Having not seen the complete score, it is difficult to form an overall picture of the work, or what aspects of it in particular may have resulted in Dolmetsch's later comments to Dalby. The recorder part is technically demanding, but it does not contain any of the avant-garde techniques that Dolmetsch was usually keen to discourage.

The author contacted Nicholas Maw enclosing the section on *Discourse* from the draft of the book text. In a letter of reply[58] Maw admitted that he had in fact forgotten writing the work all those years ago, noting that this was certainly partially a result of withdrawing it from circulation and publication at the time. He had also not been in possession of a score, but having tracked one down was not at all sure it was complete and tried to get hold of a copy of the sketches to fill out

---

[58] Letter dated 6 May 2002 from Nicholas Maw to the author.

his information on the work. At his request I also sent a photocopy of the manuscript recorder part so he could tell which version of the work Dolmetsch and Saxby had performed.

Maw additionally noted that he did not have any of the original correspondence and commented that it had been an odd sensation to read in my draft the extracts from a totally forgotten correspondence of 30 years ago. An interesting fact that Maw further drew to my attention was that, in addition to missing the Wigmore Hall premiere, he had not heard the BBC broadcast. *Discourse* is thus perhaps the only one of the composer's works of which he has not heard a performance.

It is to be hoped that the newly acquired material will enable Maw to piece the information together and perhaps feel able to make the adjustments to the second movement that concerned him all those years ago. In such an event it could be possible for him at last to hear a performance.

Walter Bergmann: Pastorella

Soprano, sopranino rec

To Carl Dolmetsch

Text: from John Attey's *First Book of Ayres* (1622).

First performance: Wigmore Hall, London, 3 March 1972. Elizabeth Harwood, soprano; Carl Dolmetsch, rec.

Published in: *For the Sopranino Recorder Player*, Sharon, Connecticut: Maganamusic Inc., 1972 (MM21).

The 1972 Wigmore Hall recital was another at which two works received their first performances. In addition to Nicholas Maw's *Discourse*, Walter Bergmann's *Pastorella* for the quite unusual scoring of soprano voice and sopranino recorder was also premiered.

The Dolmetsch archive contains two photocopies of the manuscript of the *Pastorella* that have been pasted into folded sheets of blank manuscript paper. On the front in Bergmann's hand is written:

> Walter Bergmann
> Pastorella
> For soprano voice and sopranino recorder

The score is headed Walter Berman (1971) and above the title of one copy only is inscribed: 'Dedicated to Carl Dolmetsch'. In the other copy was found a letter dated 18 December 1971 that reads:

> Dear Carl,
>
> Happy Christmas to you and the twins! This is my Christmas card for you, it will be

printed in a volume for sopranino recorder solo in America. *If you like it* I would love to dedicate the Pastorella to you. There is nobody who plays the sopranino like C.D.

Greta sends her love

Yours ever

Walter

Dolmetsch must indeed have liked the piece and clearly contacted Bergmann to thank him and to propose it be premiered at the forthcoming Wigmore Hall recital on 3 March 1972. (At this time Dolmetsch had not seen anything of the piece Nicholas Maw was composing for the same recital.) Bergmann's response in a letter dated 24 January 1972 reads most concisely and indeed economically: 'Dear Carl, / Surprised, honoured, grateful, / Walter.' On the same sheet is typed a composer's note, which was adapted for inclusion as a programme note for the premiere.

> The words of the Pastorella are taken from John Attey's 'First Book of Ayres' (1622). Much as I like Attey's songs, in his setting of this poem he has not, in my opinion, caught completely its amorous atmosphere. I hope my own attempt (dedicated to Carl Dolmetsch) gives the performers sufficient freedom to create in singing and playing the little bucolic love scene which a composer can only indicate by pitch and metre.

The second photocopy of the manuscript in the archive that bears the dedication to Dolmetsch was no doubt sent later so that player and singer had copies for the first performance. One copy (presumably that used by Elizabeth Harwood) contains annotations above the vocal line.

As Bergmann anticipated in his letter of 18 December 1971, the work was indeed published in the United States by Magnamusic in 1972 in a volume entitled *For the Sopranino Recorder Player*. In the list issued at Ross Winters's talk at the 1997 ERTA (UK) conference the work was indicated as unpublished. A number of people present ventured the opinion that it had been published (by Schott), but I believe they were referring to another work by Bergmann entitled *Pastorale* for medium voice and treble recorder (or flute) to words by Norman Cameron. It is dedicated to Alfred Deller and was published by Schott & Co. in 1947. It appeared in a revised edition in 1976.

As noted in the section on Nicholas Maw's *Discourse*, Anthony Payne's review made no mention of this work, but the review by Lorna Lewis in R*ecorder and Music Magazine*[59] described it as: 'haunting and evocative' and 'achieving within an economic melodic line qualities of mellowness and expression rarely associated with this tiny instrument.'

Bergmann's handful of compositions for the recorder show him to have had a remarkable awareness of its musical and indeed expressive potential. His two

---

[59] June 1972, **4**, p. 63.

5 Soprano Elizabeth Harwood, who, in addition to taking part in the premiere of Walter Bergmann's *Pastorella*, was the soprano soloist in the premiere of Lennox Berkeley's *Una and the Lion*.

sonatas for recorder and piano (one for treble, the other for descant recorder), are works of great originality and invention. The *Pastorella* explores a very different form and musical mood and in its eloquence shows another side of Bergmann's mastery in writing for the instrument and indeed the voice. Perhaps it was his work with Tippett in editing many of Purcell's songs that brought him into contact with one of the greatest setters to music of the English language and had an influence here.

Arnold Cooke: Suite

des, tr and t recs, optional hpd (or pn)

For Carl Dolmetsch

1 Moderato. 2 Allegretto. 3 Allegro. 4 Andante. 5 Giocoso. 6 Presto.

First London performance: Wigmore Hall, London, 1 March 1973. Carl Dolmetsch, rec; Marguerite Dolmetsch, rec; Jeanne Dolmetsch, rec; Joseph Saxby, hpd.

Published: Celle: Moeck Verlag, 1974 (E.M. 1513).

Cooke's manuscript scores and parts for both the versions with and without harpsichord are at Haslemere. The score of the trio version contains a letter from Cooke dated 11 July 1970 clearly indicating that the work was composed as a result of a suggestion from Dolmetsch:

> Perhaps you will remember that on your Christmas card to me last year you suggested a Trio for Recorders, and I replied that I would think about it. Well, I have and here it is, a little suite in six movements. I hope I have written it in the right way, the Descant transposing up an octave, the Treble written at pitch and the Tenor down an octave, and that it will work out.

The letter concludes: 'I shall look forward to hearing from you later on about the Suite, when you have had time to try it.'

At Dolmetsch's suggestion Cooke also made his arrangement of the work with a part for keyboard. The score and parts for this originally had the title 'Quartet' but this has been masked with correcting fluid and the title 'Suite' written in. The reason for the change of title is explained in a letter dated 24 November 1970 that Cooke addressed to Greta Matthews as Dolmetsch was on his annual tour of the United States:

> I have completed my arrangement of the Trio for Recorders with a part for keyboard. As there had to be a few adjustments of the parts here and there I have written out a separate set of parts for this. I have also changed the title of the work to Suite. It is after all a suite in 6 movements, and I don't want to call it simply Quartet which would confuse it with my other quartet for Recorder, Vln, Vc & Harpsichord.

Cooke continued by expressing concern about some high-lying passages for the descant:

> I am a bit worried now about some of the high passages I have written for the descant. I expect you know Mr. Edgar Hunt, who teaches the recorder at Trinity College. He has pointed out to me that the high C-sharp (D-flat) and E are unsatisfactory notes on most descants, so I feel I ought to alter these passages where they occur and perhaps in some cases put them down an octave. Would you please draw Carl's attention to this when he is back from the U.S., and perhaps he could kindly let me have his opinion about it sometime.
>
> Incidentally I think the work will probably be more effective in the quartet arrangement than as a Trio.'

The composer's programme note, the typed copy of which is also in the archive, is headed 'Trio for Recorders' and interestingly describes it as being for descant or sopranino, treble and tenor. The top part does indeed lie quite high, even in the published version, which contains a number of passages in the first, third, fourth and sixth movements that have been lowered an octave from the original version.

Comparison of the manuscript scores of both versions with the published edition enables these changes to be identified. In addition, Cooke made further changes before the work was published and the ending of the finale in particular underwent significant revision. Compare the recorder parts of the Trio and Quartet versions as included in the manuscripts (Ex. 3.20 and 3.21) and with the published edition (Ex. 3.22).

In all but the fourth and sixth movements of the published edition, the descant part does not descend below the compass of, and would be more comfortable on, a sopranino. The alto line is also high on the instrument and contains a top F# in the first movement which, because it does not descend below a C, could actually be played on a descant, although probably to the detriment of the overall effect. The tenor line remains comparatively low, and does not ascend above a top A.

Ex. 3.20. Arnold Cooke, Suite for three recorders with or without harpsichord. Last movement, final two bars as in the MS score of the trio version. Reproduced by permission of Moeck Verlag.

Ex. 3.21. Arnold Cooke, Suite for three recorders with or without harpsichord. Last movement, final two bars as in the MS score of the version with harpsichord. Reproduced by permission of Moeck Verlag.

Ex. 3.22. Arnold Cooke, Suite for three recorders with or without harpsichord. Last movement, final two bars as in the published score. Reproduced by permission of Moeck Verlag.

The programme note reads as follows:

> This work was written at the request of Carl Dolmetsch. It is in the form of a suite in six short movements. The first, an introductory movement in moderate time, makes use of dotted rhythm as is often found in such movements in old suites and sonatas. This leads into the Allegretto which is in a smooth flowing style in two sections, both being repeated. There follows a more lively movement, the first section of which is repeated, and then the Andante, where the sustained melodic lines of the first and last parts are contrasted with a staccato middle part. The Giocoso has a sprightly main theme with an ostinato type of accompaniment. It falls into three sections. The finale in quick six-eight time makes much use of repeated staccato notes. At the suggestion of Dr. Dolmetsch, the composer has also arranged this Suite with a harpsichord part.

This was almost certainly written for the first performance of the work in its trio version at a meeting of the London branch of the Society of Recorder Players in January 1971. Cooke mentioned this in a letter written to Dolmetsch on 5 January 1971, with which he enclosed the score and parts of the version with keyboard:

> Dear Carl,
>
> I am now sending you my arrangement of the Suite with a keyboard part, as you may like to see it while you are concerned with the Trio version. As you will see I have made a number of changes in the recorder parts, in particular in some of the high parts for the Descant.
>
> I should be able to make it all right on Saturday. I have a visit to make early in the afternoon in the Victoria area, so it will not be far to get to the Waldegrave Hall by 4.30. Looking forward very much to seeing you all and hearing you play.
>
> Yours ever
>
> Arnold

It has not been possible to establish when or where the version with keyboard received its premiere, but the performance included in the Wigmore Hall recital on 1 March 1973, is noted in *Recorder and Music Magazine*[60] as being the first London performance.

The reviewers in the daily papers gave the work only brief mention. That in *The Times* of 2 March 1973 noted: 'Arnold Cooke's Suite for three recorders and harpsichord seemed enjoyable to play though the overall effect was monochrome.' The *Daily Telegraph* of 2 March 1973 was more positive, mentioning the clever blending of the recorders and harpsichord.

What only becomes evident on examination of the score are the alternative notes, occasionally provided in the lower two recorder parts, to be played when the work is performed as a recorder trio without keyboard. This is not mentioned in the otherwise comprehensive review of the published edition that appeared in *Recorder & Music Magazine*.[61]

> Here we have a work which, but for its difficulty, conforms almost exactly to the Harvard Dictionary's definition of 'Gebrauchsmusik'. The keyboard part is optional and may be played on harpsichord or piano.
>
> The forms of the six movements are all transparently clear with easily recognisable historical antecedents, though it is the rhythmical vitality of the work which is one of its chief attractions.
>
> Compared with the trio by Hindemith (with whom Cooke studied) the textures are rather dense and in the middle section of the fourth movement the descant has difficulty in coming through the treble and tenor sonorities. Although the melodic writing within the texture is of a very high standard, the lighter, more transparent nature or the fifth and sixth movements come as a relief.
>
> The contrasts are well planned, with the fourth movement reaching unsuspected depths of feeling, and the finale providing an exciting climax. The work should be enthusiastically received by all who are seeking serious, technically demanding and at the same time easily enjoyable chamber music.

When the Suite was published Cooke sent Dolmetsch a copy expressing his satisfaction with the edition: 'I have just received copies of my Suite, so I am sending you one. It's nicely produced I think, printed to be playable in both versions.'

Like many of Cooke's recorder works, the Suite (or Trio) has a marked Hindemithian feel, but it is more than simply derivative of his teacher, and has that stamp of individual craftsmanship that is to be found in so much of his music and in the works with recorder in particular.

---

[60] June 1973, **4**, p. 211.
[61] March 1975, **5**, p. 25.

Gordon Jacob: A Consort of Recorders

Descant, tr, t and b recs

For Carl Dolmetsch

1 Fanfare and March. 2 Nocturne. 3 Panpipes. 4 Bells. 5 Chorale. 6 Adieu.

First London performance: Wigmore Hall, London, 1 March 1973. Carl Dolmetsch, des rec; Jeanne Dolmetsch, tr rec; Marguerite Dolmetsch, t rec; Brian Blood, b rec.

Unpublished (in version for rec qt)

Although it is clear (as it is with Cooke's Suite performed at the same recital) that Jacob's Consort was written for and dedicated to Dolmetsch (and in this case his consort also) there is no correspondence to indicate just how the work came into being, or for what occasion in particular it was composed. It does not appear to have been expressly intended for the Wigmore Hall.

The earliest letter in the archive in connection with the work is from Jacob to Dolmetsch and dated 22 March 1972:

> I have been meaning to write to you for some time to tell you that the recorder consort is well in hand, but have been rather extra busy lately.
> I hope to let you have it soon.
> The new Jacobean Suite will consist of:
>
> > 1) Fanfare & March
> >
> > 2) Nocturne
> >
> > 3) Panpipes
> >
> > 4) Bells
> >
> > 5) Chorale
> >
> > 6) Adieu
>
> They are short pieces, and the whole thing should play 12–13 minutes. 'Adieu' is all over in 40 sec!

Barely two weeks later, on 4 April, Jacob wrote to Dolmetsch enclosing the new work.

> Here is the promised Consort. I hope you will find it pleasurable and useful.
> Separate movements can of course be played if necessary or 3 or 4 only if preferred (to suit occasions) But the whole thing, as you see, doesn't play for very long.
> I'm not sure about No. 6 (Adieu). Is it based on a practicable figure for recorders? If so it ought to be quite amusing I think. If not I'll try & think of something else.

Jacob also wrote a programme note, given here in full:

This suite of six pieces was written in 1972 and dedicated to Carl Dolmetsch and his recorder consort, consisting of Descant, Treble, Tenor and Bass.

1) *FANFARE AND MARCH*
   Perhaps the Fanfare could be pictured as being sounded by Peasblossom, Mustardseed and their companions on their fairy trumpets to greet the arrival of Oberon and Titania. This is followed by a "March-past", quick and light. There is a trio section, after which the March is repeated.

2) *NOCTURNE*
   A peaceful little piece dominated by the swaying figure with which it begins. Later there is decorative writing for the Descant instrument.

3) *PAN PIPES*
   This mainly consists of a duet between Descant and Treble, the Tenor later taking over the lower part. In the last few bars the theme is briefly treated in 4-part polyphony. The piece is written in the Lydian mode though it takes it into its head to end with a Dorian cadence.

4) *BELLS*
   Rapid little chiming figures on the upper instruments are, after a few bars, found to fit in with the Westminster chimes heard below.

5) *CHORALE*
   This is the longest of these short pieces. It is a chorale prelude based on "Ein' feste berg [sic]". The chorale, which is shared between various "voices", is played against a texture of three-part counterpoint.

6) *ADIEU*
   Consisting of a little figure tossed about among the four instruments, it is all over in about 40 seconds.

The *Recorder and Music Magazine*[62] noted only that the Wigmore Hall performance of the Consort on 1 March was the first in London. The reviews in the daily papers were particularly enthusiastic, *The Times* of 2 March 1973 reporting that the work, '... best fused the players' and the hearers' pleasures: its six movements offer much aural variety even within a traditional triadic language. I especially liked the swaying Holstian nocturne with its cool melody for bass recorder and the chorale "Ein' feste Berg" always one step ahead of the obvious.' The *Daily Telegraph* of 2 March 1973 was likewise full of praise, particularly for the counterpoint of the Chorale based on '*Ein' feste Berg*'. The opening of the 'Holstian' Nocturne is shown in Ex. 3.23.

From a letter Jacob wrote to Dolmetsch on 20 March 1973 it would appear that he attended the Wigmore Hall recital:

> The O.U.P. are very interested in my Recorder Consort and want to look at it as soon as possible.
>
> I shall be grateful if you can let me have a copy of the score, also your amendments to the parts, as soon as convenient.

---

[62] June 1973, **4**, p. 211.

That was a marvellous concert and I am most appreciative of the way in which you all played my work and everything else on the programme too.

Ex. 3.23. Gordon Jacob, *A Consort of Recorders*. Second movement, Nocturne, bars 1–4. Reproduced by permission of Emerson Edition Ltd.

In the event, Oxford University Press did not publish the work, and it was the composer's reworking in a version for wind quintet, Quintet No. 1 'Serenade' that was later published by Emerson Edition (Emerson Edition 121). The recorder version remains in manuscript, and the autograph score, (inscribed 'To Carl Dolmetsch with admiration and affection') and parts, are in the archive at Haslemere, where they are kept in the envelope, postmarked 'Saffron Walden 4 Ap. 72', in which the composer first sent them.

The recorder version can be heard in a recording made by the Dolmetsch Ensemble at Loseley House in April 1976.[63]

Although Jacob wrote a number of works for recorder with keyboard or string ensemble, the *Consort of Recorders* remains his only work for recorder ensemble. His keen ear for wind sonorities produces in this version some rather unusual and effective moments for the recorders, but in either version, Jacob's craftsmanship is once more to the fore.

Martin Dalby: Páginas

tr rec, hpd

For Carl Dolmetsch

First performance: Wigmore Hall, London, 1 March 1973. Carl Dolmetsch, rec; Joseph Saxby, hpd

Published: London: Novello & Co. Ltd, 1973

Dolmetsch's 1973 Wigmore Hall recital was unique in that it contained no fewer

---

[63] Cassette: *Favourite Recorder Consorts*, Arts Recordings (ATD 8718).

than three first performances. Two were London premieres, but receiving its actual first performance was Martin Dalby's *Páginas*.

Dolmetsch first contacted Dalby in 1971 and his letter dated 1 September is of particular interest in its reference to another work requested from Robert Simpson:

Dear Martin Dalby,

I am writing in connection with my next Wigmore Hall recital, on Friday 3rd March 1972, for which Bob Simpson had promised me a new work for recorder and harpsichord.

He finds now, however, that he has so much on hand at the moment that he cannot let me have the work in time; but he has suggested that you might be able and willing to write something for this recital instead. Would you let me know your reaction to this suggestion? I would certainly welcome a work from you if you were able to take it on.

My associate artists that evening will be Elizabeth Harwood, my daughter Jeanne (recorder), David Strange (cello) and of course Joseph Saxby, my harpsichordist.

I had in mind a work for recorder and harpsichord principally, but if you felt you would like to widen your scope to include soprano and/or the other instrumentalists, this would be splendid. It occurs to me also that one quick lively movement which would be complete when played by the recorder and harpsichord alone, would be very useful to introduce to schools audiences when I am on tour.

I look forward to the pleasure of hearing from you.

Yours sincerely,

Carl Dolmetsch

Dalby was not able to accept Dolmetsch's invitation as he explained in his letter dated 29 September 1971:

I'm very honoured that Bob Simpson has thought well enough of me to suggest my name to you and very grateful that you should have asked me to write a piece for your next Wigmore recital.

Unfortunately I have already five pieces to finish by the end of next March (three small ones, and two large ones), so I think you'll understand that it would be extremely hazardous if I accepted yours. I'm sorry about this because I should very much like to write a work for you.

Dalby suggested that if Dolmetsch was still in need of someone to compose a piece for the 1972 Wigmore recital he contact either Nicola LeFanu or Thomas Wilson, but as will be learnt from later correspondence, other arrangements had already been put in hand. Dalby's letter concludes: 'I'm very disappointed to decline your kind offer. I hope one day in the future you will be generous enough to think of me again.'

Dolmetsch had already left for an autumn tour of the United States on the day before Dalby had written his reply and had thus followed up his earlier contact with Nicholas Maw who by this time had agreed to write a piece for the 1972 recital.

Greta Matthews responded to Dalby in Dolmetsch's absence and, having explained the above arrangements, concluded:

> I am almost certain that if Dr. Dolmetsch were in a position to write to you himself at this time, he would invite you to consider writing him a work for performance at the Wigmore Hall in the early Spring of 1973. This being the case, I am taking it upon myself to ask whether this is a possibility? Will you let me know?
> I look forward to hearing from you.

On 19 October Dalby replied to Greta Matthews saying that he would be delighted to write a work for the following year. Dalby was, at the time, teaching at Glasgow University and, as Dolmetsch was to be in the city adjudicating at the end of May and beginning of June 1972, arrangements were made for them to meet and discuss the new work. Following this, Dalby sent Dolmetsch a score and a tape recording of his work *Commedia* (for clarinet and piano trio).

With the impending departure for his 1972 autumn tour of America Dolmetsch wrote to Dalby on 7 September a long and particularly interesting letter. Noting that he would be away until late November and that publicity for the 1973 Wigmore recital would be put in hand during his absence, Dolmetsch continued:

> Now is therefore the time to crystallise our ideas for the work we discussed for performance on 1st March 1973. And before I go any further, thank you very much for sending the score and tape of your Commedia, so expertly played by the Music Group of London. I admired their technical precision and delicacy of ensemble: also the intricacy and craftsmanship of the composition.
> As you know, I do not want a pastiche of early music in any sense. At the same time, the work must make an immediate appeal to the audience at first hearing and I question whether so intellectual work as Commedia would get through to a predominantly early-music-loving audience such as comes to hear us at the Wigmore Hall. Maw's Discourse, for instance, conveyed absolutely nothing to them and in consequence literally left them cold.

At first reading, this last sentence may seem somewhat harsh, but I believe it is not so much a judgement of Maw's work itself, but of the context of Dolmetsch's Wigmore Hall recitals as the place for its first performance. If Dolmetsch had a problem with more advanced or what he considered to be intellectual forms of contemporary music, it was not his own attitude towards it, but what he perceived to be that of his audiences. His reference to a work requiring to 'make an immediate appeal to the audience at first hearing' may seem at odds with his intention of building a repertoire of significant contemporary music for the recorder. However the two ideals are not entirely mutually exclusive and no doubt Dolmetsch felt justified in making the point. With this in mind, the next paragraph of his letter is especially interesting:

> Although I told you that third and quarter tones are possible on the recorder, on further

reflection I would prefer to adhere to the standard twelve semitones, since we have a difficult enough task as it is to convince people that the recorder can be played in tune. Nor do I want any avant garde gimmicks alien to the character of the instrument – to my mind an affront to its innate dignity!

Little more than three years previously Dolmetsch had informed Francis Chagrin that the work he was about to write 'can be as sophisticated and avant garde as you like.' What had brought about this apparent change of attitude? Chagrin's perception of avant-garde was unlikely to have produced a very extreme composition, and Maw's work was certainly not avant-garde in character. However, the increasingly experimental nature of composition generally, and for the recorder in particular, during the 1960s and 1970s no doubt concerned Dolmetsch. Dalby was a young composer (about 30 years old at the time) and it is clear Dolmetsch wanted to ensure the new work made use of the recorder in a more orthodox manner.[64]

In addition to these stylistic constraints, Dolmetsch one again outlined the basic form he had in mind: 'We agreed in Glasgow that the work should be for recorder and harpsichord; that the duration should be approximately 10–12 minutes and that a section, or one movement should be lively in mood, suitable for playing on its own to schools audiences.'

These, together with Dolmetsch's comments in the previous paragraph of the letter, represent a very definite series of requirements (after this, in only one subsequent commission were similar requirements requested), to which he added the need for the piece to be available to begin rehearsal by mid-January.[65] He also asked if it would be possible for Dalby to let him have some idea of the form or title of the piece for the advance publicity to be released in early October.

On 17 October, Greta Matthews, having not heard from Dalby, and in Dolmetsch's absence on tour in the United States, wrote to request details of the work. At the top of the copy, in Greta's handwriting, is Dalby's Glasgow telephone number, and in the right-hand margin, also in Greta's writing, is the title 'Páginas', obviously the result of a telephone call.

On 25 January 1973 Dalby's secretary despatched the first pages of *Páginas* to Dolmetsch, noting that these were not very good but that the next copy would be better.

This was followed on 31 January by a letter from Dalby himself:

I am sorry that you have not received the complete work yet but I am afraid the ending

---

[64] In a letter to the author dated 26 January 2001 Dalby noted that Dolmetsch had not defined 'avant garde gimmicks alien to the character of the instrument', commenting that he might well have agreed with him on this point.

[65] Ibid. Dalby also commented that Dolmetsch 'did in this commission impose certain constraints and requirements but I don't think I noticed them too much at the time. Certainly I did not find them a hindrance.'

has been more troublesome than I thought it would be; however, you should receive it within the next day or so. Meanwhile, I enclose a programme note on Páginas.

The scores I sent you the other day are not, of course, the ones to be used in the performance: when the work is completed I shall have proper scores made, one bound for Mr. Saxby and the other loose sheets to enable you to turn pages more easily.

I hope that you will both enjoy playing Páginas. I look forward to hearing it in March.

Dalby's programme note reads as follows:

PÁGINAS was commissioned by Carl Dolmetsch and receives its first performance this evening. The title is Spanish, meaning pages, and the work is the third of a group of compositions based on 13th century Spanish canciones and cantigas. The mother of the group is CANCIONERO PARA UNA MARIPOSA, an instrumental sequence, where the canciones and cantigas form the basis of its melodies, harmonies and rhythms. The second, CANTIGAS DEL CANCIONERO, is an arrangement of four canciones and cantigas for five solo men's voices, spanned by vocal re-workings of some of the instrumental material in CANCIONARO. The relationship between the music of PÁGINAS and the early Spanish songs is quite different: fragments of the instrumental material appear, but beyond this the canciones and cantigas do not influence the course of the music; they are heard as echoes, their shapes bent to the contours of the language of the work.

On 5 February Dalby wrote to Dolmetsch enclosing a bound copy and one in single sheets as previously promised, adding: 'I shall also send you copies of the Spanish tunes which form the basis of the work.'

I asked Martin Dalby if it would be possible to send me copies of the Spanish tunes also. This he very kindly did and they are included as Ex. 3.24, 3.25 and 3.26.

He further explained where in the piece the tunes appear. *Sobra Baza estaba el Rey*, in addition to its clearly indicated use in the final march section, first makes

Ex. 3.24. *Sobre Baza estaba el Rey* (Romance), Anon.

Ex. 3.25. *Tristeza, quien a mi vos dió* (Villancico), Antonio.

Ex. 3.26. *Aquel caballero, madre* (Villancico), Anon.

an appearance the bar before figure 4, after which it begins to emerge more and more into a recognizable form. The ending of *Tristeza, quien a mi vos dió* is quoted three bars before figure 7, and what Dalby describes as the shadow of the tune continues thereafter. The opening of *Aquel caballero, madre* is clearly discernible four bars before figure 13.

After the first performance Dalby wrote to Dolmetsch: 'First, many thanks again for a splendid performance last week; not only was I delighted with your playing, but I was gratified to know that you like the piece.'

The review in the *Daily Telegraph* of 2 March 1973 was descriptive rather than analytical, noting the inspiration of the Spanish songs and the continuous recorder line above the incidental background sounds of the harpsichord. *The Times* of 2 March 1973 was less enthusiastic, and though initially complimentary, found the musical material of the first section did not sustain its length: '... tried hardest to break new ground [compared with the other new works in the programme]: it started promisingly with close searching interchanges between the instruments, but stayed with this material about three times too long so that interest was lost when an allegro came.'

Novello's published edition reproduces the manuscript score and recorder part in a copy of the composer's own very elegant musical handwriting. The end of the score is signed and dated '31.1.73'. (It is also very large: the pages of the score measure almost 30cm wide by 39cm high.)

The first section is marked *Libero* and has the metronomic rate of ♩ = 52–60. In this first section the recorder part contains a number of cues from that of the harpsichord, which are of considerable assistance in the complex textures and rhythms that abound.

At figure 14 we find the indication 'MARCH: SOBRA BAZA ESTABA EL RAY' and the tempo is marked as *vivace* at ♩ = 108. This is the composer's response to Dolmetsch's request for a section 'lively in mood, suitable for playing on its own to schools audiences.'[66] The entire character is quite different, being in strict 4/4 time and with much more rhythmic emphasis. It is in complete contrast to what has gone before and could indeed be played on its own.

In this work Dalby demonstrates the complete professionalism of a young composer fulfilling quite precise conditions and yet creating a very individual and personal contribution to the recorder repertoire, which also forms part of a cycle of pieces all inspired by early music. In this respect it shares a common feature, though certainly not a compositional style, with a number of the earlier pieces written for Dolmetsch.

Hans Gál: Three Intermezzi, Op. 103

tr rec (or fl), hpd (or pn)

1 Andantino. 2 Allegretto, quasi minuetto. 3 Allegro ma non troppo.

First performance: Wigmore Hall, London, 6 March 1974. Carl Dolmetsch, rec; Joseph Saxby, hpd.

Published: London: Schott & Co. Ltd, 1974 (OFB 134).

Dolmetsch must have been pleased to receive this letter dated 14 May 1973 and its enclosure from his friend Hans Gál:

> Here is something to look at for you and Joseph: kindly let me know whether it suits you as to style and technique; if so, there may be one or another more to come of little pieces such as this.
> I would not like to have the recorder replaced by the harmonica, but would have nothing against the harpsichord part to be played on a pianoforte.

---

[66] Ibid. Dalby confirmed that this was the stand-alone section requested.

Although this single movement had no title, it was the first of what were to become the *Three Intermezzi*, as a further letter from Gál dated 1 June explains:

> It came out as I guessed: there are two more pieces, and they should give nice contrasts, everyone between 4 and 5 minutes duration. Well, I cannot send you the other two for the moment being as I have not got yet presentable copies, and we are off to York tomorrow to the 'children' for a few days. But I'll attend to this as soon as I am back.
>
> I had much pleasure with the things, which, implying nothing I'll just call 'Three Intermezzi': or could you suggest a better title? A child, after all, must have a name.

In a photocopy of the manuscript score in the archive the first movement is marked 'Impromptu' in pencil, but the individual movements remain without titles in the published edition.

Just one week later Gál was able to send Dolmetsch the remaining two pieces. His accompanying letter, after regretfully having to decline an invitation to the opening concert of the Haslemere Festival continues:

> Now here is the remainder, another two pieces, belonging together with the one I've sent you. I can imagine you have your hands full with preparations for the Festival. All the same, kindly let me know in due course how the things agree with you and Joseph – I mean whether you agree with them ...

In a postscript on the reverse of the page Gál added: 'My timing is 16 min. for the three pieces. I'll send them to the copyist to get a good well readable copy. Well, meanwhile you will have to put up with my scrawl! I hope it is readable.'

Dolmetsch had to wait until September for the clean copy that came with the following letter:

> Here is a clean copy of our 'Three Intermezzi'. As you will see, there is a number of more or less small corrections in it, as they occur with a final careful scrutiny. I found a decent player who played them to me, and I am quite happy with them; more important, though, that you are happy.
>
> If you have departed already for your customary American tour, I trust Greta will keep them for you safely stored.

Dolmetsch had not yet left for his American tour, and on 19 September wrote to thank Gál for the clean copy. Until now, no mention had been made of a performance of the pieces, but the letter notes: 'Joseph and I will much look forward to playing them at our Wigmore Hall recital on 6th March 1974. We hope very much that you and Hanna will be there.'

At this point it is worth noting that Dolmetsch's own original list of the Wigmore works is somewhat confusing, as for 1974, in addition to Mathias's *Concertino*, it describes Gál's work as 'Suite for 3 recorders and harpsichord'. This would appear to be an error, especially as only three lines above is listed Cooke's 'Suite for 3 recorders and harpsichord'. It is clear from the above and later correspondence however, that it was Gál's *Three Intermezzi* that were performed at the 1974 Wigmore Hall recital.

Towards the end of January 1974 the country was in the middle of a crisis brought about by industrial unrest and a fuel shortage that had resulted in the introduction of a three-day working week. Gál wrote to Dolmetsch on 23 January in connection with the *Three Intermezzi*. The beginning and end of his letter catch something of the mood of the time, but he also makes a suggestion to assist with rehearsal.

> Time is flying, and I am thinking already of a happy occasion when I hope to meet you – if there are still trains, if there is still any light or heat or petrol in this country. Meanwhile I beg to offer a suggestion: till you have got my Three Intermezzi presentable, kindly send me a *tape* of your rendering, and I'll offer my remarks on it on the other side. In recent years I have frequently made use of this convenience which is simple and can save work.
>
> I do hope you are all well and comfortable, in spite of the three-day week and all the present mess and discomfort.

Dolmetsch obviously thought this a useful suggestion and wrote to Gál: 'Yes, I will be glad to send you a tape of the Intermezzi for your comments – these will be most helpful.' Dolmetsch also requested a programme note, which Gal forwarded almost immediately with the following comment: 'I enclose the note you wanted. – I do not think more is necessary. I have always found that the only valid information about a piece of music is a good performance, and to this I am looking forward.' The letter also includes a list of corrections to be made to the fair copy. It seems that Joseph Saxby had also contacted Gál about the new pieces, for in a postscript typed at one side of the letter Gál notes: 'Joseph's telephone call, some days ago, made me an immense pleasure: there is no greater delight than if the customer is satisfied!'

Dolmetsch and Saxby made a tape recording that was sent to Gál on 19 February with the accompanying letter:

> As promised, here is our tape of the Three Intermezzi which we have just recorded for you.
>
> Naturally, as the time of the performance approaches, we shall have added refinements and more clearly marked dynamic contrasts than will be apparent on this tape.
>
> Little slips here and there and the broken B♭ at the end of the first Intermezzo will of course not be there in our final performance, but we shall have the added benefit of your comments as well as knowing the work very fully by then.

Gál's comments, rather than being put on the reverse side of the tape, were sent in a letter dated 21 February 1974 addressed to 'My dearest both. Carl & Joseph', that contains some interesting observations.

Your tape has given me very keen pleasure – everything is splendidly in its place; speeds, transpositions etc., quite unobjectionable. I presume, Joseph, you played on your small harpsichord, – what I am missing are *some* dynamic contrasts – piano and forte etc. – but I hope some contrasts of this kind will be provided by an instrument with two manuals. All I have to remark regards some wrong notes, which partly are certainly accidental, while others are recurring. Here is a list.

I have not reproduced Gál's list of the 'wrong notes', but there are two other noteworthy comments which deal more with performance. In Intermezzo No. 2 Gál observes: 'In the trio section the double dottings both in the harpsichord and sometimes in the recorder part could be more *double*.' Also in No. 2 he notes that the harpsichord right hand from the third beat in bar 52 to bar 56 should be 'very legato!' and suggests third finger on E in bar 53. He also notes: 'I was amused to find that the duration of your tape, 16 minutes, is exactly the duration I put into my manuscript after timing the pieces.' Finally he expressed his thanks for tickets for the concert and requested an invitation to the last rehearsal at the Wigmore Hall before the performance.

Gál's programme note is given in full below.

These pieces were written last year. Though they can stand on their own, independent of each other, they form, both tonally and structurally, a kind of unity, similar to a suite or sonatina. A transparent texture prevails throughout, in accordance with the tender character of both instruments; and they unite in a duo of two marked individualities who put things in their own way an animated discussion and contribute equally to the sequence of events. As to the formal layout, the opening piece is a lyrical kind of rondo, the second a minuet and trio and recapitulation and the third movement in sonata form.

Following the Wigmore Hall recital Dolmetsch wrote to Gál on 15 March 1974:

My dear Hans,

Before another day goes by, I want to thank you again for the three gracious Intermezzi, which had such a warm welcome from our audience.

Joseph and I so much enjoyed playing these elegantly constructed pieces, which lie as well under the fingers as if you played the recorder yourself.

In case you didn't see it, I am enclosing a copy of Edward Greenfield's review in the Guardian. There was nothing in the Times or Telegraph, but if anything appears in the music journals, we will send you copies in due course.

Our love to you and to Hanna – and my very warm thanks again,

Yours as ever,

Carl

In his review in *The Guardian* of 7 March 1974 Edward Greenfield mentions the *Three Intermezzi* briefly and comments that they 'exploit the gentlest brand of neo-classicism, lyrical and light hearted.' The opening of Gál's reply in a letter dated 20 March 1974 is characteristic of his attitude to his art:

Dear Carl,

Kindest thanks for your letter and for the review, which was certainly well meant. If he only knew how little I have bothered all my life about any neo-nonsense!

The evening at the Wigmore Hall was pure pleasure indeed, glorious music (what a uniquely beautiful Telemann!) and beautifully played. As to 'Three Intermezzi', I just corrected the proofs and I hope they will be available in a short time. Schott have done it in grand style, engraved, and they will look very fine indeed. Let's hope they will sell too!

Lots of thanks again to you both, and love to all the family.

Yours ever,

Hans

Bearing in mind Edward Greenfield's comments in *The Guardian*, it is interesting to compare them with those of Margaret Campbell in her review of the concert in *Recorder & Music Magazine*,[67] in which she observed: 'The first performance of Three Intermezzi showed Carl Dolmetsch and Joseph Saxby rise to the challenge of modern music.' Gál's musical language was certainly more conservative than that of the new William Mathias work premiered at the same concert, and the challenges presented by the *Three Intermezzi* are surely in the refinement essential to their satisfactory performance.

Dolmetsch embraced a wide musical aesthetic and clearly understood, and was as entirely at one with Gál's musical language as he was with that of the composers who wrote for him in a decidedly more contemporary idiom. As mentioned in connection with Gál's *Concertino*, having developed his own distinctive musical style, he resolutely resisted the adoption of what may be considered as more fashionable or radical trends. There are perhaps comparisons to be made in this respect with Gaston Saux and Jean Françaix, and some recorder players have difficulty in reconciling these composers' works with those from the twentieth century that embrace a more radical approach. In so doing they are perhaps failing to appreciate that to create something new within traditional forms and idioms can be more challenging than constantly seeking to break new ground.

This was the last of Gál's works to be premiered by Dolmetsch at the Wigmore Hall, but the two men continued to correspond well into the 1980s. A letter from Gál dated 17 December 1985 notes: 'I am too old for travelling, but we are both in good health, and my hands are on my piano every day. Well, my latest and definitely last work, a sonatina for solo recorder, will be published by Schott.'[68]

When Gál died in October 1987, Dolmetsch wrote to Hanna, and in her very touching reply she commented: 'It was the acquaintance and friendship with you which enticed Hans to take a serious interest in and write for the recorder works

---

[67] June 1974, 4, p. 363.
[68] The Sonatina, Op. 110B, was written for John Turner and published in 1993 by Forsyth Brothers Ltd in *Pieces for Solo Recorder*, 2.

which otherwise would never have come into existence at all.' This was true of a number of the composers who wrote works for Dolmetsch, but is especially so of his good friend Hans Gál.

William Mathias: Concertino, Op. 65

tr rec (or fl), ob, bn, hpd (or pn)

Commissioned by and dedicated to Carl Dolmetsch

1 Moderato – Allegro vivo. 2 Andante mesto. 3 Allegro capriccioso.

First performance: Wigmore Hall, London, 6 March 1974. Carl Dolmetsch, rec; Anthony Camden, ob; Kerry Camden, bn; Joseph Saxby, hpd.

Published: Oxford: Oxford University Press, 1977.

Although Dolmetsch already had a work for his 1974 Wigmore Hall recital in the form of Hans Gál's *Three Intermezzi* for recorder and harpsichord, he had invited the Camden brothers to join him and was therefore keen to have a new composition in which they could also take part.

Dolmetsch had previously encountered and been impressed by William Mathias's music and thus wrote to him to enquire if he could be persuaded to write a new work for the occasion. Dolmetsch's letter is dated 20 August 1973:

> When I was playing Gordon Jacob's Suite for recorder and strings at Fairfield Halls recently, the RPO also performed your Celtic Dances which I found very enjoyable. At the same time, I was reminded of the enthusiastic praise given your works by the Californian conductor Ralph Matesky, who toured Wales with the Idyllwild Orchestra when you were in Bangor.
>
> You may know that over the past thirty-five years or so many leading composers in Britain and abroad have written for me among them Rubbra, Berkeley, Arnold Cooke, Bob Simpson, Martin Dalby, Nicholas Maw and so on.
>
> For my next Wigmore Hall recital, on 6th March 1974, I have invited the Camden brothers to join me in works by Telemann, Vivaldi and others. It would give us – and the very large recorder public – great pleasure and stimulating interest if you could be persuaded to write a work for recorder with oboe and bassoon for the occasion, with or without harpsichord?
>
> If you are able and willing to agree with my proposal, and if the work could be conceived alternatively for recorder, violin and cello, I could include it in my programmes for my 1974 autumn tour of America, to play with the distinguished violin/cello Duo Alice and Eleonore Schoenfeld, of the USC Music Faculty in Los Angeles. I have in mind a work of approximately twelve minutes' duration.

Mathias had been on holiday when this letter arrived and had spoken to Dolmetsch on the telephone before accepting his invitation, which he did in a letter dated 11 September 1973. In this, Mathias notes that it is to be a work for recorder, oboe, bassoon and harpsichord. In connection with the suggestion that it also be conceived alternatively with violin and cello in place of oboe and bassoon, Mathias comments: 'I will certainly bear this in mind in the writing, though perhaps you could leave the final judgement on this to me in the light of the way in which the work emerges. Could we say a work of 10–12 minutes if this is acceptable to you?' The letter continues by suggesting that an amount for the fee be put forward by Dolmetsch, noting: 'I am interested in writing this work, so that I do not envisage any complexities here!' Mathias was also keen to obtain guidance on writing for the recorder:

> Whilst I have, of course, written for recorder on one or two previous occasions it has been for the instrument in the hands of amateurs. As such, it would be useful if you could give me some guidance as to what is possible (and ultimately, not possible) in the hands of the virtuoso player which I know you to be. Could you (a) let me have a total range of the instrument which you use, and (b) advise me as to whether any specific key centre is more desirable than any other – this latter would in fact be useful to know before I get down to thinking about the music itself. Any further information on the nature of the instrument *in terms of your own technique* would be a help as I find such comments stimulating.

The letter concludes by requesting Dolmetsch for a suggested date for completion of the score, adding: 'I have, incidentally, little doubt that Oxford University Press will be interested in the finished composition.'

Dolmetsch responded on 16 September expressing his pleasure that Mathias was able to accept the invitation to write a new work and noted that a duration of 10–12 minutes would be perfect for the programme. In connection with the fee, Dolmetsch noted that the work was being sponsored by him personally, and in light of what he had paid to Nicholas Maw and Martin Dalby, and the 'changing economic situation', offered Mathias £75.

In answer to Mathias's request for guidance regarding technical aspects of the instrument, Dolmetsch wrote:

> I would envisage that the model of recorder involved would be the treble, whose chromatic range extends from F above middle C to g# two octaves and one third above the fundamental F. Although the instrument is chromatically complete, there are certain keys which, as with any instrument, are more comfortable than others. Particularly good keys are F major, G major and minor, A minor, B♭ major, C major and minor, D minor. Such keys as D and A major, while perfectly possible, are better suited to the flute. Notwithstanding its chromatic completeness, it is better to avoid fast chromatic work in the very lowest five semitones (where the double holes are) and the very highest notes of the compass.
>
> Should you wish to introduce the sparkling sound of a sopranino recorder for brilliant effects anywhere in the work, it is pitched exactly an octave above the treble and the music is written the same though sounding an octave higher. As I am sure you will know, the recorder is at its strongest in the upper register.

With regard to Mathias's request for a date for completion Dolmetsch noted that he would be glad to have the work at least four weeks before the concert as, due to several engagements at that time, he would not be able to work at it uninterrupted. The letter concluded by requesting a title, if possible, before the advance publicity due to go to press in October/November, and a programme note for nearer the time of the concert.

In his reply dated 21 September, Mathias considered the fee offered as perfectly acceptable as he was interested in writing such a work for recorder, and because the commission was from a private individual. He thanked Dolmetsch for his comments on the recorder and noted the other points regarding completion and a programme note. In connection with the title Mathias wrote:

> Perhaps you could let me have a few days to consider and finalise a title for publicity purposes, though I note you would like to receive such a title in time for the press, in October/November. I shall contact you in the near future regarding this, and will, of course, supply a short note for the programme at the requisite time.

During the autumn of 1973 Dolmetsch was, as usual, away on his American tour. In his absence, and having heard nothing about a title, Greta Matthews wrote to Mathias on 7 November to see if he was in a position to advise of one. Mathias replied by return, giving the title for the new work as 'CONCERTINO, for recorder, oboe, bassoon and harpsichord'.

Mathias also took the opportunity to ask: 'Is there any special feature of Mr. Saxby's harpsichord – the one to be used at this recital – which it would be useful to know about?' Greta thanked Mathias for the title and gave the following details of the harpsichord: 'The Dolmetsch concert harpsichord is a two-manual instrument, with a range of five octaves and one note – F to g – per manual. The specifications are 16ft., 4ft., 8ft., harp, coupler, harp, lute and 8ft., the last three being the upper-manual registers.'

By 3 February 1974 the *Concertino* was complete and Mathias wrote to Dolmetsch:

> Two 'advanced' Xerox copies of the new CONCERTINO are enclosed, as arranged. One can if desired be sent to the Camden brothers.
>
> The original transparencies are being sent on to Christopher Morris, Music Editor of Oxford University Press who will arrange (a) to have a satisfactory playing copy photographed for the use of the harpsichordist, and (b) to have parts copied for Recorder, Oboe and Bassoon.
>
> I am assuming generally the use of the treble recorder in the work, but have been wondering about the possibility of the sopranino version in at least certain areas of the slow movement (to convey an 'antique', mythical kind of sound). Unfortunately, there is no one here who plays the instrument *well* enough to demonstrate to my full satisfaction – at this stage therefore, the idea is merely mentioned en passant for your comments.

In a postscript Mathias noted: 'You will perhaps see that your original point with regard to possible future arrangement for violin & cello has not been forgotten, but the wind version must for now be our primary concern.'

Dolmetsch acknowledged receipt, commenting: 'I am looking forward to going through it this evening with Joseph Saxby – so far I have only looked at it, but I can already say that I like what I see. Thank you also for the dedication.' The copies of the score and parts (made by the OUP) remain in the archive.

A number of letters were exchanged regarding the performing material, tickets for the concert and preliminary rehearsals. Mathias was keen to attend the final rehearsal on the day of the concert and this is mentioned in a letter dated 21 February, which also adds:

> I am glad that all material for the CONCERTINO has been safely received from Oxford University Press, and that you are enjoying working on the piece. I did not indicate any harpsichord specification deliberately – I find that it is best to leave such matters until after rehearsal and/or first performance; or rather that it is somewhat dangerous for a composer to be dogmatic about such matters of interpretation previous to physically hearing the piece. Also, I'm assuming for the time being that you are using the treble recorder, without discounting the possible use of the sopranino in one or two places if you felt this to be desirable. This, at all events can be settled later.

The programme note for the concert is also printed in the published edition:

> The opening *Moderato* leads directly into an *Allegro vivo* much concerned with contrapuntal interplay and contrapuntal rhythms. The slow movement alternates a remote, Celtic-sounding melody on recorder (against harpsichord fifths) with expressive comments from oboe and bassoon. The elegiac nature of the music becomes even more clear as the movement proceeds, evoking a past more distant than the Renaissance. The finale is in a free sense fugal, though it also contains a broad-spanned melody for recorder and oboe against harpsichord figuration. Scope for display is given to all four instruments, and the work ends in something of a spirit of *bravura*.

Only *The Guardian* of 7 March 1974 among the daily papers appears to have covered the concert, Edward Greenfield commenting that the *Concertino* was, 'neatly turned, has the tangy flavour of Hindemith with Welsh overtones – capering contrapuntal outer movements and a Celtic lament in the middle.' Margaret Campbell in *Recorder & Music Magazine*[69] also commented on the Celtic influence in the work: '... the writing displayed the Celtic leanings of the recorder and reed instruments.'

Dolmetsch was pleased with the new piece and on 13 March wrote to Mathias:

> Before another day passes by, I want to thank you again for the splendid Concertino you wrote for the Dolmetsch/Camden Ensemble. As you will have seen for yourself, it had

---

[69] June 1974, **4**, p. 363.

a wonderfully enthusiastic reception from our audience – and I enclose Edward Greenfield's review in the Guardian, in case you didn't see it.

As promised, I will indicate in pencil on the recorder part the minor modifications which seemed desirable from a player's point of view, for you to use as you think. Would you prefer me to send the score and parts to you before they go to Christopher Morris?

With every good wish, and my warm thanks again.

Dolmetsch forwarded his observations and modifications to Mathias on 26 June 1974, and these were eventually included in the published score. First the footnote to the first page of the *Allegro vivo* regarding the use of the bell key for the high F#s at the beginning of this movement and elsewhere in the work, and also a footnote to the finale, noting that it gains in brilliance from the use, as in the first performance, of the sopranino recorder. (Mathias's desire to include the instrument eventually found an effective place.) The *ossia* in the recorder part three bars before letter J was also included at Dolmetsch's suggestion. Mathias thanked Dolmetsch, adding: 'These will certainly be very useful in view of the fact that I am keen to get this work to press (OUP) as soon as possible. It will take some time to appear as there are considerable delays involved in printing in these difficult times.' (See the section on Hans Gál's *Three Intermezzi*.) The work did not appear in print until 1977.

The remaining correspondence between Dolmetsch and Mathias in the archive is in connection with a planned recording of the work by the BBC at which Mathias was eager to be present.

Dolmetsch firmly intended to include among the new works he commissioned for the recorder those in which the instrument was integrated into a chamber music context, reflecting the practices of the baroque. Mathias's work, with its trio of wind instruments, has echoes of the scoring of chamber concertos by Vivaldi, but it also bears Mathias's own very characteristic voice.

Although for a high-baroque instrumental grouping, the now more frequent use of period instruments makes the programming of this piece a little more difficult. However, attempts to make a place for it in the recital hall would not go unrewarded.

Mathias's untimely death in 1992 robbed British music of a particular talent. His choral and organ works and an impressive collection of orchestral and chamber music are marked by imaginative sonic colour and an assured technique. The obvious influences of Bartók and Hindemith, where present, are inevitably underlined by a distinctive Celtic flavour that gives his music its individuality. Recorder players are fortunate to have the *Concertino* in their repertoire.

Alan Ridout: Sequence

rec, lute

To Carl Dolmetsch and Robert Spencer

1 Locrian Mode. 2 Mixolydian Mode. 3 Phrygian Mode. 4 Ionian Mode. 5 Aeolian Mode. 6 Lydian Mode. 7 Dorian Mode.

First performance: Wigmore Hall, London, 7 March 1975. Carl Dolmetsch, rec; Robert Spencer, lute.

Published: Hebden Bridge, Peacock Press, 2003.

For his 1975 Wigmore Hall recital, Dolmetsch was to be joined by lutenist Robert Spencer. Discussion between Dolmetsch and Spencer clearly took place regarding the possibility of their performing a new work for recorder and lute. Alan Ridout's name would seem to have been suggested in connection with this, and on 20 July 1974 Spencer wrote to Dolmetsch:[70] 'I went to see Alan Ridout on Thursday and he likes the idea of writing something for you with lute. Presumably you will suggest which recorder and length of piece. I much look forward to 7 March.'

Alan Ridout had contacted Dolmetsch about a composition for recorder as far back as 1956 (see the section on Ridout's Chamber Concerto performed at the Wigmore Hall in 1981). With Spencer's further introduction Dolmetsch now wrote in a letter dated 15 August 1974:

> I am delighted to hear from Bob Spencer that you are interested in writing a work for the two of us to play at the Wigmore Hall on 7th March next year.
>
> As you may know, I have made a feature of presenting 20th century works at these recitals since the 1930s, and I shall be most happy to add your name to the many distinguished composers who have written for the recorder.
>
> A concertante sonata with treble recorder and lute on equal terms is the kind of work I have in mind, approximately the length of an 18th century sonata but in 20th century idiom of course. The normal range of the treble is from F first space to G two octaves and one note above – four ledger lines above the treble stave. While the recorder is chromatically complete between these two extremes and can be played with dexterity over most of its compass, it is better to avoid rapid chromatic progressions over the four lowest semi-tones and the five highest semi-tones similarly.
>
> May I suggest too that while the work should be devised primarily for recorder and lute, if the lute part were made adaptable to harpsichord or piano, this would ultimately make the work accessible to a wider performing public.
>
> For a work of approximately ten minutes' duration, would you consider accepting a fee in the region of £50? I might add that the BBC has hitherto recorded all the modern works introduced at my Wigmore Hall recitals.
>
> I look forward to hearing from you and will be pleased to meet you here or in London if you feel there are any points requiring discussion.

---

[70] Spencer's interest in the music of Alan Ridout is noted in the obituary of Spencer written by John Turner in *The Recorder Magazine*, December 1997, **17**, p. 134.

6 Lutenist Robert Spencer. His enthusiasm for Ridout's music led directly to the commissioning of *Sequence*.

One wonders from Dolmetsch's explanation of recorder compass and technical details whether he remembered that Ridout had sent him the score of a concerto for recorder and string quartet back in 1956. Ridout was, however, pleased to accept this new commission and wrote to Dolmetsch on 3 August:

> I will be delighted to write the work you suggest for Treble recorder and lute, and am happy with the fee of £50 which you mention.
> I would probably like to meet you and discuss technical details etc. a little later on and will write again in a few weeks when I am clearer of present composing commitments. In the meantime, if you by any chance have copies of other works commissioned for your concerts which you consider particularly well written and successful I should be grateful to see them.

In the event, it was Ridout who sent Dolmetsch some of the recorder pieces he had written for beginners, as can be deduced from a letter Dolmetsch wrote to Ridout on 23 October in which he comments favourably on them. It is also evident from this letter that Ridout had visited Haslemere where, no doubt, the new work was discussed, although the only mention made of it is a request for a title for the soon to be produced handbills.

The next we hear of the work is in a letter from Ridout to Dolmetsch dated 26 January 1975 in which he gives the news: 'The work for you and Robert Spencer is now complete and I shall let you have it just as soon as I can write it out. I am starting almost immediately. In the meantime I am enclosing the programme note.' This is quoted in full and reads as follows:

> Sequence is in seven thematically related movements. Each movement makes use of one of the modes.
>
> Movement I (Locrian mode) presents the main material, though much decorated.
>
> Movement II (Mixolydian mode) is fast, employing irregular rhythms.
>
> Movement III (Phrygian mode) has the character of a funeral march.
>
> Movement IV (Ionian mode) is a moto perpetuo, the recorder in 7/4 time, the lute in 6/4.
>
> Movement V (Aeolian mode) consists of a melody simply accompanied.
>
> Movement VI (Lydian mode) has something of the nature of a primitive dance.
>
> Movement VII is mainly in the Dorian mode. The recorder plays a cantilena while the lute makes much use of large chords. In the coda, the modes are recapitulated one after the other, moving progressively from darkest (Locrian) to the brightest (Lydian).

Ridout's use of large chords in movement 7 is indicated in Ex. 3.27.

The review in the *Daily Telegraph* of 8 March 1975 was enthusiastic, commenting that although idioms from the past were employed, the result was not pastiche. The seventh movement, in which the recorder's floating line was accompanied by rich chords, was singled out for praise.

Ridout's letter to Dolmetsch following the premiere fully expresses his delight with the performance:

> A thousand thanks for a simply lovely performance of my piece. It could not have been more ideal and I am most grateful to you and Bob for working at it so hard.
>
> The whole programme was a delight. I heard someone say during the interval 'I can never hope to hear the recorder played more beautifully', and that sums up for me the general feeling in the audience.
>
> I loved some of the other works and think it was a most ideal form of programme. I especially liked the slow movement of the Haydn.
>
> My warm congratulations too to Marguerite and Joseph. How lucky you are to work with such lovely people!
>
> I do hope that one day you may permit me to work with you again. It has been a very heart-warming and elevating experience.

Ex. 3.27. Alan Ridout, *Sequence*, for recorder and lute. Movement 7, final eight bars. Reproduced by permission of Ampleforth Abbey Trustees.

This letter is quoted in full as it shows the obvious pleasure Ridout had derived from the collaboration, and the warmth of friendship he found with the Dolmetsch family, as will be seen also from later correspondence.

The work was recorded and broadcast by the BBC soon after. Ridout was present at the recording, as we learn from his letter to Dolmetsch dated 7 April 1975. This is, as mentioned above, indicative of the enjoyment and friendship he had found in working with Dolmetsch in particular and with the family generally.

> It was a great joy to me to hear your broadcast (for me again) on the radio this morning.

I thought it came off splendidly and hope you were as pleased as I was. I found it particularly interesting, having been at the recording, and having such a clear memory of the sounds I heard at Joseph's elbow, and then hearing the balance of the Studio manager and producer. I thought it excellent, didn't you?

Since I am writing now, I might as well mention something else that has been in my mind. I'd like enormously to write for you again in whatever combination you would find most useful (i.e. recorder and harpsichord or consort, or whatever). And this I should like to do without any form of payment if you are agreeable. I so enjoyed working with you before – felt very privileged.

My best regards to your family, and, of course, to Joseph.

In a postscript Ridout added:

You may be interested to know that Chappells wish to produce a version of Sequence for Recorder and Keyboard (for practical commercial reasons) and Bob Spencer tells me that the Lute Society would like to bring out the original version (in tablature). I believe a special publisher's agreement may prove possible.[71]

However, no keyboard version appears to have been made, and Jeanne Dolmetsch recalls that Joseph Saxby played the work on the harpsichord from the score, in which the lute part is written in standard notation (not lute tablature) and sometimes on two staves.

Dolmetsch was very grateful for Ridout's offer and replied:

It is wonderfully kind of you Alan to offer to write another work for us and we would just love to take advantage of your generosity. What would be really welcome at this stage is a work for a consort of viols. Although there are many players who work with us, the most readily available consort on the spot consists of Jeanne, Marguerite and me – in other words, two trebles and bass; or treble, tenor and bass.

We too enjoyed co-operating with you and I hope very much to be working in close partnership again on this new project.

Such a work is not mentioned again, however, until correspondence dating from December 1982.

Dolmetsch performed *Sequence* again in his 1987 Wigmore Hall recital, and on this occasion performed the sixth movement on sopranino recorder. According to one reviewer, this substitution, 'although perhaps suited to the nature of this movement, did to some extent disrupt the overall unity and flow of the work.'[72]

Dolmetsch again played the sixth movement on sopranino (presumably with harpsichord accompaniment) at his final Wigmore Hall recital in 1989. However,

---

[71] Neither Chappells nor the Lute Society published the work, and it remained unpublished in any version in the composer's lifetime. *Sequence* was played from manuscript by John Turner and Dorothy Linnell at a memorial recital for Robert Spencer given in the Church of St Bartholomew the Great, Smithfield, London, in November 1997.

[72] *The Recorder and Music Magazine*, June 1987, **9**, p. 36.

on that occasion only the sixth movement was played, as one of a series of pieces featuring tenor, descant, bass and sopranino in turn.

Ridout clearly enjoyed the challenge of writing a contemporary work for two instruments from music's past. *Sequence* contains music of much ingenuity and contrast, from the syncopations and strange mixture of time signatures in the moto perpetuo fourth movement, through the scampering 6/16 dance in the sixth, to the broad sonority of the seventh. However, a more accomplished recorder work by Ridout (at least in the opinion of this author) was to receive its first performance at the Wigmore Hall recital six years later.

Malcolm Lipkin: Interplay

tr rec, perc, gamba, hpd

To Carl Dolmetsch

1 Moderately flowing, dreamlike. 2 Very still.

First performance: Wigmore Hall, London, 5 March 1976. Carl Dolmetsch, rec; James Blades, perc; Marguerite Dolmetsch, gamba; Joseph Saxby, hpd.

Published by the composer in 1975.

There is nothing in the archive to indicate how Dolmetsch first came into contact with Malcolm Lipkin,[73] but it is evident from a letter dated 15 September 1975 that Dolmetsch visited Lipkin at his home near Crowborough in Sussex (about forty miles from the Dolmetsch home in Haslemere) at that time. It is also clear that their discussions were of a new work that was to include percussion and viola da gamba, in addition to recorder and harpsichord. This unusual scoring was proposed to suit the performers in the 1976 Wigmore Hall recital that were to include the renowned percussionist James Blades and Dolmetsch's daughter Marguerite playing the viola da gamba. Dolmetsch's letter notes:

> It was very kind of you to welcome us so warmly the other day and I am sorry our visit had to be so short.
>
> I am delighted that you like the idea of writing a work for recorder, percussion, harpsichord and viola da gamba for my next Wigmore Hall recital, on Friday, 5th March 1976. As mentioned when we were discussing matters, I would like a work of 10–12 minutes' duration but I am happy to leave this to you. Would you accept a fee of £70?
>
> The normal compass of the treble recorder is fully chromatic but avoiding chromatic acrobatics at both extremes of the range. You are very welcome to look at the resources of our double-keyboard eight-pedal harpsichord any time you are in the vicinity if you

---

[73] In a telephone conversation with the author (January 2001), Malcolm Lipkin noted that Dolmetsch had first contacted him by telephone with an invitation to write a new work for the 1976 Wigmore Hall recital.

would telephone beforehand. My daughters would demonstrate anything further you might wish to know about recorder or viola da gamba.

Dolmetsch's letter concluded by thanking Lipkin's wife for her hospitality and asking if it would be possible for Lipkin to advise of the work's title in time for the advance publicity to be issued in the autumn. The letter also noted: 'James Blades is also looking forward to hearing from you.' Lipkin replied almost immediately:

> My wife and I were delighted to meet you and your colleagues last week. Thank you very much indeed for the [information about the][74] recorder, and your letter – yes, I shall be very happy to write a new piece for you.
>
> I have been in touch with James Blades, and we shall be meeting. I hope to be in Haslemere in the near future; I shall telephone your secretary to arrange a suitable time.

Lipkin did indeed meet James Blades as the above letter indicates was the intention. In a telephone conversation with the author (January 2001), Lipkin recalled an invitation to James Blades 'den' where the eminent percussionist showed him his extraordinary collection of instruments and gave considerable assistance with the selection of those most suitable to provide the delicate effects of scoring required with such an unusual ensemble.[75]

We hear no more of the new work until a letter dated 13 January 1976 with which Greta Matthews forwarded copies of the handbills to Lipkin and requested a note for the programme, which was shortly to be sent for printing. This letter contains the first reference to the title of *Interplay*, although it is evident from a letter written to James Blades on the same day that the score was, by this time, in Dolmetsch's possession: 'I have pleasure in sending you a copy of the score of Malcolm Lipkin's 'Interplay' for the recital at the Wigmore Hall on Friday, 5th March. We think you would prefer to have a score so that you can put in your own cues.'

Lipkin forwarded a programme note (included later) and advised that James Blades had written to him to request two copies of the percussion part. The archive contains virtually all the performing material in the form of three printed scores in the composer's own edition. The first is marked 'C.F.D. copy', the second 'Guite' (the Dolmetsch family name for Marguerite) and the third 'James Blades' score'. There is also a further unmarked photocopy.

---

[74] From the original wording of the letter it appeared that Dolmetsch had given or lent an instrument to the composer, but, in the same telephone conversation referred to in note 73, Lipkin noted that he had not had an instrument with which to work.

[75] Blades advised the use of eight chime bells, and Lipkin (in the same telephone conversation referred to in note 1 recalled with some amusement that, after he had enquired if there was a particular musical or practical reason for this, Blades had explained this was the maximum number that could be accommodated in his shooting brake!

By the end of January Dolmetsch was able to invite Lipkin to a rehearsal of the work:

> We are much looking forward to putting the four parts together and I have, in fact, just arranged a rehearsal here with Jimmy Blades at 2.0 p.m. on Sunday, 29th February. Would you be able to join us for lunch that day and go through the piece with us afterwards?

Lipkin accepted Dolmetsch's invitation, and his letter so doing is the last in the archive referring to the new work. The programme note contains, in addition to an explanation of the form of the work, details of the percussion instruments employed:

> This work is dedicated to Carl Dolmetsch, who commissioned it for to-night's concert. The piece has two movements, in which the dominant feature is contrast – in the first, elements of a scherzo are juxtaposed with more dreamlike, reflective themes. In the second movement, contrasts in dynamics are explored: a very still opening erupts in an intense and forceful climax, which eventually subsides, the movement ending in calm.
>
> For the percussion, I have used instruments which balance the delicate tones of the recorder, harpsichord and viola da gamba. There are chime bells, six timbales, glockenspiel and xylophone.

The press books in the Dolmetsch archive contain no reviews of the 1976 Wigmore Hall recital from the national daily papers, but the *Farnham Herald* of 12 March 1976 contained a detailed review which of *Interplay* noted:

> This is a serious, somewhat austere piece, which when the word was fashionable would have been described as 'linear'
>
> Most impressive was the subtle blending of the percussion instruments (chime bells, small kettledrums, glockenspiel and xylophone) with each of the melody instruments in turn; noteworthy too was the careful consideration which the composer has given to the timbre and capabilities of each instrument.

The review concluded: 'It is hoped that "Interplay", so aptly titled will not have to wait long for a second performance from these exceptionally talented and sympathetic artists.'

The *Recorder & Music* magazine also noted the sensitive use of the instruments: '... Lipkin shows a good knowledge of the different instruments and has written sensitively for them, exploring the dynamic range of the recorder and gamba and using only the more delicate percussion instruments.'

The unusual forces for which this work is composed are a vital factor in the programming of further performances. Recorder, gamba and harpsichord is a frequently found instrumental ensemble, but the addition of small percussion is much less common and requires careful programming. It was thus interesting to discover in the archive an arrangement of the work made by the composer for recorder, gamba and piano, and published by him in 1978. This combination of instruments is perhaps almost as difficult to assemble in a programme as the original scoring, and will certainly lose much of its colour.[76] Despite any programming difficulties however, a work that skilfully employs the sonorities of such an unusual and colourful ensemble is deserving of the effort of bringing it together for a performance.

Alun Hoddinott: Italian Suite

rec (or fl), gui

1 Cadenza (Con fuoco). 2 Passamezzo (Moderato). 3 Gondoliera (Andante). 4 Tarantella (Prestissimo).

First performance: Wigmore Hall, London, 4 March 1977. Carl Dolmetsch, rec; John Mills, gui.

Published: Oxford: Oxford University Press, 1983.

In circumstances not dissimilar to those of the 1975 Wigmore Hall recital, in which Dolmetsch was joined by lutenist Robert Spencer, Dolmetsch was partnered in the 1977 recital by guitarist John Mills. A new work for recorder and guitar was thus sought, and on 23 August 1976 Dolmetsch wrote to Alun Hoddinott a letter quite similarly worded to that which he had sent to Alan Ridout requesting a new work with lute:

> Since the late 1930s, I have made a feature of introducing new works at my annual Wigmore Hall recitals, as you perhaps know. Among leading British composers who have written for me are Edmund Rubbra, Lennox Berkeley, Gordon Jacob, Nicholas Maw, Martin Dalby and your compatriot William Mathias.
>
> For my next Wigmore Hall recital, on 4th March 1977, I have invited the guitarist John Mills to join me and it would give us – and the considerable recorder and guitar playing public – very great pleasure if you could be persuaded to write a work for our two instruments, with or without viola da gamba and/or harpsichord, to your own preference.
>
> A concertante sonata with treble recorder and guitar on equal terms is the kind of work I have in mind, approximately the length of an 18th century sonata but naturally in your own idiom. I would like to suggest too that although the work would be designed primarily for recorder and guitar, if the guitar part were made adaptable to alternative harpsichord or piano, this would ultimately render the work accessible to the widest possible performing public.
>
> I look forward to the pleasure of hearing from you.

---

[76] In a later telephone conversation with the author (June 2001), the composer advised that he had also made an arrangement of the work for flute, cello and piano enabling a performance on entirely modern instruments.

It is likely that Dolmetsch also made contact by telephone (a Cardiff number is written at the top of the copy of the above letter) as a letter from Hoddinott dated 25 September 1976 notes: 'I look forward to writing a work for you and confirm that it should be ready (hopefully!) by January. It would be most helpful if we could meet fairly soon so that I can gather some technical information.'

Dolmetsch thanked Hoddinott for his letter and suggested a meeting in Haslemere, but of such a meeting there is no reference in any later correspondence.[77] As usual Dolmetsch also asked if it would be possible to have a title or some idea of the form of the new work for the advance publicity.

On 6 January 1977 Dolmetsch wrote to Hoddinott: 'John Mills was here last weekend – between Canadian tours – for a preliminary rehearsal of some of the early works in our programme for 4th March. He expressed great interest in the suite you are writing for us and we are much looking forward to seeing it.' By this time material for the programme was being assembled for printing, and in the same letter Dolmetsch also asked Hoddinott for a programme note. Once again it is likely that telephone contact was made as the same Cardiff number is written at the top of the copy of this letter. Of particular interest is a note written at the bottom in Dolmetsch's hand that reads: 'End of this week – Italian Suite in 5 mots.' However, this must have been a slip of the pen, as Hoddinott later confirmed in a letter to the author.[78]

Hoddinott's programme note identifies the particular influence that both inspired the music of the suite and gave it its title.

> Much of my music has been stimulated by Italian art and the Italian countryside.
>
> The fourth movement, for example, of Variants for Orchestra (1966) is an evocation of the Grotte di Pertosa near Paestum and my 2nd Sonata for Violin and Piano was written entirely during an Easter spent at Asolo in 1970.
>
> This new Suite was much in my mind during a recent visit to Florence and whilst not showing any obvious influences, nevertheless is indebted to some forms and expressions of Italian music.
>
> The opening Cadenza is a flourish to the more extended Passamezzo, originally an Italian formal dance in wide use throughout the 16th and 17th centuries. Gondoliera resembles a Venetian boating song and the final Tarantella is a fast dance which derives its name from Taranto in the old province of Apulia.

As with the 1976 Wigmore Hall recital, the only review to be found in the Dolmetsch Archive press books is from the *Farnham Herald*. The review in the issue of 11 March 1977 mentions the three dances, which, 'after an opening rhapsodic cadenza, make up this suite and are held together by the insistent dance rhythms given to the guitarist, who however has no mean share of the tune as

---

[77] In a letter written to the author in March 2002 the composer confirmed that he did visit Dolmetsch in Haslemere to discuss technical matters.

[78] Ibid.

well, but the most lively and evocative movement by far was the closing Tarantella.'

Dolmetsch was clearly pleased with the work, but felt that the first performance could be improved upon, and on 14 March wrote to Hoddinott:

> It seems incredible that more than a week has passed since so many of us gathered in the Wigmore Hall to enjoy your Italian Suite. I feel sure you know already how grateful John Mills and I are to you for writing this truly satisfying work for us.
>
> On short acquaintance, we felt we extracted a great deal from the Suite, but with a small lapse of time since our very concentrated work on it we think that we shall give a performance altogether more poised when we pick up the threads again.
>
> In fact, we would like to make a tape with one copy for yourself, one for the BBC and another for ourselves. Therefore, as soon as you can let us have back our copies of the parts (with our strange-looking markings which helped so much in the short term), we shall be glad to have them. At present, we have the necessary time for work and recording which will be denied abruptly once intensive rehearsals for the Haslemere Festival begin to get under way.
>
> With thanks again and warmest greetings to you and your wife.

Hoddinott replied the next day: 'It was good of you to write – I much enjoyed your performance of my piece and working on it with you. I'm sending back your ms. copy and look forward to hearing you play it again. OUP will publish as soon as I get a copy to them.'

In August Dolmetsch forwarded a copy of the promised tape recording to Hoddinott who replied: 'Many thanks for the tape. I have listened to your playing with the greatest pleasure – I do hope you can play my Suite occasionally. I'm going to make a very few small additions which I will send on when completed.'

Comparison of the published edition with a copy of the original manuscript in the archive reveals a few amendments, but it is the ending of the final movement where additions have been made. Bar 109 originally contained a rising figure in quavers for the first two beats and a dotted C# crotchet with a trill leading to a final crotchet D in bar 110. This was originally the final bar. In pencil below the recorder part in bar 109 Dolmetsch added a flourish, the notes of which have been incorporated into the semiquaver runs in the composer's amended bars 108 and 109. The revised bar 110 now contains the C# trills, and bars 111–14 were added to form a new ending.

In response to a letter from Dolmetsch, no copy of which is to be found in the archive, Hoddinott replied in a letter dated 16 February, but with no indication of the year. The last paragraph reads: 'I've been a bit lazy about the Italian Suite, but I've now corrected the 2nd proofs so the score should appear very soon.'

It was not until 1983 that Oxford University Press published the *Italian Suite*. When it did appear, it was not with an alternative keyboard part, as Dolmetsch originally suggested, but adapted to an equally large number of performers by the inclusion of a part for flute. This is the same as that for recorder in the final

Tarantella (except for the final two notes), but differs in the first three movements with the inclusion of many octave transpositions.

The opening cadenza is perhaps the most challenging for the recorder, beginning on a bottom F# and containing a number of passages that are perhaps more comfortable on the flute. In the more lyrical Passamezzo and Gondoliera movements, however, the recorder comes into its own.

Hoddinott's *Italian Suite* was among the earliest substantial works for recorder and guitar, a scoring for which the repertoire has continued to grow steadily.

Edmund Rubbra: Fantasia on a Chord, Op. 154

tr rec, hpd, optional gamba

Written for the tenth wedding anniversary of Valerie and Kenneth McLeish, 1977

In one movement: Tempo comodo e liberamente (Poco andante).

First performance: Wigmore Hall, London, 9 March 1978. Carl Dolmetsch, tr rec; Joseph Saxby, hpd; Marguerite Dolmetsch, gamba.

Published: Croydon: Alfred Lengnick & Co. Ltd, 1979 (4554).

It had been over 12 years since the Wigmore Hall premiere of Rubbra's Sonatina and, as Dolmetsch commented in a letter to Rubbra dated 1 September 1977, it seemed 'quite some time since we last exchanged news.' The letter continued:

> Joseph and I are setting off next month for our 19th tour of America and will be returning home at the end of November. Your Passacaglia is in our programme for this tour – and I included it in my Master Class at our summer school this year.
>
> As you may imagine, many projects have to be set in train before an absence of this length, among them being the programme for my next Wigmore Hall recital, on 9th March 1978. Our guest artist will be Gillian Sansom, a brilliant young violinist who scored a great success in our Festival this year, playing unaccompanied Bach and joining with Joseph, my daughter Marguerite (viola da gamba) and myself in trio-sonatas.
>
> The much-loved and often-played works you have written for us have not so far featured this standard 18th century instrumental combination and I am wondering whether you could be persuaded to write such a work for our recital on 9th March? A work of this nature from you would I know find a wide and highly appreciative performing public.
>
> If the suggestion appeals to you, I will immediately approach that department of the Arts Council which exists for the sponsoring of new works.
>
> Warm greetings from us all, and looking forward to hearing from you.

Rubbra responded immediately, his letter is dated 3 September 1977:

> It was very nice to hear from you & to know that you will be including my Passacaglia in your forthcoming American tour.
>
> While I would very much like to write a work for the forces you suggest, I am in a

difficulty about being able to do so, as I have already *three* commissions to fulfil! However, as it happens one of the commissions comes from a former Oxford pupil of mine (a recorder player) who wishes for a piece for his 10th wedding anniversary, & I have promised him a recorder harpsichord piece. I have today telephoned him to ask if he would like – subject to agreement of course – to have it first performed at your next Wigmore concert. He jumped at the idea! We quite understand though if this doesn't fit in with your scheme of things.

Rubbra further noted that under these circumstances it would not be necessary to seek Arts Council funding.

Dolmetsch was entirely receptive to this idea and wrote to Rubbra on 9 September:

What a splendid idea: I am delighted to fall in with your suggestion that we might premier your new recorder and harpsichord piece at my next Wigmore concert, on 9th March.

Could I make just one little request – that you would provide an optional bass part for viola da gamba (or cello) sustaining the left hand of the keyboard player?

My daughter Marguerite has become a wonderfully sensitive gamba continuo player and, in addition, this instrumental combination would make the work accessible to trio groups proliferating all over the place nowadays.

Our initial publicity will go to press (musical monthlies etc.) in October, so Greta will be glad to have a note of the work's title or form in order that she can draft advertisement, handbills etc.

As requested, Rubbra wrote to Greta Matthews on 29 September, but his advised title was not as it was eventually to appear: 'Carl has asked me to let you have the title of my new piece for treble recorder and harpsichord: this will, I think, be *Air and Dance, Op. 154*. Please tell Carl that I will add an optional gamba (or cello) part.'

The title would appear to have been changed by early November, as Greta Matthews wrote to Rubbra on the 7 November: 'Your amended title will be incorporated in our Wigmore publicity and I will tell Dr. D. about the gamba part when he returns at the end of this month – I am sure he will understand.'

Perhaps Rubbra was taking time to compose the optional gamba part, as this was only forwarded with a letter dated 30 December, by which time we learn that the score was already in Dolmetsch's possession:

Enclosed is the Gamba part of the new Fantasia. I have written it in pencil so that any emendations you suggest can be incorporated without much trouble. Hope I haven't exceeded the upward compass!

Please add to your score

(1) the rehearsal figures
(2) the two small harpsichord emendations you will find in the gamba part.

The harpsichord emendations (that repeat the left-hand chords in bars 3 and 8) have been added to Rubbra's original manuscript score in Joseph Saxby's hand.

Among the various portions of manuscript for this work in the archive are no fewer than three different gamba parts. What is probably the earliest of these is in Dolmetsch's hand and appears to be his own attempt to create a suitable gamba line based on the score already in his possession, ahead of receiving that from Rubbra.[79] The second is that in pencil referred to in, and enclosed with, the above letter. (The third will be commented on later.) Dolmetsch acknowledged receiving this gamba part in a letter dated 13 January 1978:

> Thank you so much for the gamba part of the new Fantasia – Guite [i.e. Marguerite] is delighted to have it so well in advance and the three of us are looking forward to playing through it together quite soon. I have taken note of the two points you make regarding the score.

After requesting Rubbra for a programme note and the number of complimentary tickets he would require, Dolmetsch concluded: 'We look forward to getting together with you beforehand, to make sure that we perform the Fantasia as you would wish.'

The gamba part, however, came in for some revision, as can be learned from a letter from Rubbra dated 6 February: 'I have re-thought the opening bars of the gamba part & would you be so kind as to alter the part in accordance with the enclosed ms.' This particular portion of manuscript has not been found, but the third gamba part (referred to above) appears to have been written out in full (by a member of the Dolmetsch family) incorporating the amended opening bars. It also substitutes a C3 clef in the places where Rubbra had transferred from bass clef to C4 to avoid ledger lines in the higher lying sections.

Dolmetsch was probably away on a tour, as the response to the above letter is from Greta Matthews: 'Thank you for the ms of the re-thought opening bars of the gamba part – Guite loves it and is thrilled to bits to be included in a new "Rubbra-work".'

Greta's letter concluded with some suggested dates when Rubbra might be free to attend a rehearsal and, although no reply is to be found in the archive confirming any of these, we can be certain that he did, for as noted in the section on the *Passacaglia*, Rubbra rehearsed all of his new works with Dolmetsch and attended all the first performances.

From the rehearsal it seems that Dolmetsch suggested an appropriate place where a repeat could be successfully incorporated, as a letter from Rubbra dated 3 March 1978 (just six days before the first performance) notes: 'Here's the suggested join for the repeat (which was a fine idea of yours), and also on a

---

79 Marguerite Dolmetsch has confirmed to the author that this part was indeed the work of her father.

separate sheet of m.s. paper, my suggestions for the harpsichord figuration that we discussed yesterday.'

A new portion of score indicating this revision (with a separate stave for the gamba part) has been inserted into the original score. Of the separate sheet containing the harpsichord figurations there is no trace in the archive, presumably because it was passed on to Joseph Saxby. However, there is evidence of some semiquaver figuration having been added into the score in Saxby's hand.

Rubbra's programme note for the premiere is given here in full.

> This Fantasia was written in the autumn of 1977 for the 10th wedding anniversary of a former Oxford pupil of mine, Kenneth McLeish, and his wife Valerie. It is based on the chord A D E G# C# F consisting of an intriguing collection of varied intervals, and which, being tonally uncommitted, is capable of moving into a variety of keys. The piece starts slowly with a spaced build-up of the chord on the harpsichord from the bottom note (A), and when it arrives at the top note (F) the recorder uses this note as the starting-point for a very long melodic line that is always hinting at keys but never really establishing them until a definite A major is reached. Up to this point the harpsichord continues, with only occasional breaks to reinforce the basic chord. Now, however, the music develops by emphasizing certain intervals subtracted from it. First of all, the *fourth* builds up to a climax, after which a sudden dynamic change to *mp* introduces a new theme on the recorder, accompanied by persistent *thirds* in quavers and guitar-like reiterations of the first three notes of the basic chord. The music now increases in pace and force until an *allargando* brings it round to the beginning, a short Coda allowing this climax to die-down to a more ethereal use of the prevailing harmony. The music ends unexpectedly in F#, a key that is logically prepared if the F natural of the above chord is enharmonically changed to E#.
>
> The viola da gamba part is designed to add sustaining lines and colour to both of the predominating instruments.

The gamba part indeed does more than simply sustain the harpsichord left hand and, though sometimes performing this function, also doubles the recorder line at the lower octave and occasionally has entirely independent material.

The *Haslemere Herald* of 17 March 1978 carried a review of the premiere, commenting that the work 'proved a delightful, whimsical, bitter sweet piece in contrast to the classical repertoire' and showed 'how the older combination of recorder, harpsichord and gamba can come alive with modern music.' The *Daily Telegraph* of 9 March 1978 announced that this thirty-third Wigmore recital marked the forty-fifth year of the partnership between Carl Dolmetsch and Joseph Saxby and noted this as surely one of the longest associations in musical history. The paper did not, however, carry a review of the recital. Edgar Hunt noted of the piece: 'The chord ... provides the warp on which the composer weaves his patterns, a web of sound with which he mesmerizes the listener.'[80]

Unusually there is no correspondence in the archive from the time of the first

---

[80] *Recorder & Music*, June 1978, **6**, p. 54.

performance, but on 23 August 1978 Dolmetsch wrote to Rubbra enclosing a tape recording of the work:

> In consort with Joseph and Marguerite, I have just had the great pleasure of recording your Fantasia on a Chord. It brought back memories of the warmth with which it was received at the first performance last March. We gave it another performance at the AGM of the Dolmetsch Foundation in April and it was again very well received.
>
> I am sending a copy of the tape to the BBC – and here is one for your own archives.
>
> I hope your new symphony [No. 11, Op. 153] is making good progress. When you have a little spell between major works, we would still love to have a consort for three viols, for the twins to play with me.
>
> Warm greetings from all here.

The response from Rubbra, dated 13 September, is of particular interest, as hearing the work again seems to have stimulated him to make some fundamental changes to the work's rhythmic structure:

> I am very grateful to you for sending me the tape containing my new Fantasia, for, listening to it objectively, I have been able to pin-point an aspect of it that has been worrying me ever since the first performance. The material remains the same, for I am very happy about this, but I am re-shaping its rhythmic presentation. I am sure that, when you get the revised manuscript, you will feel that the increased suppleness has improved the piece enormously.
>
> The corollary of this is, of course, that I would not like further performances to take place until the revisions are complete, for I would naturally like a broadcast to be of the finished new version. I am sure you will agree. When the m.s. is ready I will send it to my publishers & ask them to send you a photo-copy.

Comparison between the original and revised versions does indeed show that many rhythmic changes were made in the reworking. The opening bars demonstrate this quite clearly, being originally cast in common time (Ex. 3.28). Because it is recast in 3/2 and halves the original note values, the first two bars of the revised version represent six bars of the original. It will also be noted that the gamba's entry was originally made in the first bar, whereas in the revised version it is delayed until bar three. Even the original tempo indication of *Andante quasi impovisatore* did not remain unchanged, although the metronomic rate remains intact.

Later in the piece the harpsichord textures were also subject to revision. The harpsichord part at bar 32 of the original version appears as indicated in Ex. 3.29. The equivalent bar 16 of the revised version and the succeeding bars have had semiquaver figuration added. Detailed study of both manuscripts reveals many subtle changes throughout.

This was Rubbra's last work for recorder, and though not specifically written for Dolmetsch, it is quite naturally linked with him through its first performance, the addition of the gamba part and the inclusion of a repeated section.

Ex. 3.28. Edmund Rubbra, *Fantasia on a Chord*, bars 1–6 of the composer's original version. By permission of Alfred Lengnick & Co. (a division of Complete Music Ltd). Published version available from William Elkin Music Services.

Ex. 3.29. Edmund Rubbra, *Fantasia on a Chord*. Harpsichord part, bar 32 of the original version.

Unlike most of Rubbra's other works with recorder, the *Fantasia* is not founded on a melody from the music of an earlier period. However, it does have a link with the *Cantata pastorals*, that work being founded on a characteristic five-note scale, this on a particular chord. In each case the works develop from a very basic musical root.

It has been observed that, by the time of the composition of this work, Rubbra was perhaps beyond the height of his compositional powers. *Fantasia on a Chord* is not as accomplished a work as the *Meditazioni* or the *Passacaglia*, but it should nevertheless not be dismissed, and performances of it will reveal the composer's skill at creating a work from the most basic and modest musical material.

Rubbra was among those composers with whom Dolmetsch had a long and musically productive friendship. The five previously composed works together with the *Fantasia on a Chord*, and also the *Notturno* for recorder quartet written for the Dolmetsch children, represent a significant body of pieces that Dolmetsch noted in a letter to the author were 'varied enough in fact to make an entire Rubbra programme.'

Lennox Berkeley: Cantata 'Una and the Lion', Op. 98

Soprano, rec, hpd, gamba

Text: Edmund Spenser, *Faerie Queen*, Canto III, verses 5–9

First performance: Wigmore Hall, London, 22 March 1979. Elizabeth Harwood, soprano; Carl Dolmetsch, rec; Marguerite Dolmetsch, gamba; Joseph Saxby, hpd.

Published: J & W Chester/Edition Wilhelm Hansen London Ltd, 1979.

If 12 years had elapsed between the composition of Rubbra's Sonatina and his *Fantasia on a Chord*, no fewer than 23 years separate the premiere of Berkeley's *Concertino* and his cantata, *Una and the Lion*, written for Dolmetsch's 1979 Wigmore Hall recital.

Unfortunately there is no correspondence in the archive relating to the work, but there is a copy of the published score (a reproduction of Berkeley's manuscript inscribed 'For Carl with love and a great many thanks – Lennox'). It is from the programme note for the first performance that we can learn a little about the form and origins of the piece:

> The text of the cantata is from Spenser's 'Faerie Queen' Canto III verses 5 to 9.
> The three instruments form mainly an accompaniment to the voice except in the Sarabande, during which the voice is silent. The vocal part is chiefly what one might call melodic recitative in which the instruments share the thematic development.

To this note is added the following: 'This work has been commissioned by Carl Dolmetsch with funds made available by the Arts Council of Great Britain.' Dolmetsch was successful in securing Arts Council funding for a number of the new works performed at the Wigmore Hall around this time. Marguerite Dolmetsch recalled a visit to London for a rehearsal in the presence of the composer.

The opening bars, with high trills for sopranino recorder and viola da gamba above harpsichord arpeggios, create an atmosphere of tension to herald the soprano's entry with the words:

> It fortuned out of the thickest wood
> A ramping lion rushed, rushed suddenly,
> Hunting full greedy after savage blood.

The music reflects the menace with harpsichord chords and viola da gamba arpeggios punctuated by fragmentary answering phrases on the recorder. However, as the lion draws closer to his prey (a virgin princess), his mood changes and in Spenser's words:

> His bloody rage assuaged with remorse,
> And with the sight amaz'd, forgot his furious force.

The music too grows calmer; the sopranino recorder is replaced by the treble instrument and in duet with the viola da gamba preludes the words:

> Instead thereof he kist her weary feet
> And lickt her lilly hands with fawning tong.

Eventually, the recitative-like vocal line and the accompaniment take on a more defined rhythmic character and in 3/4 time lead to an instrumental interlude. This takes the form of a gentle and elegant sarabande (marked *Andante* and ♩ = 54) – Berkeley at his most instrumentally subtle.

Again in a more recitative-like style, the soprano sings of the princess's wonder at the beast's change of mood in response to her 'sad estate', and then in an expressive passage in 3/4 accompanied by all three instruments the princess ponders her desertion by her champion knight. The lion takes pity on her, and in a final section in 12/8 (*Andante con moto*) the soprano sings of his faithfulness as the princess's companion:

> From her faire eyes he took commandment
> And even by her lookes conceived her intent.

In addition to an enthusiastic review in the *Daily Telegraph* of 23 March 1979 that regarded the work as an unusual one to have been requested from its composer, the *Haslemere Herald* of 30 March 1979 carried a review, both positive and informed. It noted that the cantata:

> ... is an elegiac setting of words from Spenser's 'Faerie Queen', and describes how a chaste princess, deserted by her champion knight, subdues by her virtue an angry lion who thereafter becomes her faithful companion. The refined poetry is well matched by Berkeley's transparent scoring, flowing melodies and impressionistic harmonies in which, again and again, come echoes of his French teachers.

Edgar Hunt, writing in *Recorder & Music*,[81] commented on what appeared to be

---

[81] June 1979, **6**, p. 183.

problems with the scoring: '... although there were some beautiful sounds in the calmer moments, the more energetic sections seemed frustrated, as if the composer had expected the harpsichord to give more resonant support to the ensemble.' A full harpsichord sonority is indeed essential for an instrumental balance that would however be completely destroyed by the substitution of a piano.

In *Una and the Lion*, as in many of his works, Berkeley showed himself to be a fine setter of words and a master of delicate instrumental colour.

Michael Berkeley: American Suite

tr rec (or fl), bn (or vc)

1 ♩ = 66 – 2 [Without tempo indication]. 3 Moderato (♩ = 100) – Allegro, (♩ = 118–120). 4 ♩ = 76.5 Presto (♩ = 150). 6 ♩. = 40.

First performance: Wigmore Hall, London, 28 March 1980. Carl Dolmetsch, rec; John Orford, bn.

Published: Oxford University Press, 1980.[82]

It seems entirely likely that it was Dolmetsch's long association with and recent commission from Lennox Berkeley that led to a work from Michael. There can be few occasions in any musical circumstances on which works have been commissioned in successive years from a composer and his composer son.

The only letter extant in the archive is from Michael Berkeley to Dolmetsch enclosing a copy of the *Daily Telegraph* review of the Wigmore Hall premiere. However, the programme note for the first performance is especially informative about the origins and inspiration of the piece:

> In 1977 I made my first visit to the USA and stayed with several families, many of whom had children who played the recorder. Instead of singing for my supper, I composed for it. When Carl Dolmetsch asked me for a work, I decided to weld these unaccompanied melodies into a Suite for recorder (or flute) and bassoon (or cello). Thinking of Carl Dolmetsch's reputation as a teacher as well as a player, and of my own gratitude to Bartók for his 'Mikrokosmos' I decided to try and write a work for children that would not speak down to them and that would therefore also be rewarding for accomplished players. Combining simplicity and individuality is not easy, which is why Bartók shines like a bright star over so much 'Music for Children'. However, I hope I have gone a little way in the right direction.

As with Lennox Berkeley's cantata *Una and the Lion* of the previous year, the

---

[82] There is no copy of the actual manuscript of Michael Berkeley's *American Suite* in the archive, but the published score available for hire from Oxford University Press is a reproduction of the composer's manuscript. It is inscribed '25/II/80 WALES' after the final bar.

programme also states: 'This work has been commissioned by Carl Dolmetsch with funds made available by the Arts Council of Great Britain.'

The individual movements are not given titles (neither in the score nor the recital programme) and in some cases only a metronome mark is given in preference to a tempo word marking.

The recorder alone opens the work with a brief folksong-like prelude to the more energetic main section of the first movement. Scored for both instruments, this begins in 3/8 time but soon changes to 2/4. An episode for solo bassoon follows and the movement concludes with a restatement of the 3/8 – 2/4 material. This leads seamlessly into the second movement, which begins with both instruments exchanging the pair of notes on which the previous movement ended. Eventually 4/4 crotchets on the bassoon form a repeated note accompaniment to a stepwise rising and falling melody for the recorder. Recorder and bassoon exchange roles as the movement proceeds, but it eventually dies away on a recorder bottom G# (the note on which it began), but not before a *sforzando* low G♮ interjection on the bassoon.

Lightly stepping quavers for the bassoon introduce the third movement and form the accompaniment for another folk-like melody for the recorder marked *cantabile*. A brief bassoon solo leads to a quicker section (marked *allegro*) featuring a livelier recorder melody with repeated note accompaniment for the bassoon. There are some staccato exchanges and rising arpeggio figures in double octaves before a return to the *moderato* opening material, this time with the bassoon having the *cantabile* melody, the recorder providing the quaver accompaniment. A varied reprise of the *allegro* material brings the movement to a close.

The fourth movement is a calm song-like episode before the *Presto* fifth featuring, after the bassoon's introduction, a recorder melody in 3/4 over a bassoon drone. The melody is repeated by the solo bassoon and the movement ends much as it began with staccato quavers, but on both instruments.

Perhaps because this is a work composed with children in mind, the last movement has something of the nature of a lullaby about it and moves along gently in a very slow 3/8. The recorder's opening melody is repeated by the bassoon and the entire movement is founded upon it. The ending is marked 'much slower, more deliberate' with both instruments in unison.

As previously noted, the only letter from Berkeley in the archive is that enclosing a copy of the review from the *Daily Telegraph* of 29 March 1980. About the *American Suite* it was brief but enthusiastic, noting that it contained music for children of a quality not often found at the time, and which recalled Nielsen in its outdoor freshness.

Sometimes, the exchanges of solo passages and use of the instruments in octaves make the textures sound somewhat thin, but on the other hand this may reflect the composer's striving for a simplicity that does at times provide genuine appeal. The availability of the performing material for hire only is undoubtedly a factor preventing more players from becoming acquainted with the work.

Alan Ridout: Chamber Concerto

rec, str qt

For Carl Dolmetsch

1 Espressivo. 2 Giocoso. 3 Ground. 4 Vivace.

First performance: Wigmore Hall, London, 26 March 1981. Carl Dolmetsch, rec; Amici String Quartet: Lionel Bentley, Robert Hope Simpson, Nicholas Dowding, Bernard Richards.

Unpublished.[83]

In 1956 the 21-year-old Ridout submitted the score of a chamber concerto for recorder and string quartet to Dolmetsch with a request that it be considered for performance. In the accompanying letter Ridout presented his musical credentials, noting that he had studied at the RCM with Howells and Jacob, and that he had also received lessons from Tippett. He further noted that as a student he had won a Royal Philharmonic Prize and a Patrons Fund Award for composition. The letter concludes: 'A good deal of my music has been heard in London and elsewhere including a Violin Concerto, a Concerto for Strings, an Overture and much chamber music. A published choral work was performed recently by 500 voices at a Royal Concert in St. Paul's and was later broadcast.'

Dolmetsch kept the work for some time, as he did not, as explained in a later letter to Ridout, have much opportunity at that time to work with a string quartet. Eventually, however, he did try it through with the Martin Quartet, after which it was returned, and with which Greta Matthews enclosed a letter that noted:

> Mr. Dolmetsch asked me to say that he likes the work, and suggests that you submit it to the Cheltenham Festival or perhaps to the committee for the promotion of New Music. If it should be accepted, he would be pleased to give the work its first performance if you wished.
>
> Mr. Dolmetsch says there are one or two places where the recorder goes into its lower range and might be covered by the strings. He suggests you put the recorder up an octave at these points – he mentioned low F's and G's.

Dolmetsch may appear to have been somewhat dismissive of a young composer who obviously showed considerable talent. However, as Greta Dolmetsch explained in a conversation with the author, in his continuing efforts to build a contemporary recorder repertoire Dolmetsch felt it necessary at that time to involve composers who were more firmly established.

Later, of course, Ridout *did* write a work for Dolmetsch, and *Sequence* for recorder and lute was given its first performance at the 1975 Wigmore Hall recital. Now, six years later, Dolmetsch's 1981 Wigmore Hall recital was to include a number of

---

[83] MS No. J30 in the catalogue of Ridout's works in the Ampleforth Abbey Library.

baroque concertos with recorder and strings, and there was thus an opportunity to include a new work for recorder with string quartet. Whether Dolmetsch recalled Ridout's earlier work for this scoring it is not possible to determine.

The archive contains two photocopies of the manuscript score of the new Chamber Concerto and a set of manuscript parts in another hand. After the final bar, the score that is in Ridout's hand of the 1970s and 1980s bears his characteristic calligraphic initials and the place of composition (Canterbury), but, unusually, no date. It is intriguing to wonder if any material from the 1956 Concerto had been included in the new work.

Quite by chance, soon after locating the copies of the score and parts, the author was contacted by Robert Scott, a friend of Ridout with considerable knowledge of his works. However, he had not seen a score of the 1981 Chamber Concerto and Jeanne Dolmetsch thus sent him a copy together with copies of the manuscript parts. He thought the handwriting in the parts bore some resemblance to that in a number of early works. However we agreed that this in itself was insufficient evidence to link the two concertos, and that only the discovery of a score of the earlier one (of which there seems to be no trace) would establish with certainty whether there was any shared material.[84]

There is only one letter in the archive that from its date must surely be in connection with the new concerto. It is from Ridout to Dolmetsch and is dated 9 December 1980. The opening reads: 'Enclosed is a photo[copy] of the new work which I hope you will enjoy. If it seems right to you it will easily convert, at a later date, for String Orchestra and/or for Recorder and harpsichord.' Neither of these arrangements appears ever to have been made. The reference to a 'new' work is significant in light of the above mentioned discussion regarding its possible link with the 1956 work.

The composer's programme note reads:

> I have long been an admirer of Carl Dolmetsch and his considerable pioneering work in this country and abroad of the recorder, and for the music of the 16th, 17th and 18th centuries; and I decided in the Chamber Concerto to try to make a personal portrait of him as a tribute. The four movements are in turn affectionately expressive, bright, ruminative (over a ground bass) and lively.

Ridout had only recently completed two other concerted works for recorder and strings. The Concerto for treble recorder, strings and percussion (completed on 29 September 1979) was commissioned by Southern Television and funded by South East Arts. The first rehearsals and first performance by Evelyn Nallen were filmed for a programme entitled *Music in Camera* in January 1980.

---

[84] In a conversation with the author in June 2001 Colin Hand recalled that Ridout had sought his advice during the composition of the Chamber Concerto and was of the opinion that it was an entirely original work.

For the second, Ridout was requested for a work for recorder with strings (keeping the string parts to approximately Grade 5 level in difficulty) as part of the centenary celebrations of Jersey College for Girls. *Concertante Music* was completed on 26 May 1980 and Evelyn Nallen gave the first performance in September of that year. The work is in five movements and makes use of descant, treble and sopranino recorders. The Chamber Concerto for Dolmetsch's 1981 Wigmore Hall recital thus completed a trio of recorder concertos with different scorings composed within a period of about 18 months.

The first movement is a sort of slow syncopated dance – almost a twentieth-century reinterpretation of sarabande elements (Ex. 3.30). A long recorder cantilena unfolds over sustained harmonies on muted strings, but the individual members of the quartet have moments where they too join in the melodic development.

Ex. 3.30. Alan Ridout, Chamber Concerto for recorder and string quartet. First movement, bars 1–4. Reproduced by permission of Ampleforth Abbey Trustees.

Mutes are removed, but the strings are directed to play pizzicato for most of the light, transparently scored second movement. It is full of lively musical ideas that almost tumble over one other as each follows in quick succession. There is a contrasting section in which the strings, now *arco*, have the melodic interest, while the recorder has interjectory flourishes. A return to the opening material follows, after which the movement is brought to an abrupt but effective close.

In the slow third movement (Ex. 3.31), the ground upon which it is founded appears eight times, though in true Purcellian fashion, having begun on the cello, it appears later in the first violin and viola parts. String tremolandos and dotted rhythms, again somewhat reminiscent of Purcell, are among the contrasting textures of this haunting movement, above which the recorder has a stream of expressive and decorated melody. It ends quietly and mysteriously on a recorder low A accompanied by upper string harmonics.

The finale is a rondo combining all the energy of the second movement with even more brilliant writing for the recorder in its upper register above the lightly scored quartet now playing *arco* (Ex. 3.32). The ending is similarly unmistakable reminder of that of the second movement.

Study of the recorder part and a cassette containing a recording of the first performance revealed two places in the final movement where Dolmetsch had

Ex. 3.31. Alan Ridout, Chamber Concerto for recorder and string quartet. Third movement, bars 1–7. Reproduced by permission of Ampleforth Abbey Trustees.

Ex. 3.32. Alan Ridout, Chamber Concerto for recorder and string quartet. Fourth movement, bars 1–6. Reproduced by permission of Ampleforth Abbey Trustees.

wisely and effectively raised the recorder part by an octave, providing brilliance and improving the balance with the string ensemble. He also added a flourish of semiquavers to the recorder's final descending passage.

An anonymous review in *Recorder and Music*[85] commented:

---

[85] June 1981, **7**, p. 38.

... according to the composer's note he 'tried to make a personal portrait of Carl Dolmetsch as a tribute'. We find it difficult to see a portrait in the music. It was certainly interesting to listen to, with its succession of suspensions in the first movement and unusual ground bass in the third, and with lively second and fourth movements; but time and further performances will decide its place in the repertory.

A review in the *Farnham Herald* of 3 April 1981 was much more assured of the work's merits and its place in the repertoire:

> ... this slow and expressive movement [the Ground] is full of technical interest for both the student of recorder playing and the student of orchestration, and composition, ending as it does with high harmonics on the violins. The final Vivace demonstrates that the composer has fully grasped the essentials of concerto writing for the recorder, for never once did we lose the sound of 'la flûte douce' even when accompanied by modern violins. This fine work is worthy not of another hearing, but of many: with Edmund Rubbra's 'Fantasia on a theme of Machaut' and Gordon Jacob's Suite, it must rank as one of the finest works of its genre.

Perhaps the musical portrait of Dolmetsch is not immediately apparent, but the Chamber Concerto is an effective work that manages to fill the scoring of recorder and string quartet with a wealth of colour and musical ideas.

Donald Swann: Rhapsody from Within

rec, hpd

To Carl Dolmetsch & Joseph Saxby to celebrate 50 years' partnership

Part 1: Molto movimento. Part 2: Rhapsodico. Part 3: Ritmico.

First performance: Wigmore Hall, London, 2 April 1982. Carl Dolmetsch, rec; Joseph Saxby, hpd.

Published: Hebden Bridge: Peacock Press, 2002 (PD 04).

Donald Swann's manuscript keyboard score and recorder part of *Rhapsody from Within* are held in the archive at Haslemere. The score contains the characteristic markings for articulation, registration and fingering pencilled in by Joseph Saxby and it is clearly from this that the first and earliest performances were given. There is also a photocopy of a very neatly written copyist's score which, though containing a few differences from Swann's original manuscript, was obviously derived from it and, for the most part, remains faithful to it.

The earliest letter in the archive relating to the work is dated 29 September 1981 and is from Greta Matthews to Swann:

> Dr. Dolmetsch left on Sunday for San Francisco, at the start of his current American tour. He asked me to tell you how very pleased we are that you are going to write him a

work for performance at his next Wigmore Hall recital, on Friday 2nd April 1982.
We do hope you will be able to keep that evening free.

Inside the autograph score, and presumably sent with it, is an undated letter from Swann on headed notepaper from the Queen's Hotel, Leeds. The letter (which is a little difficult to decipher in places) reads:

> Dear Mr. Dolmetsch,
>
> I eventually worked[?] out the recorder part on tour in Leeds. I hope it arrives safely. My writing is a bit of a puzzle, but it is an *indication* ... I so hope Rhapsody from Within will work out well. Looking forward to seeing you on the 18th at 3.
>
> Yours ever
>
> Donald Swann

By far the most informative document in the archive concerning the work is Swann's original programme note, which contains two paragraphs not printed in the final version in the recital programme. It is given here in full:

> Engaged on a mystical opera 'Candle Tree' about St. Boniface (inventor of the Christmas Tree), I used *all* the recorders (for an eighth century glade!) and was led to meet their 'parents', as it were, the Dolmetsch's of Haslemere. At this point Carl Dolmetsch asked for a new work for his 1982 Wigmore Hall recital and thrilled me by saying it should be inscribed 'to celebrate a half-century of collaboration between Carl Dolmetsch and Joseph Saxby'.
>
> The title 'Rhapsody from Within' occurred at once to me as I wished to draw on a lower river of the mind. Shy of the two instruments' association with another age (albeit later than the 8th century!) I appealed to the subconscious to help me respond 'out of time'.
>
> I rarely write other than for voice and piano, but had long been aware that when Carl Dolmetsch plays the recorder it is indeed like a voice, and I knew I could rely on Joseph Saxby to de-pianify any mannerisms I couldn't avoid. This he did and I thank him.
>
> And so I found, as I began on the opening movement, that the two instruments were serenading each other happily through the keys, and the work fell into place. I used the treble recorder throughout, except in the third movement when the tenor enters to contribute a lower melody.
>
> Part I (in 12/8) establishes the rhapsodic dialogue until eventually the recorder pulls up an F major scale in the penultimate bar and says 'let's rest, it's our home key'.
>
> Part 2 starts with the harpsichord playing a rubato introduction a l'española and then settles back to accompany a 'tune' on the recorder. Is it a Mediterranean, is it a Corfiote Tune? I hope it is mine. But as Samuel Butler says: 'It's a wise tune that knows its own father.'
>
> In the final movement both the instruments engage the jazz stop and alternate this, here and there, with a touch of South American cross-rhythm (the tenor recorder's contribution). The treble returns to complete the work on his top G, while the harpsichord descends through the keys in triplets to discover that he too was heading for the final G major chord.

An anonymous review in *Recorder & Music*[86] commented on the pianistic character of the keyboard part, noting that *Rhapsody from Within* was 'an interesting work, but we wondered whether the composer might not have been happier writing for the piano – he seemed to be seeking a more sustained quality than that offered by the harpsichord.'

Following the first performance Dolmetsch wrote to Swann on 17 April:

> Time has flown since our Wigmore Hall concert and it has been on my conscience that I should have written before to say how very grateful Joseph and I were to have such a beautiful work from you to celebrate our 50 years' partnership.
>
> You will have seen for yourself how warmly the audience responded to the piece and we shall look forward to opportunities of playing it on many more occasions. The next one is, in fact, on 1st May, at the AGM of the Dolmetsch Foundation, in the Museum in Haslemere. For these occasions, I always provide our members with a short concert and 'Rhapsody from Within' will be a special treat for them. If you were free that afternoon, you would be very welcome to come, though I know full well how busy you are.
>
> With warmest greetings from everyone here and my grateful thanks again.

Dolmetsch was obviously pleased with the work, even if it did require Joseph Saxby to 'de-pianify' Swann's mannerisms in the keyboard part.[87] This seems to be reflected in the instrumentation given at the head of the copyist's score, which reads: 'For Recorder or Flute and Piano (Original Performance – Harpsichord)'. When Piers Adams came to record the work on his *Shine and Shade* CD (which also included four other 'Dolmetsch' works), pianist Julian Rhodes very sensibly played the keyboard part on the piano, to which it is undeniably better suited. However, in his biographical note written for the published edition Leon Berger made the rather interesting observation: '... when the piece is played, as conceived, with a harpsichord accompaniment the *tremolandi* sections approach the sound of a cimbalom.' In the same note Leon Berger also drew attention to the wide-ranging musical references in the work that a casual listener may not at once recognize:

> There are Sullivanesque moments and also shades of Mendelssohn and Saint-Saëns. Above all, the piece is unified by a distinctive recurring motif – a direct homage to Poulenc's FLUTE SONATA; the sudden woosh of its upward flourish appearing variously in the recorder or the piano treble and bass parts, and slower elsewhere in more measured scales.

In the CD booklet Piers Adams noted:

---

[86] June 1982, 7, p.146.

[87] A cassette was later discovered at 'Jesses' containing a recording made in the studio there in April 1982 of Carl Dolmetsch and Joseph Saxby playing *Rhapsody from Within*. Even with Joseph Saxby's valiant efforts to 'de-pianify' the keyboard part, the harpsichord is quite clearly stretched to the limit.

It may come as a surprise to see the name of Donald Swann on an album of serious classical music. To most, he is immortalised as one half of the celebrated songwriting duo Flanders and Swann but it was as a 'classical' composer that he strove for recognition in the later years of his life.

Piers Adams further noted that the composition of *Rhapsody from Within* resulted in 'a charming and unashamedly tuneful work which proudly carries the flag of English eccentricity.' It is indeed a particularly idiosyncratic, but at the same time, charming work, full of fun and energy.

When I interviewed Piers Adams for *The Recorder Magazine* in 1994, shortly after the *Shine and Shade* CD had been recorded (and just three months after Swann's death),[88] he commented on Swann's striving for recognition as a serious composer adding, 'I hope this recording posthumously helps!' There is no doubt that the recording did make the work known to a wider audience.

At the time of writing publication is imminent and will bring *Rhapsody from Within* fully into the repertoire. This will enable it be enjoyed by players seeking an unusual but appealing work that, while characteristic of the composer, is somewhat removed from the witty songs for which he is more usually and affectionately remembered.

Gordon Jacob: Suite (Trifles)

tr rec, vn, vc, hpd

For Carl Dolmetsch

1 Largo. 2 Allegro. 3 Adagio molto. 4 Allegro.

First performance: Wigmore Hall, London, 24 March 1983. Carl Dolmetsch, rec; Carmel Kaine, vn; Anna Carew, vc; Andrew Pledge, hpd.

Published: 2000, Ampleforth: Emerson Edition (Edition 355).

When Ross Winters gave his talk entitled 'The Dolmetsch Legacy' to the European Recorder Teachers Association (UK) conference in May 1997, the accompanying list of Wigmore Hall premieres he had prepared from a list drawn up by Dolmetsch himself contained a number of unpublished works. Among those that looked of special interest was a suite for recorder, violin, cello and harpsichord by Gordon Jacob, first performed in 1983. The excellence of his Suite for recorder and string quartet, written for Dolmetsch in 1957, made the prospect of another work for recorder with chamber ensemble an enticing one.

In June 1998 I made my first visit to Haslemere to collect photocopies that

---

[88] 'Piers Adams in conversation with Andrew Mayes'. Leon Berger has confirmed in a note to the author that shortly before Donald Swann died he had been able to hear the Piers Adams/Julian Rhodes recording of *Rhapsody from Within* and was delighted with it.

Jeanne Dolmetsch had made to enable me to make a closer study of all the correspondence between Dolmetsch and the composers who had written works for him. It was also my first opportunity to investigate the manuscripts of twentieth-century works in the archive, but there was only sufficient time on that occasion to inspect those for recorder with keyboard.

When I read through the letters, only one from Jacob of about the date of the Suite's first performance was to be found, but it did not refer directly to the work. Dated 8 December 1982, it reads:

Dear Carl,

I hope the enclosed will do. So glad you're doing it and it was nice to have a word on the phone.

All good wishes

Gordon

However, another letter from Jacob to Dolmetsch dated 29 April 1971 intrigued me. It read:

Dear Carl,

I hope you will find a use for the enclosed.
I called the pieces 'Trifles' in the first place because they are short and unpretentious. Afterwards I added the titles in brackets as a sort of pun on the word, but you needn't use these titles if you don't want to!
Anyway they come with affectionate greetings

from Gordon

There was no indication of the instrumentation or any other information about the pieces, and I was a little puzzled as to their identity. However, during my next visit to Haslemere I was able to inspect the manuscripts of the works for recorder with strings, still hoping to locate that of the unpublished Suite. What I found made everything quite clear.

In a brown manila envelope addressed to Carl Dolmetsch, bearing a Saffron Walden postmark and marked 'Trifles' in Carl Dolmetsch's handwriting, were the manuscript score and parts of a four-movement work by Gordon Jacob scored for treble recorder, violin, cello and harpsichord. In addition to the manuscripts were photocopies of the score and violin and cello parts, and on the front of these parts, again in Dolmetsch's hand, was written: 'First performance 1983 Wigmore Hall'.

Trifles and the Suite are one and the same composition, as further indicated by the fact that the original titles on the manuscript score and recorder have been masked by pieces of paper with the title 'Suite' written on them. In the score and recorder part, the titles of the individual movements referred to by Jacob in his letter of 29 April 1971 had similarly been obscured by blank paper. In the manuscript violin and cello parts, however, these titles remained uncovered. These are in French and read as follows:

1 Le buffet
2 La trifle au vin de Jerez
3 La trifle à l'anana – très douce
4 La trifle à l'anglais

The tempo markings retained for the Suite were at the head of each movement, and pencil markings in the score and parts indicated that these had been played from.

Almost certainly the short letter of December 1982 will have been in connection with the programme note Jacob wrote for the first performance that reads:

> This work, written for and dedicated to Carl Dolmetsch, is in four movements: Largo, Allegro, Adagio molto, Allegro. It is therefore in the form of a sonata of late 17th and early 18th century origin by composers such as Vivaldi, Telemann, Tartini etc. This form has always appealed to the present composer who has used it in several other works from time to time. But no return is made to the idioms of that period. The last movement, a lively piece in 6/8 time, has a short coda marked Presto. This is one of several works written by Gordon Jacob for Carl Dolmetsch. They include a Suite for Recorder and String Orchestra, a set of Variations for Recorder and Harpsichord and a Consort for four recorders.

The national daily papers were tending not to cover Dolmetsch's Wigmore Hall recitals by this time, but a review in *Recorder & Music* noted enthusiastically:

> The new suite displays to the full the composer's characteristic sensitivity to the demands and capabilities of the instruments, which are made to blend in an entirely satisfactory whole. The performers captured every nuance of mood in this generally restrained work, from the antique melodies of the slow movements to the general ebullience of the finale, with its wry (possibly unintentional?) hint at a popular tune.[89]

Unfortunately there is no other correspondence in connection with this work, and thus two questions remain to be answered. The first is why it should have taken so long after the composition of the work for it to receive its first performance. During the 1960s a number of new works for treble recorder, violin, cello and harpsichord received their first performances at the Wigmore Hall, when Dolmetsch was joined by Alice and Eleonore Schoenfeld and Joseph Saxby. Perhaps it was with this particular ensemble in mind that Jacob wrote the work, especially as he had not been able to rescore the Variations to include violin and cello parts in the 1963 Wigmore recital as suggested by Dolmetsch (see the section on that work). Although Dolmetsch continued to give recitals with the Schoenfeld

---

[89] June 1983, **7**, p. 267. The reviewer is identified as 'S.M.G.' [Shelagh M. Godwin].

sisters during his tours of America, they did not take part in a Wigmore Hall recital after 1971. Indeed none of the new works performed in the 1970s featured a string ensemble. The 1983 programme, however, with a number of baroque solo and trio sonatas including various combinations of the treble recorder, violin, cello and harpsichord ensemble, provided an ideal opportunity to perform Jacob's work.

The second question is why Dolmetsch should have felt it necessary to drop Jacob's original title for the work and those of the individual movements. Although the overall title and the whimsical French titles seem in keeping with the character of the pieces, perhaps Dolmetsch felt they were not entirely appropriate for the Wigmore Hall. As Jacob had noted, 'you needn't use these titles if you don't want to!'[90]

During a subsequent visit to Haslemere in May 1999 Jeanne Dolmetsch kindly permitted me to make a photocopy of the manuscript score and parts. This enabled me to make a detailed study of the work, but also gave me an opportunity to arrange an informal play-through with friends; this was, at the time, the only way I would be able to hear it.[91]

The first movement, just 12 bars long, is scored without the harpsichord and forms a gentle prelude with the recorder carrying most of the melodic material in very leisurely semiquavers ($\flat$ = 66) above the strings.

Having remained silent for the first movement, the harpsichord enters first in the second, followed closely by the violin and the cello with hints of a melody, but it is the recorder, entering last, which has the theme proper. The movement continues with much rhythmic flexibility and instrumental textures enriched by alternations between pizzicato and *arco* playing for the strings.

In the trio section that follows, the cello introduces another main theme and is soon joined by the violin (playing an octave *below* the cello), the recorder entering later with a second theme linked to the first by a little triplet figure. This leads back to a reprise of the first section, the abrupt ending of which, although it has been heard already, seems to come out of nowhere.

The third movement, in a basic ABA form, is indeed 'très douce'. This is especially true of the modified reprise of A, in which the recorder has a decorated version of the opening theme, with the violin playing a counter–melody high above. The ending is particularly atmospheric, the violin's high e''' hanging magically on its own as the recorder falls silent and the cello's pizzicato notes and the harpsichord's final C major chord die away.

---

[90] Greta Dolmetsch later confirmed in a conversation with the author that this was indeed the reason for the change of title, noting: 'One does not play Trifles at the Wigmore Hall!'

[91] The author playing recorder together with Susan Marshall, violin, Brenda Buckley, cello, and Christine Stanton, harpsichord, gave what was possibly only the second performance of the work in a recital in Thornham Parish Church, Norfolk, on 29 July 2000 as part of the King's Lynn Festival Fringe.

The folk-like melody in E minor that opens and permeates the finale seemed familiar, but at first strangely unidentifiable. It is indeed an English folktune, which Christopher Burgess immediately identified as *The Keys of Canterbury* – hence presumably the movement title 'La Trifle à l'anglais'. The folktune (already hinted at in the trio section of the second movement) is introduced in lively style in all the voices. The tempo then slows to almost half that of the opening and, now in C minor and in augmentation, the tune is played on the recorder above a much varied harmonic accompaniment by the violin and cello. To this the harpsichord adds brief interjections of a fragment of the tune in diminution. An atmospheric *Adagio* leads to the whirlwind coda, reminiscent in character of the closing bars of the earlier Suite and the Variations for recorder and harpsichord.

Although the recorder part is less demanding technically than any of the others Jacob wrote for the instrument, and the piece generally does not have the substance of the earlier Suite with string quartet, it is composed with all Jacob's usual craftsmanship, and is very satisfying to play for the entire quartet.

Jeanne Dolmetsch and I felt that the piece deserved to be published, and in the knowledge that Emerson Edition had published many of Jacob's works towards the end of his life and also published York Bowen's Recorder Sonata, I contacted June Emerson to discuss the possibility of publishing *Trifles*. Her initial thoughts were that the work might have derived from or been arranged to become the *Four Fancies* for flute and string trio, but a comparison revealed no resemblance. June Emerson then contacted Jacob's widow Margaret, who thought that the work was just a 'little something' done for Dolmetsch but never published, and encouragingly agreed to its publication if Emerson Edition would be prepared to take it on. June Emerson considered this a good thing to do and thus, some 30 years after its composition, Jacob's *Trifles* finally came into print. This new edition restored the original title of the work, not least to avoid confusion with the earlier Suite, and also those of the individual movements, as they do seem to relate to the musical character.

The location of the manuscript of this work and its publication have been among the exciting developments to have come out of the research for this book.

Colin Hand: Concerto cantico, Op. 112

tr rec, str qt

To Carl Dolmetsch

First performance: Wigmore Hall, London, 23 March 1984. Carl Dolmetsch, rec; Florizel String Quartet: Lionel Bentley, Robert Hope Simpson, Martin Smith, Heather Harrison.

Unpublished: withdrawn by the composer.

Colin Hand's association with Dolmetsch went back many years before the commissioning of this work. His *Sonata breve* for treble recorder and piano was dedicated to Dolmetsch on his sixtieth birthday in 1971, and the *Divertissement*, Op. 100 for two recorders and harpsichord was written for the 1981 Dolmetsch tour of the United States. In addition, the *Sonata piccola*, Op. 63, the *Petite suite champêtre*, Op. 67, and the *Plaint* for tenor recorder and harpsichord all have Dolmetsch connections, the last two having been recorded by him.

Dolmetsch's request for a work for his 1984 Wigmore Hall recital (the fortieth) was initially made in a telephone conversation, as a letter from Hand dated 25 August 1983 confirms:

> It was a good thing (as Pooh would have said) that we had a telephone conversation last week as I had confused your 40th Wigmore with the 60th H.[aslemere] Festival which does make a difference to the time available for writing a new piece! Anyhow, having cleared that up I should be delighted to produce a new work for your Wigmore Hall recital on Friday, March 23rd, 1984.
>
> If I can just recap and confirm – you would like a short, concerto for solo recorder and string quartet with the option of performance using a larger group of strings with double bass, and lasting between 12 and 15 minutes.
>
> I shall begin work on the concerto in mid-September when we return from our holiday, and I will let you have a score in early January if that arrangement is acceptable to you. I will also let you have the official title of the piece by the beginning of November in time for your publicity campaign.

On 20 September 1983 Dolmetsch acknowledged receipt of and thanked Hand for his letter:

> Anticipating that you and Margaret are newly home from your holiday – and literally on the eve of my own departure to Colombia with my son – I send you a word of thanks for your letter encapsulating terms of reference (as Pooh would not have said) for the new work you have agreed to write for my 40th Wigmore recital.
>
> An approach has been made to the Arts Council of Great Britain, who will no doubt let me know the results of their deliberations in due course which we in turn will pass on to you. Fingers crossed everyone.

Dolmetsch had received Arts Council funding for the commissions for the 1979, 1980 and 1981 recitals and was obviously hopeful that such funding would again be available, but, as will be discussed later, this was not to be forthcoming.

By October 1983 Hand was at work on the new concerto and wrote to Dolmetsch, as he had previously promised, to inform him of the details:

> According to my records you will soon be needing to know the official title of your new work for the Wigmore Hall recital. After throwing out the material for the first attempt, on Margaret's advice – 'it's too spiky and it's certainly *not Carl*' – I have turned to a theme that has been in my sketch books for some time and which I think has plenty of potential, and your new work (which, to date, satisfies Margaret!) is now well under way. Its title is CONCERTO CANTICO for Treble Recorder and Strings. As the

adjective implies, I am emphasising the singing quality of the recorder – an extension of the human voice – and there are references to your own ornithological interests in quasi-birdsong passages. In short, I intend that it should be a happy piece for a happy occasion. After all, 40 Wigmores with an annual newly commissioned work is no mean achievement.

Although Hand had promised the score of the new work for early January he was able to write to Dolmetsch on 30 November 1983: 'Here's the new Concerto prematurely delivered a month before the agreed date.' The letter later comments on the style of the work:

> I hope the piece is not too jolly! The trouble with employing eclectic composers is that the end product can assume almost any form or style, but I think that, knowing you, I need make no apologies for what is in effect a piece of light music – quite unsophisticated. After all there's plenty of grimness in much of today's music – and elsewhere for that matter.
>
> I have just one humble little request: *please* don't be tempted to play the last section on a sopranino. Apart from the fact that I abhor the instrument, it would leave such a big gap between solo and strings with a resultant balloon, i.e. a hollow middle to the music.

Dolmetsch was no doubt pleased to have the concerto earlier than expected but on 29 December 1983 wrote to Hand with disappointing news about the application for Arts Council funding: 'This sad little note reached me earlier this month, but as I didn't want to cast a shadow over your Christmas merry-making, I have held it back until now.' Dolmetsch expressed his inability to understand the ways of the Arts Council in terms that will be familiar to anyone who has had an application of this kind rejected. Significantly he also noted that the 1983 Wigmore Hall recital had made a loss. The letter continued:

> But I don't want you to be a casualty in this and I think it would be fairer to you if I were to ask you to make me a proposition, remembering that I am delighted with the Concerto and wish to play it. Having 'put you in the picture' as it were, I am sure we can arrive at some mutually acceptable arrangement in this. When you have had a little think about it, will you let me have your suggestions?
>
> Our love to you both, and we wish you and Margaret the best of Good Fortune in 1984.

Hand was quick to respond, and wrote to Dolmetsch on 2 January 1984, thanking him for the Arts Council communication, and noting that he was not entirely surprised by their rejection of the application. Hand's views on the reasons were a little more phlegmatic than Dolmetsch's, and the letter continued:

> ... I would also add that, had I known the outcome of your application to the Arts C., I would still have wanted to accept your commission – and certainly for the *40th* Wigmore – and I am pleased that the work was safely delivered before I learnt of their reply.
>
> I assure you, I do not feel a casualty of the exercise, and after twenty or so years

during which you have been very generous in promoting my music, I am so pleased that you like my latest offering. However, I *will* make a proposition as you suggest because I know you will feel happier if I were to do so. It's in two bits.

1. My present publishers are not at the moment enthusiastic about taking on a work of the nature of Concerto Cantico involving a set of string parts and a piano reduction of them which I plan to do, so I intend to publish it myself in Lindis Edition after you have launched it. I am now preparing the parts, and in order to cater for suitable page turns and ample cues, and avoid note crowding I have had to have some large-sheet manuscript paper printed by a Maidstone firm that will ultimately print the published copies for me.

Would it be fair to ask if C.D. [Carl Dolmetsch] Concerts would like to stand the cost of preparing the first set (available in time for Wigmore rehearsals) for your own use and for your library? The special order would run to about £5 for Ms. and £10 for printing.

2. The other bit of my proposition is to ask if I could be sent a programme (or Photocopy) whenever you perform the work in public so that I can use it for a PRS [Performing Rights Society] return that I make every six months. Many proprietors of concert halls fail to send in complete PRS returns and so many composers are notifying the Society themselves. However, a new ruling (from Summer 1983) states that programmes or other documentary evidence is now required in addition to chapter and verse relating to performances. I'm afraid it's a bit of a fag, but it is the only means whereby a composer can claim his dues.

Love to all at Jesses from Margaret and self and every good wish for 1984 including the Ruby Wigmore and the Diamond Festival.

With understandable gratitude, Dolmetsch wrote to Hand on 18 January:

I was so very pleased to have your kind and understanding letter and to know that, while we share the disappointment of being turned down by the Arts Council, it makes no difference so far as 'the object of the exercise' is concerned.

Your proposition in answer to my suggestion strikes me as both very generous and reasonable and I agree without reservation to both bits, 1 and 2. I would only add bit 3 of my own, which is that you must let me be responsible for your and Margaret's fares to and from London 'on the day'. It is absolutely mandatory that you both be there and won't hear of anything to the contrary. In due course, let me know the amounts involved for bits 1 and 3 and I will send a cheque to cover post haste.

On 2 February 1984 Hand wrote to Dolmetsch enclosing a copy of the recorder part and noting that the string parts would follow soon. He also noted some amendments to the recorder part including the addition of a 'flourish' that he felt to be required before the recapitulation. The letter concludes by assuring: 'there will be no further alterations prior to the 23rd!'

Hand duly sent the parts, which, in a letter confirming their arrival, Greta Matthews reported: '... the boss man says they are *beautiful* to play from.' The same letter also confirmed details of two performances of Hand's *Divertissement* in America in 1981, presumably in order that these could be sent to the Performing Rights Society.

For the first performance Hand wrote the following programme note:

Concerto Cantico is a concerto da camera for Treble Recorder and String Quartet or small String Orchestra with optional double bass. It is in two movements, the second having a slow introduction with a cadenza. As the title implies, the music emphasises the singing quality of the recorder, and, for that matter, the strings also, and there are several passages throughout the work that draw upon the character of birdsong, a subject close to the heart of the dedicatee. The concerto is built upon the monothematic principle and in particular upon a five-note tail-piece to the main theme of the first movement. This five-note group used in inversion and augmentation provides the contrapuntal introduction to the piece before appearing as an ending to the first theme. The same five notes in combination provide the harmony for the slow introduction to the second movement and the main tune of this finale is another version, this time in jig rhythm, of the same melodic germ.

The work was conceived with the *treble* recorder in mind, and it is the composer's expressed wish that it be used as the solo instrument throughout.

Following the first performance Hand wrote to Dolmetsch:

This is just to say an official big thank you for a most enjoyable recital last Friday and for giving 'Cantico' such a good send-off. I thought the strings supported you admirably and the overall balance was most successful. I think perhaps a string quartet is the ideal number of 'ripieno' members for any treble recorder concerto, and speaking for my own work, I feel that a small string orchestra plus double bass might make life a bit hard for the soloist to break through. Anyhow, I shall be making a keyboard arrangement in due course so as to make Cantico available to a wider public, but I think it will have to be for piano (with its sustaining pedal) rather than for the plucked sound of the harpsichord. I will let you have a copy when it is done. I do not know if my publishers would be interested in taking it – there are a lot of economic cuts in those directions these days – but if not, I shall produce it under the Lindis title. By the by, is it going into the Festival this year – I see the Florizel are playing – or have you any plans for any further performances? Do let me know if so.

Dolmetsch replied four days later:

Your splendid letter gave me much pleasure and my reply has been delayed only because I wanted to send you the crit. from our local Herald. Have you seen any others I wonder? Should there be yet more, I will send copies as they appear.

Yes, Friday went off very well indeed for all concerned and I was so pleased that we had a capacity audience for the launching of 'Cantico'. Although there are no immediate plans for a further performance, it will certainly go into the C.D. touring repertoire. You may be right about small forces being best for the treble, though I have coped with quite large chamber orchestras 'in and among', as Rachel says. In practice, two violins don't make twice the noise of one!

The review in the *Farnham Herald* of 30 March 1984 mentioned in Dolmetsch's letter gave an enthusiastic appraisal of the work:

... the name 'recorder' was derived from the verb 'to record' – to sing like a bird. The genial Dr. Hand allows his music to do just this. Concerto Cantico is a beautifully constructed work, rhythmically and harmonically a work which shows a sympathetic understanding of the timbre and homogenous blend of treble recorder and strings.

Hand did not, however, agree with this critic's assessment of the work, which he felt had been written too quickly, and despite Dolmetsch's welcome for the *Concerto cantico* and the impression it had made on the audience, elements remained with which the composer was not satisfied. Eventually he withdrew the work, and although copies of the score and parts remain, he would not wish any attempt to be made to resurrect it.

Colin Hand is a composer who understands well the ways of the recorder and writes for it consistently and idiomatically, but he is also perhaps his own sternest critic, and will not permit what he perceives as a work containing weaknesses in material and structure to remain in the repertoire. However, he is also wise enough not to discard themes and ideas that have potential, and the main melodic material of *Concerto cantico*, which he considers do encapsulate his musical personality, may one day find their way into a new work probably in concertante form.[92] If such a work does eventually come from his pen, it is likely to receive a warm welcome from the recorder world.

Michael Short: Sinfonia

tr rec, hpd, str qt

To Carl Dolmetsch

1 Introduction (Moderato). 2 Andante. 3 Finale (Allegretto).

First performance: Wigmore Hall, London, 3 April 1985. Carl Dolmetsch, rec; Bernard Partridge, vn; Antonina Bialas, vn; David Lloyd, va; John Stilwell, vc; Joseph Saxby, hpd.

Unpublished.

As with his commissioning of Colin Hand for a new work for the 1984 Wigmore Hall recital, Dolmetsch turned the following year to another musician whom he had known and worked with over a number of years. Michael Short had been the composer in residence at the Dolmetsch Summer School for ten years by this time (he was to perform this duty for a total of 19 years) and had written a sonatina for treble recorder and piano for Dolmetsch and Saxby in 1979.

Short wrote on 21 September 1984 to thank Dolmetsch for the invitation evidently made in a telephone call:

What a wonderful surprise and honour to be asked to write a piece for your next

---

[92] This information was contained in notes enclosed with a letter dated 25 June 2001 from Colin Hand to the author.

Wigmore Hall concert! I only hope that I will be able to produce something worthy of the occasion and of such fine performers.

I think February would be a good target date, and I will do my best to have the piece completed by then, to give you enough time to prepare it for the concert.

Short noted that owing to a reorganization at the college where he taught he was about to be relieved of much of his administrative responsibilities to concentrate on teaching composition, and this would provide the time required for composing the new piece. The letter concluded:

> The combination of string quartet, harpsichord and recorder is a very attractive one, and I hope that I will be able to do justice to your commission. I will keep you informed as to progress (and may have to ask one or two technical questions!).
>
> Meanwhile, all best wishes, and thank you once again for your kindness in thinking of me.

Dolmetsch replied in a letter dated 28 September 1984, unusually and uniquely, suggesting a title for the new work:

> Very many thanks for your letter, and we are all delighted to hear that you like the idea of writing a work for my next Wigmore Hall recital, on 3rd April 1985. How very fortunate that the re-organisation of your college work coincided with my telephone call.
>
> Unless you prefer a more exotic title, I rather like the sound of 'sinfonia' which I think will give you considerable freedom of form. If it is to be in separate movements, like the sinfonias of Alessandro Scarlatti, you might like to think in terms of a lively finale which could be played on its own in a recorder and harpsichord reduction on those occasions when one doesn't have a string quartet about one.
>
> Having enjoyed your Sonata so much, also the work you wrote for the Scottish Baroque,[93] I shall look forward with great interest to the new piece.

On 12 February 1985 Short wrote to Dolmetsch enclosing the new piece:

> Herewith the new Sinfonia, as promised.
>
> I don't know whether it is the kind of thing you were hoping for, but it has turned out different from what I was expecting. I had intended to do something rather radical and experimental, but in the event the piece turned out to be simply a lightweight entertainment piece – perhaps 'Divertimento' would be a better title than 'Sinfonia'.
>
> Anyway, it is now yours for what it is worth, and I look forward to hearing you play it.

The letter concluded by noting that it would be necessary to have the harpsichord tuned to equal temperament due to a number of enharmonic changes.

Short's programme note for the Wigmore Hall premiere reads as follows:

---

[93] The piece referred to is Michael Short's *Concert Music* for string orchestra, commissioned by the Dolmetsch Organisation for performance in Chichester Cathedral.

This piece was written at the request of Carl Dolmetsch and was composed in January 1985. It is in three short movements, in which the basic material is looked at in slightly different ways. A slow introduction leads to a vigorous first movement in which rhythmical motifs are juxtaposed with lyrical phrases. The slow movement leads without a break into the finale, which seems at first to be a rondo, but in fact leads back into the opening mood of the slow introduction.

The beginning of the slow introduction is indicated in Ex. 3.33 and the *vivace* section into which it leads in Ex. 3.34.

Ex. 3.33. Michael Short, *Sinfonia* for treble recorder, harpsichord and string quartet. First movement, bars 1–8. Reproduced by permission of the composer.

Ex. 3.34. Michael Short, *Sinfonia* for treble recorder, harpsichord and string quartet. First movement, bars 21–29. Reproduced by permission of the composer.

Ex. 3.34. continued

There is no further correspondence until after the first performance when Dolmetsch wrote to Short on 22 April:

> Belatedly, I am writing to thank you again for the splendid Sinfonia you wrote four our 41st Wigmore Hall recital. It captivated the players as well as the audience; its message was immediate and they absolutely lapped it up, as you must have realised from their enthusiastic response. I had, in fact, intended to send you the first review which should have appeared in our local press, but wouldn't you know it got held over because that particular reporter was on holiday and it remains on her desk! However, I will send it on to you in due course, together with reviews as they arrive.

Dolmetsch expressed his wish to perform the work again outside London, but noted the expense of putting such a work on, and offered to defray the expenses Short had himself incurred in connection with travel to rehearsals and the performance. Dolmetsch concluded: 'Thank you again Michael for another excellent contribution to the recorder repertoire, which really ought to be published and made available to as wide a public as possible.'

The review of the concert in *The Recorder and Music Magazine*[94] did no more than mention that the work received its first performance. More detailed was that in the *The Herald* (Haslemere), referred to above, which appeared on 3 May 1985:

> After the interval came a modern Sinfonia (first performance) by Michael Short. I found this very intriguing. Quite different of course from the classical pieces we had heard, the strings formed not so much a harmony or counterpoint as a shifting texture, a weaving of sounds into a coloured web as a background to a silvery thread of melody from the treble recorder which changed, twisted, intertwined, rose and fell against a darker cloud of string tones and harpsichord in a most striking and beautiful way, concluding by a return to the initial melodic theme. It was given no key title, as this would not have been appropriate.

---

[94] June 1985, **8**, p. 182.

Short's reply of 11 May, though acknowledging the apparent enthusiastic reception of the piece, again expressed misgivings, as noted when he first sent the score:

> Thank you very much for your letter of 22 April, and please excuse the delay in replying: we have been away on holiday, and then I have had a busy time at the beginning of the summer term at college.
>
> I very much appreciate your kind words about my piece, and I am glad that the audience seemed to like it as well. The performance was of course excellent – all that a composer could want – and it was a pleasure to work with a soloist and ensemble who were prepared to put in so much work to make the piece a success.
>
> Having said that ...(!), I have to tell you that I am dissatisfied with the Sinfonia – it turned out to be quite different from what I had originally planned. I think I had in mind something much more radical and hard-edged, but somehow in the writing this notion got transmuted into something that sounded more like Ravel dished up for recorder than anything else. Mind you, I think it must have been the first time Ravel has ever been played on a recorder!
>
> The problem is that in my compositions I am always trying to find a kind of music which is just right: perhaps this is a hopeless task and such music doesn't really exist, but sometimes I feel as if I have come near to it, although this didn't seem to happen in the case of the Sinfonia. However, I think it was quite successful as a 'one-off' piece and seemed to give the audience some pleasure (I have received a couple of congratulatory letters), so it can't be all bad.

These are sentiments that must be familiar to many composers, but are particularly so to Short who is a prodigious reviser of his own works.

Dolmetsch's reply of 23 May was understanding and encouraging:

> Speaking as one perfectionist to another(!) I think most creative workers take pleasure in their achievements while at the same time are convinced they could do better next time. Clearly, the Sinfonia got through to the audience much more readily on first hearing than it might have done if it had been more radical and hard-edged. Philip Evry was still enthusing when I saw him at Brentwood a week or so ago.

Michael Short contributed a tribute for *The Recorder Magazine*[95] following Dolmetsch's death, and during my contact with him in connection with this I asked him about the *Sinfonia*. He confirmed that he still had the score (a photocopy is also in the Dolmetsch archive), and that it remained his intention one day perhaps to revise it. Short further commented that his publisher had not been very interest in producing a work of this kind. (This brings to mind Colin Hand's similar comments in connection with his *Concerto cantico*.)

An inspection of the score reveals that publication (with or without any revisions the composer felt it necessary to make) would provide a welcome addition to the very small repertoire for this particular scoring.

---

[95] December 1997, **17**, p. 132.

Arnold Cooke: Divertimento

des and tr recs, vn, vc, hpd

To Carl Dolmetsch

1 Allegro moderato. 2 Allegro. 3 Andante. 4 Allegro vivace.

First public performance: Wigmore Hall, London, 3 April 1986. Carl Dolmetsch, des rec; Jeanne Dolmetsch, tr rec; Bernard Partridge, vn; John Stilwell, vc; Joseph Saxby, hpd.

Unpublished.

As with Gordon Jacob's Suite (*Trifles*) for recorder, violin, cello and harpsichord, 12 years separate the composition of Arnold Cooke's Divertimento and its first performance. Cooke sent a copy of the work to Dolmetsch with a letter dated 8 November 1974:

> I am sending you a copy of the score with parts of a chamber work I have recently written. This exists in two versions, one for Flute, Oboe, Violin, cello and Piano, and the other for Descant Recorder, Treble [Recorder], Violin, cello and harpsichord. The differences between the two versions only amount to slight variations in the scoring. I thought the second version would be something you might be able to play sometime with Joseph and your friends the Schoenfeld sisters, whose splendid performances with you I remember so well at the Wigmore Hall.

This mechanically reproduced copy of the score remains in the Dolmetsch archive, together with manuscript parts in Cooke's hand. The score contains Joseph Saxby's characteristic markings for registration and fingering.

Unfortunately, as noted in the section on the above-mentioned Gordon Jacob Suite, the Schoenfeld sisters did not take part in any of the Wigmore recitals after 1971, and this is almost certainly why the work had to wait a number of years before receiving its first public performance at the Wigmore Hall. From later correspondence, however, it is evident that the work did receive a private performance at a Dolmetsch Foundation meeting.

The next mention of the work is in a letter from Cooke to Dolmetsch dated 21 May 1976 in which he noted that he had sent a copy of the score to Robert Simpson at the BBC with the suggestion it be broadcast by the Dolmetsch Ensemble.

On 25 September 1985, Dolmetsch wrote to Cooke to enquire about the Divertimento:

> In November 1974 you very kindly sent me the score and parts of a Divertimento set for descant and treble recorders, violin, cello and harpsichord. According to your letter, this was a slightly adapted version of a work for flute, oboe, violin, cello and piano. We performed the Divertimento at a Dolmetsch Foundation Meeting to which I believe you came.
> Am I right in believing that our version has not yet received a public performance? If

that is so, we would like to give it a première at my 42nd Wigmore recital on 3rd April 1986.

For ease in identification, here is the opening of the first movement.

I shall look forward to hearing whether we can call ours a 'first performance'.

Cooke replied on 27 September:

Thank you very much for your letter of the 25th about my Divertimento for Descant & Treble Recorders, Vln, Vc & harpsichord. I remember that you performed it at a Dolmetsch Foundation Meeting.

Yes, I am sure you are right that the work in this version has not yet received a public performance, and I am delighted that you wish to give it a première at your 42nd Wigmore Hall recital on 3rd April 1986.

It so happens that this version is at present being published by Anglo-American Music Publishers of 4 Kendall Avenue, South Croydon, Surrey. It has not yet been issued, but I hope perhaps it will be by next spring.

On 31 December 1985 Cooke sent Dolmetsch a programme note for the work and once again mentioned its imminent publication, which he hoped would 'be in print and available by the time of your concert.' Despite the hopes expressed in this and his earlier letter, the work did not appear in print by the time of the concert, or indeed, as far as I have been able to establish, at all.

Cooke's programme note is very detailed and is given here in full:

This work exists in two versions. The first original one is for Flute, Oboe, Violin, 'cello and piano. This second one is dedicated to Carl Dolmetsch. The work is one of the few by the composer based on twelve-tone serial techniques.

> I. Allegro Moderato. The first movement begins with a repeating accompaniment figure on the harpsichord, introducing a melody for the Treble Recorder. This is then repeated in a setting for the full ensemble. A second subject of a staccato, rather spiky nature follows. Later, another theme with wide leaps is introduced by the treble recorder. After some development, based mainly on the first subject, the first part of the movement is recapitulated, and it ends with a quiet coda in slightly slower tempo.
> II. Allegro. The second movement is a type of scherzo with a steady pulse in 3/4 time. The first section is constructed mainly in short repeated figures. A second section has more sustained melodic phrases. The third section is a varied recapitulation of the first. There is no Trio or contrasting part.
> III. Andante. This opens with an extended melody on the Treble Recorder with smooth accompaniment figures on the Violin and Harpsichord. Further melodic phrases follow with more activity in the accompaniments. Then the first subject is repeated on the Descant recorder, accompanied by Violin, 'cello and Harpsichord. The final section has the opening melodic phrases played in canon at the fifth by the Recorders.
> IV. Allegro Vivace. A lively staccato figure, played by the ensemble in octaves, introduces the subject matter of the last movement. More melodic phrases follow, with chords and accompaniments on the Harpsichord. A second subject

appears based on arpeggio figures. Yet another with repeating triplet phrases is heard on the Recorders, with a swaying, legato, chordal accompaniment on the Harpsichord. There follows some development, eventually leading to the recapitulation of the first part of the movement. This is then completed by a final section in rather quicker tempo.

Though detailed, Cooke's note does not give a full impression of the complexity of the work. Rather than basing it on a single tone row, Cooke introduces several, sometimes combining two simultaneously. The rows are used very freely and are frequently reversed, inverted and transposed.

In addition to the manuscript score and parts in the archive, there is another treble recorder part in Jeanne Dolmetsch's hand in which three of the tone rows used in the first movement have been written in pencil (Ex. 3.35) and their appearances in various forms identified.

Ex. 3.35. Arnold Cooke, Divertimento for descant and treble recorders, violin, cello and harpsichord. Three of the tone rows noted by Jeanne Dolmetsch in her MS recorder part.

Row A opens the work, where it is played by the treble recorder. It is stated twice, the second time with rhythmic variation, after which it appears a third time but in its reverse form. When the full ensemble enters at bar 19, row A is used in both its original and a transposed form simultaneously (Ex. 3.36).

Row B as indicated in Ex. 3.35 is as it first appears in the treble recorder part, but its entry seven bars earlier on the violin is a minor third lower. It also appears in inversion on the descant recorder four bars after the violin's entry.

Row C is first heard on the treble recorder but in combination with row A on the descant recorder (Ex. 3.37).

In the second movement, row A makes its first appearance at bar 10 on the descant recorder, though in a somewhat varied and extended form. It appears again in the treble recorder part four bars later, and typically of the freedom with which the rows are used, the notes C and A are reversed.

The 'extended melody' with which the third movement opens is actually a variant of a fourth row that appears in the cello part at bar 60 in the first movement,

Ex. 3.36. Arnold Cooke, Divertimento for descant and treble recorders, violin, cello and harpsichord. First movement, bars 19–22 of the score. Reproduced by permission of Julia Earnshaw.

Ex. 3.37. Arnold Cooke, Divertimento for descant and treble recorders, violin, cello and harpsichord. First movement, descant and treble recorder parts, bars 68–70. Reproduced by permission of Julia Earnshaw.

where it is combined with row A on the violin. Row A's appearance in the third movement is somewhat disguised but can be detected in the 'smooth accompaniment figures' on the violin at bar 9 (Ex. 3.38).

The treble recorder's melody at this point begins with a phrase somewhat perversely made up of 11 notes of the chromatic scale, with C omitted. However, it continues with a reversal of the row with which the movement opened.

The fourth movement is rondo-like, with its initial unison theme forming yet another tone row (Ex. 3.39).

After the opening statement the treble recorder enters with a further variant of row A. What Cooke refers to as a 'second subject ... based on arpeggio figures' is actually another row. Row A continues to appear in various forms throughout the movement, at one point with some of its notes enharmonically altered.

Even this further elaboration of Cooke's programme note gives only a hint of the tour de force this work presents in the manipulation of the rows in combination with related material.

Ex. 3.38. Arnold Cooke, Divertimento for descant and treble recorders, violin, cello and harpsichord. Third movement, violin part, bars 9–12. Reproduced by permission of Julia Earnshaw.

Ex. 3.39. Arnold Cooke, Divertimento for descant and treble recorders, violin, cello and harpsichord. Fourth movement, bars 1–4 of the score. Reproduced by permission of Julia Earnshaw.

In letters dating from the end of March, arrangements were made for Cooke to attend the final rehearsal at the Wigmore Hall on the afternoon of the recital, Dolmetsch noting: '... your advice and recommendations would be both welcome and very helpful.'

Following the performance itself Cooke wrote to Dolmetsch on 5 April:

> I would like to thank you and your colleagues most warmly for the splendid first performance of my Divertimento which you gave on Thursday at the Wigmore Hall. I thought the character of the work was beautifully brought out by the lively and well-balanced playing of the recorders, the violin and 'cello, backed up by the excellent harpsichord of Joseph Saxby. I am proud to have written this work for your ensemble and to have dedicated it to you.

The review in *The Recorder and Music Magazine*[96] noted that the work 'was the composer's arrangement of a work originally conceived for other instruments – a

---

[96] June 1986, **8**, p. 299.

fact which might explain some problems with balance, the treble recorder, for instance, sometimes struggling to be heard in a part presumably originally written for oboe.' The review does not comment on the work's structure which, in adopting serial techniques, moves away somewhat from the world of Hindemith so often encountered in Cooke's works with recorder. Though arranged from another work, it bears the authority of the composer himself.

It is of interest to have another work by Cooke based on 12-tone techniques, as the *Serial Theme and Variations* for solo recorder was previously considered to be his only work to use serial procedures.

For there to be a complete edition of all Cooke's works with recorder, the Divertimento requires to be published, but it is not just for the sake of completeness, as it is a work of considerable invention that shows another and less familiar side of Cooke's musical language.

Lionel Salter: Air and Dance

tr rec, pn

To Carl Dolmetsch after 25 years!

[1] Air. Andante piangevole. [2] Dance. Allegro moderato ma giocoso.

First performance: Wigmore Hall, London, 27 March 1987. Carl Dolmetsch, rec; Lionel Salter, pn.

Unpublished in recorder version. Published as *Air and Scherzino* for ob/sax and pn, Ricordi.

There are no letters in connection with this work in the archive, but it does contain the manuscript score and a separate manuscript recorder part, possibly in Dolmetsch's hand. The score is inscribed 'To Carl Dolmetsch after 25 years!' The significance of this is noted in the composer's programme note:

> These two movements, which are thematically linked, were written for Carl Dolmetsch, as a token of my esteem and affection, after I had appeared as a soloist at his Haslemere Festival for 25 consecutive years. In 43 years' concert giving in the Wigmore Hall, Carl Dolmetsch has premièred 50 works specially written for him, thereby endowing his instrument with a substantial future to complement its honourable past.

Lionel Salter played a prominent part in the Haslemere Festivals, appearing as conductor, accompanist, continuo player and soloist on harpsichord, fortepiano and piano, often in the same event, in addition to supplying numerous programme notes. His diaries reveal that he performed 78 solo works in the festivals between 1961 and 1989.[97]

---

[97] Information provided by Lionel Salter's son Graham in a note to the author, March 2002.

The three-note rising phrase D–E–F with which the recorder and then the piano open the Air is the musical idea on which the entire piece is constructed. Ex. 3.40 indicates different forms of the motive as it appears in bars 3 and 7 of the recorder part.

Ex. 3.40. Lionel Salter, Air and Dance for treble recorder and piano. Air, bars 3 and 7, showing rhythmic variants of the D–E–F motif.

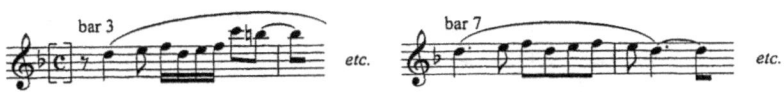

While the Air is in D minor, the Dance is in D major and begins *attacca* with a short piano introduction, the right-hand melody of which, and indeed the descending bass, are immediately recognisable as a variant of the opening of the Air. A syncopated and leaping figure introduced at bar 9 in the recorder part is a new idea that is to return on a number of further occasions.

One sharp is dropped from the key signature for a trio section marked *scherzando*. Like the first part of the movement, this has an occasional strategically placed bar in 5/8, but with a quite different rhythmic effect. The trio ends with four bars in 3/8 that lead back into the dance and eventually to a coda that begins with the syncopated figure noted earlier. In the coda the rising three-note figure in both its minor and major forms is prominent in the recorder part. It is also to be heard in the piano accompaniment (reminiscent of that at the end of the Air) to the recorder's top D, on which the Dance closes, coming to rest, as does the Air, on a D major chord.

A review of the first performance was published in *The Recorder and Music Magazine*:[98]

> The two movements of the work are thematically linked. The *Air* has a lyrical, mournful opening, with the recorder and piano parts interweaving and answering one another. The movement was reminiscent of Frank Bridge's piano music. The lower register of the treble is skilfully exploited and the movement ends with a short cadenza. The *Dance* is constructed in a traditional manner, with the first part returning after a middle section in which Lionel Salter employs syncopated patterns. Piano and recorder were well balanced throughout the work and it will make a useful addition to the recorder repertoire, particularly for those looking for alternative pieces for examination syllabuses.

Of course 'useful' additions to the repertoire can indeed also serve as examination pieces and in this way boost acceptance of a work (and sales), but a solely pedagogic purpose should not be the implication.

---

[98] June 1987, **9**, p. 36.

Salter certainly did not set out to break new ground stylistically or harmonically, but the Air and Dance has an unassuming charm, and the use of a melodic fragment as the basis for both movements gives the work a satisfying and tightly knit unity.

Jean Françaix: Quintette

rec (or fl), 2 vn, vc, hpd

Dédié à Carl Dolmetsch

1 Largo. 2 Allegro. 3 Sarabande. 4 Scherzo. 5 Rondo (Prestissimo).

First performance: Wigmore Hall, London, 12 April 1988. Carl Dolmetsch, rec; Bernard Partridge, vn; Antonia Bialas, vn; Zoe Martlew, vc; Andrew Pledge, hpd.

Score published: Paris: Schott SARL, 1990 (ED 7644). Parts also available.

The earliest letter in connection with this work in the archive is neither from Dolmetsch nor Françaix, but from a recorder player from Vincennes in France, Cécile Michels, whom Dolmetsch had met at the Golden Jubilee Festival of the Society of Recorder Players in Newcross on 4 April 1987. Dolmetsch had clearly asked for the address of Jean Françaix, and in her letter dated 20 April Cécile Michels was able to provide this, having obtained it from Charles Limcuse, for whom, she noted, Jean Françaix had written two compositions for recorder and guitar. Cécile concluded her letter: 'I sincerely hope you can convince Mr. J. Françaix to write other compositions for recorder!'

With his letter of thanks to Cécile Michels, Dolmetsch enclosed a copy of that which he had written to Françaix. It is dated 2 September 1987 and contains so much interesting information that it is quoted here in full:

Dear Monsieur,

By way of introducing myself, I wonder whether you remember meeting my father, Arnold Dolmetsch, during the early 1930s? In his later years, he made a pilgrimage to France to see once again the friends of his youth. Your father-in-law had attended the Lycée in Le Mans at the same time as Arnold Dolmetsch, and later played the 'cello in a trio in which my father was the violinist.

My father remembered meeting you at Monsieur Provost's house, when he was greatly impressed by your ability to improvise on the piano in the style of very early Welsh Bardic harp music, which he had recently transcribed from the original manuscript. My father told me also that you were shortly going to Berlin to conduct one or your compositions there at the beginning of your successful career.

During the late 1930s when many leading composers were writing for us, it occurred to me that you might be persuaded to write a work for the recorder (flûte-à-bec). Unhappily, World War II intervened and I lost touch. Most of the composers who have written for me have been British – Lennox Berkeley, Herbert Murrill, Edmund Rubbra, Cyril Scott, Gordon Jacob, Antony Hopkins, Joseph Horovitz, Francis Chagrin, Arnold Cooke and many more – but the list includes also some from France, notably Georges Migot and Gaston Saux.

My first recorder recital in London's Wigmore Hall was in 1939, and annually since 1946 I have given the first performance of a contemporary work specially written for the occasion. My 44th recital in the Wigmore Hall will be given on 12th April 1988 and it would be a great honour to introduce a work composed by you if you are able to consider writing for me. I shall be supported by two violins, 'cello and harpsichord, and a work for solo flûte-à-bec in combination with all, or any of these instruments would be ideal, in duration 7–10 minutes. My programme on 12th April will include works by Bach, Vivaldi, Marais, Salieri, Pleyel and Albinoni.

Although my father was borne in Le Mans and I in Fontenay-sous-Bois, I have lived in England since the age of three years; though I speak and read French with ease, I express myself better on paper in English. I hope you will excuse my writing in this language and that you will reply in French if you prefer to do so. The next time I visit France, it would give me great pleasure to meet you in Paris if I may?

Please accept my cordial greetings and good wishes,

    Yours sincerely

    Carl Dolmetsch

It would appear that this letter went astray in the post, as another letter from Dolmetsch to Françaix dated 5th October 1987 reads:

I was delighted to make your acquaintance by telephone last week and it gives me very great pleasure that you have agreed to write a work for my next recital in London's Wigmore Hall on 12th April 1988.

My direct approach to you by telephone must have been a great surprise, for which please accept my apologies; but you will see from the enclosed copyletter that I had previously written to you on 2nd September, and this letter must have gone astray in the post.

As promised, here is the range of the two principal sizes of recorder. The alto is the more important in the historical repertoire, but the higher soprano model is very effective where appropriate. My supporting string ensemble will be two violins and violoncello.

By separate post, I am sending you a cassette of some of my performances of baroque and modern works, which may be of interest to you.

I was happy to hear that you remembered my father's visit to Le Mans, now more than 55 years ago.

A further telephone communication took place, following which Dolmetsch wrote to Françaix on 28 November 1998. This letter contains details of a number of important developments in connection with the new composition:

I was very pleased to be able to talk to you again by telephone and to know that you had received the cassette of baroque and modern works for the recorder. It gave me great pleasure to learn that you had enjoyed the performance and I hope it will help you to assess the standard to which we work.

In regard to your new composition, it is very kind of you to say you will approach Schotts of Mainz to discover if they will contribute financially to (as well as publish) the new work; but please be assured that I will guarantee the commission in any case.

The other question is whether to include a viola in the score. Although I had planned the programme without a viola (to save some expense in a very costly promotion), if you think it artistically important to your new composition, please tell me and I will engage a viola player and find parts for him to play in other works as well.

Since your new composition will create an auspicious "entente cordiale" situation at my 44th Wigmore Hall recital, I will approach the cultural department of the French Embassy in London, in the hope that France will be diplomatically represented, perhaps by the Ambassador himself.

I shall look forward to hearing the title of the new work; in the meantime, I have had to proceed with publicity printing and have called it simply "New work".

Françaix's reply, dated 3 December 1987, noted the omission of the viola and how he intended to overcome this: 'In order to avoid our *Entente cordiale* becoming a *Mésentente cordiale*, I am renouncing the Viola, with its pomp, and all its works. I am going to see to it that my 2nd violin spends part of its life playing the 4th string in the 1st position.' Later in the letter his comments are somewhat revealing. If non avant-garde composers sometimes experienced neglect of their work, Françaix had evidently encountered this, certainly in his homeland and, and as he amusingly points out, in England also:

As my music is guaranteed not to have any consecutive fifths or octaves, it is not played in Paris, where it does not benefit from any government subsidies. I am pleased to say that this is not the case in London where it is played every 29th February.

In the hope that you like what you hear of my music, may I congratulate you once again, dear Sir, on your great talent.

Dolmetsch spent some time at the beginning of 1988 in South America, but was keen to obtain funding for the new work from the Arts Council of Great Britain. In his absence, Greta Matthews sent Françaix the application form with a letter dated 10 February 1988 asking if he would be kind enough to complete the required sections and return it for signature by Dolmetsch on his return. Françaix returned the form with a letter dated 15 February 1988:

Dear Madam,

Please find attached the questionnaire duly completed for the "Arts Council of Great Britain".

"Your" Quintet for recorder, two violins, cello and harpsichord is presently in the hands of the copyist. I have put my heart and soul into it.

However, before I send it to you Mr. Dolmetsch must, as a matter of form, sign the contract with my publisher, Schott of Mainz, as I myself am under contract with them.

Yours sincerely,

Jean Françaix

P.S. I have not completed question 19 of the questionnaire, as I have never received any orders from Great Britain.

Greta assured him, in a letter dated 17 February 1988, that Schott London had made contact, and the wishes of Schott Mainz would be fully complied with.

On 2 March 1988 Françaix sent Dolmetsch a copy of the harpsichord part with a letter containing some interesting insights into his own feelings about his music:

> Dear Sir,
>
> In order to save you time I am sending you the harpsichord part of my "Quintette" with corrections in pencil, before the final printing.
>
> Please do not be put off by the complex sequence of complicated chords, once you have the parts for the other instruments everything will become clear (imagine that you are accompanying a Mozart air and you don't know the vocal part!)
>
> The problem with my music is that you hear every single note, and you need time to 'digest' them all.
>
> I will send you the score and all the other material once the agreed sum has been paid.
>
> Yours sincerely,
>
> Jean Françaix
>
> P.S. I will also send you the recorder part.

Dolmetsch evidently responded as requested and asked the composer for a suitable programme note. A postcard from Françaix dated 20 March 1988 accompanied this, in which he requested Dolmetsch to forgive him for his 'cheeky little harmonies' and to accept the dedication.

There is one further letter in the archive from Dolmetsch to Françaix written before the first performance. It is dated 6 April 1988, by which time the *Quintette* was in rehearsal. Dolmetsch was clearly thrilled by the new work:

> My colleagues and I have now had our first complete rehearsal of your splendid Quintette and we are all charmed and delighted with your new work. You have certainly put your heart into it, as well as your consummate skill and humour and I know it will electrify our London audience. I can say with absolute truth you Quintette is one of the best that has ever been written for the recorder in modern times.
>
> At this first rehearsal, we made a cassette recording for you which I send you now. We shall of course increase the tempo of the Rondo in performance. Because there are one or two instances where the lowest notes of the recorder are not very strong and might not be heard over the other instruments, I have suggested slight modifications at the octave above, which I hope will meet with your approval.
>
> Thank you for sending a note for the printed programme. A copy will be sent to you as soon as it is ready.

Dolmetsch had mentioned in a previous letter his intention to contact the French Embassy in London in an attempt to secure diplomatic representation at the Wigmore Hall recital. This appears to have been successful as the letter continued:

> Among the guests at the Wigmore Hall will be the Cultural Attaché at the French

Embassy, Mons. Patrick Vittet-Philippe; also the Director of the Institut Français, Mons. Michel Monory. I have spoken as well to Mons. François Turmel, Head of the BBC French Service, who are going to broadcast an interview with me on the BBC French Service, probably on a Sunday. I hope you will be able to hear it.

With warm greetings and my most sincere thanks again for your wonderful Quintette.

With a copy of the published edition of the *Quintette* in the archive is a page of music manuscript in Dolmetsch's hand headed 'Quelque Petits ALTERNATIFS', containing the suggested alterations referred to in the second paragraph of his letter above. These mainly raise the recorder part by an octave to avoid passages in its lowest register, but were not incorporated into the published edition of the work.

Françaix replied on 20 April 1988 (and thus after the premiere of the work) with a number of comments on the recorded performance:

Dear Sir,

Thank you very much for sending me the tape recording of "our" Quintette: magnificent performance!

I too, in memory of your father, have put all my heart and soul into it ...

There were just two small mistakes in the performance.

1. At the beginning of the Sarabande the violins should be played pizzicato for 4 bars
2. In the 4th bar after figure 36 the violins should play

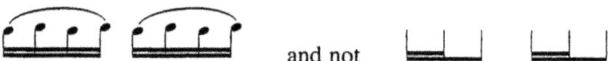 and not

The *Coda*, right at the very end, should be *slower*.

Finally, on a more general note, there is too much violin and cello, the harpsichord (which you play so remarkably well!) must be heard. In the dialogues, the recorder should be heard equally with the 1st violin. (But perhaps on the tape it was because of the microphone). Therefore my dear strings, play often '*sul tasto*'!

I hope your concert at the Wigmore Hall was a great success. Of course with such marvellous performers how could it not be, and I am the lucky beneficiary.

I apologise for all the difficulties with my composition, however I must say that you have overcome them very well and I greatly admire you all.

Jean Françaix

P.S. After Austria, I was on the Côte d'Azur, hence my delay in responding.

The note supplied by the composer (originally in French, but translated for inclusion in the programme) is something of an artistic credo and is included here in full:

Admirable as our epoch may be for its scientific progress, artistically I find it atrocious for its snobbism and vulgarity: its sculpture is dislocated, its architecture monstrous and its music nightmarish. Proud to be rooted in traditions of the past, I do not faint in horror at the sound of a common chord and as though it were an act of terrorism.

In asking me to write a work for the recorder and the harpsichord – and not for electric guitar or electric organ – Carl Dolmetsch has perhaps divined where my sympathies lie.

My Quintette is composed to his brief, from the heart but controlled by the mind: while it is in classical form I hope the public will appreciate that it has a personality of its own. As in my life, my score is based on the cardinal virtues: Faith in its invention; Hope that its voice is true; and the Charity to reward the listener for his time.

Following the first performance, the work received brief but enthusiastic comment in a review published in *The Recorder and Music Magazine*: '... in the classical tradition but with the wit and beauty of phrase that one associates with Françaix – a welcome addition to the repertoire.'[99]

As Françaix's programme note mentions only that the work is in 'classical' form, a brief analysis is given here.

The opening Largo is for muted strings and harpsichord until the very last bars, where the recorder holds a pair of trilled notes to allow the removal of the mutes, before a short semiquaver run leads into the *Allegro*. The first subject of this is a syncopated tune for the recorder above a pizzicato accompaniment of crotchets on the beat for the violins, and quavers off the beat for the cello. The harpsichord enters four bars later with a similar rhythmic formula. These elements, together with a distinctive little upward moving phrase at the end of the recorder's theme, are briefly developed before a second subject moving mostly in crotchets is again given to the recorder. It is accompanied by the cello, with the harpsichord supplying syncopated chords. The cello repeats its accompanying melody, this time pizzicato, while the violins play a motive entirely in quavers. After considerable interplay and further development, the movement ends with a rising scale of F major over two octaves for the recorder, featuring a basic rhythmic pattern heard earlier in the movement.

The Sarabande's opening phrase is given to the recorder above the violins and cello. It then falls silent while the strings intone a long series of phrases (rhythmically related to that of the recorder at the opening) over a harpsichord accompaniment that specifies the 16-foot register for the left-hand octaves. When the recorder enters again the music takes on a more conversational character involving all the instruments. Eventually the strings and harpsichord return to their opening theme while the recorder adds wisps of melody and brings this gentle movement to a close.

Although in 5/8 throughout, the Scherzo falls into two distinct sections. The first, scored for strings and harpsichord alone, features a melody for the first violin. There is a four-bar link with a repeated note figure for the recorder and two bars of semiquavers for the harpsichord, establishing a rhythmic ostinato that is to permeate the entire second section. The strings continue with relentless 5/8 quavers while the recorder's melody is so subtly phrased as to seem hardly in 5/8

---

[99] June 1988, **9**, p. 154.

at all. The opening section is repeated and leads to a very short coda founded on a combination of elements from both sections.

The rhythmic structure of the final Rondo is based on bars of 7/4 divided into groups of 4 and 3 crotchets either side of an intermediate dotted bar line. It opens for the strings alone but the recorder and harpsichord soon join in the energetic quavers which, apart from a short section about halfway through, marked *Adagio subito* and *Dolcissimo* and scored for the strings and harpsichord alone, suffuse the entire movement. The character is similar to that of the *Allegro* and it ends similarly in an ebullient F major.

The published score is a facsimile of the composer's manuscript dated, after the final bar, '20.I.88'. The handwriting bears all the confidence of the work itself, unmistakable in its Gallic elegance and wit and, while inhabiting the worlds of Poulenc and Ibert, fully characteristic of Françaix's own distinctive style.

It remains not only a valuable addition to the repertoire, but also among the most accomplished works with recorder in its genre.

Alan Ridout: Variants on a Tune of H.H.

des (or t) rec, hpd

For Carl Dolmetsch

Theme: Cantabile. Var. 1: Fancy on One Note. Var. 2: Conversation. Var. 3: Plaint (Meno mosso). Var. 4: Toccatina (Brillante). Coda.

First (public) performance: Wigmore Hall, London, 27 October 1989. Carl Dolmetsch, rec; Sir David Lumsden, hpd.

Published: Hebden Bridge, Peacock Press, 2003.

Alan Ridout's *Variants on a Tune of H[erbert] H[owells]*, as the score is headed, was sent to Dolmetsch with a postcard dated 15 February 1988:

> Dear Carl,
>
> A little work for Descant Recorder and Harpsichord for you and dear Joseph to play. I hope you like it.
>
> With love to you, Greta
>
> and your family
>
> Alan

The piece was not the result of a commission, but almost certainly a spontaneous expression of the desire to write something else for Dolmetsch that Ridout had first noted at the time of the composition of *Sequence*. A photocopy of the manuscript is in the archive at Haslemere. It bears Ridout's characteristic calligraphic initials, place of composition (Canterbury) and date (14 February 1988) after the last bar. In addition to the score there is a photocopy of the recorder part, also in Ridout's hand. The score contains a prefatory note of considerable interest:

> The tune employed in this work was composed in about 1934 for Anne Lawrence. Howells called it 'Pipe Tune' and wrote it in the presence of the young Miss Lawrence. There were originally two unaccompanied pieces. Neither were published or collected, and this one was written out from memory by Ruth Dyson (who had known Miss Lawrence) on 11th April 1987.

Howells's 'Pipe Tune' is shown in Ex. 3.41. (The phrasing is as it appears in Ridout's manuscript.)

Dolmetsch had been away in South America at the beginning of the year, and found the new piece on his return. He wrote to Ridout on 2 March to thank him:

7   Harpsichordist Ruth Dyson, who wrote out Howells's 'Pipe Tune' from memory, enabling Alan Ridout to use it as the theme for his *Variants on a Tune of H.H.*

My dear Alan,

It was a delightful surprise on coming home from S. America to find your charming variations on Herbert Howells' theme awaiting me.

Herbert was a dear friend for many years, since 1937 in fact, and I often wished he

Ex. 3.41. Herbert Howells, 'Pipe Tune' as it appears in the manuscript of Alan Ridout's *Variants on a Tune of H.H.* Reproduced by permission of the Herbert Howells Estate.

had written something for us. Now you have provided this combined with your own variations and now we have a superb "confluence" of musical inspiration.

Joseph and I played through the work this morning and we plan to include it in the little concert which forms part of a week-end course at Westham College, in Shakespeare country – our 41st consecutive year there. I would also like to play it to the Dolmetsch Foundation members at the AGM on 23rd April; would you be able to come that afternoon?

Thank you again Alan for the kindly thought. Everyone here joins me in affectionate good wishes.

Yours as ever,

Carl

Whether the above performances took place, or indeed if Ridout was able to attend that given at the Dolmetsch Foundation AGM, cannot be determined from any information in the archive, but Dolmetsch did include the *Variants* in his Wigmore Hall recital of 1989. Although not noted as such in the programme, this would have been the first public performance, and Dolmetsch's own list of Wigmore Hall first performances notes it as the new work for 1989.

The 1989 Wigmore Hall recital was a very special occasion, marking as it did 50 years since Dolmetsch's first two recitals given in the hall in 1939. It was, in fact, within a matter of a month, 50 years since that in which the first public performance of the Berkeley Sonatina had been given.

Ridout's *Variants* formed the second of a series of four pieces played together featuring the four other common sizes of recorder in addition to the treble used extensively in the remainder of the programme. For the sopranino, the sixth section of Ridout's *Sequence* was played; for tenor, Colin Hand's *Plaint* and for bass, Dolmetsch's own *Tempo di gavotta*. This last was particularly appropriate, as the first recital in 1939 had included his Theme and Variations, written in the absence of any suitable contemporary compositions. How the situation had changed 50 years later!

Edgar Hunt's review of the recital in *The Recorder and Music Magazine*[100] made no comment on Ridout's piece, but did mention the presence in the audience of Joseph Saxby, who had by this time virtually retired from public performance.

Ridout himself was there, and he wrote to Dolmetsch on 31 October to express his thanks:

> Dear Carl,
>
> Thank you so much for those wonderful performances and the whole wonderful concert. I thought that the RAM strings and Sir David Lumsden gave superb support and added something special to a very special evening. 50 years is really an amazing achievement, and I felt so proud to be a part of the evening.
>
> I always love writing for you and much hope to do so again. My many congratulations for a most memorable concert, and my many thanks for being so encouraging to my work.
>
> Yours ever
>
> Alan

Carl Dolmetsch's 1989 Wigmore Hall recital was to be his last and brought to close a unique chapter in the history of the recorder. No wonder Ridout felt such pride at being involved.

In the absence of a description in the programme note, a brief analysis follows:

> Theme: Herbert Howells 'Pipe Tune' (marked *cantabile*), is given out by the recorder above a suitably simple accompaniment.
>
> Variant 1 (Fancy on One Note): Makes a feature of the repeated A's that open the theme in the recorder part, and the same note is reiterated almost for the entirety of the harpsichord accompaniment.
>
> Variant 2 (Conversation): Fragments of the theme are exchanged between the harpsichord and the recorder, those on the recorder having a particular rhythmic emphasis.
>
> Variant 3 (Plaint): Marked *Meno mosso*, the tune is subject to rhythmic variation and inverted above a very chromatic accompaniment on the harpsichord (Ex. 3.42).
>
> Variant 4 (Toccatina): The score is marked *brillante* but the recorder part has the indication *Vivace*. The tune is contained on the appropriate beats of the bar in almost *moto perpetuo* staccato semiquavers on the recorder. The harpsichord accompaniment is similar to that in the initial theme, simple enough to allow the recorder's semiquavers not to be obscured, but with more written-out broken chords to add to the sonority.
>
> Coda: Eight bars that play on the quaver figure contained in the fourth bar of the tune and concluding with the particular upward-moving third F to A.

Ridout's *Variants on a Tune of H.H.* is a charming and well-crafted piece, although some of its interest is without doubt a result of Herbert Howells's tune. Consequently, and because the scoring is for descant recorder and keyboard (a

---

[100] December 1989, **9**, p. 353.

Ex. 3.42. Alan Ridout, *Variants on a Tune of H.H.* Variation III, bars 1–4. Reproduced by permission of Ampleforth Abbey Trustees.

combination that still does not have a comparable repertoire with that for treble recorder) its publication is welcomed. This also provides another step towards a complete edition of Ridout's works for recorder, an important task since his untimely death in 1996.

Chapter 4

Works not premiered at the Wigmore Hall

The new works premiered at the Wigmore Hall represent a little over half of the music composed for Dolmetsch. Among the remainder are some significant pieces, which, though not premiered at the Wigmore recitals, were published and in some cases have become frequently performed works in the recorder repertoire. Others, from miniature celebratory occasional pieces from friends and colleagues to some large-scale works, remain in manuscript.

If there was a tendency for the Wigmore works gradually to set the recorder within a chamber music context, then the remainder continued to be mainly for recorder and keyboard. There are a few early exceptions for recorder ensemble plus a recorder duet and a number of solos.

Of the ensemble pieces, those by Cecily Lambert and Shelagh Godwin are for the usual SATB recorder quartet, while the quartet by Santiago Velasco is for SSTB. The trios by Thomas Pitfield and Hans Gál are for SAT, while that by Gaston Saux is for AAT. The duet is Georges Migot's Suite for descant and treble. The only published solo is the *Suite exotique* for descant by Jean Temprement.

The scoring of the works for recorder and keyboard are as follows:

Descant recorder and harpsichord	3
Descant recorder and piano	4
Treble recorder and harpsichord	10
Treble recorder and piano	6
Tenor recorder and harpsichord	1
Tenor recorder and piano	1
Bass recorder and harpsichord	2

Of the works for treble recorder and piano, the *Romanza* by Santiago Velasco Llanos is alternatively set for ATB recorder trio. Franz Reizenstein's Partita for treble recorder and piano is described in detail in the section on the works of the 'ten' composers having come about as a result of Manuel Jacobs' pre-war initiative.

Colin Hand's *Divertissement* is the sole work in the entire Dolmetsch canon to include two recorders and keyboard and makes use of different recorder pairings in each of its three movements. However, it was later withdrawn by the composer.

Perhaps the most unusual scoring to be found is in Zvi Herbert Nagan's Trio for descant recorder, violin and viola. Mention should also be made of the Introduction and Caprices for recorder (using bass, treble and sopranino) and strings by Darrell Davison, composed in 1983.

Among the occasional dedicatory pieces is a rather touching fragment contained on a single sheet of the wide-staved manuscript paper used by Gordon Jacob as his sight deteriorated in later life. It was to mark Dolmetsch's 70th birthday and is headed: 'A 70-note unfinished tune for Carl's ...ieth birthday.' The scoring is for 'recorder of any shape or size' and the melody, of 12 $^1\!/_2$ bars' duration, founded on F major and marked *Andante con moto*, does indeed break off tantalizingly after exactly 70 notes. At the foot of this little unfinished piece Jacob wrote: 'With cordial greetings from Gordon, and with best wishes for at least 30 more notes.' In the top right-hand corner is written in Dolmetsch's hand: 'August 1981'.

Ten years later Dolmetsch's eightieth birthday was celebrated in a somewhat similar fashion by Michael Short. *Les quatre vingts: fantasie sur le nom 'C.D.' pour sopran flûte-à-bec seule* uses exactly 80 notes but, unlike Gordon Jacob's birthday tribute, is complete. For the first two bars, only the dedicatory notes appear, but this miniature solo eventually makes use of the full range of the descant recorder up to top D. In a letter of thanks Dolmetsch noted that he had enjoyed playing it through, adding: 'It's quite amazing how far eighty notes will go.'

Dolmetsch's eightieth birthday was also celebrated by his harpsichordist friend and Haslemere Festival colleague William Godfree with *A Birthday Present*. This 20-bar miniature for recorder and piano is headed *Andante con moto*. It opens with a piano figure that continues as an ostinato, over which the recorder's melody is founded on the dedicatee's initials CFD. The piece concludes with a chromatic ascending phrase for the recorder.

Birthdays seemed to form a good excuse for such musical tributes and the happy coincidence that Dolmetsch's initials formed three musical notes certainly did not go unnoticed. The shortest such tribute is undated and is a *Fuga à 3* ascribed to 'Anon. Master of the 20th century'. Just four bars of music forming a perpetual canon are written on a short strip of manuscript paper and are the work of Walter Bergmann.

Of a more substantial nature, the Suite for Recorders (SATB) by Shelagh Godwin is in three movements (*Alla marcia, Andante, Allegro*). It appears to have been composed originally for pipes and the finale is a new movement to suit recorders. The manuscript is dated 1983 and is inscribed: 'To the Dolmetsch Ensemble in tribute to many happy years past and to come'. It is the work of a Dolmetsch family friend and former secretary of the Dolmetsch Foundation.

In the case of a number of works, besides the manuscripts, some correspondence or programme notes remain in the archive to give further details of how they had their origins. (Michael Short's *Giocata* was a special commission.)

As much detail as the surviving material (and contact with composers and performers) permits is included, though in many cases it has not been possible to establish the date or place of a first performance, or indeed if one took place. The works are described as far as possible in chronological order where the dates can be determined, but in the case of Christopher Wood's manuscripts none are dated.

Since beginning work on this book a number of the unpublished works have appeared in printed editions. The work of publication is a continuing process and it is likely, and to be hoped, that a number of works covered in this section will eventually be published.

Christopher Wood: Sonata di camera, Op. 18

[tr] rec, hpd

To Carl Dolmetsch and Joseph Saxby

1 Andante tranquillo. 2 Molto adagio. 3 Recit ad lib – Cadenza: Lento (rec solo) – Allegretto (hpd) – Tempo allegro giocoso.

First performance: date and location unknown.

Unpublished.

The autograph manuscript of this work is one of three by Christopher Wood in the archive. None of them is dated and one does not bear an opus number.

The first movement opens with a harpsichord ostinato, above which the recorder enters with a rising semiquaver arpeggio founded almost entirely on this material.

The second movement marks a change of key to B major (awkward for treble recorder). Here the recorder weaves an intricately decorated line over another harpsichord ostinato.

Cadenzas for recorder solo and harpsichord open the multi-sectioned third movement before recorder triplet figures lead to the final *Allegro giocoso* featuring busy semiquaver movement for the recorder above repeated quaver chords on the harpsichord. As in the first, most of this movement is founded on the material of its opening.

Christopher Wood was a harpsichordist of the Haslemere circle (he deputized for Joseph Saxby at the first public performance of Lennox Berkeley's Sonatina at the Wigmore Hall in November 1939) and the keyboard writing contains many large chords low in tessitura that sound well on the harpsichord. Wood obviously had an instrument in mind on which pedals controlled the registers and with some sort of sustaining device present. The score thus contains some unusual directions such as: $\frac{1}{2}$ 8', $\frac{1}{4}$ 8' and *sust. ped.*

Though dedicated to Dolmetsch and Saxby, the score does not contain any of Joseph Saxby's characteristic markings; perhaps Dolmetsch played the work with Wood himself.

Christopher Wood: Concertante in E, Op. 50

des rec, hpd

To Jeanne Marie Dolmetsch and Marguerite Mabel Dolmetsch. Written for Carl Dolmetsch

1 Allegro con brio. 2 Lento maestoso. 3 Allegro vivace ma non troppo. 4 Largo maestoso. 5 (Fuga) Poco allegro.

First performance: date and location unknown.

Unpublished.

This is almost certainly the latest of the three works by Wood in the archive, and represents a substantial concert solo for recorder and harpsichord of impressive proportions.

The first movement opens with a harpsichord ostinato, above which the recorder gives out a melody containing groups of grace notes that seem to be a characteristic of Wood and that appear in the fugal subjects of the final movements both of this work and of the *French Suite*. In the *Lento maestoso* second movement it is again the harpsichord that begins with four introductory bars containing a rising figure above which the recorder has fanfare-like motives. As in Wood's *Sonata di camera*, the keyboard part in this and the fourth movement contains the direction *ped.*, indicating the intended use of a sustaining mechanism fitted to some Dolmetsch harpsichords of the period.

It is once again with an ostinato figure for the harpsichord that the third movement opens. The recorder's melody in a gentle 6/8 begins low on the instrument and is directed to be played 'as soft as possible'.

The fourth movement, like the second, is headed *maestoso*, and its opening bars are even more declamatory and sonorous, with large rising chords for the harpsichord.

The finale is a fugue founded on a subject similar in character to that forming the finale of the *French Suite*. It begins on the harpsichord, and when the recorder eventually enters at bar 14 it is with a fifth voice. The conclusion is a bravura affair with top Es for the recorder and ending on this note, the use of which Dolmetsch clearly promoted, having written it in his own Theme and Variations and encouraged York Bowen to include in the finale of his Sonata.

Christopher Wood: French Suite

des, tr and t recs

To Carl, Marie and Natalie Dolmetsch

1 Pétit prelude (Lento tranquillo). 2 Movement agité (Allegro leggiero). 3 Pastorale langoureuse (Andante espressivo). 4 Retrospectif (Lento – Allegro – Lento – Allegro leggiero – Presto non tanto). 5 Tourbillons (Presto) et fugue (Allegro moderato ma un poco grazioso).

First performance: date and location unknown.

Unpublished.

If the *Concertante* in E is the latest of Wood's works, then this suite is probably the earliest, though without a date or opus number this cannot be affirmed with certainty. Like the *Concertante* in E, it is a large work in five movements and features a fugue in the finale. The manuscript score also contains separate parts for descant and tenor recorders but that for the treble is missing. An important note written by the composer on the front page directs: 'To be played as one work – and pieces must not be played from it'.

The first movement opens with a dialogue between the descant and treble recorders above a repeated low E for the tenor. The repeated-note figure moves up to the descant line, and the treble's rhythm at bar 3 is later developed in a 'pétit' prelude that is a total of 61 bars in length.

There is a distinctly agitated feel to the opening of the second movement as all three instruments move with the same incessant rhythmic pattern. A central section of calmer but nevertheless motivic quaver movement follows, in which the flat is dropped from the key signature. This leads to a da capo of the first section and a concluding coda.

The pastoral third movement flows along in A major with the upper instruments moving in parallel at the opening.

Various elements of the first three movements are brought together in the fourth, aptly titled *Retrospectif*. It opens with the rising motive of the first movement *Lento* but now in 3/4 time. An *allegro* section making use of the incessant rhythm from the opening of the second movement follows, but the tempo slows again while the 6/8 theme from the third movement is reintroduced. At the indication *presto non tanto* a new idea emerges in the form of a rising figure that leads to the final and fifth movement. The *Tourbillons* section is marked *presto* and develops the rising figure with which the previous movement has ended.

In the fifth-movement fugue the busy subject containing grace notes is given out by the tenor and moves mostly in semiquavers (as the fugue in the *Concertante*). The treble is next to enter and finally the descant. After careful working out, the music leads back to a restatement of the *Tourbillon* to conclude a recorder trio conceived on a large scale.

Anthony Bernard: Prelude and Scherzo

tr rec, hpd

For Carl Dolmetsch

[1] Prelude (Grave). [2] Scherzo (Allegro scherzando).

First performance: Haslemere Hall, 1941. Carl Dolmetsch, rec; Anthony Bernard, hpd.

Published: Hebden Bridge: Peacock Press, 2001 (PD 02).

The manuscript score and recorder part of this piece (dated January 1941) is in the Dolmetsch archive. Contained within the manuscript is a tribute to Anthony Bernard written by Dolmetsch at the time he made a recording of the piece. It is dated 10 October 1990 and contains an account of the work's beginnings:

> In the early 1920s Haslemere Music Society – a local body of enthusiastic amateur players – appointed Anthony Bernard as their conductor, coach and mentor, a position he held for over 20 years during which time he became a much-loved friend to all.
>
> Among his many talents, Anthony was a gifted and fluent composer, a pupil of John Ireland. I well remember a January evening during the wartime blackout when he arrived unheralded on the doorstep, clutching a manuscript score. 'I've written a piece for you', he said, 'and it's built on the initials of three generations of Dolmetschs' – AD (Arnold), CD (Carl) and FECD (François Eugene Carl, my 3-month-old son).
>
> There and then I seized my recorder, seated Anthony at the harpsichord and we revelled in the first utterances of a work which was to become a historical milestone. Together we gave the first public performance during 'Warships Week', a national event devoted to raising money for more battleships to defend our merchant convoys. Anthony's 'piece' which was an instant success consisted of a Prelude and Scherzo, the one romantic and colourful, the other playful and joyous. At intervals since I have performed the work on numerous world tours with Joseph Saxby;[1] it was first broadcast from BBC Bristol, during an air raid!
>
> And now, both my son and Anthony Bernard's piece have reached the half-century; but the main reason for recording the Prelude and Scherzo now is in commemoration of a dear and greatly-admired friend whose centenary falls on 25th January 1991.

Dolmetsch wrote to Mary Beatty on the same day as writing his tribute, stating his intention to record the piece, probably in early December. In a letter of thanks, Mary Beatty noted that the only time she had heard the piece was in Haslemere Hall during 'Warships Week'. There is also a Christmas card from her thanking Dolmetsch for the cassette (made with harpsichordist Nigel Foster).

Among the correspondence in the Dolmetsch archive is a letter from Bernard to Dolmetsch dated 18 May 1941 requesting that he be sent the manuscript (by Herbert Murrill at the BBC) so that a copy could be made for his own use. In a letter to Dolmetsch dated 26 May 1943, Bernard noted: 'Elizabeth Poston tells me that you are playing our piece again soon. I shall look out for it.'

The Prelude opens in arresting manner with the harpsichord alone, and the recorder follows with a variant based on the same notes, but with the first C sharpened. For much of the Prelude, the harpsichord accompaniment is founded on arpeggio figures and, though quite clearly intended for harpsichord, has the

---

[1] Among the tours on which Dolmetsch performed the piece was that to the United States in the autumn of 1970, a report of which is contained in *The Recorder and Music Magazine* of March 1971, **3**, p. 337.

direction *ped.* in places, indicating the presence of a harpsichord sustaining device sometimes also called for in works by Christopher Wood. At the beginning of the elaborate recorder cadenza that follows, the manuscript score has an octave appoggiatura to a high A, but in the recording referred to above Dolmetsch starts on a minim low A, after which there is a pause before he continues with the remainder as written. Jeanne Dolmetsch has confirmed that this was the way her father usually played it. This leads to the Scherzo which, like the Prelude, is introduced by the harpsichord. The recorder's theme (mostly in 2/4) presents the 'initials' in a different order, and the little rhythmic figure found in its third and fourth bars characterizes the entire movement. At bar 103 the key signature changes to two sharps and it is in the major tonality the work is brought to a cheerful conclusion.

Martin Shaw: Sonata in E♭

rec (or fl), hpd (or pn)

For Carl Dolmetsch

1 Allegro moderato. 2 Theme and Variations (Andante espressivo). 3 Allegro con spirito.

First performance: date and location unknown.

Published: London: J.B. Cramer & Co., 1942 (15242).

The idea that Martin Shaw should write a sonata for recorder and harpsichord seems to have come from Carl Dolmetsch in the first instance, as we find in a letter dated 5 October 1941 from Shaw to Dolmetsch:

> My daughter – to whom her visit to Haslemere gave great pleasure – tells me that you suggested that I should write a Sonata for Recorder and Harpsichord(?) I would like to have a try. Perhaps you would send me the range both of Recorder & the other instrument – or whatever combination you would prefer.

Dolmetsch clearly sent Shaw the information he required and work must have progressed quickly, as on 15 December 1941 Shaw wrote to Dolmetsch: 'Here is the Sonata. It may not be Recorder–Harpsichord music at all & I shall quite understand if you find it is not in the right genre.'

A number of Shaw's subsequent notes at this time were written on postcards and are not dated. However, they coincide with a change of address, and from the new address printed at the head of the cards and the content generally the order can be satisfactorily deduced. It is after a reminder to Dolmetsch of the change of address, on a postcard clearly written shortly after the above letter, that Shaw asks: 'Do let me know how you now feel about the Sonata & don't spare me if you find it doesn't suit the instruments. "I can take it." Best wishes for the New Year.'

Although no copy of any letter from Dolmetsch giving his thoughts on the work appears to have survived, another postcard from Shaw notes: 'So glad it seems all right', and suggests a meeting at Cramers, 'when we could arrange adjustments.' Dolmetsch must have further suggested that one of the movements could stand on its own as the card from Shaw concludes: 'Yes – Theme & Variations would make a separate number.'

From yet another postcard we learn that the meeting at Cramers was arranged for 24 February 1942. Shortly after, on 27 February, Shaw wrote to Dolmetsch:

Dear Mr. Dolmetsch,

I have made the adjustments & sent off the MS to Cramers who are publishing the Sonata. I have told them the concerts are in June & asked them to have the work published by the middle of May which they think there should be no difficulty in doing.

It was so pleasant to meet you & Mr. Saxby the other day & I am greatly looking forward to the concerts.

Every good wish

Sincerely

Martin Shaw

By the way what is the *lowest* note in the harpsichord? Would you very kindly drop me a card with this information?

Cramers must have set about the publication of the sonata almost immediately as on 4 April Shaw wrote to Dolmetsch: 'I am enclosing with this the 1st proof of Sonata. Would you very kindly glance through the flute part? I think it's all right but I would like your confirmation. If you would return it to me as quickly as possible I would be grateful.'

In addition to a copy of the published edition of the Sonata in the archive is a publisher's proof of another movement headed 'II Scherzo', the pages of which carry at the bottom the initials 'J.B.C & Co.' and the reference 15242 – the same as that of the published edition. At the top of the first page written in Carl Dolmetsch's handwriting are the composer's name and a note underneath: '*Unpublished* (not included in sonata 1941)'.

This Scherzo, in G major, is a long movement. The Scherzo itself (in 3/4 time, ♩. = c. 92) is almost 180 bars in length, not including the indicated repeats. It is followed by a trio section (in E minor and marked *poco meno mosso*, ♩. = c. 72) of some 50 bars, after which the Scherzo is repeated da capo. It is not clear why this movement was omitted from the Sonata, as there is no mention made of it in any of the correspondence, and the proof even contains a number of corrective annotations. It is substantial enough to stand as a piece on its own, although it was the Theme and Variations that Dolmetsch suggested could in fact do so.

By the time of the recital proposed for June 1942 (mentioned in Shaw's letter of 27 February), at which the premiere was to have been given, Dolmetsch was unwell and unable to take part. Joseph Saxby was involved in civil defence duties and was likewise unavailable. In a letter from Shaw to Dolmetsch dated 21 June 1942 we read:

> I do hope you're all right again, It was sad not to see and hear you, though no more delightful substitute than your mother could be imagined, and the same is of course true of Christopher Wood. Your mother won all hearts & her interpretations were greatly loved. C. Wood is splendid. He is such a good musician as well as executant & we liked having him stay here very much. He will no doubt tell you all about it.

It may appear from this that the sonata was premiered by Dolmetsch's mother Mabel, but as she was a player of the viol and not the recorder, the programme of the recital must have been revised to accommodate this.

No other details of a first performance are to be found in the remaining correspondence, but in the list of new works performed at the Wigmore Hall compiled by Dolmetsch, the Shaw Sonata is noted to have been premiered at a recital given in 1941. However, no programme for such a recital has been found in the archive, and if, as Dolmetsch later recorded, the 1984 recital was the fortieth, this would not permit the inclusion of a recital in 1941. It is clear, however, that Dolmetsch was able to give a broadcast performance of at least the Theme and Variations from the sonata, as an undated postcard from Shaw thanks Dolmetsch for letting him know about the broadcast, 'which I shall look forward very much to hearing.' Shaw sent another undated postcard to Dolmetsch after the broadcast:

> Just a line to say thank you for V. fine playing of my Th. & Var. & do tell Y. Bowen I hope he enjoyed playing me as much as I enjoyed hearing him.
> Alas I could only hear a few bars of his work as I had to leave for church where I am responsible for the music, please tell him. So I missed him & you & L. Berkeley much to my upset.

The published edition describes the work as being for flute or recorder and piano, no doubt for commercial reasons, but Shaw's original scoring intentions are clear from footnotes to the first page of the score and the recorder/flute part referring to various *ossias*. That in the score reads: 'It is important to note that the passages marked "ossia" are to be played if the sonata is performed by recorder and Harpsichord.' There are a number of passages where *ossias* are marked specifically for the harpsichord, and in connection with this it is worth recalling Shaw's query regarding the lowest note on the instrument. In the recorder/flute part the wording is slightly different: 'it is important to note that the passages marked "ossia" are to be played only if the sonata is performed by Recorder.' The alternatives for the recorder avoid high F#/G♭ and raise some low-lying passages.

The work opens in 3/4 with a short keyboard introduction, the melody of which is immediately repeated by the recorder an octave higher, but there is a twist at the end and the time signature changes via a single bar of 2/4 to the 6/8 in which most of the movement is written. The second subject makes use of a rapidly rising scale and a repeated note figure. The opening 3/4 passage does not return until the recapitulation, after which there is an immediate return to the prevailing 6/8. The end of the movement makes use of the repeated quaver figure from the second subject on a high E♭.

A set of variations on the theme *Beata nobis gaudia* (the Office Hymn for Whitsunday) forms the second movement; the plainchant melody, rationalized into a 3/4 metre, is given out by the solo recorder. In the first variation the theme is fragmented and a triplet figure is introduced in the second. The theme remains in the recorder for the third variation, in which it is accompanied by harpsichord semiquavers. The time signature is changed to 2/4 and the flats disappear from the key signature in the fourth variation, in which the melody is decorated and high on the recorder. In the fifth variation there is another change of time signature to 9/8 and the melody is subject to the recorder's predominant rhythm of ♩♪ ♩♪ ♩♪. The sixth variation restores the three-flat key signature and is an ad lib cadenza for recorder solo that leads to the finale.

As in the first movement, there is a keyboard introduction, the energetic 3/4 rhythm being immediately taken up by the recorder. Rhythmic energy characterizes the entire movement, which also contains some interesting modulations. Shaw did not change the key signature, so that the recorder part in bar 28, while still in three flats, has a sharp before every note. The energy is maintained to the very end and the recorder holds a high E♭ trill above semiquaver figuration in octaves on the keyboard.

Some of the writing in Shaw's Sonata does not fall very comfortably on the recorder, but this should not prevent players from acquainting themselves, if not with the entirety of this fine work, at least with the Theme and Variations.

William Wordsworth: Theme and Variations

tr rec, hpd

For Carl Dolmetsch and Joseph Saxby

Theme (without tempo indication but marked ♩ = 156). Var. 1: Legato. Var. 2: Scherzando. Var. 3: L'istesso tempo. Var. 4: Andante. Var. 5: Allegro. Var. 6: Allegro. Var. 7: Vivace – Largamente – tranquillo – resoluto.

First performance: date and location unknown.

Unpublished.

The archive contains the composer's autograph manuscript of the work dated May/June 1947 at the head of the score and signed and dated '18.VI.47' at the end.

A note also at the head states: 'mm [metronome] marks are only rough guides W.B.W.'

It has not been possible to establish the location or date of a first performance, or indeed if one took place, but the score does contain Joseph Saxby's characteristic markings for registration and has clearly been played from. The recorder part however does contain some unidiomatic features, and from conversations with the Dolmetsch family I learned that these may well have been the reason for Dolmetsch's apparent neglect of the work.

The somewhat angular theme of 27 bars is stated by the recorder over a chordal accompaniment on the harpsichord, the harmonic structure of which is to pervade the entire work.

Variation 1 moves the initial rising quavers of the theme's first bar to the harpsichord left hand and in the second immediately inverts them. The recorder's minims in the second and third bars continue with the outline of the theme and at the fourth join in the quaver motion and harmonic progression.

Variation 2 fragments the theme's opening and the note progression of its second and third bars are compressed into a bar of the prevailing quaver rhythm. The characteristic harmonic and melodic progression of the fourth bar pull the variation back on track.

Variation 3 brings a change of key signature and the basic melodic shape is contained in semiquaver motion for the recorder and in the harpsichord right hand.

Variation 4 introduces yet another change of key and the less recorder friendly key signature of five sharps. The rising motive of the theme's opening is transferred to a smooth flowing 12/8 time in the recorder part while the harpsichord accompanies with large arpeggio chords.

At the opening of the *allegro* Variation 5, the theme as such has disappeared, but over an accompaniment of sextuplet figures on the harpsichord the recorder has a rising phrase featuring trills and inverts the progression found in the theme's second and third bars.

Variation 6 brings yet another change of key signature – to five flats – and a change of time to 3/4. The harpsichord's rhythmic accompaniment spreads out from a single note while the recorder has its own motive above and appears to have abandoned the initial theme entirely.

Variation 7 develops into an extended finale in several sections, the first of which has a key signature of two sharps and a time signature of 2/4. The metronomic rate however remains unchanged and the rhythmic pulse of the previous variation is maintained. It should also be noted that this is almost exactly half that of the original statement of the theme and as such the new 2/4 time relates directly to it, the rising semiquavers representing the quavers found at the very beginning. In the next two bars the characteristic falling fourths of bars two and three of the theme are inverted.

This is followed by an arpeggiated section marked *largamente* ($\JoinedRelation = 56$) for the solo harpsichord, then a cadenza-like phrase for the recorder leads to a further chordal passage for the harpsichord before the recorder has its own extended cadenza. A return is then made to the one-flat key signature of the opening and a section marked *tranquillo* features the falling fourth motive in minims on the recorder above the harpsichord's chordal accompaniment. The music arrives at a final *resoluto* in D major and the recorder's concluding upward arpeggio ends on a high F#.

There is no correspondence from the time of composition, but in March 1976 William Wordsworth wrote to Dolmetsch noting that the Scottish Music Archive was anxious to make a copy of the piece and had requested the loan of the manuscript. Dolmetsch duly had a photocopy of the manuscript made and forwarded it to Wordsworth, who acknowledged receipt on a postcard dated 25 May 1976:

> Many thanks for sending me the photo-copy of my Theme and Variations. I had quite forgotten about it until I was asked if I had ever written anything for recorder and remembered that I'd written this piece for you and Joseph Saxby. (Hence the fact that it is missing from the enclosed brochure) I will send a copy to the Music Archive in Glasgow who will be able to make a copy of it.

The problematic final high F# is characteristic of some of the difficulties presented by the work. Under similar circumstances Dolmetsch frequently offered technical advice to composers. Whether he did on this occasion it is impossible to tell, but if so, perhaps the composer felt that the necessary amendments would have compromised the textures or structure of the piece. Whatever may or may not have occurred, the Theme and Variations contain many original ideas and it is thus unfortunate that the work does not fall more comfortably or idiomatically onto the solo instrument.

Ivor Walsworth: Sonata

tr rec, hpd

To Carl Dolmetsch

In one movement, but in several sections to be played without a break.

First performance: Royal Festival Hall Recital Room, London, 27 April 1961. Carl Dolmetsch, rec; Joseph Saxby, hpd.

Unpublished.

The autograph manuscript (dated 1950) of this single-movement work is in the archive, but unfortunately no correspondence in connection with it appears to have survived.

A period of 11 years separated composition and first performance (which took place in a recital at which York Bowen's Two Pieces for three recorders and harpsichord also received their first performance). The composer contributed the following programme note for the premiere:

> This short work, written after hearing one of Carl Dolmetsch's broadcasts, is mainly lyrical in character, with moments of repose. It is designed to afford the opportunity of displaying that limpid beauty of tone so characteristic of the recorder, and also the almost bird-like agility of which the instrument is capable.

Dolmetsch added: 'This duo-sonata is in one movement divided into sections of contrasting tempi. The passages of florid decoration, alternating with those of more contemplative mood, serve to enhance the rhapsodic nature of the work.'

The beginning is marked *moderato quasi lento* (2/2, ♩ = 84), but this is applies only to the first of a number of sections that are to be played continuously. Much use is made of a theme/motive indicated in Ex. 4.1.

Ex. 4.1. Ivor Walsworth, Sonata for recorder and harpsichord. Recurring theme/motif.

An *Allegro* in 6/8 follows and alternates with sections marked *meno mosso*. This is succeeded by a *Lento molto* in 4/4 before a return to *moderato quasi lento* and a restatement of the opening material. A passage marked *rit. e perdendo al fine* leads to the conclusion in G minor.

This is a work original in its style and structure, characterized by especially light textures in the keyboard writing.

Ivor Walsworth was head of the BBC Transcription Service (outside broadcasting) and was married to the pianist Joan Davies.

Joseph Saxby: Improvisation

tr rec solo

For Carl

In one movement: Andantino.

First performance: date and location unknown.

Unpublished.

The single sheet of paper that contains this work is, in its way, among the most fascinating manuscripts in the archive. It is dated '18.2.51', underneath which is written 'Derby', presumably the place of its composition. It would appear to be the only surviving piece written by Joseph Saxby, at any rate for recorder.

In brackets below the title is written '(CD)', and these letters appear again above the first two notes of the work (although the C is sharpened). This same rising semiquaver figure on the same notes is to be found elsewhere, most significantly five bars from the end. (Incidentally, one is led to wonder if the sloping line after the D in this bar represents a glissando up to the F that follows.) At the end of the work Saxby has written: 'This is but an attempt to write a slight piece for solo recorder and is to be played with complete freedom by the performer; not going by the bar line, but rather the phrase! (sic)'

Perhaps there is a hint here of the many discussions on interpretation that must have taken place between the two men, whose musical collaboration, even at this date, was approaching 20 years. The piece contains many indications of dynamics and articulation (and ornaments too) and is short enough to include here in its entirety.

We are left to imagine what Carl Dolmetsch himself made of this miniature.

8 The manuscript of Joseph Saxby's *Improvisation*.

Thomas Pitfield: Deva Suite

rec trio (des, tr, t)

To Carl Dolmetsch

1 Chester Waits' Tune (Allegro). 2 Air (Moderato semplice). 3 In Folksong Manner (Andante teneramente). 4 Finale: Jig and Trio (Allegro).

First performance: date and location unknown.

Published: London: Boosey and Hawkes Ltd, 1956 (18228).

There is only one brief letter referring to this work in the archive. This is from Thomas Pitfield to Dolmetsch and is dated 3 February 1989. It reads as follows:

> A voice out of the blue!
> John Turner tells me you would like a copy of Deva Suite – herewith wrapped up in my latest booklet.
> Through J.T.'s intervention, I have written a number of recorder works, amongst these a concerto for a Bowdon Festival, a solo sonatina and several suites (I still keep busy with all my vices)
> Wellwishings also to Joseph Saxby.

Alas, no manuscript of the work is to be found in the archive, nor indeed the copy of the published score referred to in the above letter.[2]

The work is an agreeable though not particularly outstanding piece of writing for recorder trio, and it is perhaps the two brief inner movements that contain its best and most characteristic music. The Chester Waits' tune used in the first movement, or at least a variant of it, appears in the trio section of the Jig and Trio finale.

The direction 'solo' above the treble line seven bars from the end of the Air appears to indicate that the work may be played by more than one instrument per part. However, it is more likely that the composer intended the melody, a variant of that opening the movement on descant recorder, to be clearly heard at this point, (especially as it is also marked *mp* in contrast to *p* in the other parts).

It is frequently the case that composers make their acquaintance with the recorder in small-scale pieces such as the *Deva Suite* and subsequently write much more substantial and accomplished works for the instrument. Pitfield's concerto referred to in his letter to Dolmetsch and his *Three Nautical Sketches* certainly bear witness to this.

---

[2] I am grateful to John Turner for the loan of a copy of the published edition of the Suite, which is now out of print.

Cecily Lambert: Eclogue

rec (or fl), kbd

To Carl Dolmetsch

In one movement, marked 'freely, expressively'.

First performance: date and location unknown.

Unpublished.

The 11 pages of the composer's manuscript keyboard score, together with a separate recorder part, are dated November 1957. The piece, which is in a single substantial movement, is marked 'freely, expressively' and begins with eight bars for the recorder alone. Initially in 4/4 time, the later introduction of bars of 3/4 and 5/4 provide rhythmic fluidity and much use is made of a little quintuplet figure with which the work opens. A number of thematic ideas are developed and at bar 46 the score is marked *scherzando*, the piano introducing a theme hinted at some dozen bars earlier by the recorder. The piano part is more than mere accompaniment and frequently shares the thematic material with the recorder in addition to providing an expressive and at times chromatic harmonic foundation.

This would appear to be the earliest of three pieces Cecily Lambert dedicated to Dolmetsch or members of the family, it being followed by *Aubade*, published in 1962, and the unpublished *Bergomask*, also dating from 1962, both for recorder quartet.

Cecily Lambert also had a recorder tutor and three collections of easy pieces and arrangements for recorder published by Forsyth Brothers of Manchester.

Georges Migot: Suite for Two Recorders

des rec (or fl), tr rec (or cl)

To Carl Dolmetsch

1 Allant. 2 Grave. 3 Finale: décidé.

First performance: date and location unknown.

Published: Kassel: Bärenreiter-Verlag, 1958 (Edition 3225).

It is likely that this is another work resulting from a meeting with the composer during Dolmetsch's tour of France in 1956. The published edition dates from the same year as that of Migot's *Sonatine* (given its UK premiere in Dolmetsch's 1961 Wigmore Hall recital).

The first movement has a metronome mark of $\quarternote$ = c. 96–100 and begins on the second beat of a 4/4 bar with a rather angular melody for the descant. There is no key signature, but all the Fs are sharpened, both in the descant part and in the treble, which is in the same mode and moves mainly in quavers and in contrary motion to the descant. At bar 5 the beginning of the opening melody is repeated *en echo* but is soon varied. The phrasing of the two lines overlaps and groups of quavers are soon beamed across the bar lines. A triplet figure is introduced later in what is quite a brief movement just 41 bars in length.

As in the first movement the second also begins on the second beat of a 4/4 bar. The *Grave* tempo indication is qualified by a metronome marking of ♩ = c. 66–69. Unlike the first movement, however, the two parts move quite independently. The treble enters first in mainly crotchet motion; the descant has triplet figuration and once again a wide-ranging and somewhat angular melodic line.

In the Finale (in 3/4, ♩ = c. 116) it is again the treble that begins, and its two-bar phrase, characterized by semiquaver two-note appoggiaturas that infuse the entire movement, is immediately repeated by the descant. Migot once again employs unusual phrase lengths with groups of quavers beamed across bar lines, and introduces a triplet figure as the movement develops.

The writing is not especially idiomatic for recorders and one wonders whether Migot actually conceived the piece for recorder duet, as it is certainly equally well suited to the alternative scoring for flute and clarinet. The playing score presents the music an octave lower than it will sound on recorders, obliging the treble to transpose up an octave. The pitch is therefore as the piece would sound on flute and clarinet, but in this form is not very practical for reading on a B♭ clarinet either.

Much of what can be said of the *Sonatine* also applies to the Suite, and although there is movement and rhythmic interest in both parts, the character of the melodic lines seems curiously elusive.

Arthur Milner: Suite

tr rec, pn

For Carl Dolmetsch

1 Dance (Allegretto). 2 Intermezzo (Andante espressivo e rubato). 3 Jig (Allegro).

First performance: date and location unknown.

Last movement only published: London: Novello, 1960.

The archive contains the manuscript score of the complete Suite and a letter from Milner to Dolmetsch dated 27 June 1958:

> Dear Carl,
> I have written the enclosed *Suite for Treble recorder and piano*, specially for you if you will honour me [by] accepting the dedication.
> If, however, after trying it over, you don't care for it, or find it unidiomatic for the recorder, please don't hesitate to say so: I shall quite understand. But, now that I am

getting more stuff accepted by publishers, I would like to do something for one whose playing has so often given me such intense pleasure.

If you accept the dedication, will you please return the MS so that I may suitably inscribe it before trying it out on a publisher?

Which publishers are most interested in recorder music? Up to the present my stuff has been done by Stainer and Bell, Augner, Ashdown and Novello, but I don't think any of them go in much for recorder music. Your advice would be appreciated here.

Warmest regards,

Yours ever

Arthur

Dolmetsch obviously accepted the dedication (which the manuscript now bears) and in the above letter underlined the name Novello noting at the foot, 'Novello has just begun a series.' He must have conveyed this information to Milner, as it was Novello who eventually published, not the whole suite, but the final movement only (retitled Gigue), and then in an edition indicated for violin and piano. A footnote on the first page of the published score (a copy of which Milner signed and sent to Dolmetsch in April 1960), informs us: 'This piece may be performed on treble recorder without alteration.'

Of the unpublished movements, the opening Dance is in 6/8 time and flows along over a carefully worked-out accompaniment. The recorder part includes a number of *ossias* to avoid high F#. In the second movement, titled Intermezzo, the recorder enters after two bars of piano introduction featuring a right hand ostinato in quavers. The final Jig (or Gigue) is in 6/8 time. The recorder's initial theme with its repeated note figures suits the instrument well.

It was presumably the association of jigs with the violin and the opportunity to spread a wider instrumental net that led Novello to publish this movement on its own. If, as Dolmetsch noted, Novello was at the time starting a series of recorder publications, it is indeed unfortunate that it did not see fit to include Milner's Suite in its entirety. It is an attractive work of a type that certainly has a place in the repertoire and even now would benefit from publication in full.

Gaston Saux: Pour une églogue Virgilienne (Pièce pastorale)

2 tr recs, t rec/3 tr recs

Au Mâitre Carl Dolmetsch

Single movement: Andante rustico.

First performance: date and location unknown.

Published: Paris: Aug. Zurfluh, 1961 (A.1059 Z).

This work, Saux's first for recorders, is scored for two trebles and tenor or alternatively three trebles, and dates from 1959. It was published specially by Zurfluh for a recorder competition (Concours National Union Française des Œuvres Laïques d'Education Artistique, 1961). A copy of the published edition is in the archive, and on the cover is written in pencil in Dolmetsch's hand: 'Brought back from France by Richard [Dolmetsch] April 1961'. Inside the score has been inscribed by the composer:

A l'éminent musicien, au merveilleux interprète Carl Dolmetsch l'auteur est heureux de dédier cette pièce pastorale en toute affectueuse amitié!

Gaston Saux Avril 1961

It is likely that Dolmetsch had met Saux during a tour of France in 1956. Marguerite Dolmetsch has confirmed that Richard had taken part in a music competition in France in 1961, but this appears to have been the 'Royaume de Musique' rather than the competition for which Saux's work had been composed.

The piece opens with the first treble on its own playing a flowing eight-bar melody in D major. It is then joined by the other two instruments, which accompany with a triplet figure in thirds. The parts enter again imitatively with a theme based on the opening melody, the tenor's entry being delayed for 11 bars. These elements are exchanged and developed over the 84 bars of the work – a gentle pastoral making use one of the recorder's traditional musical associations.

Saux's music is conservative in style but suits the recorder well. In the remaining years of his life (Saux died in 1969) he composed a further 19 works including recorders, among them four recorder quartets.

Elna Sherman: Air de souvenir

t rec (or des rec), pn

To Carl Dolmetsch and Joseph Saxby

Single movement: Andante.

First performance: date and location unknown.

Unpublished.

The manuscript of this work, dated December 1959, is to be found in a folder in the archive that contains a number of other manuscript works by American recorder player Elna Sherman.[3] Although the score is marked for tenor or descant recorder, the separate recorder part notes the instruments in reverse order.

After five bars of introduction the recorder enters with a melody featuring a

---

[3] An obituary of Elna Sherman by Natalie Palm was published in *The American Recorder*, 6 (1), Winter 1965, p. 19.

syncopated figure, the rhythm of which is derived from the inner parts of the keyboard introduction. The opening sets the mood for the remainder of this 62-bar piece. At the foot of the page containing the recorder part is the title *Polonaise*, but no further music is written and a note by the composer declares: 'This was to follow, but have not had time to copy it.' This would imply that the movement had indeed been composed.

The other pieces in the folder comprise a substantial three-movement sonata for tenor recorder (or oboe) and keyboard; a setting for high voice and descant recorder of *Willow Whistle* after a poem by Ethel Romig Fuller (on the reverse of which is written 'Christmas greetings to the Dolmetsch rising generation from Elna Sherman 1959'); and a theme and set of 12 variations for solo descant recorder on the Anglo-American sea shanty *Blow the Man Down*, dated spring 1957.

The sonata visits some less friendly recorder keys (E major and B major), but a letter enclosed with the score notes: 'Natalie Palme is taking it to Idyllwilde when she goes to study recorder, and plays it on the tenor very well.'

Jean Temprement: Suite exotique

solo des rec or other wind inst

1 Rizière (dedicated to Jean Henry). 2 Jonque funèbre (dedicated to Carl Dolmetsch). 3 Lotus d'or (dedicated to Carl Dolmetsch). 4 Chobo (dedicated to Richard Dolmetsch). 5 Dance du dragon (dedicated to Carl Dolmetsch).

First performance: date and location unknown.

Published: Paris: Aug. Zurfluh, 1961 (A.1066 Z).

John Turner first drew my attention to this suite, with three of its five movements dedicated to Carl Dolmetsch, before I had located a copy of the published edition in the archive. The copy at Haslemere was sent to Dolmetsch by Jean Henry with a letter dated 4 April 1961.

It is evident from a letter to Dolmetsch from Temprement dated 20 February 1960 that his conversion to the recorder and the inspiration for the suite were the result of attending a concert at the Salle Récamiex in Paris in which Dolmetsch and his son Richard had taken part and for which he had written a review in the *Revue moderne*.

Temprement's letter continued by noting that although originally sceptical about the instrument he was now convinced of its potential and wanted to compose various pieces for it. In the meantime he enclosed a piece, *Le charmeur de serpents*, composed for the flute, that he wanted to be played on the recorder just as it was, without any changes, or if these had to be made, kept to a minimum. Jean Henry had made a few suggestions that Temprement had marked in pencil, but he considered these strayed too far from the original. Henry had further suggested that the piece should be played on an alto recorder, but Temprement gave his authority for the piece to be transposed provided it did not affect the original feel of the piece.

The manuscript of the piece is in the archive and contains Jean Henry's suggestions as noted by the composer. As the accompanying letter later explained, the piece was originally conceived not only for flute but also with an accompaniment of string quartet, oboe and clarinet. Temprement offered to send the parts, but noted that the piece could also be played as a solo. For future compositions he asked Dolmetsch if he had a preference for a particular ensemble, noting that he planned to write pieces for solo flute, a flute ensemble, flute and wind instruments and flute and orchestra.

If, as seems likely, Temprement's reference to the 'flute' was intended to mean recorder, his plans for the instrument were ambitious, but of these, only the solo *Suite exotique* appears to have been realized.

Although the cover of the published edition indicates the work as being for recorder (or other wind instrument), the separate movements are all headed 'pour flûte à bec soprano solo' and make use of the full compass of that instrument right up to high E♭.[4]

The first movement, 'Rizière' (paddy field), is mostly in a moderate 3/4 and, as might be expected, makes use of a pentatonic scale. A central section in common time makes more intervallic exploration, with hints of a whole-tone melody, before a return to 3/4 time and a speeding up of the tempo towards the last few bars, marked *rapide*. At the point at which the tempo increases the score is marked *en roulant* and a footnote explains: 'en faisant rouler la langue sur le palais' – an indication for flutter tonguing.

'Jonque funèbre' depicts the progress of a funeral barge in three clearly defined sections but without any time signature or barlines. The first section is directed to be played at ♩ = 72, and the wide-ranging melody makes much use of the interval of a minor third. This interval also characterizes the central section marked *Più vivo* (♩ = 108). The final section is marked *Lento* (♩ = 69) and although the minor third persists, there is a falling chromatic phrase shortly before the end.

There are likewise no time signature or barlines in the next movement, 'Lotus d'or', which after beginning at ♩ = 80, followed by a short section marked *Più lento, più leggero*, continues for the remainder *Più vivo*. The omission of bar lines provides considerable rhythmic freedom, but there is an overall melodic unity stemming from the opening melody interrupted by some pentatonic arpeggios and chromatic inflections.

---

[4] In a letter to the author dated 27 July 2000 Edgar Hunt recalls of Temprement: 'I seem to remember that, as a player, his performances were limited to his own compositions! There came a time when people wanted to play the bass viol, but could not afford to buy one; so he started to teach them to make "bass viols" – more like coffins than musical instruments!'

'Chobo', like the preceding two movements, is devoid of time signature or bar lines and is again in three distinct sections, in this case with an ABA structure, the A sections being quicker. The composer similarly appears to have devised a distinctive mode from which his melodies are derived.

The rapid and exciting 'Dance du dragon' is in 2/4 time, but even within this there are some unusual rhythmic patterns that need to be worked out carefully. However, the main forward driving energy is created by semiquaver groupings ($\quarternote$ = 132) with repeated notes (mostly E's) – particularly effective recorder figuration. A slower section ($\quarternote$ = 66) brings a moment of calm, before a return of the opening formula ends the piece and the suite energetically.

Zvi Herbert Nagan: Trio

des rec, vn, va

Written for and dedicated to Carl Dolmetsch

1 Cheerful Pastoral (Giocoso alla pastorale). 2 Monologue (Moderato). 3 In Various Moods (Theme and Variations). 4 Finale (Dance): Moderato – Allegro.

First performance: Date and location unknown.

Unpublished.

A mechanically reproduced copy in the archive of the composer's manuscript score of this unusually scored work is dated 1960.

The first movement is in 6/4 time, has a metronome marking of $\dottedhalfnote$ = 56 and opens with the recorder alone, almost immediately to be joined by the strings. Double stops in both the violin and viola parts enrich the texture and the music moves along with pastoral ease.

A pastoral character also pervades the opening of the second movement, entitled monologue, as the strings play mainly drones above which the recorder has a flowing melody in 9/8 time. Later the strings begin to participate more in the recorder's movement.

'In Various Moods' is the heading of the third movement, and these are achieved in a theme and variations. The theme itself is quite extended and passes to the violin in the second variation.

The finale is a dance that after a three-bar introduction launches into the dance proper. Both the introduction and the dance have thematic links with the theme used for the variations.

This is such an unusually if not uniquely scored piece that certainly possesses originality on that account. The recorder writing lies comfortably and, together with that for the two string instruments, results in a satisfying work that is nevertheless in a thoroughly conventional musical style.

H.A. Peter: Präludium

tr rec, pn

To Mister Dr. Carl Dolmetsch

First performance: date and location unknown.

Unpublished.

Perhaps this work resulted from a Dolmetsch/Saxby Scandinavian tour (the autographed manuscript score dated 1960 contains the composer's Swedish address), although the archive also contains the manuscript (dated 1951) of a work entitled *Giga* by Peter for the same scoring that does not bear a dedication to Dolmetsch.

The single movement is marked *moderato*, is in 4/4 time and moves mainly in semiquavers in the recorder part. The opening bars are representative of the textures encountered throughout, the piano providing a rhythmically insistent accompaniment to the recorder's busy melodic line.

In addition to the score there is a manuscript recorder part that contains a seven-bar section indicated to be added after bar 28 not included in the score, and two bars' rest at bars 23 and 24 where the recorder part continues in the score. This leads to the supposition that the work may not have received a performance.

The piece moves along somewhat conventionally but with a baroque-inspired energy that would suit the alternative use of harpsichord as the accompanying keyboard instrument.

Cecily Lambert: Aubade

rec qt

To Carl Dolmetsch

Single movement: Moderato.

First performance: date and location not certain.

Published: London: Universal Edition, 1962 (UE 12639).

This short work, 36 bars in length, occupies just two pages in the published edition. There is no copy of the manuscript in the archive, and only one letter from the composer that refers to it.

The lower three instruments play a two-bar introductory phrase in 3/2 time, but the time signature is then immediately changed to 6/4, which persists (apart from a single bar of 3/4) for the remainder of the work. The descant enters in bar 3 with a melody that provides the character of the entire piece, and elements of it are exchanged between all the parts throughout.

A later variant of this opening idea, including a triplet figure, is introduced by the treble and is taken up in a slightly varied form both by descant and bass. The work ends with an ascending scale containing F# and B♭ for the descant over a D major chord, though not before two bars of quadruplet grouped minims in the bass, featuring flattened and sharpened leading notes, provide last moments of harmonic tension.

Though dedicated to Carl Dolmetsch, it seems to have been the Dolmetsch children who played the piece, and both Jeanne and Marguerite remember that Richard's expressive interpretation of the descant line brought an atmosphere to the work that might not have been at first apparent from the printed score.

Jeanne and Marguerite were unable to recall the date of a first performance, but thought it may well have taken place (as a number of other pieces around the early 1960s) at a January meeting of the London branch of the Society of Recorder Players in the Waldegrave Hall. Cecily Lambert certainly mentions having heard a performance in her letter dated 24 February 1962, with which she enclosed a companion work, *Bergomask*, significantly dedicated to the Dolmetsch children (Chapter 5).

David Dorward: Concert-Duo

des rec, hpd

For Carl Dolmetsch and Joseph Saxby

1 Tempo giusto. 2 Lento. 3 Vivace.

First performance: The Great Drawing Room, Arts Council of Great Britain, 4 St James's Square, London, 7 December 1962. Carl Dolmetsch, rec; Joseph Saxby, hpd.

Published: Wilhemshaven: Heinrichsofen Verlag, 1977 (N1427).

No correspondence in connection with this work is to be found in the archive, but it does contain the autograph manuscript score, signed and marked Edinburgh 8 October 1962.

I contacted David Dorward to seek more information on the origins of the piece, but he was unable to remember the exact circumstances under which he received the commission. He did recall, however, that it was not until after the concert in which the work received its premiere that he met Carl Dolmetsch and Joseph Saxby. Dorward further noted that he had virtually no connection with the recorder prior to writing the piece.[5]

In early April 2002 Ross Winters contacted me with news that, among the papers of his late father, Leslie Winters, he had found a number of letters that gave

---

[5] Letter to the author dated 21 February 2001. Dorward mentions having had a plastic descant recorder on which he amused himself by improvising.

much information about the piece.[6] Inspection of these did indeed provide the information regarding the commission that Dorward had been unable to recall.

Leslie Winters' first letter to Dolmetsch, dated 10 May 1962, notes that the executive committee of the Macnaughton Concerts, of which he was a member, was drawing up plans for the 1962–63 season. One particular idea was the presentation of a concert of new music for old instruments; Dolmetsch and Saxby were invited to participate. Some suggestions for pieces that might be included were put forward, but there was no mention at this stage of the new work by Dorward.

Further correspondence was exchanged over subsequent weeks regarding the programme and Dolmetsch was invited to organize the remaining non-recorder items in the programme. The commission from Dorward is first noted in a letter to Dolmetsch dated 20 June, in which Leslie Winters advises:

> We have asked David Dorward to compose a work lasting for approximately ten minutes for you to play with Joseph Saxby as a first performance, and subject to the approval of both yourself and the committee we shall be very pleased if you will undertake to learn the work for next season's concert. David Dorward's style is not unduly 'advanced' and I think he will probably produce a work which is agreeable to you. If you will be good enough to consent to do this we shall be grateful if you can let us know as soon as possible WHICH recorder you would like it composed for.

Organizational commitments for the Haslemere Festival delayed Dolmetsch's response, but on 13 July 1962 Greta Matthews replied on his behalf providing the following information:

> In regard to the new work for recorder and harpsichord to be written by David Dorward, Dr. Dolmetsch says that if it is to be mainly pastoral and lyrical in character, it should be for the tenor recorder – this does not mean that all traces of vivacity should be excluded. On the other hand, if the work is to be of a more lively and sparkling nature, it should be definitely for the descant recorder. Dr. Dolmetsch specifies these two because so much of the modern repertoire is for the treble recorder.

Leslie Winters communicated this information to Dorward in a letter dated 15 July 1962. No further mention of the new work was made in the remaining correspondence, which dealt mainly with the drafting and finalization of the programme. Besides the new work by Dorward the other pieces including recorder were: Rubbra's *Passacaglia sopra 'Plusieurs regrets'* for recorder and harpsichord, Walter Bergmann's *Pastoral* for alto voice and recorder, Hindemith's *Abend-Konzert* for three recorders and Herbert Murrill's Sonata for recorder and harpsichord.

A programme note describes the three movements of the *Concert-Duo* as

---

[6] These letters (including those quoted from in this section) are now in the possession of Ross Winters.

'quick concertante', 'slow passacaglia' and 'rondo', but these do not appear in the manuscript or the published edition, both of which include only the tempo markings given in the heading of this section.

The *Concert-Duo* is a large-scale concert work scored, as suggested by Dolmetsch, for the descant (soprano) recorder, and specifically, because the concert was for old instruments, the harpsichord rather than the piano.

The first movement is propelled from the very beginning by energetic Walton-like rhythms[7] and after only three semiquaver harpsichord chords the recorder enters with a rising figure that infuses the entire movement.

Syncopated right-hand chords above a ground bass in 3/4 time (the passacaglia of the original movement title) form the harpsichord's introduction to the middle slow movement.[8] When the recorder enters it is with an intricately decorated melody, the textures of which the harpsichord also gradually assimilates.

Eventually the music leads to a solo section for the harpsichord marked *cadenza – tempo rubato* and ending on a C minor chord. The final 11 bars are a total contrast, seemingly stripped of all the previous decorative elements. The harpsichord writing is reduced to just two parts, the left hand maintaining the ground bass (now transposed up a fifth) and the right hand having a melody mainly in quavers that feels like a theme of which the recorder's first entry has been a variation. When the recorder enters for the last six bars it is with the ground bass in its original key, forming a melody above the harpsichord's continuing two-part counterpoint – a most effective conclusion.

Although the finale starts as a lively jig with recorder and harpsichord sharing the 6/8 quaver movement, this is interrupted by a solo section of nine bars for the harpsichord alone, marked *Poco meno mosso*. The time changes to 2/4 (♩ equalling a ♩. of the 6/8) and the key signature to four flats, but there is soon a return to 6/8 and the music accelerates to the opening tempo as the recorder restates the opening material above a single line for the harpsichord. There is a further duple time and *Poco meno mosso* interruption starting with the harpsichord, soon joined by the recorder with figuration derived from that of the harpsichord right hand. Once again the 6/8 metre returns, with acceleration to the original tempo, this time led by the recorder with a rising scale figure taken up by the harpsichord two bars later. There is no re-appearance of the slower duple time section and the jig-like music races to a brilliant conclusion on a high C for the recorder and resonant C major chords on the harpsichord.

A review by Leslie Winters of the concert, published in the *Dolmetsch Foundation Bulletin*, notes of the *Concert-Duo*: 'David Dorward writes in a direct

---

[7] Letter to the author dated 21 February 2001. Dorward describes the piece as 'neo-classical' Stravinsky.

[8] Ibid. Dorward comments that the instruction for the harpsichord right hand noted in the manuscript and the proofs as 'pochis. arpeg'. had been translated into 'something rich and strange' ('pochis. atgeg.') in the published copy.

and attractive idiom and the piece was well conceived for the recorder. It was a work that made an immediate appeal although one felt that that possibly the composer's invention flagged somewhat in the final movement.'[9]

The work was not published until 1977 and a review by Ross Winters was included in *Recorder & Music*:[10]

> As is often the case with non avant-garde repertoire the most revealing and most convincing movement is the second. It is an anguished and impassioned outpouring. One senses the attempt to communicate deep feelings and that despite the apparently tranquil ending, release and resolution have not been really experienced. By contrast, the outer movements have less to say. The first is fairly lyrical with some rhythmic imagination. The last is another of those attempts to be light-hearted which remain unconvincing, although partly redeemed by the slow interludes. Having said all this, however, it compares favourably with many published contemporary works as a substantial and serious addition to the repertoire of the descant recorder.

Despite any shortcomings noted by the reviewers, the *Concert-Duo* is noteworthy for the idiomatic writing for both instruments.

The work has found an enthusiastic champion in John Turner who has broadcast it twice.

Felix Werder: Gambit

tr rec, hpd

To Carl Dolmetsch and Joseph Saxby

In one movement.

First performance: date and location unknown.

Unpublished.

From the autograph, dated 'Melbourne III. 65' and located in the Dolmetsch archive, it would appear that, like Butterley's *The White-Throated Warbler*, Werder's *Gambit* resulted from the Dolmetsch/Saxby tour of Australia in 1965. Unfortunately there is no associated correspondence.

The work is in a single movement in bars mostly of 6/8 but with some in 5/8. The opening five bars, marked $\rfloor = 52$, lead to the main body of the work, marked *poco più mosso* at $\rfloor = 63$. In style it is fragmentary and brittle, with quite complex rhythmic structures that on paper, at least, are reminiscent of Martin Dalby's *Páginas*, composed for Dolmetsch's 1973 Wigmore Hall recital.

Although melodic development is perhaps a less prominent feature than the

---

[9] *Dolmetsch Foundation Bulletin*, April 1963, p. 6.
[10] March 1979, p. 154.

exploration of rhythmic structures and transparent recorder/harpsichord textures, the recorder's opening theme is momentarily re-introduced at the fourth below (bar 27). However, considerable use is made in both recorder and harpsichord parts of short rising motives that permeate the entire work and provide its original character.

The manuscript score contains Joseph Saxby's characteristic markings for fingering and registration, and the rhythmic complexity of the piece is underlined by Dolmetsch's annotation of the recorder part with marks to indicate the location of quaver beats within the bar.

Werder was born in Berlin in 1922, the son of a cantor and liturgical composer at a leading Berlin synagogue. In 1935 he fled to England before a further move to Australia in 1940. His list of compositions contains works for many different ensembles, large and small, and includes a considerable quantity of chamber music, much of it for wind instruments, and some featuring unusual instrumental combinations.

Gambit would appear to have been Werder's only previous composition for recorder, but the author's contact with him in connection with the work in August 2001 stimulated the writing of another piece, *Twelfth Night*, for recorder and piano, for John Turner.

Carl Dolmetsch: Two Dances

b rec, hpd

[1] Tempo di gavotta. [2] Borey.

First performance: Haslemere Festival children's concert, Haslemere Hall, 1966 (Borey only). Carl Dolmetsch, rec; Joseph Saxby, hpd. Date and location of the first movement's premiere unknown.

Unpublished.

These two pieces were composed at separate times and probably not intended to form a pair. The reason that Dolmetsch wrote them lay simply in the very limited repertoire for bass recorder and keyboard. In some of his recitals, especially those for schools, Dolmetsch liked to demonstrate all sizes of recorder and would therefore include one or the other of these little pieces, which were written to show that the bass recorder could play a lively melody in addition to its usual bass-line role.

The manuscript score and part of the *Tempo di gavotta*, both in pencil, are undated and headed 'Anon. English'. Similarly, its companion piece, the *Borey*, is headed 'Anon.' and the manuscript score and part, marked 'For Haslemere Festival children's concert 1966', are dated '11.6.66'. Both are dances based on old forms with which Dolmetsch will have been very familiar. The *Tempo di gavotta* is in binary form with section repeats. The *Borey* is in a single repeated section, and there are what appear to be sketches for a varied repeat attached to the recorder part on a separate sheet.

Jeanne Dolmetsch confirmed that despite the anonymous attributions, both pieces are the work of her father. They must have been heard on countless occasions and Dolmetsch included the *Tempo di gavotta* (with its true authorship ascribed) in a sequence of pieces featuring in turn sopranino, descant, tenor and bass recorders in his very last Wigmore Hall recital in October 1989.

The programme note on that occasion for the *Tempo di gavotta* reads: 'Prompted by the scarcity of solo music for bass recorder, Carl Dolmetsch has written this lively Gavotte exploiting the entire compass of the instrument, displaying a range far wider than is usually met in consort playing.' (Up to top G.)

Though composed for a particular purpose, these jolly dances would no doubt be enjoyed by many bass recorder players were they to be published at some time in the future.

León J. Simar: Concerto '1741'

tr rec, hpd

To Carl Dolmetsch

1 Allegro. 2 Largo. 3 Presto.

First performance: date and location unknown.

Unpublished.

A mechanically reproduced copy of the manuscript in the archive is dated September 1966 and is inscribed: 'Pour M. Carl Dolmetsch, avec l'expressions de mes vifs sentiments de sympathies et d'admirations. Cali November 1966 León J. Simar'.

'1741', the year of Antonio Vivaldi's death, is the clue to the style of this work, which is a piece of enthusiastically contrived pastiche of Italian baroque concerto elements. It is a three-movement chamber concerto for recorder and obbligato harpsichord in a distinctly baroque style. An attractive piece if approached in the spirit in which it was clearly composed.

From a conversation with François Dolmetsch in July 2000 I was able to learn more of Simar. He appears to have been a composer of much talent and promise – a winner of the Prix de Rome in his youth. However, his wartime Nazi sympathies created problems for him in his native Belgium, and he therefore took up residence in South America. The *Concerto* 1741 was probably composed as a result of one of Carl Dolmetsch's visits to Colombia.

Colin Hand: Sonata piccola, Op. 63

tr rec (or fl), hpd (or pn)

To Carl Dolmetsch

1 Preludio (Allegro agitato). 2 Cantilena (Andante piangevole). 3 Burlesca (Allegretto giocoso).

First performance: Los Angeles USA, September 1966. Carl Dolmetsch, rec; Joseph Saxby, hpd.

Published: London: Boosey and Hawkes Ltd, 1968; Lindis Edition (distributed by William Elkin Music services), 1981; Hebden Bridge: Peacock Press, 2001.

There is no correspondence in connection with this work in the archive, but there is the manuscript score together with a copy of the Boosey and Hawkes edition signed by the composer. The Boosey and Hawkes edition bears a dedication, but not the manuscript or the later Lindis edition, in which it was omitted in error when the work was reset. This was observed and the printer asked to add it, but failed to do so, unfortunately producing the first two thousand copies without it.

The origins of the piece go back some years before it reached its final form, and what now forms the final movement, together with a short introduction, was performed as *Introduction and Burlesque* in a BBC radio broadcast by recorder player Philip Rogers and pianist Josephine Lee on 9 October 1957. The *Burlesque* made use of the main theme and some material from a previously composed work for clarinet and piano entitled *Integration*.[11]

Early in 1966 Colin Hand was invited by Edwin Alton to attend a recital in Clitheroe, Lancashire, given by Carl Dolmetsch and Joseph Saxby. After the recital Hand was introduced to Dolmetsch, who invited him to write a new piece for recorder. Hand turned to the *Burlesque* and replaced the previous short introduction with two new movements to form the *Sonata piccola*.[12] Dolmetsch took the work with him on his 1966 US tour where, in addition to its premiere, it received six further performances.

As he had suggested for a number of other works, Dolmetsch proposed to the composer the use of the sopranino in place of the treble recorder for the final movement. Hand was not, however, in favour of this, considering the resulting gap between solo line and accompaniment to be unsatisfactory.

The Preludio in 6/8 time opens with a two-bar introduction for the keyboard featuring a right-hand ostinato. This continues for the next six bars while the recorder announces the opening theme, which gives prominence to the interval of a rising seventh and makes use of syncopated rhythms. The little ♩. ♩♪ figure at the close is to become important as the movement progresses. At its next entry the

---

[11] This information was given to the author during a visit to the composer in June 2001.
[12] Ibid.

recorder introduces another motive derived directly from the opening keyboard ostinato. After developing this material over running keyboard figuration and in exchanges with the keyboard right hand, the recapitulation is delayed until just nine bars from the end of the movement, which closes with a rising seventh from D to C for the recorder.

As its title suggests, the Cantilena (in 3/4 time) contains an almost uninterrupted flow of melody for the recorder over an accompaniment that at first is chordal and rhythmically insistent. This becomes gradually more involved as the right hand joins in the melodic material. Eventually the recorder falls silent for just eight bars while the keyboard continues with the main theme above semiquaver arpeggios that persist when the recorder re-enters. Eventually the keyboard chords return in the keyboard right hand while the left hand has an ostinato in octaves based on a fragment of earlier melody, with which the recorder too brings the movement to a close.

A rhythmically insistent keyboard introduction also opens the *Burlesca* finale, and the recorder enters after just two bars with an angular but jocular theme (mainly in 2/2 time but including a single bar of 1/2), fragments of which are interjected by the keyboard right hand. There is a relaxation of tempo and mood in a *Poco meno mosso* central section, in which the recorder introduces a new theme. At first the keyboard is content to accompany with rhythmic fragments, but eventually it discovers that this theme will work in canon and follows the recorder at a crotchet's distance. At the resumption of the opening tempo the keyboard accompaniment takes on a more intricate texture while the recorder restates the opening theme. This recapitulation is, however, truncated and the movement comes to an abrupt but satisfying close, *senza rit.*

Hand's writing for the recorder in this work is expertly crafted and it has much in common with his earlier and equally idiomatic Sonatina No. 1, Op. 41, composed for Philip Rogers.

Christopher Edmunds: Pastorale and Bourée

des rec, pn

For Carl Dolmetsch with greetings for 1968

[1] Pastorale (Andante e dolce). [2] Bourée (Allegretto comodo).

First performance: date and location unknown.

Published: Hebden Bridge: Peacock Press, 2002 (PD 03).

This would appear to have been among Dolmetsch's favourite pieces and was recorded by him with Joseph Saxby during their seventeenth American tour in 1974.[13]

---

[13] *The Contemporary Recorder*, Orion Master Recordings, cassette OC 692.

In addition to the composer's autograph manuscript score and recorder part (dated January 1968), both in the Dolmetsch archive, there is what appears to be the proof of a trial run for a published edition, but this was never made generally available. A modern edition edited by Jeanne Dolmetsch and the author was eventually published by Peacock Press as the third title in the *Carl Dolmetsch 20th century Recorder Archive* series. There are a number of minor differences between the score and the recorder part in terms of articulation and phrasing, and the part has had further such additions made in pencil by Dolmetsch.

The *Pastorale* (in 9/8 time, ♩. = c. 60) is in A major and opens with a gentle two-bar piano introduction that immediately sets the mood for the entry of the recorder with a flow of melody that is to continue virtually uninterrupted for the entire movement.

At the very end of the movement the score is marked *cadez*, and some form of improvisatory link to the *Bourée* is perhaps required. In the recording Saxby provided a keyboard flourish and Dolmetsch a brief recorder cadenza that is written out at the end of the manuscript recorder part. However, it is possible to play the bar linking the two movements without any additions and simply stretch out the tempo (as indicated by the composer's direction *ad lib*) to provide a satisfactory rhythmic spring off its final note to begin the *Bourée*.

The *Bourée* is in A minor and no metronome mark is given to supplement the *Allegretto comodo* tempo indication. The piano part is marked *delicato*. The shape of the recorder's opening melody is a little reminiscent of that of the *Bourrée* in Reizenstein's Partita, but Edmunds's is characterized by octave leaps. This formula is maintained until the direction *dolcissim.* brings a change of mood, though the octave leaps persist and give a unity to the movement as a whole, which ends calmly and quietly, but still maintaining a dance-like character.

The opening *Pastoral* has something of the gentle romantic qualities found in the first movement of York Bowen's Sonatina, and the lively but not over energetic *Bourée* forms an ideal contrast. The entire work is a well crafted and delightful miniature, a worthy companion piece to Edmunds's earlier single-movement Sonatina for descant recorder and piano, dedicated to Edgar Hunt.[14]

Colin Hand: Petite suite champêtre, Op. 67

des rec (or fl/ob), pn

1 Entrée (Andante e poco maestoso). 2 Danse-Pastorale (Allegretto). 3 Tambourin (Allegro commodo ma con energia). 4 Danse-Finale (Allegro giusto).

First performance (in qt arr): Haslemere Museum (Dolmetsch Foundation AGM), 1968. First performance of rec and pn version, 1972.

---

[14] Published London: Schott & Co. Ltd, 1941.

Published: London: Boosey and Hawkes Ltd, 1971 (19965).

This work was not the result of a commission, but, in the words of the composer, 'just written' in 1966. It was sent to Dolmetsch, who suggested in a letter written to Hand in April 1968 that an arrangement for recorder, violin cello and harpsichord would be a welcome addition to the repertoire of the Dolmetsch/Schoenfeld ensemble. Hand completed this arrangement (of which a manuscript score and parts is in the archive) almost immediately. Also with the performing material is a part for tenor viol as an alternative to the cello, and it is likely that it was in this arrangement the work received its first performance.

The published version is with the original descant recorder and piano scoring, in which form Dolmetsch recorded the work with Joseph Saxby during their seventeenth concert tour of the United States in 1974.[15] Although the original version is entirely satisfactory, the quartet arrangement is a colourful alternative, in which the descant recorder adds a piquant voice that suits the rustic nature of the music admirably.

The first movement is a sort of stately bourrée starting on an upbeat and founded on rising fourths and fifths. It occupies a brief 24 bars and leads *attacca* into the *Danse-Pastorale*, a lilting movement in 3/8 with some unusual but effective phrase lengths. The *Tambourin* bustles along in 2/2 over a piano accompaniment that provides both drone and rhythmic drive. The otherwise regular progress is interrupted by some strategically placed bars of 1/2 that emphasise the repeated-note figure at the end of phrases or add a cheeky octave leap. A central episode marked *Poco più sostenuto* provides a contrast of texture and melody, then leads to a da capo restatement of the energetic opening section to bring the movement to close. The *Danse-finale* moves with an ease that belies its 7/4-6/4 time signature and, at the end of a work with a mainly modal feel, closes firmly in G major.

A strong dance element is present throughout the suite, and it is not only in the overall title of the work and its individual movements that the rustic charm of the French baroque is recalled, albeit with a distinctly twentieth-century musical accent. A charming miniature in either version well crafted for the recorder.

Hans Gál: Divertimento Op. 98

des, tr and t recs

1 Melodia (Allegretto tranquillo). 2 Rigaudon (Andante grazioso). 3 Rondino (Allegro).

---

[15] *The Contemporary Recorder*, Orion Master Recordings, cassette, OC 692.

First performance: date and location unknown.[16]

Published: London: Schott & Co. Ltd, 1972 (OFB 120).

Although this work does not bear a dedication either in the manuscript (a photocopy of which is in the archive) or in the published edition, the correspondence that has survived indicates that it was indeed composed for the Dolmetsch family.

Copies of the score were sent to Dolmetsch with a most friendly accompanying letter dated 15 May 1969 that reads as follows:

Dear Carl,

I hope that the enclosed gift of a comfortable, idle week will prove suitable for the "Flauto Dolce" series: as far as I can judge it should not be difficult and enjoyable to play. Well, I add two Xerox copies to the original, and it would be very nice indeed if you could get our dear young mutual friends J. & G. for a running through. Give them a kiss from me! (No: two)

Love from

Hans

It is clear that, together with Jeanne and Marguerite, Dolmetsch did try the piece through almost immediately, and gave his thanks and enthusiastic comments in a letter to the composer dated 28 May 1969:

My dear Hans,

What a lovely surprise: My girls and I played through your new Divertimento twice with enthusiasm and pleasure. We liked it immediately, and even more the second time. The technical demands will make it accessible to many players, yet it is by no means lacking in sophistication for the more advanced. The tempi you indicate work out very naturally; but for the Rigaudon we think you must have meant crotchet 126, not quaver. At least we played it at crotchet 126 and felt it would make every sailor dance!

I will certainly send one photocopy to Universal Edition with my active recommendation to publish; then we will wait to see what happens.

With warm thanks again for the kindly thought and our love and greetings to Hanna, yourself and the young couple.

As ever

Carl

Gál responded immediately expressing his delight that the piece had been well received, and explaining the slower tempo for the Rigaudon to be correct. His letter is dated 31 May 1969.

---

[16] Jeanne Dolmetsch was not able to recall the precise details of a first performance but thought this was likely to have been given at a meeting of the Dolmetsch Foundation.

My dear Carl,

I am delighted to learn that, once more, we seem to agree: I must confess, reluctantly that I am inordinately fond of that new piece. Now let's hope that U.E. will share our favourable opinion!

126 for the quaver is correct: try it so with capriciously stiff quavers, and you will see that it clicks. Well, played with virtuosity, the double speed could make a nice effect, but I doubt whether middling people would get over the semiquavers without a hitch, or several ...

Love and 100 thanks to the first performers!

Yours ever,

Hans

In the event it was Schott who eventually published this happy example of Gál's musical craftsmanship, trio writing being a form of which he was particularly fond.

Although it may appear from Gál's letter that performers have the composer's authority to perform the Rigaudon at $\downarrow = 126$, his daughter Eva explained to me that the comment '... the double speed could make a nice effect ...' was a characteristically ironic but gentle insistence that the piece should be played exactly as indicated.

Colin Hand: Plaint, Op. 72

t rec, hpd (or pn)

Single movement: Adagio espressivo e con molto rubato.

First (private) performance: Birmingham. Paul Clark, rec; the composer, pn.

First public performance: Dolmetsch Summer School, 5 August 1971. Carl Dolmetsch, rec; Joseph Saxby, hpd.

Published: London: Schott & Co. Ltd, 1973 (Edition 11147).

This work, like the *Sonata piccola*, has a link with the *Introduction and Burlesque* composed for Philip Rogers's BBC radio broadcast in 1957. As noted in the section on *Sonata piccola*, the original introduction was discarded on the composition of the additional two new opening movements, but the theme from it was used in a work composed sometime later for solo guitar. This work too was to be withdrawn, but on looking at the theme again towards the end of 1970 Hand saw it had more potential than had hitherto been realized, and thus it eventually came to form the most effective basis of *Plaint*.

The new piece was sent to Dolmetsch as a New Year gift, and with a photocopy of the manuscript in the archive is a letter from Hand to Dolmetsch dated 9 January 1971:

My dear Carl,

A little New Year offering – there appears to be so small a repertoire for tenor recorder that I decided to write this 'Plaint'. It may be apt for viol (if not for voyces!)

Yours as ever

Colin

In a letter dated 12 January 1971 Dolmetsch thanked Hand for this lovely surprise, noting that in playing it through he had been taken with its 'romantic wistful style'. Having given the first performance in August 1971, Dolmetsch included the work in his US tour later that year, and in further recitals in 1972.

Although the published edition gives the piano as an alternative accompaniment, a composer's prefatory note reads: 'The keyboard part should be played on the harpsichord whenever possible, but if the piano is used, the texture of the music should always be clear, and overdue use of the sustaining pedal should be avoided.' The keyboard textures, when played on the harpsichord, permit the tenor recorder line to come through clearly even in the lower part of its compass, of which Hand makes expressive use.[17]

The first seven bars form a recitative-like introduction mainly for the recorder, with a sparse but telling contribution from the harpsichord. This leads to the main body of the work, based on two melodic elements. The first is founded on falling phrases, the second, by contrast, rising and more intense in expression. At first the harpsichord provides only a chordal accompaniment on the offbeats of the 2/4 bars, but as the movement progresses this becomes increasingly involved, eventually introducing semiquaver movement to intensify the return of the main theme. The recorder, now in its high register, rises to a top D just before a restatement of the very opening notes and a long-held final note with written-out inverted mordant bring this haunting work to a very satisfying close.[18]

A review by Herbert Hersom of the published edition in *Recorder & Music*[19] described it as: 'a very useful and attractive piece'. It certainly remained a firm favourite of Dolmetsch and was included in his recording made with Joseph Saxby during their seventeenth concert tour of America in 1974.[20] It was also in the programme of his very last Wigmore Hall recital in October 1989 where it formed

---

[17] The composer also made an arrangement for tenor recorder and guitar.

[18] The composer's own article on the work including details of its origins and some guidance on performance were contained in Hand, 'The Composer writes'.

[19] March 1974, **4**, p. 331.

[20] One aspect of this recording and of subsequent performances of which Colin Hand disapproved was the downward and upward flourish Dolmetsch added to the recorder's high B (superimposed with a pause) in the penultimate bar (and marked in pencil in the copy of the manuscript score in the archive). Hand considered this destroyed the climax to the recorder part and did not reflect the composer's style, the flourish making use of notes that were not within the melodic framework of the piece.

part of a series of pieces featuring in turn sopranino, descant, tenor and bass recorders.

Although the repertoire for tenor recorder has continued to grow, *Plaint* remains a particularly effective contribution to it and has received many performances. It is the composer's personal favourite among his many recorder compositions.[21]

Colin Hand: Sonata breve, Op. 78

tr rec, pn

To Carl Dolmetsch with affection on his 60th birthday: August 23rd 1971

Single movement in several sections: Poco agitato – Andante quasi recitativo – Allegro con moto – Più mosso – Tempo ad lib – Allegro scherzando.

First performance:[22] Boston, (Lincolnshire), 25 April 1974.

Published: London: Schott & Co. Ltd, 1977 (Edition 11265).

The origins of the *Sonata breve* are of particular interest as it had its genesis in a work for solo recorder that Hand entitled *Sonata alla Cadenza*, a photocopy of the manuscript of which remains in the archive. It makes use of sopranino, descant, treble and tenor recorders and the dedication on the manuscript is as that for *Sonata breve*. Inside the front cover is a detailed programme note that explains the concept and structure of the work. It is quoted here in full, as something of the original structure and virtually all the thematic material were to find their way into the *Sonata breve*:

> *Sonata alla Cadenza* is a derivative work, built almost entirely on the intervals of the perfect fourth and the major seventh together with its inversion, the minor second. Furthermore, it is monothematic, all the melodic material originating from the first subject through the process of thematic metamorphosis.
>
> Structurally it is an experimental work, attempting to combine two classical principles, namely Sonata Form with its three main divisions of exposition, development and recapitulation, and the traditional plan of the three movement sonata with its contrasting speeds, quick – slow – quick.
>
> Whilst *Sonata alla Cadenza* is a single movement work and should be regarded as such, it falls into four clearly defined sections. The first one corresponds on the one hand to a Sonata Form exposition with two subjects joined by a transitional passage and rounded off by a codetta, and, on the other hand, to a quick, first movement of a complete sonata.
>
> A short, recitative-like link leads to the second section serving the dual function of the development in Sonata Form structure, and the slow movement of the traditional multi-movement sonata plan.

---

[21] See article referred to in note 2 above.
[22] As the accompanied version of the *Sonata alla Cadenza*.

The third section is a cadenza proper which, in Sonata Form can be regarded either as an extension of the development section or as a cadenza per se positioned between the close of the development and the recapitulation as in the eighteenth century solo concerto plan.

The fourth section serves both as recapitulation in Sonata Form terms, being a transcription into 6/8 time of the original alla breve exposition, and as a quick finale in the three-movement plan. A short Coda based upon the 'codetta' at the end of the first section brings the work to an exciting finish.

Apart from changing speeds and time signatures from section to section, variety is further introduced by the use of four different sizes of recorders.

Treble recorder	Allegro poco agitato ($\quarternote$ = c. 120) ¢
Tenor recorder	Andante quasi recitativo ($\quarternote$ = c. 52) 3/4
	Andante con moto ($\quarternote$ = c. 92) 3/4
Treble recorder	Cadenza ad lib ($\quarternote$ = c. 92) no time signature and dotted bar lines (this portion may be omitted). Take descant in right hand for Adagio for descant and treble.
Descant recorder	Allegro scherzoso ($\dottedquarternote$ = c. 152) 6/8 leads to Presto alla breve, the final section for sopranino recorder. (There are alternatives for descant in two places should a sopranino not be available.)

Dolmetsch wrote to express his thanks and appreciation of the new work, noting that he had played it through but was 'not up to tempo yet'. Hand replied on 2 July 1971 in a letter that also enclosed a revised final section:

> Many thanks for your letter; so pleased you like Sonata alla cadenza. I am sending you an amended page 8 [the final page of the work] as I decided that a repetition of the opening sentence on page 7 would:
> a) give the small recorder a few more bars and a more satisfactory lead-in, and
> b) it would improve the structural balance at this point.
> Hope you approve, in which case perhaps you would like to replace the original page 8 with the enclosed one.

The section at the end of the cadenza requiring simultaneous playing of descant and treble instruments was an interesting innovation and David Bedford made use of the same device in a transition between movements in his recorder concerto written for Piers Adams in 1993–94.

Hand was not, however, entirely satisfied with the work, and in a letter to Dolmetsch dated 12 December 1972 explained his reasons for rewriting it for recorder and piano. 'I have rewritten your "birthday present" of Aug 1971 as I have never really been happy with a work in which the Treble Recorder had to provide its own support. This new version therefore comes to you with the same good wishes as expressed in the original manuscript.'

At this stage, the sections of the work for C instrument had been transposed to suit treble recorder fingering, but the solo cadenza remained. This too caused Hand some concern, however, as during the course of composition he had discussed the form with Gordon Jacob, who considered the cadenza could endanger the overall unity. When Hand submitted the work for publication in 1974 the cadenza also seemed to present a problem for Schotts, who felt it was too long and difficult. They further noted that a section for solo recorder in a work otherwise for recorder and piano was not likely to prove popular, and were not inclined to publish it in its present form. Hand therefore finally omitted the cadenza and eventually resubmitted the work, noting that the original title would no longer be appropriate. For a while no suitable new title came to mind, but in the end Hand suggested *Sonata breve* as a reference to the work's short duration.[23]

In its revised and published form, the *Sonata breve* shows no trace of the keyboard part's having been grafted onto a solo work. If anything the more concentrated form achieved through the various revisions and the omission of the cadenza do indeed enhance the monothematic structure and make for a more concise work overall. The return of the opening theme in its original form in the concluding coda provides a particularly satisfying close.

The published work was reviewed in *Recorder & Music*:

> [It is] over in a matter of five minutes, but it shows Colin Hand's excellent craftsmanship in the ways his ideas follow one another with a particular preoccupation with the interval of a fourth. It is not easy, but should be an admirable test for the open class of a music festival – something for the competitors to get their teeth into, plenty of variety and about the right length.[24]

However suitable as a competition piece, the *Sonata breve* is worthy of serious attention simply on its musically creative merits. It was included in a programme of English recorder music on a CD recorded by Ross Winters in 2000 in a performance enthusiastically received by the composer.[25]

Antony Hopkins: Fifty-Fourth Festival Fanfare

tr rec, pn

For Carl and Joseph

First performance: Haslemere Hall, 21 July 1978. Carl Dolmetsch, rec; Joseph Saxby, hpd.

Unpublished.

In 1978 Antony Hopkins was invited to open the 54th Haslemere Festival, and the text of his opening speech was included in the programme for that of 1979.

---

[23] The information noted in this paragraph was given to the author during a visit to the composer in June 2001.
[24] September 1977, 5, p. 373. The reviewer is F.O.M.
[25] *English Recorder Music: the Dolmetsch Legacy* (BMS425CD).

Hopkins noted that at the 54th Festival, the Dolmetsch/Saxby partnership had been going palindromically for 45 years. His fanfare composed for the occasion was thus founded on fifths and fourths and was included as a gesture to the twentieth century. A footnote to Hopkins's text informs us: 'A Fanfare for recorder and harpsichord specially composed for the occasion by Antony Hopkins was then performed.'

The composer's manuscript score (dated 27 June 1978) is in the archive together with a manuscript recorder part. There is also a photocopy of the part in which Dolmetsch has made a number of changes, mainly to avoid notes low in the recorder's compass that might have been obscured by the accompaniment. Although the piece was performed with harpsichord, the score is indicated *Pf* and contains markings for pedalling.

The Fanfare is just 20 bars long and suitably festive in style, beginning in 4/4 but containing further various time signatures. There is also a brief cadenza for the recorder marked *brillante ma in tempo*. This is clearly an occasional piece that, because of its brevity, does not ideally lend itself to publication, although it is certainly of interest.

Michael Short: Sonatina No. 1

tr rec, hpd

For Carl Dolmetsch and Joseph Saxby

1 Prelude (Lento non troppo). 2 Moto perpetuo (Vivo). 3 Aria (Andante). 4 Burlesca (Vivo).

First performance: Haslemere Museum Lecture Hall, 27 October 1979. Carl Dolmetsch, rec; Joseph Saxby, hpd.

Published: London: Studio Music Co., 1986.

Besides the manuscript of this work, the archive contains correspondence between Short and Dolmetsch regarding its composition and first performance. It would appear from the letter dated 13 September 1979 accompanying the new work that Joseph Saxby had been an influence on its composition. As Short noted:

> As a result of some prodding from Joseph, I have concocted a Sonatina for treble recorder and harpsichord which I enclose herewith.
>
> There is a Prelude, a Moto Perpetuo, an Aria (also a bit moto perpetuo) and a Burlesca.
>
> I regard this as a draft score, so please feel free to make any alterations, especially regarding phrasing, ornamentation, etc., which you may wish to make.
>
> I hope it will give you some amusement.

Dolmetsch was obviously pleased to receive the new work and wrote to Short on

20 September 1979: 'What a happy surprise! Thank you so much for writing a Sonatina for Joseph and me – as soon as we have had a chance to play through it together, I will write to you again.'

This Dolmetsch did on 2 October: 'Joseph and I read through your Sonatina the other day and enjoyed it tremendously. It is very colourful and lies well for the recorder. Since you invite my comments, may I at this stage suggest that the third movement (Aria) might benefit from a little judicious cutting?' Dolmetsch further noted his plans to introduce the work at the Dolmetsch Foundation Autumn meeting on 27 October 1979 and invited Short to be present.

Short responded positively to Dolmetsch's enthusiastic comments and suggestions in a letter dated 6 October:

> Thank you very much for your letter: I am glad to know that you and Joseph have tried through the Sonatina and found it to be playable.
>
> As regards the Aria, I think you are right – it does go on a bit too long, and therefore some cutting would be in order. Unfortunately I don't have a complete copy, only my rough sketches, so I am unable to make any precise suggestions, but will leave it to you to do what you think is best. There is also the possibility that the tempo may be a little slow: if it is not done at the right speed it will sound tedious.

Short also expressed the hope that he would be able to attend the première, and indeed did so, expressing his thanks for the performance in a letter dated 28 October 1979: 'This is just a line to thank you and Joseph for your performance of the Sonatina yesterday. I am particularly grateful for your improvements in matters of ornamentation and dynamic contrast which make all the difference to a piece of music.' The letter continues: '... I will perform the necessary surgery as soon as I can, and let you have it back. If I could pop down to Haslemere to hand it over in person, we could perhaps discuss one or two points if you have the time.'

On 13 November Short sent Dolmetsch the score and recorder part that had received some 'surgery', noting in his accompanying letter:

> I hope the recorder part is readable in spite of the alterations: the keyboard part got into such a mess that I had to write it out again. I have tried to insert all of Joseph's pencil annotations in the appropriate places, but it is possible that one or two of them have disappeared in this process, for which I apologise.
>
> Apart from transposition of the opening phrase, most of the changes consist of cutting out superfluous material, and I hope you will agree that the result is more concise than the rather long-winded original.[26]

---

[26] The score is as the published edition, but the cuts Short made are evident in the manuscript recorder part. In the second movement some 25 bars have been removed between figures 2 and 3, a number of bars before figure 5 and three bars before figure 7. In the third movement four bars have been cut before figure 11 and three bars from before figure 12. Cuts and amendments are also evident in the fourth movement, where portions of manuscript paper have been pasted over some lines and odd single bars have been cut.

In conclusion Short mentioned his intention to send copies of the Sonatina to one or two publishers in an attempt to secure its publication. The Sonatina was indeed published by Studio Music some years later, a welcome addition to the repertoire, well crafted and in a musical idiom suiting the recorder/harpsichord scoring most effectively.

Short's three-movement Sonatina No. 2 for unaccompanied treble recorder, but also in a version with keyboard accompaniment, was composed for Anne Frances Ellis. It has not been published.

Colin Hand: Divertissement, Op. 100

2 recs, hpd (or pn), optional gamba

For Carl, Jeanne and Joseph. For their American tour, October 1981

1 Poco allegro e con energia (tr rec, t rec/2nd tr rec). 2 Andante ma non troppo (sopranino rec, tr). 3 Andante quasi recit. (hpd solo) – Allegro giusto (2 des recs).

First performance: Salt Lake City USA, 6 October 1981.

Withdrawn by the composer.

The manuscript score and parts, a copy of a proposed published edition[27] of the work and a little correspondence in connection with it are all to be found in the archive. Although there is nothing in the correspondence to indicate Dolmetsch's request for a new piece for the 1981 American tour of the Haslemere Trio, it is clear that this was the reason for its composition. It is also evident that although the scoring for two recorders and harpsichord would be the performing forces on the tour, Dolmetsch had seen the potential for further performances on occasions when Marguerite would be present, and requested an optional viola da gamba part.

Colin Hand sent the work to Dolmetsch with a letter dated 19 August 1981 written in the form of a short verse:

My dear Carl,
For a suitable title I racked my brains
And thought of "A THREE PIECE SUITE"
But then, on reflection,
I realised this diction
Would leave out the optional Guite!

---

[27] In notes contained with a letter dated 25 June 2001 to the author, Colin Hand explained that a run of just a few dozen copies was produced under the Lindis imprint, but no attempt was made to promote the edition and no copies were sold. On the withdrawal of the work, the entire run was destroyed apart from the composer's own copy and that in the Dolmetsch archive. The composer would strongly discourage any future attempt to perform the work.

.....so it's a DIVERTISSEMENT

Hope you like it.

Yours ever

Colin

The letter also noted that the gamba part was to follow.

A comprehensive programme note by the composer is fixed in the back of the manuscript score and reads as follows:

> In this work the recorder players change instruments during the course of the piece. It is basically in three sections. The first begins with a Fanfare introduction proceeding to a fugal section and concluding with a shortened form of the introduction. There are no definite sub-titles to the sections, but the composer had certain programmatic ideas in mind and these have been noted at the end of each section, thus following the example of Debussy in his 'Preludes'. The first is based on the mental image of 'Petites Trompettes'.
>
> In the second section the first recorder player has a highly ornate part for sopranino over the melody played on the treble. Here the composer has been influenced by Couperin's Nightingale, a work that Carl Dolmetsch has made very much his own. The idea behind this section is 'La Rossignol s'éville'.
>
> The last section is preceded by a harpsichord recitative during which the recorder players each change to a descant and indulge in a lively scherzo built upon the mental picture of 'Un Jouet', a stylistically Gallic equivalent of the English 16th century 'Toye'. The work ends with the original fanfare over a busy harpsichord part.
>
> The choice of title Divertissement derives from an attempt to provide a light hearted, not too sophisticated piece that is easily digestible by players and hearers a like. At least that was the intention.

Performances of the new work were well received in the United States, the *Recorder and Music Magazine* quoting from a review in a local Salt Lake City newspaper:

> As if to quash the notion that recorders and harpsichords are the stuff of dusty musicology, the Trio premiered a 'Divertissement' for two recorders and harpsichord written by contemporary English composer Colin Hand for the current U.S. tour of the Haslemere Trio. The piece is pleasant, sunlit music, dissonant but very accessible, and a worthy showpiece for Dr. Dolmetsch's panache.[28]

A tape recording of the piece made on the tour was sent to Colin Hand, to which he responded in a letter dated 13 December 1981.This gave guidance on the interpretation of some of the ornamentation and clearly led the composer to make some adjustments to the score.

---

[28] March 1982, **7**, p. 123.

Thank you so much for the tape recording. I am pleased that the new piece appears to be giving so much enjoyment to players and audiences, particularly as it was written at great speed without time for second/third/etc. thoughts!

At least the tape gives me the opportunity of looking more critically at my efforts to balance the parts. For this reason I suggest that the harpsichord tremolo (page 16) does a short decrescendo, so allowing their [the recorder's] semiquavers to come through. And one point if I might make it: please – all trills should start on the note, not on the note above, in this piece at least, and the decorations on page 9, third and fourth staves (in the cadenza passage) are modern mordants i.e. *three* notes only ⌒ etc. (the only function of these is decorative).

I look forward to hearing a live performance sometime but in the meantime it was most encouraging to receive a number of appreciative letters from both sides of the Atlantic.

It is interesting to note the composer's comments on the trills. Dolmetsch being schooled in early music performance will almost unconsciously have started the trills on the upper note, and many recorder players used to playing baroque sonatas have to make a decisive effort to change to the later convention for trills when playing contemporary music.

Despite the appreciative letters, the more Hand looked at the score, and later listened to the tape (as he noted in the letter above), the more misgivings he had about the piece, considering it often rather too predictable, harmonically uninteresting and in places lacking balance of ensemble. As a result he eventually withdrew the work, but the thematic ideas from the second and third sections were preserved in his *Sonata concisa* for treble recorder and piano, composed in 1986 for John Turner.[29]

Elizabeth Cooper: Sonatina in G, Op. 8

des rec, pn

To Carl Dolmetsch

1 Capriccioso e vivace. 2 Siciliana. 3 Rondo.

First performance: date and location unknown.[30]

Unpublished.

The Rondo forming the finale of this work originated as a single movement for solo recorder to which, with Dolmetsch's encouragement, a keyboard accompaniment was added later. With the score is a letter from Elizabeth Cooper

---

[29] In notes contained with a letter dated 25 June 2001 from Colin Hand to the author.

[30] In a letter to the author dated 22 February 2001 Elizabeth Cooper noted she had learnt from Joseph Saxby that Dolmetsch and he had played the Sonatina at one of their more private concerts, but could not recall where.

to Dolmetsch dated 24 September 1982 that reads: 'Thank you so much for prodding me into writing the accompaniment for the Rondo – it was just what I needed!'

The score is inscribed 'A little memento of Chichester 1982', Elizabeth Cooper having attended the Dolmetsch summer school that year.[31] A photocopy of the manuscript score of the complete three-movement work bears the inscription: 'For dear Carl with all good wishes and thanks for all the help and encouragement'; it is undated.

The first movement opens in 7/8, with an insistent rhythmic phrase for the recorder above an accompaniment of quaver chords (in which F#s begin to appear) placed strategically, though not uniformly, within the metre. Bars of 3/8, 6/8 and 9/8 lead to a section marked *furioso* in which the key signature changes to one flat and the time signature to 5/8. The recorder has idiomatic figuration containing repeated top As that is soon taken up by the piano. Four bars in 12/16 time, but eventually featuring semiquaver duplets, transform the rhythm as the music moves into 4/4 and two transitional bars for the piano that make use of harmonics. The one-sharp key signature is restored along with a tempo indication of *andante*; the piano has an E minor melody marked *cantabile* that is soon taken up by the recorder over an increasingly resonant piano accompaniment. In a rhythmically reverse process, bars of 12/16 and 9/8 lead back to a recapitulation of the opening material, but the 3/8 and 6/8 bars conclude with an ascending G major scale for the recorder and a final G major chord spiced by an added seventh. In the space of just 66 bars the music has moved through three distinct moods, but the structure within which this is achieved is logical and satisfying.

A single gently rocking bar introduces the recorder's expressive E minor melody in the Siciliana (a transposition and augmentation of part of the first movement's opening theme). The music moves through some unusual modulations, but eventually finds its way back to a restatement of the opening melody and, via a short coda, to a close on an E major chord.

The 2/4–3/8–3/4 time signature of the final Rondo underlines the composer's obvious predilection for less orthodox rhythmic structures. The Rondo theme itself and the three couplets (that move into related keys) are mainly in 2/4, but the introduction of the occasional bar of 3/4 or 3/8 produce some unusual phrase lengths. Harmonically the movement is less adventurous, but it provides a satisfying conclusion after the preceding two, which, it should be remembered, were actually composed, later.

Though rooted in a conventional harmonic language, this is a well structured and concise work that publication would introduce to a wider number of players, and further supplement the descant recorder/piano repertoire.

---

[31] Ibid. Elizabeth Cooper entered the Sonatina in the competition for players organized by Dolmetsch at the Summer School. He had been complimentary about it and requested a copy.

Following the early encouragement received from Dolmetsch for the Sonatina, Elizabeth Cooper has continued to compose for the recorder, and three books of pieces/studies have been published, two for descant and piano by Kirklees Music and a third for treble and piano by Peacock Press.

Reginald Johnson: Sonatina domestica

des rec, pn

For Carl Dolmetsch and Joseph Saxby

In one movement: Allegro.

First performance: date and place unknown.

Unpublished.

The manuscript of this work is signed by the composer and inscribed: 'Carl – his copy / from / Reginald Johnson – his perpetration.' In the manuscript is a friendly letter dated 8 February 1983 from the composer to Dolmetsch that gives a very clear indication of the circumstances and the occasion for which the piece was written. It reads as follows:

> My dear Carl,
>
> Having regard to the longstandingness (is there such a word?) of our association I felt that I should like to do something beyond making a delightful visit to Town to honour the fifty years of collaboration between you and Joseph. For a long time I could not think what it should be; but in the end (although I know that I am not one of the World's greatest composers) I decided to follow the example of Robert Bridges and say,
>
> > "I too will something make
> > And joy in the making."
>
> And now it is done, and having been vetted by my (much) younger critics and passed as acceptable I send it to you with a Shakespearean envoi –
>
> > "a poor thing, but mine own!"
>
> I hope that it may be of some small use on occasion. Joseph will have his own copy – as he has his own plate![32]
>
> As ever
>
> Reginald

---

[32] The reference to 'his own plate' is in connection with two specially made plates commissioned by Shelagh Godwin from German potter Mary Wandrausch to celebrate 50 years of the Dolmetsch–Saxby musical partnership. Both are now kept in the kitchen at 'Jesses'.

The opening is a rhythmic dialogue between the two instruments that, though having a one-flat key signature, has a distinctive A minor/G minor feel to the tonality. The first section is repeated. Later the recorder introduces an idiomatic repeated note figure that is used again at the end of the work. Though an occasional piece, and despite the composer's apprehension, the *Sonatina domestica* is an engaging miniature.

Reginald Johnson was indeed a long-standing friend of the Dolmetsch family. As schools music advisor for the county of Dorset, he organized a rolling programme of recitals that, over a period of some 20 years or so, brought Carl Dolmetsch and Joseph Saxby to every school in the area every three years. A particular party piece on occasions was his performance for four hands at the harpsichord with Joseph Saxby, but he also made a number of arrangements for recorders and edited some of Gabrieli's music for Universal.

Darrell Davison: Introduction and Caprices

rec, str orch

[1] Introduction (Andante) (b rec). [2] Caprice I: (Allegro) (tr rec). [3] Caprice II [without tempo indication] (sopranino rec).

First performance: Haslemere, 1983. Carl Dolmetsch, recs; Strings of the Haslemere Music Society; Darrell Davison, conductor.

Unpublished.

Darrell Davison's father Arthur was the organizer of series of concerts for children in the Fairfield Halls, Croydon, and the paper on which most of the correspondence relating to this work was written bears the letterhead 'Arthur Davison Orchestral Concerts for Children'. Darrell Davison was conductor of the Haslemere Music Society at the time of this composition and wrote the piece to be performed with Carl Dolmetsch as soloist.

The archive contains a manuscript score of the work and two recorder parts, one each in the composer's and Dolmetsch's handwriting.[33] In a letter dating from February 1983 the composer described it as a 'mini recorder concerto' and noted that he felt it demonstrated some of the facets of the different recorders. He also noted that he had been careful in the balance of the orchestration, often reducing to one desk per part where there was the possibility of swamping the recorder sound.

The opening introduction for bass recorder is in 3/4 with a metronome rate of $\downarrow = 72$. The string accompaniment is light, with no violins at the opening and

---

[33] There is also a manuscript of a keyboard reduction of the string orchestral accompaniment.

all but the front desk of the violas and cellos playing pizzicato. A recorder cadenza leads to Caprice I (2/4, ♩=160) scored for treble recorder. The main theme features an alternation between triplet and dotted figuration for the soloist and makes use of some interesting trills for the strings, the adjacent notes indicated to be played downwards by the outer player of each desk and upwards by the inner player. Caprice II (also in 2/4) is scored for sopranino and is a virtuosic *moto perpetuo* without a tempo indication, but which is marked in the recorder part 'practice at 180'. The recorder part consists almost entirely of semiquavers.

The original recorder part has many fast chromatic passages at both the top and bottom extremes of the instrument's compass in a way that Dolmetsch frequently advised against. The recorder part written in Dolmetsch's hand attempts to obviate these as far as possible by octave transposition and it is significant that in another letter from the composer he refers to having met Dolmetsch to sort out problems.

Even with the modifications made to the recorder part in Caprice II, Jeanne Dolmetsch noted that it was 'very difficult' and that it provided her father with a number of technical problems. He nevertheless spent a considerable amount of time working on it in an attempt to create on the recorder the effect the composer clearly had in his mind, but which was more readily obtainable on a string instrument and with string playing techniques. However, the composer's efforts to write a transparent accompaniment to balance the recorder are for the most part successfully realized.

Santiago Velasco Llanos: Romanza

tr rec, kbd

Single movement: Andante.

First performance: Sala Beethoven, Cali, Colombia, 7 November 1984. Carl Dolmetsch, rec; kbd player not known.[34]

Unpublished.

The manuscript score in the archive bears no dedication, but the place and date of the first performance have been written at the head of the first page in Dolmetsch's handwriting, after which is noted: 'and again in Bogota on Wed 14th November 1984'.

---

[34] The note written by Dolmetsch on the manuscript does not give any indication of who played the keyboard at the first performance. François Dolmetsch thought it might have been Andrew Pledge, but Pledge himself could find nothing among programmes in his possession to confirm this. Although he did take part in a South American tour he could not recall having performed this particular work. (Author's telephone conversation with Andrew Pledge, May 2002.)

It will have been on a trip to South America to visit his son François that Dolmetsch will have been introduced to this piece.

It is in 6/8 time, 68 bars in length and with a metronome indication of $\downarrow. = 72$. The recorder's melody is announced above an accompaniment of a repeated chordal figure over a descending bass. Though beginning in C and maintaining much the same texture throughout, the music does undergo some interesting modulations before returning to C for the conclusion.

Inside the score, in addition to the part for treble recorder, are parts for tenor and bass recorders that can replace the keyboard and enable the piece to be played as a recorder trio. François Dolmetsch considered this betrayed the work's possible origins as a string trio. As a recorder trio the piece takes on an entirely different but equally appealing character.

Santiago Velasco Llanos: Homenaje a J.S. Bach (Fuga doble)

rec qt (SSTB)

First performance: date and location unknown.

Unpublished.

Carl Dolmetsch gave the premiere of Velasco's *Romanza* for recorder and keyboard in Colombia in 1984 and his association with the composer, through Dolmetsch's son François, clearly dates from this time. An envelope in the archive contains the manuscript score and parts of the fugue together with a letter dated 14 January 1986 from François Dolmetsch to his father that notes:

> I enclose Santiago Velasco's revised and 'corrected' score. He very much enjoyed the tape I brought back to Colombia and is enthusiastic about the idea of playing the piece at a meeting of the SRP.
>
> It would be interesting perhaps to do this and perhaps make another tape so that he could hear it in a more polished performance.

Velasco's enthusiasm is clear from a letter from Cali dated 10 January 1986, also enclosed with the score. In it he notes how the cassette enabled him to correct the score and parts, and gave authorization for the work's inclusion in the Dolmetsch concerts and for subsequent publication. He also acknowledged the great honour this would represent for a Latin American composer who would like his work to be recognized.

Although the score does not bear a specific dedication, the Dolmetsch family associations with the work are very clear and the individual parts are marked with the names of the players to which they were assigned:

1° Flauta Soprano – 'Papa'
2° Flauta Soprano – 'Jeanne'

Flauta Tenor – 'Guite'
Flauta Bass – 'Brian'

The two fugue subjects have a distinctly Bachian flavour. At the beginning (in F major) the parts enter in the order tenor, soprano 2, soprano 1 and bass, but the key signature changes to four sharps at bar 27 in preparation for the second subject in E major. This is introduced first by soprano 2 at bar 33 and then by soprano 1 at bar 40, bass at bar 47 and tenor at bar 54. The key signature reverts to one flat at bar 69 and the subjects are finally combined at bar 109, just 20 bars before the end.

The less orthodox recorder quartet scoring of SSTB was, as François Dolmetsch has confirmed, a result of the work's being conceived initially for strings. The transcription for recorders also resulted in portions of the bass part extending very high into its compass.

Although in the style of Bach, the modulation before the entry of the second subject adds an unusual (and technically more challenging) touch. However, there is an almost relentless logic to its structure that perhaps detracts from the overall effect.

Michael Short: Giocata

des rec, hpd

To Carl and Joseph

In one movement: Moderato ad lib ($\downarrow$ = c. 84).

First performance: Westham College, West Midlands, 21 March 1987. Carl Dolmetsch, rec; Joseph Saxby, hpd.

Unpublished.

A photocopy of the manuscript of the work in the archive contains a note giving details of its origins: 'Commissioned by Westham Adult Residential College with assistance from West Midlands Arts to mark the 40th Annual recorder course presented there by Carl Dolmetsch and Joseph Saxby.' The manuscript copy was sent to Dolmetsch with a letter from the composer dated 23 January 1987. This was brief and offered generous scope to the performers in the event of practical difficulties:

Dear Carl,

Herewith the piece for Westham College – I hope that it is playable. If you don't like anything in it – change it!
Excuse haste – will be in touch later.
All the best to you and Joseph

Yours

Michael

Also with the manuscript copy is the composer's programme note that, in addition to describing the character of the work, gives an explanation of the unusual title:

> If the word Sonata comes from 'suonare' (to sound), then Giocata (pronounced 'Joe Carter') can be derived from 'giocare' (to play – as in a game). By good fortune, the first two syllables are also those of the names *Jo*seph and *Ca*rl, to whom the piece is dedicated. The music is playful throughout – motifs appear, are toyed with, disappear, and sometimes re-appear later – the whole in a light-hearted, improvisatory style.

With the rather limited repertoire available for descant recorder and harpsichord compared with that for treble, publication of Michael Short's *Giocata*, typical of his musical ingenuity, would be a welcome addition to it.

Chapter 5

Works written for the Dolmetsch children

It is not surprising that, being brought up in a house full of music making, the Dolmetsch children soon developed into musicians themselves. François, Jeanne, Marguerite and Richard were able to form a recorder quartet or a trio of recorders with keyboard, and both ensembles were scored for in a handful of works specially written for them. Of these, only Cecily Lambert's *Bergomask* remains unpublished.

The earliest piece, dating from 1950, is by Herbert Murrill and is dedicated to the young Jeanne and Marguerite. The remainder, written for all four children, date from the late 1950s and early 1960s, but only a few years remained before the tragic and untimely death of Richard in 1966 robbed the family ensemble of perhaps its most talented member.

It seems appropriate to include details of these works here as it is surely through Dolmetsch's previous contact with their composers that they were written. York Bowen, Herbert Murrill and Edmund Rubbra were significantly the first three composers to write new works for Dolmetsch's Wigmore Hall recitals when these resumed in the late 1940s.

Both Cecily Lambert and Peter Crossley-Holland (at Dolmetsch's invitation) contributed works to Universal Edition's *Il flauto dolce* Dolmetsch Recorder Series: Crossley-Holland a seven-movement *Little Suite* for descant recorder and piano (or descant and two treble recorders without piano), *Breton Tunes* for recorder(s) with or without keyboard and *Irish Tunes* for three recorders. Cecily Lambert's *Aubade* for recorder quartet is dedicated to Carl Dolmetsch (see Chapter 4).

Hans Gál's *Quartettino* for recorder quartet (S, S, A/T, T/B) was another work inspired by the family consort that also appeared in Universal Edition's *Il flauto dolce* Dolmetsch Recorder Series.

Rubbra's *Notturno* occupies a central position chronologically between the first and last three of his six recorder compositions premiered by Dolmetsch at the Wigmore Hall.

Although works for recorder quartet are numerous, the original repertoire for three recorders and keyboard is rather small. The significance therefore of York Bowen's and Crossley-Holland's works in particular underlines the welcome inspiration provided by the young Dolmetsch family ensemble.

9 Richard, Jeanne, François and Marguerite Dolmetsch. A photograph of the family consort taken in the mid-1950s.

Herbert Murrill: Piece for my Friends

2 tr rec, hpd

For Jeanne and Marguerite

First performance: date and location unknown.

Published: London: Universal Edition Ltd, 1957 (UE 12575).

This little piece originated not long after the first performance of Murrill's Sonata for recorder and harpsichord. The manuscript was sent to Dolmetsch with a letter, dated Whit Monday 1950, with which Murrill also returned the recorder part of the Sonata. After his thanks for the loan of this, Murrill continued:

> ... and here also is the promised piece for my two friends. There are places for them to sign their names on the cover, so as to make it *really* theirs. I myself would not take the responsibility of placing one or t'other *first*, so it must be worked out chez nous.
>
> Alas the piece is no good. It is more difficult than I meant it to be and I don't expect the young ladies can do it for some little time yet. If indeed this is so, I must try again, and this can be 'second steps.'

Dolmetsch wrote to Murrill on 4 June to thank him for the piece:

> How very, very kind of you to send such a lovely surprise to our little daughters – they are absolutely thrilled with their special piece of music. It really is exceedingly good of you to have been bothered about it and to be better than your word! I don't think it is going to be too difficult for them, it is just a matter of learning it bar by bar and they have already made a start on it. It is a grand incentive to use you as bait by saying that as soon as they can play it we shall ask you down here again. How nice it would be to have a grand try out, tous ensembles, with the composer at the harpsichord. We shall look forward to it as the occasion for another happy reunion in Haslemere.[1]
>
> By the way, as regards seniority, Jeanne-Marie saw the daylight twenty minutes before Marguerite opened her eyes, so *they* have accordingly inscribed their names in the spaces so beautifully provided.

On 4 July Murrill responded:

> Bless those twins! They are good to work so hard at the little duet. Kiss them for me and say I look forward to a grand performance with them. They will be wanting a harder piece soon! *You* yourself must be tired of the little duet, though I think it contains one (1) good idea! That is, the phrase after the first double-bar of the first section. Four bars or so, there, are tolerable. But, for the sake of my reputation, pretend to the twins that it is all good.

---

[1] Jeanne and Marguerite explained in a conversation with the author that in the event a trip to London was arranged for them to play the piece with the composer. The visit also involved lunch and a visit along with Murrill's daughter Carolyn to a swimming pool.

Murrill's manuscript of the piece is a charming document. The title on the front page appears as 'Piece for Two Recorders and Harpsichord for my friends' and is signed below by the twins, as noted in Dolmetsch's letter above, in the spaces provided by the composer himself.

The 'one good idea' to which Murrill refers in his letter of 4 July, and the 'tolerable' four bars are as indicated in Ex. 5.1.

Ex. 5.1. Herbert Murrill, *Piece for my Friends* for two treble recorders and harpsichord. Bars 9–14, containing the composer's 'one good idea'. Reproduced by kind permission of Universal Edition (London) Ltd.

Murrill was being somewhat self-critical and Universal thought fit to publish the work. It is among only a small number of pieces from the contemporary repertoire scored for two recorders and keyboard. Quite by chance, another piece from that small repertoire, written just four years later, was also for two sisters. The work was Harald Genzmer's Sonata for two treble recorders and piano, and the sisters were his own.[2]

Peter Crossley-Holland: Albion

des, tr and b (or t) recs, hpd (or pn)

For Jeanne, Marguerite, François and Richard Dolmetsch

1 Organum for St Andrew (In the style of a chanted prayer). 2 Witches' Dance (Lively and vigorous). 3 Mist on the Ben (Sustained and remote). 4 Down on Yon Bank (With courtly elegance). 5 The Nameless (Lively and playful).

First performance: Royal Festival Hall Recital Room, London, 30 April 1959. Jeanne Dolmetsch, Marguerite Dolmetsch, François Dolmetsch, recs; Richard Dolmetsch, hpd.

Published: London: Universal Edition Ltd, 1960 (UE 12600).

Peter Crossley-Holland's *Irish Tunes* for three recorders (two descants and treble)

---

[2] This information was contained in a letter to the author from Alison Baldwin written after she had visited Harald Genzmer in Munich in January 2000. Genzmer's Sonata was published in 1956 by Schott & Co. Ltd, Mainz.

were published by Universal in the Dolmetsch Recorder Series in 1959 (UE 12595) at Carl Dolmetsch's instigation. Thus when he began to make preparations for a concert to launch the ensemble made up of his four children it was to Crossley-Holland that he turned for a new work to be scored for descant, treble, and bass or tenor recorders with harpsichord. The composer was keen to continue with the Celtic idiom explored in *Irish Tunes* and sought inspiration in some ancient Scottish tunes to produce a five-movement suite entitled *Albion* (an old name sometimes given to Scotland).

For the opening movement the composer wanted music with a medieval atmosphere and asked Denis Stevens if he could find a suitable chant in the former St Andrews (now Wolfenbüttel) manuscript[3] (Ex. 5.2).[4] Crossley-Holland did not quote the chant exactly, but used its contours and atmosphere as a starting point for the opening movement, which he titled *Organum for St Andrew*.

Ex. 5.2. Opening of the Matins Response for the Feast of St Andrew (from the Wolfenbüttel manuscript).

The remaining movements were based on melodies found in the Skene manuscript (1615–20), the earliest known manuscript of traditional Scottish music.

The second movement, *Witches' Dance*, uses the melody of *Kilt thy coat Maggie*, and the third movement, *Mist on the Ben*, sets the melody *Lady Cassiles Lilt*. For this movement Crossley-Holland made use of fingered tremolos on pairs of notes a third, fourth or fifth apart to emphasise the remote atmosphere, after being advised by Dolmetsch of suitable fingerings. *Down in von Bank* (or 'Doun in yon Banke') makes use of another original melody, while that upon which the final movement is based is without title and hence called *The Nameless*.[5]

---

[3] Wolfenbüttel, Herzog August Bibliothek, MS 677.

[4] Dr Nicole Crossley-Holland, the composer's widow, kindly lent me a copy of the chant written out on a fragment of manuscript paper that in addition to the heading contains a note that reads: 'Consulted before writing 1st movement of *Albion Suite* – No. 91.' The Latin text underlay reads: '*Vir iste in populo suo mitissimus apparuit sanctitate autem et gratia plenus iste est qui assidue orat pro populo et pro civitate ista.*' Fixed to this with a paper clip was a smaller piece of paper on which was written a translation: 'That man appeared most gently to his people for he also prays continually for his people and for his country is full of [sanctity and] grace.'

[5] The information contained in these opening paragraphs is taken from an article that the composer had all but completed at the time of his death. It was published in *The Recorder Magazine* in 2002, together with a foreword and additional notes by John Turner, as Crossley-Holland, 'Sounds from the wood'.

The composer's own programme note for the first performance reads as follows:

> This Suite is written for Jeanne, Marguerite, François and Richard Dolmetsch. It is called 'Albion' (an ancient name for Scotland) because each of its five movements was inspired by material from early Scottish manuscripts. No. 1, combining unusual rhythmic freedom with a style stemming from the mediæval organum, is an invocation suggested by two fragments of plainchant found in a 13th century manuscript once in St. Andrews. No. 2 is a setting of a piper's tune danced by some lively witches who were tried in 1659. The melody of No. 3, echoing the music heard by belated travellers in fairy-haunted spots, is re-written from a traditional tune of the Casilles Family. The tune in No. 4 is partly taken from an air of courtly elegance from a 17th century manuscript. The playful opening section of No. 5 is freely based on some 17th century material having no name. The idea of the Nameless suggested the rest of the movement.

Following the first performance Dolmetsch wrote to Crossley-Holland expressing his 'appreciation for your major part in the success of our concert'. The letter continued:

> We were all immensely pleased with the enthusiastic reception of *Albion* and were delighted that you and all your family were with us to share its success. Did you see the Times notice on Saturday I wonder? As a matter of fact the children themselves are so fond of the Suite that they are going to play it tomorrow at the AGM of the Dolmetsch Foundation.

The original manuscript of the suite is not in the archive, but it does contain a copy of the published edition. A review of this by Lily Taylor was included in the *Recorder News*:

> This inventive suite consists of five contrasting pieces of no great technical difficulty. The opening 'Organum for St. Andrew' looks tricky with its changing time signatures, but a crotchet beat remains the same throughout to simplify this. 'Witches' Dance' is a vigorous and lively piece, and 'Mist on the Ben' a calm and mysterious contrast. 'Down on yon bank' has the elegance of a stately minuet and the final 'The Nameless' is rollicking and exuberant, and a little more difficult. The keyboard part (harpsichord or piano) is interesting and the player must be en rapport with the recorders throughout.[6]

Dolmetsch wrote to Crossley-Holland on 21 April 1969 to inform him of and invite him to another performance:

> Dear Peter,
>
> It seems a very long time since we last met, but I thought you might like to know that we propose to play your Albion Suite again on Saturday next, at the AGM of the Dolmetsch Foundation – 3.00 pm in the Haslemere Museum Lecture Hall. For us it will

---

[6] September–October 1960, New Series, No. 30, p. 8.

be a nostalgic performance. If you are free on Saturday, and would enjoy a breath of country air, do come down and join us – you would be warmly welcomed.

All best wishes,

Yours as ever,

Carl

Richard Dolmetsch's death in 1966 and the memories of his participation in the Dolmetsch children's ensemble's first performance of the work almost exactly ten years earlier would indeed have made this a nostalgic performance.

Albion dates from about three years after another suite for recorder(s) composed by Crossley-Holland and published by Universal. It is entitled *A Little Suite* and is scored for descant recorder and piano or alternatively, descant recorder with two treble recorders without piano. It contains six movements some of which, as in *Albion*, have evocative titles such as *Dream*, *Cavalcade* and *Dusk*.

Works for or including recorder continued to form part of Crossley-Holland's compositional output. Among these were a number of songs with recorder obbligato and the substantial *Invocation at Midsummer* for tenor recorder solo written for John Turner and published by Forsyth Brothers in 1996. It would appear from sketches found among the composer's papers after his death in April 2001 that he was working on a concerto for recorder sometime around September 1999 or shortly before. Alas, other tasks intervened, and the work did not progress beyond these tantalizing fragments.[7]

Edmund Rubbra: Notturno, Op. 106

rec qt (des, tr, t, b)

For François, Jeanne, Marguerite and Richard Dolmetsch

Single movement: Andante, poco lento (3/2, ♩ = c. 72).

First performance: Royal Festival Hall Recital Room (now the Purcell Room), London, 28 April 1960. Richard Dolmetsch, des rec; Jeanne Dolmetsch, tr rec; Marguerite Dolmetsch, t rec; François Dolmetsch, b rec.

Published. Croydon: Alfred Lengnick & Co. Ltd, 1962 (4051).

A copy of the published edition in the archive is inscribed: 'To Carl & the family from Edmund 27.1.62'. The archive also contains a photocopy of the manuscript score that is undated. This contains a significant difference from the published version in the descant part three bars after figure 4, which has been raised by an octave (including high D♭) in the published edition and is marked *sempre staccato*.

---

[7] Crossley-Holland, 'Sounds from the wood', note 6 (by John Turner).

The original descant part is in unison with the treble six bars after figure 4. Otherwise the published edition follows the manuscript very closely.

For the first performance the composer wrote the following programme note:

> In this piece I have tried to exploit the 'cool' sounds of recorder tone, by keeping the texture and harmonies bare against the main theme, first stated by the tenor recorder. This sustained three-two theme (in C minor, with F-sharp prominent) is treated as a Passacaglia. It appears in all four recorders, is sometimes inverted, and at one point both the normal and inverted forms appear together. There is cumulative movement, and at the final statement of the theme the descant recorder accompanies it with a dancing theme in four-four based on a diminution of the cadence bar of the main theme.

Some sections are marked 'solo', but this is to emphasise the melodic line as it passes from one part to another rather than indicating the possibility of performance by a larger recorder ensemble. An alternative scoring for a wind quartet of piccolo, flute, oboe and B-flat clarinet is also indicated in the published score.

The opening tenor melody and bass accompanying figure, featuring repeated notes and octave leaps, are indeed the foundation on which the entire piece is built. However, this material is subtly developed, and even the treble quaver figures that accompany the later simultaneous presentation of the original theme in the tenor against its inversion in the bass can be seen to be derived from the very first three notes of the bass's initial theme. Characteristically, Rubbra introduces a new idea featuring semiquaver movement in the descant, and later treble part to accompany the tenor's final statement of the theme.

The piece has many of Rubbra's compositional fingerprints, and a number of motives show a resemblance to similar ideas in the *Passacaglia sopra 'Plusieurs regrets'*, (composed not long afterwards). Those most immediately evident are the ostinato-like accompanying quaver figures and the rising chromatic phrase in the treble part, two bars before figure 4, that comes out of nowhere and transforms the immediate character of the prevailing harmony.

No doubt the young Dolmetsch ensemble will have warmed to Rubbra's atmospheric writing, and recorder consort players generally are fortunate to have the *Notturno* in the repertoire, for the opportunity it provides of first-hand acquaintance with Rubbra's recorder compositions.[8]

---

[8] They should also acquaint themselves with Rubbra's Air and Variations, Op. 70, composed in 1950 for the Pipers' Guild. Though written for a quartet of bamboo pipes it can be performed satisfactorily on recorders.

Hans Gál: Quartettino, Op. 78

2 des recs, tr rec (or t rec), t rec (or b rec)

1 Alla marcia (Allegro). 2 Tempo di minuetto (Andante grazioso). 3 Gigue (Allegretto vivace).

First performance: Location and date unknown.

Published: London: Universal Edition Ltd, 1960 (UE 12622).

There is no correspondence in the archive relating to this work or a manuscript, but it does contain at least two copies of the published edition.

As noted in the section on the *Concertino*, Op. 82 (Chapter 3), it is likely that Dolmetsch first met Gál during a visit to Edinburgh. During the late 1950s Gál also visited the Dolmetsch family at Haslemere (a clear recollection recounted to the author by Jeanne Dolmetsch) and was no doubt impressed by the young family consort. The *Quartettino* seems to have been his response to their talents, and its publication by Universal in their *Il flauto dolce* Dolmetsch Recorder Series coincides with that of other works for the children composed by Peter Crossley-Holland and York Bowen.

The *Quartettino* does not appear to have been among the works that were premiered at a series of recitals given by the Dolmetsch family in the Recital Room of the Royal Festival Hall in the late 1950s and early 1960s. Jeanne Dolmetsch does, however, recall the piece being performed by the family consort, and Eva Fox-Gál (the composer's daughter) believes it was also taken up enthusiastically by members of the Edinburgh branch of the Society of Recorder Players.

The energy of the opening march is further enlivened by the syncopations resulting from notes tied across the bar lines, and the lower parts in the central section also provide a strong rhythmic accompaniment to the first descant's melody. The *Tempo di minuetto* (just three pages of music) has all the elegance of Gál's writing in this form, while the subtlety of the final Gigue requires the players' attention to the composer's carefully indicated articulation and phrasing.

It is unfortunate that this piece is not presently in print, especially as the alternatives in its scoring would enable it to be enjoyed by many players who would otherwise not have an opportunity to experience Gál's music at first hand in his works with solo recorder.

York Bowen: Two Pieces

des, tr, b/t recs, kbd

To François, Jeanne, Marguerite and Richard Dolmetsch

1 Andante grazioso. 2 Allegro scherzando.

First performance: Royal Festival Hall Recital Room, London, 27 April 1961. Jeanne Dolmetsch, Marguerite Dolmetsch, François Dolmetsch, recs; Richard Dolmetsch, hpd.

Published: London: Universal Edition Ltd, 1962 (UE 12638).

A photocopy of the composer's manuscript of these two pieces is in the archive together with two copies of the published edition. For the first performance the composer wrote the following short programme note:

> These two short pieces were written experimentally in order to judge the effectiveness of more than one recorder with the addition of harpsichord. Both are of a fairly simple nature, the first exploiting the legato and melodious style of playing and the second more in the form of a scherzo or caprice. Three different sizes of recorder are intended in the combination.

A review by Lily Taylor of the published edition of the two pieces was published in *The Recorder and Music Magazine*:

> Many contemporary compositions for the recorder are beyond the ability of average players, but here we have a trio with keyboard accompaniment which will readily capture the affection of slightly less versatile ones. The eloquent Andante pursues a simple course from a quiet opening, with imitative solo passages throughout. The descant player has some top Cs and Ds which are easy enough, and although top F is possible the publishers have wisely given an alternative part for bars 43 and 44 where this note occurs.[9] The two-in-a-bar allegro scherzando is a witty and nimble fantasy touching top E (the fingering for this note is given together with a suggestion that it may be played an octave lower). Mention of these slight difficulties should in no way deter consort players from performance, with an accompanist of moderate ability.[10]

The first of the two pieces opens with the top two instruments in octaves, but this lasts only as far as bar 11, after which the writing frequently pairs two of the recorder lines against a more independent third. The keyboard has entirely its own material and, though certainly playable on a harpsichord, is at times somewhat pianistic.

The direction (solo) in the treble and bass parts in three places perhaps indicates the composer's intention that the piece could be played with more than one instrument per part, though is more likely simply to emphasise the prevailing melody at these points.

In the *Allegro scherzando*, chords in a percussive rhythm for the keyboard open the movement (cues of this in the recorder parts refer to the keyboard, rather

---

[9] The published edition in the archive inspected by the author does not contain these alternatives or the fingering for top E in the *Allegro scherzando* or a suggestion for its downward octave transposition.

[10] August 1963, **1**, p. 56.

strangely, as 'continuo'). This is immediately answered by the descant and treble recorders with a phrase, the basic shape and rhythm of which reminds of the opening of the finale of the Sonatina for recorder and piano.

York Bowen's harmonic language is unmistakable throughout both pieces, which date from not long after the second Wigmore Hall performance of his Sonatina for recorder and piano. Once again the composer is not afraid to write top Es and Fs for the descant as he had done in the finale of that work. However, as noted in the above review of the two pieces, these high notes can be substituted (and are probably better for so being in this context) and should not be a discouragement to performance, either as a pair or singly, of these characteristic works for an unusual scoring.[11]

Cecily Lambert: Bergomask

rec qt

To the Dolmetsch Quartet: Guite, Jeanne, François and Richard

Single movement: *Allegro scherzando*.

First performance: date and location unknown.

Unpublished.

The manuscript score and parts of this work are to be found in the archive. The score also contained the following letter dated 24 February 1962:

Dear Carl,

After I heard the performance of my 'Aubade' for recorder quartet I decided I must write another to be its companion piece. The enclosed 'Bergomask' is the result.

We do hope very much that you will be able to come and visit us soon – it would be delightful to welcome you here.

With kindest regards to Guite, Jeanne, François and Richard and to Joseph.

and all good wishes to you

Very sincerely

Cecily

The piece, scored for descant, treble, tenor and bass recorders, is in a single movement headed *Allegro scherzando*. It is not founded on the traditional Bergamasque tune but on an original melody that is introduced by the descant after a four-bar introduction in crotchets in the lower three parts.

---

[11] The *Allegro scherzando* was performed on its own by Carl Dolmetsch, Marguerite Dolmetsch, Brian Blood and Joseph Saxby in a concert attended by the author in July 1986.

Treble and tenor also soon become involved with the development of the opening theme but the bass remains firmly in rhythmic support. At bar 42 the two-flat key signature is dispensed with, the score is marked *dolce* and an entirely new idea is introduced. A theme in falling thirds and quavers in the descant is followed at a distance of just a crotchet by the same theme in inversion in the tenor. After just a beat and a half, the treble enters with the theme in augmentation and the bass answers in inversion. However, this excursion into more complex counterpoint is short-lived, and some brief imitation in the top three parts leads to short melodic passage based on the falling thirds for the descant, accompanied by the remainder of the quartet. A semiquaver rising scale for the descant brings a bold unison restatement of the opening theme and the two-flat key signature reappears as the theme, now back in the original key, begins a recapitulation of the entire opening section. At the point where the *dolce* section occurred the first time round, another semiquaver descant rising scale leads to a short coda based on the very opening notes and the work ends on a G major chord.

Some of the descant part lies high on the instrument (occasional top Ds) and very precise intonation and ensemble are essential for a successful performance of the piece that is in very marked stylistic contrast to its companion work – the *Aubade* referred to by the composer in the letter above.

Chapter 6

Unfulfilled invitations

There has always been a fascination within the musical world with the fragments, sketches and unfinished works left behind by composers at the end of their lives. In recent years, the careful realization by Anthony Payne of Elgar's sketches for his Symphony No. 3 come to mind, but there are, of course, many other examples.

Almost as fascinating are the speculations in connection with works that might have been, but for one reason or another never came to be composed. Of a projected *Prélude, scherzo e paraphrase finale à L'après-midi d'un faune*, Debussy completed only the exquisite *Prélude*, making us wonder just how the other movements would have sounded.

Dolmetsch's efforts to secure new works for his Wigmore Hall recitals did not always prove fruitful, and the archives contain correspondence with a number of composers who, in varying circumstances, were unable to respond to Dolmetsch's invitations.

Sometimes they were simply too busy, as is most clearly evident from brief correspondence with Thea Musgrave dating from 1965. Dolmetsch wrote to the composer in August that year with an invitation to write a new work for his 1966 Wigmore Hall recital. In her reply, Thea Musgrave had to refuse the invitation, noting that the composition of a full-length opera on which she had been working for one-and-a-half years had necessitated her postponing or turning down no less than ten commissions that she would have to return to on completion of the opera.

The guitarist John Mills was to take part in the 1977 Wigmore Hall recital, and a letter from Dolmetsch to John McCabe dated 30 July 1976 included a request for a new work for recorder and guitar. McCabe's reply, dated 5 August 1976, regretfully explained that compositional commitments over the next two years would prevent him from accepting the invitation. His works for recorder composed subsequently show a complete affinity with the instrument.

It is also evident from the letter Dolmetsch wrote to Martin Dalby requesting a work for the 1972 Wigmore Hall recital that Robert Simpson was, owing to the amount of work on hand, unable to complete a piece for recorder and harpsichord in time. As a result, Simpson had suggested Dalby be invited to fulfil the commission.

Likewise Peter Racine Fricker reluctantly had to turn down an invitation to write a new work for the 1959 Wigmore recital (for which, in the event, Robert Simpson composed his Variations and Fugue) and referred to four works needing to be completed by the end of the year, including 'a biggish piece for piano and orchestra'. Fricker noted, however, that he would 'like to do a work sometime' (he had by this time composed his Suite for three recorders), and this prompted Dolmetsch to repeat his invitation the following year. Fricker's response to this second invitation is particularly revealing of how such a workload could affect a composer's well-being and state of mind. His letter (dated 13 July 1959), in which he admits it is unlikely that a work will be forthcoming, concludes:

> I have not been feeling at my best recently after several years of prolonged and concentrated work – rather run down in fact, mentally and physically. I feel that I need to take things rather more easily for a time. I do hope you will understand and that you will be able to find a new work for your concert.

Fricker's Suite for recorder trio is well known to recorder players, and it is interesting to speculate on the sort of work he would have produced for the forces Dolmetsch had in mind (recorder and string quartet) – especially as he had studied with Mátyás Seiber, whose own *Pastorale* of 1941 is scored for recorder, violin, viola and cello.

Dolmetsch's correspondence with Sir Arnold Bax, relating to an invitation to write a new work for the 1953 Wigmore Hall recital, reveals the somewhat different but equally real problems it is possible for a composer to experience.

It is evident from the beginning of a letter from Dolmetsch of November 1952 that Bax had attended a concert at the Royal Festival Hall in which Dolmetsch had taken part. The letter continues:

> I need hardly say how delighted and honoured I felt by your kind response to my suggestion that you might write a work for the recorder. It would greatly enhance its modern literature. If this could be in Coronation year and in time for our Wigmore recital on 8th May it would be wonderful, and as we are touring New Zealand later that year, we would introduce the work to our audiences in that country also. Broadcasting of the work would also be a certainty, and the now formidable body of recorder players would clamour for its publication (hoping it wasn't going to be too difficult for them!).
>
> Most works by modern composers to-date have been written for recorder and harpsichord (or piano), but there is a considerable demand for recorder and string quartet (or string orchestra) with harpsichord on the lines of the Telemann concerto we played on Saturday. May I leave that for your consideration, and also say again that the work need not be a very long one, as I know how busy you must be.

The letter concluded with details of the compass of the treble recorder and advised that in passages where accompanied by strings the recorder should generally remain above its middle register to avoid any danger of it being covered.

Bax's short reply is dated 23 November 1952:

Dear Carl Dolmetsch

Thank you for your letter and the technical details of the recorder. I will really try to do something about it before the spring.

Yours very sincerely

Arnold Bax

Dolmetsch replied by return expressing his delight at the prospect of a new work from Bax's pen:

Dear Sir Arnold,

Thank you very much for your letter from which I am delighted to learn that you plan to have the new work for recorder written by next spring. I shall look forward with eager anticipation to receiving and performing it.

Meanwhile we shall be arranging the advance publicity fairly soon. May I with your permission announce that my programme will include a new work by yourself?

I feel it is indeed auspicious that it should be you who will be writing a new work for our English Flute in Coronation year.

With kindest regards,

Yours sincerely

Carl Dolmetsch

By the middle of January 1953 Dolmetsch had heard nothing in connection with the new work and wrote to Bax to enquire about progress, again asking if an announcement that it was being written could be made. A few days later Dolmetsch received Bax's very poignant reply.

Dear Carl Dolmetsch,

Thank you for your letter. I am sorry to say that I am in very bad composing form and no ideas for a piece for you have visited me although I have thought about it a good deal. It would be of no use for you to announce anything for May as I have still to write another coronation piece. Perhaps later on I hope to but I rather feel that it is time for me to retire. I can never be anything but a romanticist and that is all out of date!

Yours sincerely

Arnold Bax

Dolmetsch wrote a sympathetic reply expressing the hope that Bax would 'soon strike a rich composing vein again'. However, 'another coronation piece', *What is it Like To Be Young and Fair* for SSAAT voices, setting words by his brother Clifford, composed for *A Garland for the Queen*, was his last completed work; Bax died in October 1953.

The letter cited above is further, painful testimony to the well documented disillusion felt by the ageing Bax during the last years of his life, when the post-war musical world grew to regard his music as increasingly 'out of date'.

With more of Bax's chamber music again being performed it is intriguing to speculate how he might have written for the recorder. The harpsichord, had he scored for it, might have proved to be something of a challenge, but the inclusion of strings would have surely provided lyrical inspiration. A work in Bax's rich romantic style for recorder and string trio (perhaps with the addition of his particularly favoured harp in chamber music scoring) would surely have held a unique place in the repertoire.

Another fascinating correspondence, but for totally different reasons, is that between Dolmetsch and Benjamin Britten, dating from the mid-1950s and early 1960s. Dolmetsch's several letters give a clear indication of the determination and enthusiasm he brought to his quest to enhance the recorder repertoire with works by important composers. Mention has already been made in Chapter 2 of Britten's possible place among the 'ten' composers approached by Manuel Jacobs in 1939 to write works for recorder, and reference to this later correspondence with Dolmetsch is made there.

In his efforts to encourage Britten, Dolmetsch took the very practical step of making him a present of two recorders, a descant and a treble.[1] Unfortunately there is no accompanying letter from Dolmetsch in the Britten-Pears Library, nor any copy in the Dolmetsch archives. Britten thanked Dolmetsch for the recorders in a letter dated 20 January 1954 written from his home at 4 Crabbe Street, Aldeburgh:

Dear Mr. Dolmetsch,

I have to thank you for the very welcome present of two superb recorders which arrived yesterday. I am afraid my technique is, as yet, very inadequate, and I do not feel in the very few hours I have had playing on them since their arrival that I have fully exploited their possibilities, but I have realised in a very short time a little of their exceptional quality, and thank you more than I can say for the kind thought and generosity of your gift.

I have always been fascinated by the sound of recorders and cannot understand why I have not tried to play any of them before. It was, in fact, our very active music club here, with its energetic consort, that spurred me on, and I am much enjoying my beginners efforts. I am also discovering for myself some of the possibilities of the instrument which will be invaluable when I start to write for them, as I hope to soon.

Peter Pears has tackled the bass recorder which, of course, is a more difficult affair, but he has several months start over me, and before long I hope we shall be playing duets.

With many thanks,

Yours sincerely,

Benjamin Britten

The Aldeburgh Music Club's 'energetic consort', with which Britten sometimes

---

[1] Although a number of recorders, including three made by Robert Goble in the mid-1950s, remain in the Britten-Pears Library, those sent by Dolmetsch do not unfortunately appear to be among them.

played, thrived under the enthusiastic direction of Imogen Holst, and it was she who initially introduced Britten to playing the recorder. He became joint editor with her of Boosey and Hawkes's series 'Music for Recorders'.

Dolmetsch followed his present with an invitation to Britten in a letter dated 29 September 1954 to write a work for recorder and harpsichord for performance at the 1955 Wigmore Hall recital.[2]

Dear Mr. Britten,

When our friend Imogen Holst visited us here last March in connection with the Perotin ms which you are including in your series of publications for Boosey & Hawkes, she mentioned to me your interest in the recorder as a recital instrument and said that you were considering composing for it.

You may already know that I give an annual recorder recital at the Wigmore Hall and include in the programme a work by a contemporary composer. Composers who have already written for me include Martin Shaw, Lennox Berkeley, York Bowen, Herbert Murrill, Cyril Scott, Edmund Rubbra, Antony Hopkins and now I would very much like to add your name to the list. Would you consider writing a short work for recorder and harpsichord for my next recital early in February? I would be very honoured to give it its premiere in my programme.

I shall look forward to having your views on my suggestion.

Yours sincerely,

Carl Dolmetsch

Unfortunately, Britten's musical commitments were such that he was unable to accept, and he wrote to Dolmetsch on 7 October:

Dear Mr. Dolmetsch,

Thank you for your kind letter. I hope one day to be able to write a piece for you to play at your annual recorder recital, but I much fear that my commitments are so great that it will not be possible for next year; but quite sincerely I must say that it will give me great pleasure to write a serious piece for recorder and harpsichord. I am planning at the moment a rather unsophisticated work for mixed recorders, and another reason for the delay is that I want to see how successful I am in writing for the instrument before I tackle a more elaborate piece.

May I say how much pleasure I have got these last months from playing the instruments you so kindly sent me?

With best wishes,

Yours sincerely,

Benjamin Britten

---

[2] This letter and the others Dolmetsch wrote to Britten cited below are all held in the Britten-Pears Library, Aldeburgh, UK.

The 'rather unsophisticated' work to which Britten refers is the *Scherzo* for recorder quartet, completed in 1955 and dedicated to the Aldeburgh Music Club consort. Despite Britten's assessment, it is a finely crafted piece of recorder consort writing.

Dolmetsch replied to Britten's letter just five days later, clearly in the hope of maintaining the interest expressed by the composer and further making an offer of technical advice.

> Dear Mr. Britten,
>
> Thank you very much for your letter from which I am very pleased to learn that you contemplate writing a serious work for the recorder and harpsichord some time in the future. Over and over again recorder players and others have asked me when your name is going to be added to the growing list of contemporary composers for the instrument. Being a player yourself now, you will know from experience the great potentialities of the instrument which on first acquaintance appears so simple.
>
> I shall look forward to hearing from you again as soon as you feel able to consider writing a recital piece and should there be any technical points regarding the instrument on which I could help you, please let me know as I should be only too happy to do so.
>
> With kind regards,
>
> Carl Dolmetsch

It was no doubt in the hope of stimulating Britten's interest further that Dolmetsch invited him to the 1955 Wigmore Hall recital at which Rubbra's *Fantasia on a Theme of Machaut* for recorder, string quartet and harpsichord was to receive its premiere. Dolmetsch's letter dated 31 January added the suggestion that Britten might also consider writing a work for recorder and strings.

> Dear Mr. Britten,
>
> I wonder whether you are likely to be within easy reach of London on Friday 11th February? If so, I feel sure you might be interested to hear the new Fantasia for recorder, strings and harpsichord which Rubbra has just written for me and which I am playing on that date with the Martin Quartet at the Wigmore Hall.
>
> If there is any chance of you coming do let me know and I will be pleased to send you complimentary tickets. We shall be giving the first broadcast of the work in the Third Programme on 15th April; I add this in case you are unable to be in Town for the recital but would like to hear the Fantasia.
>
> When I approached you some little time ago about a work for recorder from your pen, you said that it is your intention to write for the instrument sometime. Is there any hope of you producing a work in time for my recital in February 1956? I fully appreciate how busy you are, but at the same time assure you how eagerly the thousands of present-day recorder players are looking forward to such a solo work. We are becoming fairly well provided with contemporary works for recorder and harpsichord, or piano; our need now is for more works with strings.
>
> With kind regards,

Yours sincerely,

Carl Dolmetsch

Unfortunately Britten was unable to attend the concert of 11 February, as noted in his reply to Dolmetsch dated 4 February 1955. In this letter Britten expresses interest in the suggestion of recorder and strings, but explains that compositional commitments and a winter tour would prevent his immediate attention to such a work. The letter concludes:

> I was interested in your suggestion of a work for recorder and strings. I am afraid it will have to wait a time since my plans for composition are full for this year, and next winter I am undertaking a six months tour. But when I return, and incidentally get more acquainted with the recorder as an instrument, I will certainly consider the idea again with, I hope, some result.

Britten's *Alpine Suite* for recorder trio was composed for the injured Mary Potter (an artist friend of the composer and member of the Aldeburgh Music Club recorder consort) during a skiing holiday in 1955 and no doubt contributed further to his getting 'more acquainted with the recorder as an instrument', but whatever consideration he may have given to a composition for recorder and strings, unfortunately no such work was to come into being.

A few years were to pass before Dolmetsch again contacted Britten to request a work for recorder. A significant anniversary was to be celebrated, as Dolmetsch's letter of 27 March 1962 explains:

> Dear Benjamin Britten,
>
> When you first began writing for the recorder, your works gave much joy to enthusiasts everywhere – and by 'everywhere' I mean this quite literally. But every so often, people ask me why your name is missing from the list of moderns now writing solo works for the instrument and I remember from our correspondence of a few years ago that it was your intention to do so.
>
> Joseph Saxby and I are now in the 30th year of our collaboration. If I could persuade you to write us something for recorder and harpsichord, we would perform it at the Wigmore Hall in February next year. Our recital would then be in the nature of a double celebration. The work need not be long – Rubbra's latest, a passacaglia, runs for some five minutes.
>
> Hoping that I may hear from you soon and that many besides myself now see a long-felt wish come true.
>
> Yours sincerely,
>
> Carl Dolmetsch

Unfortunately Britten was unable to fulfil Dolmetsch's latest request. His reply, dated 2 May 1962, began with apologies for the delay in answering, noting his recent release from hospital. It continued:

> Some day I really do hope to write a piece especially for you, but I am afraid there is no chance of my doing it in time for your recital in February next year. I have an enormous amount of commitments, including a great deal of composition, and I dare not undertake any more at the moment.
>
> I am sorry to write so negatively, but you know I wish you and your great work continued success.

There appear to have been no further attempts by Dolmetsch to persuade Britten to compose a work for recorder. The lack of such a work from Britten is a constant source of regret to recorder players, as his rapid assimilation of the instrument's qualities were clearly indicated by his ingenious scoring for it in *Noye's Fludde* (1957) and *A Midsummer Night's Dream* (1960). It is also clear from his letters to Dolmetsch that although he did maintain a genuine interest in the instrument, unfortunately this did not translate into the work Dolmetsch and indeed all other recorder players sincerely wished it had.

Correspondence between Dolmetsch and Sir Malcolm Arnold dating from August 1958 reveals discussion regarding a piece (possibly a chamber concerto for recorder and string quartet) for the 1959 Wigmore Hall recital. However, the work was not composed. Dolmetsch certainly knew Arnold's Sonatina for treble recorder and piano (dedicated to Philip Rogers), and a copy of the published edition signed by the composer in 1953 is in the archive. Much later (in 1988), though not for Dolmetsch, Arnold did compose a concerto for recorder and orchestra.

Whatever enquiries may have been made of, or discussions held with other composers in connection with Dolmetsch's quest to establish and enhance the recorder's contemporary repertoire, no record has been preserved.

With the exception of Arnold Bax, the compositions of all the composers mentioned above include works for recorder. It is thus with some interest that we consider what the repertoire might now further contain had they all been able to fulfil Dolmetsch's invitations.

Chapter 7

Idiomatic and technical considerations

Many recorder players to whom I have put the question: 'What first attracted you to the recorder as a musical instrument?' have answered that it was initially its sound rather than its repertoire. What are the characteristics of recorder sound that make it unique and are fundamental to the most idiomatic music composed for it? Being somewhat uncertain myself, I questioned a number of players on the subject. They were able to provide some examples of what they considered to be effective idiomatic writing from the twentieth-century repertoire, but often concluded their brief selection and thoughts with: 'I don't think I have been entirely helpful, have I?' or words to that effect. (In fact their comments were more often than not of considerable assistance.) It is indeed not always straightforward to provide answers in the context of actual pieces, and attempting to compile a work-by-work assessment of idiomatic writing would prove too subjective an exercise to serve any real purpose. It is perhaps easier to think in general terms of what makes the recorder sound most effective, and there is no substitute for actually playing this repertoire and 'getting among the notes' to experience this at first hand.

The composer Donald Bousted included a mission statement for the recorder in an article on composing for the instrument in which he summed up many of these characteristics very succinctly.[1] Among these he noted:

> It is completely agile throughout its range and most interchanges between pitches are possible, even at high speed. The sound resembles a pencil line drawn on high-grain paper; clear and focussed, yet beautifully uneven and wayward. The dynamic range is vast (remember that dynamics are relative).
>
> Unlike the orchestral woodwinds, the recorder responds immediately to the breath of the player. This gives it an unprecedented ability to play highly sophisticated and intricate rhythmic patterns to the extent that a new kind of rhythmic composition is possible.

Later, Bousted observes: 'In addition, the roots of the instrument as an extension of the human voice, made from natural materials which have always been close to man's survival and development, create a certain intimacy; an introspective, though not always melancholic quality.'

If asked to provide an example of idiomatic recorder writing from the entire

---

[1] Bousted, 'An Instrument for the 21st century'.

repertoire, it is likely that many players' thoughts will turn immediately to Telemann. The best of his recorder parts seem to capture the very essence of the instrument in a way hardly matched, certainly by his contemporaries, and the brilliance is frequently achieved in music that is nevertheless not particularly technically demanding.

It is worth commenting that idiomatic appropriateness and technical difficulty are not necessarily directly proportional, and it is quite possible for technically demanding writing to be completely idiomatic (and conversely for technically easy pieces to be unidiomatic). This is certainly not confined to the recorder.

What in particular about Telemann's recorder writing provides its idiomatic qualities? The following extracts from the first and last movements of the well-known F major sonata for treble recorder and continuo from *Der getreue Musikmeister* (Ex. 7.1 and 7.2) will serve to indicate.

Ex. 7.1. G.P. Telemann, Sonata in F major from *Der getreue Musikmeister*. First movement, recorder part, bars 8 and 9.

Ex. 7.2. G.P. Telemann, Sonata in F major from *Der getreue Musikmeister*. Third movement, recorder part, bars 1–6.

Certainly the agility to which Bousted refers is evident here, and similar figuration is to be found in a number of contemporary works, where it serves the recorder equally idiomatically. The dazzling finale of David Bedford's Recorder Concerto composed for Piers Adams in 1993–94 makes use of repeated notes and leaps in a Telemannesque tour de force – an excellent example of technically demanding though totally idiomatic recorder writing

Compare the above extract from the first movement of the Telemann with Ex. 3.17 from Arnold Cooke's Quartet for treble recorder, violin, cello and harpsichord of 1964 and Ex. 3.18 from the same composer's *Little Suite* No. 1 for treble recorder solo.

Compare also the above extract from the third movement of the Telemann with the opening of the finale of Cooke's Quartet (Ex. 7.3).

Cooke's recorder writing does sound effective on the instrument, and this was noted by Walter Bergmann in his review of the 1960 Wigmore Hall premiere of

Ex. 7.3. Arnold Cooke, Quartet for treble recorder, violin, cello and harpsichord. Third movement, recorder part, bars 1–4. Reproduced by permission of Schott & Co. Ltd.

Cooke's Divertimento for recorder and string quartet: 'It seems to be a miracle that Mr. Cooke, who does not play the recorder himself, could write so unfailingly well for this instrument. He seems to be a composer who knows his craft and who wants to write for and not against the instrument (and audience).'[2]

Cooke's figuration does indeed resemble Telemann's, but should certainly not be considered in any way as pastiche, as a study of the underlying harmonic scheme will indicate.

However, the recorder's agility is but one of its facets, and the 'pencil line drawn on high-grain paper' – that essentially pure but nevertheless 'wayward' sound, is also central to its character. Telemann's (and indeed Handel's) slow-movement arioso-like melodies frequently explore the vocal qualities of the instrument. In the contemporary repertoire also, this quality (intimate and introspective as Bousted observes) certainly comes into its own in slow and expressive music, and is possessed of an innocence that lends a particular poignancy to many of the slow movements that would be lost if played on another instrument. Those in the sonatinas of Berkeley, Leigh and York Bowen, the *Scottish Suite* by Norman Fulton, and in Gordon Jacob's Suite and *Trifles* are excellent, though not the only examples. It remained a characteristic cherished by the composers writing for Dolmetsch into the last decade of the Wigmore Hall recitals, the first movement of Ridout's Chamber Concerto being a case in point.

If Cooke, as in the examples above, consciously (or perhaps unconsciously) made use of what appear to be baroque idioms, Gordon Jacob noted, following the composition of his Suite for treble recorder and string quartet, that he had 'treated the recorder as a perfectly normal musical instrument, which it is, and not in any way as a museum piece.'[3]

Dolmetsch was frequently at pains to stress that he did not want a pastiche of early music in the new works, and Jeanne Dolmetsch has informed me that he considered the pieces composed for him by Jacob, Rubbra and Cooke worked particularly well. Rubbra's works that make use of themes from the music of an earlier age do so in an entirely contemporary language, although study of these and the scores of Jacob and Cooke (and Murrill and Gardner among others) reveal

---

[2] *Recorder News*, March 1960, New Series, no. 28, p. 1.
[3] Letter, Jacob to Dolmetsch, 2 March 1958.

music that nevertheless looks familiar and inviting to the recorder on the printed page.

By comparison, some of the earlier works from the late 1930s are sometimes considered to be not as idiomatic, and have drawn the criticism that they are actually better suited to the flute.[4] Many of the published editions did indeed indicate the flute as an alternative solo instrument to the recorder (Reizenstein's Partita included separate parts for recorder and flute). This was surely as much a commercial as an artistic consideration in the early years of the publication of recorder music. Among the earliest published works alternative passages are sometimes found that avoid the problematic high F# of the recorder, but this should be viewed more as a technical consideration and not necessarily an indication of unidiomatic writing. If some of these earlier pieces do sometimes exhibit rather less idiomatic characteristics, it should be borne in mind that unlike the composers of the eighteenth century, composers of the late 1930s, and to an extent those of the immediate post-war period also, were far from familiar with the recorder. It is thus a testament to the craftsmanship of these pioneer composers that much of the music is effective and that some of it has stood the test of time and remained in the repertoire.

When the reviews of the new works in the broad sheets are examined, there is little if any reference to idiomatic writing, though for the earlier works, as might be expected, it was the then somewhat unfamiliar sound of the recorder that drew most comment. When idiomatic details are mentioned, it is in the context of the expressive limitations the instrument was considered to possess. Later, as the recorder became more prevalent, there was more emphasis on general musical structure, though the effect of the instrument was also sometimes referred to. The recorder is still perceived by some as lacking in dynamic and expressive qualities, but as Donald Bousted observes, 'dynamics are relative' (talk to any clavichord player).

Even in *The Recorder and Music Magazine*, where idiomatic considerations would perhaps be expected to come under discussion in reviews, especially of the published editions, they are mentioned only infrequently. Gordon Jacob's Suite is described as 'superbly written for the recorder'.[5] Perhaps within the recorder world the ability of the music to suit the instrument was taken for granted, although it must be said that in this respect some works were more successful than others.

Although, as stated earlier, technical difficulty is not directly related to idiomatic writing, technical considerations do play an integral part. Hans Gál's writing for the recorder in his *Three Intermezzi* drew from Dolmetsch the

---

[4] Ironically, the charge that much of this repertoire is better suited to the flute has not prevented some players from performing such overtly flute-orientated pieces as Debussy's *Syrinx* or Poulenc's Flute Sonata on the recorder.

[5] *Recorder News*, October 1959, New Series, no. 26, p. 12.

comment that they 'lie as well under the fingers as if you played the recorder yourself.'[6]

What made Telemann's recorder writing particularly idiomatic was the sheer practicality of it. The way in which it fits so naturally onto the instrument technically is what makes it so appropriate and convincing aurally. Within the idioms of baroque music this can be accomplished with relative ease. Tonality is often confined to keys that do not stray far from the fundamental of the instrument, and the passage-work resulting from the harmonic and melodic structures embraces intervals that usually form part of common chords: cross and forked fingerings are thus less frequently encountered. The same passage in a remote key should still *sound* idiomatic, but would not be so technically.

The harmonic structure of twentieth century music and thus also its melodic contours result in intervals and progressions that do not always fall quite so readily under the fingers. Dolmetsch typically advised Francis Chagrin that 'provided the notes are all obtainable within the compass of the recorder ... I do not mind how modern your chosen idiom may be.'[7] Bousted also correctly observes that 'most interchanges between pitches are possible, even at high speed.' However, at a point where the bounds of practicality are approached the natural idioms of the recorder may cease to be as effective.

There is also within twentieth-century music a tendency towards more frequent and radical modulations that result in enharmonic accidentals. This does not in itself create a technical difficulty, but the system by which recorder fingering generally flattens the note above rather than sharpens the note below can in some circumstances make the music initially more difficult to read. This is perhaps a psychological consideration, but in the performing parts Dolmetsch occasionally resorted to writing in equivalent enharmonic notation that, while not strictly in accordance with musical convention, made note recognition more immediate.

Unorthodox and complex rhythms associated with contemporary composition can be technically challenging but are not by their nature unidiomatic. Indeed, as Bousted notes, the recorder has 'an unprecedented ability to play highly sophisticated and intricate rhythmic patterns ...' Rhythmic complexity was a feature sometimes to be found in early music and can be just as, if not more, exciting in a contemporary context.

Even among the more successful works in this repertoire there are sometimes examples of unidiomatic technical difficulties: slurring across register breaks, diminuendos in passages rising towards the highest notes of the compass, ornaments (especially trills) on awkward adjacent notes, or very high notes beyond the usual upper range of the instrument. These may not seem especially problematic when compared with the technical difficulties encountered in the avant-garde repertoire, but in more conventional works they do represent a

---

[6] Letter, Dolmetsch to Gál, 15 March 1974.
[7] Letter, Dolmetsch to Chagrin, 23 April 1969.

challenge. Sometimes it may be necessary to make compromises if the underlying character of the music is to be preserved.

Dolmetsch was keen for there to be clear lines of communication between composer and performer and performer and audience, and valued time to get to know the detail of a new work. Performing material in the archives testifies to this, and the marking 'AF' (alternative fingering) is sometimes to be found where Dolmetsch wished to achieve a particular effect of dynamic or timbre that can be realized only on the recorder. Additional phrasing and articulation are also frequently found added in his performing recorder parts. Players today setting out to interpret this music will also need to be prepared to spend time becoming acquainted with its language and exploring how best the composer's intentions are to be realized. As with Dolmetsch, this may involve making use of alternative fingerings and other technical devices of which the composers were unlikely to be aware.

Individual players will find pieces with which they identify more easily than others, and what they perceive to be idiomatic or expressive writing will no doubt influence their choice. However, as Jeanne Dolmetsch commented after reading an early draft of this chapter: 'There are always a few major talents who can make *anything* sound well on the recorder – suitable or not!'[8]

As noted at the beginning of this chapter, the players I questioned about this had their own ideas on idiomatic elements, but Evelyn Nallen offered the very practical advice of considering fundamentally: does the music sound well on the recorder? This is not as simple as it may at first appear, and from discussions with Evelyn, the author was made very aware of the scrutiny to which she subjects a piece ahead of its inclusion in a recital programme or recording. Our own judgement may sometimes be coloured by our enthusiasm for the instrument, but that enthusiasm is perhaps the key, as the ultimate success or otherwise of performance lies to a large extent firmly and literally in our hands.

---

[8] Letter, Jeanne Dolmetsch to the author, 13 March 2002.

Chapter 8

Harpsichord or piano(?)

The words that head this chapter are sometimes to be found on the title pages of the published editions, particularly of the earlier pieces in the repertoire. Although they represent a natural desire on the part of the publishers to appeal to the widest possible market, some works do contain alternatives provided by the composers to suit the different instruments. The question mark added in parenthesis is representative of the debate that has often surrounded the keyboard accompaniments: what really were the composers' intentions instrumentally?

Harpsichords are now to be found in far greater numbers than in the relatively recent past. Even as little as 25 or so years ago, the presence of a harpsichord at a recital would attract a large gathering of inquisitive members of the audience at the interval rather in the way a rare and special sports car can still attract a group of admiring schoolboys. To an extent, growing familiarity during subsequent years has brought about something of a reaction, as if the sound that once seemed exciting and unusual, and representative of a different age of music making, has become more commonplace. Certainly there appear to be an increasing number of performances and recordings of Bach, Scarlatti and their contemporaries on the piano, though it is less certain whether this has had any influence on the use of the harpsichord in the twentieth-century recorder repertoire.

In contrast, the relative scarcity of harpsichords in the late 1930s had an effect on the scoring certainly of the pieces composed as a result of Manuel Jacobs's initiative. Without exception these were published for recorder and piano,[1] and yet some received early performances with harpsichord. Both Joseph Saxby and Christopher Wood were primarily harpsichordists (although this did not prevent Saxby from enjoying playing on a good piano) and, as noted in Chapter 3, the first performance of Lennox Berkeley's Sonatina was given with harpsichord. However, this was not the only work from this group of pieces to be performed in this way, and Saxby's markings in the performing scores preserved in the archive reveal that he also played the Sonatinas by Walter Leigh and Peggy Glanville-Hicks on the harpsichord. This may not be easy to imagine when we have become

---

[1] The cover of the edition of Reizenstein's Partita, Schott & Co. OFB 1014, indicates incorrectly 'for treble recorder and harpsichord'. However, the title at the head of the work is given as 'for treble recorder and piano'. This was brought to the author's attention by Margaret Reizenstein during a telephone conversation in March 2002.

so accustomed to hearing these works with piano, but attempts to play them with harpsichord can indeed be revealing.[2]

Among the first works to be composed specifically for Dolmetsch was Martin Shaw's Sonata of 1941 for recorder and harpsichord. Shaw clearly had some doubts as to the suitability of the music for the instruments, noting in a letter to Dolmetsch that it 'may not be recorder-harpsichord music at all'.[3] The published edition contains *ossias* for the harpsichord, and the keyboard part does sound effective on the instrument. In a discussion with the author about the use of the harpsichord in this repertoire David Gordon made the interesting observation that Shaw was among a number of composers (Rubbra included) whose familiarity with church music, and thus a contrapuntal style, was an influence that assisted their music to suit the harpsichord more readily.

Anthony Bernard's Prelude and Scherzo of 1941 includes the indication *ped.* in a number of places, but these do not infer piano scoring, but rather the use of a harpsichord sustaining device. Christopher Wood's *Sonata di camera* similarly contains not only the marking *sust. ped.*, but also $\frac{1}{2}$ 8', $\frac{1}{4}$ 8', indicating the use of another device found on some earlier Dolmetsch harpsichords that varied the strength with which the strings were plucked and thus the dynamic level.

When Dolmetsch re-established the Wigmore Hall recitals after World War II it was York Bowen's Sonatina that was the first new work to be premiered (see Chapter 3). Although Dolmetsch had initially requested a work with harpsichord, the composer's doubts as to the ability of the keyboard writing to suit the instrument, so clearly expressed in correspondence at the time, resulted in a work for recorder and piano, to which it is undeniably better suited. For York Bowen, the accomplished pianist, 'habit and instinct' led naturally to piano textures and sonority.

The next new work, Rubbra's *Meditazioni sopra 'Cœurs désolés'*, was certainly composed for and first performed with harpsichord, but the published edition gives the piano as an alternative and the composer expressed his own preference for performance with piano (see Chapter 3). The published editions of Rubbra's *Cantata pastorale* and *Passacaglia sopra 'Plusieurs regrets'* also indicate harpsichord or piano, but the published editions of the Sonatina and *Fantasia on a Chord* specify harpsichord only. This is also the case with the *Fantasia on a Theme by Machaut*, where the harpsichord forms part of a larger ensemble. However, Rubbra's comment to Dolmetsch in connection with this work is significant: 'Shall you use a larger harpsichord than the one you used for the first performance of the "Meditazioni"? It seems to me this new work needs a bigger sonority and greater variety of registration.'[4] Certain expectations of harpsichord sonority were also expressed by other composers (and reviewers), as will be noted later.

---

[2] See Chapter 3, note 1 to section on Berkeley's Sonatina.
[3] Shaw to Dolmetsch, 15 December 1941.
[4] Letter, Rubbra to Dolmetsch, 29 December 1954.

Murrill's Sonata was given its first performance with the composer at the harpsichord and there is no discussion about the instrumentation as such in correspondence during composition, although Murrill described the keyboard part at the beginning of the second movement as 'very light'.[5] Harpsichord or piano are indicated in the published edition and in a letter enclosing a copy of this Murrill commented: 'I do hope the recorder players won't be put off by the flautists or the pianists by the harpsichordists!'[6] His intention that the work could be played on either is further reinforced by the alternative indication for the final keyboard note(s) of the first movement. Harpsichord sonority does however suit the textures well.

Only the piano is mentioned in the published edition of Cyril Scott's *Aubade* and the writing is certainly pianistic. As with some of the pre-war works, however, the first performance was given with harpsichord, as the review in *The Times* of 12 May 1952 confirmed, referring to a harmonically stimulating harpsichord part. The published edition of Antony Hopkins's Suite likewise mentions only the piano (and pedalling is indicated in the final movement), but, as with the Scott, Saxby played the first performance on the harpsichord.

The alternative scoring with flute and piano in the published edition of Berkeley's *Concertino* represents what is virtually another arrangement of the work. (The same can be said of Cooke's unpublished Divertimento of 1974, which received its first public performance in the arrangement with recorders and harpsichord at the 1986 Wigmore Hall recital.)

All the remaining new works premiered at the Wigmore Hall that involved keyboard (with the exception of Lionel Salter's Air and Dance, in which the composer played the piano) featured the harpsichord. Some, including Norman Fulton's *Scottish Suite*, Gordon Jacob's Variations, John Gardner's *Little Suite*, Mathias's *Concertino* and Hans Gál's *Three Intermezzi*, give the piano as an alternative to the harpsichord in the published editions, clearly to capture a wider market.[7] In the case of Gál's work he specifically mentions in a letter to Dolmetsch that he 'would have nothing against the harpsichord part to be played on a pianoforte.'[8] However, having heard a tape recording of Dolmetsch and Saxby playing the piece he commented: 'I presume, Joseph, you played on your small harpsichord, – what I am missing are *some* dynamic contrasts – piano and forte etc. – but I hope some contrasts of this kind will be provided by an instrument with two manuals.'[9] This would appear to be another instance, as with Rubbra mentioned

---

[5] Letter, Murrill to Dolmetsch, 20 February 1950.

[6] Letter, Murrill to Marie Dolmetsch, 17 February 1951.

[7] The edition of Gordon Jacob's *Trifles* published by Emerson in 2000 gives flute and piano as alternatives to recorder and harpsichord for similar reasons, although the manuscript does not mention either.

[8] Letter, Gál to Dolmetsch, 14 May 1973.

[9] Letter, Gál to Dolmetsch, 21 February 1974.

above, of a composer seeking greater sonority and dynamic contrast from the harpsichord, or at least a small one. Similarly, Edgar Hunt's review of Berkeley's *Una and the Lion* commented that 'the more energetic sections seemed frustrated, as if the composer had expected the harpsichord to give more resonant support to the ensemble.'[10] Perhaps the more resonant sound of later harpsichords based on historic originals would have provided the sonority some of the composers were seeking. (See the comments attributed to Frank Martin in Chapter 9.)

Another instance of harpsichord sonority being questioned occurred with Donald Swann's *Rhapsody from Within*, the reviewer wondering 'whether the composer might not have been happier writing for the piano – he seemed to be seeking a more sustained quality than that offered by the harpsichord.'[11] Although for large portions of the work this is the case, the cimbalom effect noted by Leon Berger (see chapter 3) will not be realized on the piano.

Nigel Butterley's *The White-Throated Warbler*, Stephen Dodgson's *Warbeck Dances*, Martin Dalby's *Páginas* and the *Quintette* by Jean Françaix were all conceived with the harpsichord clearly in mind, the Dalby and Françaix works specifically indicating the use of the harpsichord's 16' and 4' registers. The title page of the manuscript score of Alan Ridout's *Variants on a Tune of H.H.* indicates the work as being for recorder and harpsichord. The first keyboard stave indicates harpsichord or piano, but the composer has included directions for the use of the harpsichord's lute stop and 4' register in two of the variations, making clear that harpsichord sonority was primarily intended. Colin Hand also stresses in a prefatory note to his *Plaint* that the harpsichord should be used whenever possible rather than the alternative piano, and pedalling kept to a minimum if the piano is used.

Two other works require special comment. Arnold Cooke's Quartet of 1964 was composed to be premiered at the 1965 Wigmore Hall recital by Dolmetsch and Saxby with the Schoenfeld sisters, and is thus scored for recorder, violin, cello and harpsichord. The title page of the composer's manuscript mentions only the harpsichord, but the cover and title page of the published edition indicate piano. At the head of the work and in front of the first keyboard stave the harpsichord is given only as an alternative, surely a case of the publisher attempting to seek a wider market.

Malcolm Lipkin's *Interplay* exists in three versions. The original, for recorder, percussion, viola da gamba and harpsichord, requires harpsichord sonority in the light scoring with small percussion instruments. A second version replaces the percussion and harpsichord with piano, and a third is a complete rescoring for flute, cello and piano. In the second version, the piano is something of a compromise, but in the third, piano sonority is required with the modern flute and cello.

---

[10] *Recorder & Music*, June 1979, **6**, p. 183.
[11] Ibid., June 1982, **7**, p. 146.

As noted above, the option of the piano is available, certainly where the composer or the publisher (though this may not have been with the composer's direct authority) has indicated it as an alternative to the harpsichord. However, much care will need to be taken by the pianist, and sparing use of the sustaining pedal made if dynamic balance is to be maintained. For the recorder player, matching the inherent expressivity of the piano presents its own challenge.

Some recorder players find the recorder (especially treble) and piano combination less satisfactory than recorder and harpsichord for some of this particular repertoire. Piano sound lacks the upper partials possessed by that of the harpsichord, and in combination with the recorder provides less of a contrast in timbre. Sometimes this is exploited to imaginative effect in works for which the scoring is specifically for piano. The passage in the second movement of the Sonata in E♭ by Hans Ulrich Staeps,[12] in which the recorder and piano right hand play in parallel fifths and blend to create an unusual tone colour, is unlikely to work in the same way with harpsichord. A section at letter F in the second movement of Walter Bergmann's Sonata for treble recorder and piano[13] uses the recorder to form what is in effect a bass line to piano figuration played *ottava* in the right hand. Only by using the harpsichord's 4' register on its own could notes in this tessitura be obtained, but this would not produce the effect the composer clearly had in mind.

Overcoming the various problems faced by both players in this repertoire requires a developed rapport. The Dolmetsch-Saxby partnership represented a very special musical relationship in which major contributory factors were Saxby's unfailing ear for the characteristics of harpsichord sonority and his instinctive feel for accompaniment. Study of the performing material reveals how carefully (and copiously) he added markings to indicate not only changes of registration, but also of fingering to achieve variations in articulation. Saxby's keen ear also led him to add octave doublings and filling out of chords to provide richer sonority where the music required it. Such additions are also to be found marked in Saxby's performing scores and would have been especially appropriate on some of the smaller harpsichords or the 'jet spinet' used for performances on tour. It is no doubt Saxby's familiarity with the early keyboard repertoire that influenced his appreciation of what sounded most effective. Large chords low down on the harpsichord possess a remarkable richness but are not always so well suited to the piano. The harpsichord's transparency is much easier to balance with recorder sound; however, the greater sustaining power of the piano is sometimes an advantage and is certainly required to realize the composers' intentions in such works as Bowen's Sonatina and Scott's *Aubade*.

Being able to compare at first hand and experiment with the different effect that harpsichord or piano can impart to the music is fascinating if arrangements can be

---

12 Vienna: Universal Edition, 1957.
13 London: Schott & Co. Ltd, 1974.

made for both instruments to be available. This was something I was able to experience while first playing through Gordon Jacob's *Trifles*, when both were purposely tried, and for which, in our opinion, the harpsichord seemed better suited.

It is important to appreciate that the keyboard parts in so much of this repertoire are more than simply accompaniment (although accompanimental skills are nevertheless of great importance). Counterpoint and thematic material are shared and developed with the solo instrument, as are rhythmic structures. On occasions when the keyboard provides a harmonic foundation only, it is frequently the shifting harmonic patterns that give expressive direction to the melodic line. These points need to be understood and appreciated as much by recorder players as their partners at the keyboard, and apply equally to the harpsichord as to the piano.

Some of the earlier works published with the piano as the primary keyboard instrument can certainly be played on the harpsichord, but the player will have to be prepared to experiment and summon up every last subtlety of harpsichord technique if a convincing performance is to result. Similarly, if the piano is used, a very sympathetic approach is essential, but as York Bowen observed, 'if handled gently (as some of us *can*!)' the balance can indeed 'be made perfect',[14] or it can come reasonably close. Recorder players will need to be ready to adapt to the very different musical environments that harpsichord and piano provide. Harpsichord sound can vary considerably from one instrument to another and that of earlier twentieth-century instruments from those of more recent construction. (This is discussed in more depth in Chapter 9.)

Whether harpsichord or piano is used, a musical relationship needs to be forged between keyboard and recorder player in which both are prepared to work towards a performance expressing the intellectual and emotional aspects of a work while making clear the individual contributions of both instruments. This is likely to take time, and in conversation with the author, Greta Dolmetsch recounted her fascination at hearing Dolmetsch and Saxby gradually bringing all the elements of a new work together over many hours of discussion and rehearsal. This repertoire frequently demands such commitment.

---

[14] Letter, York Bowen to Dolmetsch, 28 September 1946.

10 Carl Dolmetsch and Joseph Saxby in a discussion during rehearsal. (The echo key fitted to Dolmetsch's instrument is clearly visible.)

Chapter 9

Performance – questions of 'authenticity'

The place of the recorder in the early music revival is of considerable significance. It is among those instruments that seem to symbolize the increasingly serious efforts during the twentieth century to recreate the music of the past on its own terms. The thinking behind that revival has not stood still, and continuing research has brought about changes not only in performance practice but also in the construction and playing techniques of the instruments used for the interpretation of early music.

The modern recorder has in the course of research into its construction, based on surviving instruments from the past, been subject to numerous changes since the earliest examples were made. This has increased its suitability for the performance of early music, but not in all circumstances equally so for the performance of twentieth-century repertoire. The instruments of 60 or so years ago, when some of the earliest significant new works for recorder where being composed and performed, display a number of clearly discernible differences from the historic copies being made today. This is not to say that the earlier models are inferior, simply different.

Among the differences, perhaps the most fundamental is the shape of the windway. Recorders with the wider and rectangular windway typically found in older instruments will, when compared with later instruments with narrow, curved windways based on seventeenth- or eighteenth-century models, produce appreciably different sound and playing characteristics. Other differences in fingerhole construction (undercut on seventeenth- and eighteenth-century instruments) and bore design further contribute to an overall tonal dissimilarity.

The harpsichord has, if anything, undergone even more radical changes during the period of the early music revival. Gone are the heavy case construction, metal frames and complex jack mechanisms of earlier models, to be replaced by instruments of much lighter construction based much more closely on historic examples. The accompanying difference in sound is likewise of greater contrast, a somewhat thinner sound resulting from heavy construction compared with the comparative resonance of more recent historic copies.

Should such differences in the basic characteristics of the instruments of half a century ago be taken into consideration when performing the music composed at that time? I must admit it was something to which I had given little if any thought

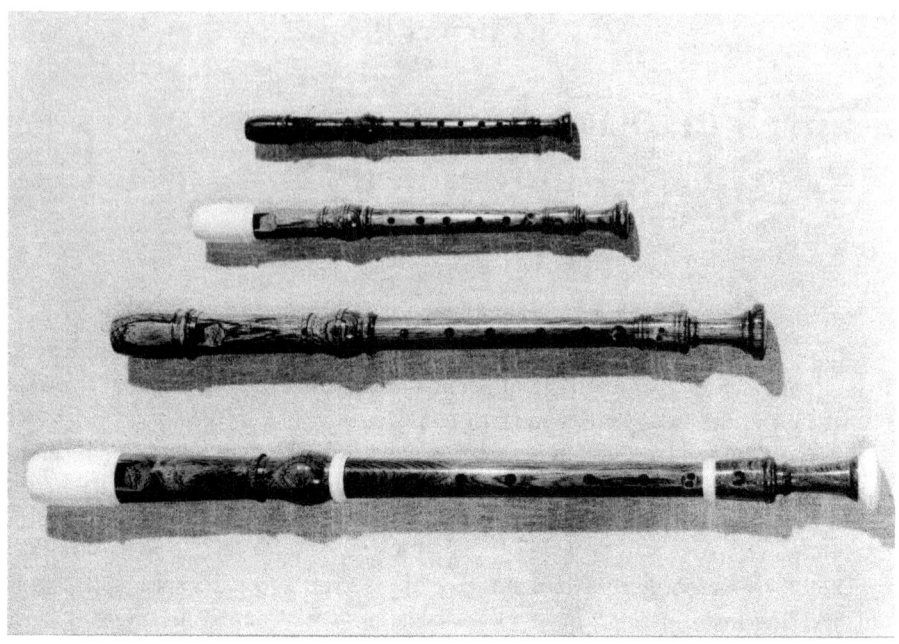

11 Recorders from the Dolmetsch workshop: tenor, treble, descant and sopranino.

until I attended a lecture recital given by Evelyn Nallen at the 1997 Festival of the Society of Recorder Players in St Albans. In the course of this, Evelyn played Rubbra's *Passacaglia sopra 'Plusieurs regrets'* on a Dolmetsch recorder dating from about 1953 accompanied on a harpsichord of quite modest dimensions.

Carl Dolmetsch's own recorders, made in the Dolmetsch workshops, were of the type just described, that is with a wider, rectangular windway. There are a number of photographs of Dolmetsch holding and playing such instruments, and those that belonged to him remain in the possession of the Dolmetsch family.

Joseph Saxby played on keyboard instruments also made in the Dolmetsch workshops. These varied in size and design, depending on the recital location, from a small single manual spinet-like instrument (known affectionately as the 'jet spinet' owing to its ease of transportation – even by air) used on tour, to the large, two-manual concert harpsichord played in many of the Wigmore Hall recitals. Examples of both these types of instruments remain at Haslemere and elsewhere. The small spinet had a single 8' register and a harp stop.

The specification of the Dolmetsch concert harpsichord is described in a letter[1] responding to enquiries about the instrument from William Mathias in 1973 as cited on p. 149: '… a two-manual instrument, with a range of five octaves and one

---

[1] Greta Matthews to William Mathias, 7 November 1973.

note – F to g – per manual. The specifications are 16ft., 4ft., 8ft., harp, coupler, harp, lute and 8ft., the last three being the upper manual registers.'

Foot pedals were employed to control the various registers, as on most harpsichords of the period, a feature rarely found on harpsichords being made at present. Likewise, 16' registers are now almost universally absent.

The tone of earlier Dolmetsch harpsichords is certainly more robust than that of the typical German Serieninstrumente of the 1950s and 1960s, and the construction more along historic lines, but it is nevertheless different in character from that of the instruments of more recent manufacture by other makers.

There is no doubt that the researches of the early music movement have led to an increased understanding of early performance practice and instrument construction that, when constructively and sensitively adopted, can provide a totally fresh appreciation of the music. At worst, however, convoluted and irrelevant arguments can arise (angels and pinheads come to mind) that seem to add little to the musicality or indeed any aspect of performance.

With this in mind, the answer to my earlier question has to be a guarded 'yes' – guarded because 'authenticity', or what I would prefer to term 'historical awareness', should not be regarded as the only important factor in the performance of this or indeed any music from the past, even the recent past, where first-hand evidence is more readily available.

Recorder players seeking to get closer to an original sound for this particular part of the twentieth-century repertoire may well find that the use of a 'period' instrument assists in their overall performance and interpretation.[2] Harpsichordists may similarly find inspiration from an instrument contemporary with the music, if indeed they can find one, for examples are becoming increasingly rare. It is worth noting that in some of the works discussed in earlier chapters the scores include specific directions for the use of the harpsichord's 16' register.[3]

What of other recorder devices such as the bell key, the echo key or the tone projector, all of which Dolmetsch added to the instrument to overcome very particular problems? The presence of a bell key will indeed enable the high F#s sometimes found in this repertoire to be obtained more easily, and the high D–E trill. The echo key, though effective in extending the dynamic range of the

---

[2] In October 2001, with a view to experiencing this for myself, I purchased a second-hand Dolmetsch treble recorder (instrument No. 10740, dating from about 1963). It was refurbished in the Dolmetsch workshop and had a bell key fitted (salvaged from a recorder of similar age). The instrument is in satin wood with an ivory mouthpiece, materials that Marguerite Dolmetsch informed me were her father's favourites and used for his 'master' instruments. Exploring the repertoire on a recorder that has similarities with Dolmetsch's own concert instrument has been revelatory.

[3] Directions for the use of controls to vary the strength with which the strings are plucked and even of a sustaining device are to be found in some of the scores of works by Christopher Wood and Anthony Bernard. Such devices were to be found on a few harpsichords made in the Dolmetsch workshop: see Chapter 8.

12 · One of Carl Dolmetsch's concert instruments, a treble recorder fitted with a bell key.

instrument, has not found universal acceptance. As far as the tone projector is concerned, its value or practicality will depend entirely on the acoustic conditions of the place of performance and the player's own personal preferences.

I believe that serious attempts to play this repertoire on instruments from the period should be encouraged if the resulting performances genuinely enhance our appreciation and understanding of the music. However, performance on recorders and harpsichords of the types in use 50 or so years ago can create distinct problems for the players (and listeners) of today, and there is a quite natural tendency to resort to the familiar territory of more modern-style instruments. Piers Adams noted in connection with his *Shine and Shade* CD that modern baroque copy recorders had not proved entirely satisfactory. However, rather than a Dolmetsch type instrument, the treble and tenor used were made by Michael Dawson to a more 'modern' design with a wider bore and what Adams described as an 'unusually rich flute-like sound.'[4]

It is, however, interesting to reflect on the similar problems for players – and indeed to an extent the hostility – period instruments encountered when first used in the performance of baroque and classical music. It has taken a while for techniques to be relearnt and re-established, but standards of performance of baroque and classical music on period instruments, perhaps once thought to be unattainable, are now for the most part taken for granted. The problems posed by the use of appropriately contemporary instruments in twentieth-century repertoire reflect those encountered by the players who first performed this music. Players today in attempting to overcome these same problems may well discover things about the music that would not be apparent from performance on more modern instruments. This has certainly been the case with the music of the past, and the artistic and practical arguments put forward to justify the use of period instruments in earlier repertoire must surely have a bearing when considering the performance of twentieth-century music.

However, it has to be admitted that in some respects earlier harpsichords were not entirely satisfactory. Frank Martin wrote initially for a large mid-twentieth century instrument, but on first hearing a harpsichord constructed after historic originals is reported to have commented that he wished he had been aware of such sounds before composing for the harpsichord.

Would the composers writing for the large harpsichords of the mid-twentieth century and recorders from the same period have had such a clearly formed idea of the instrumental sound that they would not have found later instruments based on historic models equally acceptable? It is unlikely that we shall ever know for certain, but there is without doubt potential for much more discussion and exploration in this area.

If period instruments are employed for this repertoire, however, they should not

---

[4] Mayes, 'Piers Adams in conversation; cf. Piers Adams's notes to the CD *Shine and Shade*, Tremula Records, 1994.

under any circumstances be used as camouflage for inadequate performance of any kind, and such basics as good intonation, ensemble and balance remain absolutely essential, even if sometimes more difficult to achieve.

Excellent performances can be, and indeed are, achieved on the more recently made style of instruments. A well-voiced modern recorder with a good singing tone, and a well regulated, crisp-toned and resonant modern harpsichord are, in committed hands, entirely suited to do justice to this repertoire. Nevertheless, acquaintance with the sound and playing characteristics of recorders and harpsichords from close to the period when a work was composed may well influence the way in which the music is approached and played on modern instruments.

For players performing this repertoire today, there is no substitute for attempting to gain a genuine feel for the underlying style of the music (though this cannot be assumed to be the same for the work of many composers over a period of more than 50 years) and this will be achieved through careful study of and increased familiarity with it. From a practical point of view, a good balance between the instruments and the clear audibility of all a work's musical constituents, even bearing in mind the final sentence of the paragraph above, are perhaps as important as what might be considered the 'right' sound.

The instruments used are indeed only a part of the interpretation of twentieth-century repertoire and a number of other elements also need to be considered.

One that frequently stimulates debate is vibrato, as there is perhaps a tendency to use this more sparingly than hitherto in the performance of music from all periods. There is certainly a perception that Dolmetsch himself played with more vibrato than a number recordings I have heard would seem to indicate. The use of vibrato to lend expression to particular notes has always been an important weapon in the recorder player's armoury and can add weight to dynamic contrast. This is as important in twentieth-century repertoire as in that from any other period and requires careful consideration.

Ornamentation is also of considerable significance and interest. In the correspondence with a number of composers it is clear that in performance Dolmetsch had added ornaments to the melodic line of a new work. Rubbra in particular expressed his approval of those added in *Meditazioni sopra 'Cœurs désolés'* and asked Dolmetsch to mark them in the manuscript score ahead of publication.[5]

There is much discussion in the correspondence with Herbert Murrill regarding the little cadenza that appears towards the end of the second movement of his Sonata. This grew out of a Dolmetsch improvisation, and he seems to have added cadenzas at similar points in a number of other works. In his own copy of the score of Walter Leigh's Sonatina, Dolmetsch wrote 'short cadenza' at the pause over the recorder's D at bar 79 in the final movement. Written out on a small piece of manuscript paper attached to the recorder part is a cadenza, to be found in Ex. 9.1, that also presumably started life as an improvisation.

---

[5] Letter, Rubbra to Dolmetsch, 11 May 1949.

Ex. 9.1. Cadenza for the last movement of Walter Leigh's Sonatina for treble recorder and piano, written out by Carl Dolmetsch on a portion of MS paper and inserted into his copy of the recorder part.

It is perhaps not entirely stylistically appropriate, although it clearly shows an intention that no doubt found its way into other pieces, but for which written-out examples have not survived, or were not ever committed to paper.

Dolmetsch's addition of ornaments and cadenzas in his interpretation of early music seemed to have spilled over almost unconsciously into his performances of modern repertoire. A number of recorded performances, in particular those of him playing York Bowen's Sonatina, Gordon Jacob's *Trifles* and Alan Ridout's Chamber Concerto, when compared with the scores, demonstrate this very clearly. In *Trifles* we hear a deliciously languid appoggiatura added to the last note of the first movement, and in Ridout's concerto a number of short repeated phrases in the quick second movement are effectively decorated in the repetitions. The final descending passage at the end of the last movement becomes a bravura flourish with the addition of semiquavers. None of these appear in the parts, and are quite effective in context.

However, not every composer was sympathetic to Dolmetsch's addition of ornamentation, and the downward and upward flourish added to the high B superimposed by a pause in the penultimate bar in his performances of Colin Hand's *Plaint* was not approved of by the composer.[6] John Gardner is another composer who does not welcome addition or alteration of his musical text, and attention should also be paid to the note by Nigel Butterley in the Orpheus Music edition of *The White-Throated Warbler*, in which he discourages elaboration and improvisation. Players may consider the addition of ornamentation in at least some of this repertoire, and a certain amount of such 'personalization' is in keeping with its spirit, but this should be done with caution and taste.

As mentioned at the outset, the recorder is an instrument with its roots in the past, and it is a happy characteristic that some improvisatory elements of the performance practice from that past can enhance the performance of its twentieth-century repertoire. This is clearly something that appealed to Dolmetsch, and which subsequent interpreters, with due respect for the character of the music and what can be determined of the composers' intentions, may also recognize and enjoy.

---

[6] See note 20 in Chapter 4.

Chapter 10
Past, present and future

Among the works composed for Dolmetsch are a handful that from the time of their first performance and publication have maintained a place in the recorder repertoire. Berkeley's Sonatina, Rubbra's *Meditazioni sopra 'Cœurs désolés'* and Jacob's Suite for treble recorder and strings received immediate critical acclaim and represented, together with other works from the 1930s, 1940s and 1950s, the successful synthesis of what had been considered an 'early' instrument with a mainstream contemporary musical idiom. Recorder players besides Dolmetsch, at least those with the required technique, took them into their repertoire, and together with works being composed on the continent by such composers as Harald Genzmer, Hans Ulrich Staeps, Henk Badings and Jens Rowher, a significant new repertoire began to be established.

However, members of the succeeding generation of players increasingly considered that such music did not wholly represent the recorder's contemporary voice. Works such as *Muziek voor Altblokfluit* (1961) by Rob du Bois,[1] *Sweet* (1964) by Louis Andriessen[2] and *Gesti* (1966) by Luciano Berio,[3] all written for Brüggen, and Jürg Baur's *Mutazioni* (1962),[4] composed for Michael Vetter, represented a radical departure in approach to recorder composition, making use of what have become known as extended or alternative techniques.

The late 1960s and 1970s also saw the emergence of a Japanese school of recorder composition. Equally demanding and innovative in its approach, it is represented by such works as *Fragment* (1968) by Makoto Shinohara,[5] *Black Intention* (1975) by Maki Ishii[6] and *Meditation* (1975) by Ryohei Hirose.[7]

Increasingly the recorder sound world of Rubbra, Murrill, Jacob, Cooke and their contemporaries seemed to represent an outmoded form of expression to the new generation of players: Franz Brüggen, in an interview published in 1974 considered it, at that time, to be retrogressive.[8] As Ross Winters has observed: 'In

---

[1] Mainz: Schott & Co. Ltd.
[2] Mainz: Schott & Co. Ltd.
[3] Vienna: Universal.
[4] Wiesbaden: Breitkopf and Härtel.
[5] Mainz: Schott & Co. Ltd.
[6] Tokyo: Zen-On Music Co. Ltd.
[7] Tokyo: Zen-On Music Co. Ltd.
[8] Horner, 'Franz Brüggen on contemporary music for the recorder', p. 353.

my student days in Amsterdam, there was no question of playing these English works. It was almost damning enough to call them English and write them off as pastoral, pseudo-Baroque music.'[9]

Greta Dolmetsch noted in a conversation with the author that as a young recorder players in the 1920s Carl Dolmetsch, together with his brother Rudolph, had experimented with what would now be regarded as extended techniques simply for fun, but he was unable to find a place for them in his music making at that time and indeed subsequently. Throughout the years of the Wigmore Hall recitals the works premiered by Carl Dolmetsch remained in a more mainstream musical language. His comment in a letter written to Martin Dalby in 1972 referring to 'avant-garde gimmicks alien to the character of the instrument – to my mind an affront to its innate dignity!'[10] is an indication of his frustration with the direction new music for the recorder was taking. He expressed a similar view in a telephone conversation with the author in 1995.

However, he was prepared to embrace a wider musical aesthetic than might initially be apparent. We find aleatoric fragments in Hovhaness's Sextet, serialism in Butterley's *The White-Throated Warbler* and Cooke's Divertimento (premiered in 1986), amplified harpsichord and bitonality in Chagrin's *Preludes for Four* and highly complex rhythmic and textural structures in Dalby's *Páginas*.

It was perhaps among the growing number of non-professional players that interest in the contemporary mainstream repertoire might have been expected – and indeed was – found. However, the recorder parts make higher technical demands than the average baroque sonata, and the keyboard parts require a level of technique not encountered in playing a continuo realisation. They also require an understanding of the keyboard's particular role in this repertoire that is more than simply accompaniment. If the recorder/keyboard repertoire presented technical difficulties for the non-professional, the works with strings or other instruments had practical implications; the ensembles for which they were scored were not always easy to assemble in an amateur context. The music thus seemed trapped between the disinterest of the more progressive professional element and the limited technical ability of many non-professionals.

It would be an inaccurate simplification to assert that the emerging avant-garde was solely responsible for there being less interest in the substantial musical mainstream that did of course continue to exist, and in which Dolmetsch was content to remain working. This was, after all, music he enjoyed playing, by composers who, in many cases, were old friends. Within the recorder world he was certainly not alone, but there was a movement that sought to assert the instrument's continuing renaissance by adopting a position at the cutting edge of contemporary music, and reinforcing it by a rejection of non avant-garde elements.

---

[9] Winters, 'The Dolmetsch legacy'. Paper given at the European Recorder Teachers Association (UK), May 1997.

[10] Dolmetsch to Dalby, 7 September, 1972.

This is a curiously paradoxical position, as those who took it were also part of the continuing early music revival, firmly of the belief that music was not evolutionary, but that the music of one age did not supersede that which had come before. Why then should the music of the recorder avant-garde apparently render the contemporary mainstream repertoire obsolete?

Even the musical mainstream is subject to changing fashion. For York Bowen, Cyril Scott, Gordon Jacob and Edmund Rubbra, as for many composers of their generation, the years immediately following their deaths seemed to bring about a neglect of their work from which it is only just beginning to emerge.

Although interest in and performance of the recorder's mainstream contemporary repertoire has to varying degrees been maintained, by the late 1980s and early 1990s a more discernible rekindling of enthusiasm was becoming apparent.

Ross Winters (for whom Alan Bush composed his recorder sonata) had for some time included works by, among others, Rubbra, Bergmann, Berkeley and Hopkins in his recital programmes (he had performed the Hopkins Suite at a Macnaughton concert at the age of just ten). In the following years during his early teens, Ross received much encouragement and support from Walter Bergmann, no doubt a significant influence on the development of his interest in the mainstream contemporary repertoire. A BBC Radio 3 broadcast included the Berkeley and Rubbra Sonatinas, and his continuing enthusiasm for the repertoire was reflected in his paper 'The Dolmetsch legacy', given at the European Recorder Teachers' Association UK conference in 1997.[11] His commitment found further expression in his CD of English recorder music containing nine pieces from the Dolmetsch repertoire released by the British Music Society in 2000. Ross's infectious enthusiasm for this repertoire was certainly a major contributory factor to the writing of this book.

Piers Adams's CD *Shine and Shade* released in 1994 was also representative of the changing attitude. The title of the CD was that of Stephen Dodgson's work for recorder and harpsichord composed for the English recorder virtuoso Richard Harvey and included in the programme. Besides this and Edward Gregson's *Three Matisse Impressions* the remainder of the pieces were from Dolmetsch's Wigmore Hall repertoire and featured works by Fulton, Rubbra, Bowen, Berkeley and Swann. As if to underline his commitment to the music Adams's liner note commented: 'Considering the huge upsurge in interest in the recorder in the past few decades, it is remarkable that such high quality music by English composers of stature has been largely neglected in favour of indifferent baroque sonatas and avant-garde experimentation.'

There were other players also making a significant contribution to the non-avant-garde renaissance. Canadian-based recorder player Alison Melville recorded a programme of music from the English, German and Austrian non avant-garde

---

[11] Later forming the basis for his article 'The Dolmetsch legacy'.

repertoire on a CD entitled *Fruit of a Different Vine*, released in 1998. Its French title, *Parfums d'un jardin secret*, is perhaps more expressive, and like Piers Adams, Alison nailed her colours to the mast in her liner note. Referring to the many pieces dating from the decades following the recorder's revival early in the twentieth century she commented: 'Relatively little of this music is heard in performance, and even in this current age of esoterica on CD, recordings of it are few.' Later in the note Alison added: '... it has always been fun to explore these attempts to fit the recorder – which, like all instruments, has its limitations – into the language of the mid-twentieth century.'

Evelyn Nallen is another player prepared to programme works from this repertoire in her wide exploration of recorder music as a whole. Alan Ridout, Carl Rütti and Roxanna Panufnik are among the composers to have written works for her, some of which she has recorded on an as yet unreleased CD covering 60 years of recorder music with keyboard player David Gordon (who composed the most recent work in the programme). The programme also included four works from the Dolmetsch repertoire.

The mainstream contemporary repertoire has also been explored in the recital programmes of English recorder player Caroline Jones.

Practical interest in the repertoire has also been shown on the continent. Kees Otten (for whom over 30 new works were composed, including the powerful sonata for recorder and harpsichord by Henk Badings) with his wife Marina Klunder and an ensemble of their friends, recorded a very international programme of twentieth-century repertoire including works by Hindemith, Genzmer Leigh and Staeps.

The young German recorder player Michael Hell from Hanover has devised and performed programmes based entirely on the works initiated by Manuel Jacobs and composed for Carl Dolmetsch. His diploma thesis made an in-depth study of the music, which he tellingly referred to in correspondence with the author as remaining largely 'taboo repertoire' in his native Germany.

In singling out particular players who have contributed to the emerging revival there is a real danger of unintentional omissions. However, no appraisal would be complete without acknowledgement of the indefatigable efforts of John Turner. His live and broadcast recital programmes, including many works not only from the Dolmetsch repertoire, but also the mainstream contemporary repertoire as a whole, would be impressive on their own. Yet in addition, and to his great credit, Turner has continued in Dolmetsch's tradition of encouraging composers to write new works for the recorder. The number he has premiered is now approximately 350 and continues to rise. He has included some of them on a number of CDs that also feature recordings of the Rawsthorne Suite, Walter Leigh's Air, Robert Simpson's Variations and Fugue and Arnell's Quintet (The Gambian).

It should be stressed that none of the above players has rejected avant-garde elements as a result of their interest in the mainstream contemporary repertoire. Rather they have sought to explore to the full the wide range of music that twentieth-century composers have written for the recorder in a variety of idioms. This has gone a considerable way in bringing the instrument to a maturity that has no need to factionalize or pigeonhole, but rather embrace a diversity that has emerged as a positive asset.

New composition for the recorder around the turn of the twenty-first century reflects that diversity. An even wider range of influences is at work, including folk, jazz, minimalism, and elements not only of the mainstream, but also of the avant-garde. Microtonality, live electronics and the electro-acoustic recorder are also areas of significant development.

Important in the move towards a synthesis of avant-garde techniques with a more expressive musical language are works such as Hans-Martin Linde's *Music for a Bird* (1968)[12] and particularly his *Amarilli mia bella* (subtitled 'Hommage à Jacob van Eyck') of 1971[13] and *Una follia nuova* (1989),[14] both founded significantly on themes from the music of an earlier age. All are for solo recorder, a particular characteristic of the avant-garde, but the extended techniques employed here serve to add colour and expression rather than being the sole foundation.

The works of German composer and recorder player Markus Zahnhausen take this process even further. The three pieces that comprise his *Lyrische Szenen* (1992)[15] for solo recorder, Zahnhausen states in his notes on performance, 'should be regarded as standing squarely in the romantic tradition.' In these, extended techniques are used sparingly, but in his *Lux aeterna* (1992–94),[16] also for solo recorder, use is made of finger holes for transverse flute embouchure, flageolet tones and for a portion of the work the player is required to whistle rather than play. In addition to these somewhat disturbingly unorthodox playing methods, quarter-tones are employed melodically to great expressive effect in what the composer refers to as 'super-chromaticism'. For all this, the piece achieves a stillness and emotional intensity in its simplicity.

Among other more recent compositions, Anthony Gilbert's recorder concerto *Igórochki* (1991–92)[17] and Hans Stadlmair's *Sonata pastorale* (1996)[18] stand out for their creative originality. The soloist in Gilbert's concerto makes use of sopranino, soprano, alto, tenor and bass recorders and the remarkable accompanying ensemble consists of percussion (vibraphone, marimba, crotals and handbells), cimbalom, guitar and string quartet. Stadlmair's substantial (24-minute) sonata also uses five sizes of recorder from sopranino to bass, partnered

---

12 Mainz: Schott & Co. Ltd.
13 Mainz: Schott & Co. Ltd.
14 Mainz: Schott & Co. Ltd.
15 Wolfenbüttel: Möseler Verlag, 1997.
16 Wolfenbüttel: Möseler Verlag, 1995.
17 London: Schott & Co. Ltd.
18 Wolfenbüttel: Möseler Verlag.

by a fortepiano. This unusual scoring produces some extraordinary and dramatic affects.

Although these two works have been mentioned particularly, they are but representative of an approach to recorder composition found in many other contemporary pieces that while totally innovative remains mindful of the instrument's techniques and traditions.

In taking but the briefest look at more recent recorder composition an attempt has been made to provide a context in which to view the Dolmetsch repertoire at the beginning of the twenty-first century. The earliest works are now as far removed from the present time as Handel's *Messiah* is from Beethoven's First Symphony. It is all too easy to forget this and make the mistake of considering all twentieth-century non-avant-garde recorder repertoire from the same musical standpoint. Successful performance of the recorder works from 40, 50 of even 60 years ago depends on a grasp of their musical language, which can be far removed from that of more recent works, and in an entirely different world from the avant garde. Seeking its particular musical vitality and expressiveness is a challenge, but one to which the recorder players of today, and indeed the future, should rise, for it has its own rewards.

How then should we assess Dolmetsch's influence on the establishment and growth of a contemporary recorder repertoire? His earliest efforts to encourage the composition of significant new works, and the enthusiasm with which he promoted and performed them in programmes alongside the earlier repertoire associated with the instrument are fundamental. However, other elements are equally influential, though perhaps not as immediately obvious. From the outset Dolmetsch realized the importance of encouraging accomplished composers (and not necessarily those who had composed for the recorder previously) if significant works were to be created, a philosophy that has increasingly continued to enhance the repertoire.

It is worth noting how many of the composers who wrote works for Dolmetsch, including those for whom it was not their first encounter with the recorder, continued to compose for the instrument. Gordon Jacob, Gaston Saux, Thomas Pitfield, Arnold Cooke, John Gardner, Hans Gál, Richard Arnell, Stephen Dodgson, Alan Ridout, Alun Hoddinott, Colin Hand and Michael Short, among others, all contributing to the expanding repertoire, sometimes as a result of encouragement from the next generations of players.

Dolmetsch's unwillingness to adopt an avant-garde approach should not be seen as wholly reactionary. His continued encouragement of composers working in a less experimental musical language resulted in some fine pieces that would not otherwise have come into being. The fact that they were contemporary with some of the important works from the avant-garde does not invalidate their musical worth. Dolmetsch's was not a lone voice, but certainly representative of a wish for the continued development of the recorder repertoire without the abandonment of the instrument's traditions and basic techniques.

There is a particular area where Dolmetsch sought to encourage new repertoire and in which his influence has possibly yet to be fully realized. Works for recorder with a chamber ensemble of strings or winds and sometimes including voice featured prominently in the Wigmore Hall recitals. This integration of sonorities, while reflecting baroque practice, also provided new possibilities for the recorder in a chamber music context. John Turner has also been keen to encourage compositions (and arrangements of previously composed works for recorder and piano) with recorder and chamber ensemble, especially string quartet (and including the voice), but this is musical territory where potential for exploration remains in abundance. Much of the avant-garde repertoire was, as noted above, for solo recorder. Although sometimes highly effective and featuring the creation of exciting and at times dramatic new sounds, this position of relative isolation has not been conducive to the development of the recorder in contemporary chamber music. This is all the more puzzling, as a considerable amount of new music has been composed for recorder ensemble.

A particular criticism of contemporary recorder repertoire as a whole is the lack of really important and significant pieces; indeed the recorder repertoire in its entirety is frequently regarded as containing very little truly 'great' music. Dolmetsch very wisely observed: 'We welcome the fact that composers of our time are writing for our instrument, but at the same time we cannot automatically hail every work from a modern pen as a masterpiece. Discrimination is essential to the selection of music in any age and is a fundamental precaution not confined to the field of recorder music alone.'[19]

In attempting to establish and extend the contemporary recorder repertoire Dolmetsch did succeed in obtaining a body of works among which are some highly significant pieces. Although 'not every work from a modern pen' can result in a masterpiece, this should not detract from the continuing effort to encourage the composition of new music for the recorder. Dolmetsch's own contribution in this field must be regarded as seminal and exemplary.

---

[19] Dolmetsch, 'The recorder's 20th century repertoire', p. 249.

Bibliography

Adams, Piers, notes for CD *Shine and Shade*, Tremula Records TREM 103-2, 1994.
Bergmann, Walter, 'Recollections of Benjamin Britten', *The Recorder Magazine*, **5** (9), March 1977, 286 only.
Bousted, Donald, 'An instrument for the 21st century', *The Recorder Magazine*, **21a** (4), Winter 2001, 141–45.
Bridge, Joseph Cox, 'The Chester recorders', *Proceedings of the Musical Association*, **27**, 1900–01 (quoted in Kinsell, 'J.C. Bridge and the recorder', p. 159).
Cole, Hugo, 'Simpson, Robert', *New Grove Dictionary of Music and Musicians*, ed. Stanley Sadie, London: Macmillan, 1980, **17**, 331–32.
Crossley-Holland, Peter, 'Sounds from the wood', *The Recorder Magazine*, **22** (2), Summer 2002, 53–56 [with a foreword and additional notes by John Turner].
Davies, Malcolm, 'The recorder music of Gaston Saux', *The Recorder Magazine*, **19** (3), Autumn 1999, 87–89.
Davis, Alan, *Treble Recorder Technique*, London: Novello, 1983.
Dolmetsch, Carl, 'An introduction to the recorder in modern British music', *The Consort*, **17**, 1960, 47–56.
——, 'The recorder in evolution', *Recorder Magazine*, **16** (2), June 1996, 55–56.
——, 'The recorder's 20th century repertoire', *Recorder & Music Magazine*, **2** (8), February 1968, 247–49.
Foreman, Lewis, 'Recorder music', in Lewis Forman (ed.), *Edmund Rubbra, Composer: Essays*, Rickmansworth: Triad Press, 1977, 71–75.
Hand, Colin, 'The composer writes', *Recorder & Music*, **5** (3), September 1975, 89.
Horner, Keith, 'Franz Brüggen on contemporary music for the recorder', *Recorder & Music*, **4** (10), June 1974, 352–54.
Hunt, Edgar, *The Recorder and its Music*, London, Eulenberg, 1977; (rev. repr., Hebden Bridge, Peacock Press, 2002).
——, 'The recorder music of Edmund Rubbra', *The Recorder & Music Magazine*, **8**, (10), June 1986, 296–97.
Jacobs, Manuel ('Terpander'), 'The Recorders', *Musical Times*, **79** (1147), September 1938, 653–56.
Johnson, Edward (ed.), *Robert Simpson: Fiftieth Birthday Essays*, London: Triad Press, 1971.

Kinsell, David, 'J.C. Bridge and the recorder', *Recorder & Music*, **5** (5), March 1976, 157–59.

Martin, Anne, *Musician for a While: a Biography of Walter Bergmann*, Hebden Bridge: Peacock Press, 2002.

Mayes, Andrew, 'Piers Adams in conversation with Andrew Mayes', *The Recorder Magazine*, **14** (4), December 1994, 116–18.

Mellers, Wilfrid, 'Rubbra's recent chamber music', *The Listener*, **47**, (1211), 15 June 1952, 809 only.

O'Kelly, Eve, 'The recorder revival ii: the 20th century and its repertoire', in John Mansfield Thomson, and Anthony Rowland-Jones (eds), *The Cambridge Companion to the Recorder*, Cambridge: Cambridge University Press, 1995, 152–66.

——, *The Recorder Today*, Cambridge: Cambridge University Press, 1990.

Rowland-Jones, Anthony, *Playing Recorder Sonatas*, Oxford: Clarendon Press, 1992.

——, *Recorder Technique*, 6th impression, Oxford: Oxford University Press, 1971.

Thomson, John Mansfield, *Your Book of the Recorder*, 2nd edn, London: Faber and Faber, 1974.

Thorne, J.O., 'Hans Gál: a seventy-fifth birthday tribute', *The Recorder & Music Magazine*, **1** (10), August 1965, 303 only.

Turner, John, notes for CD *Aspects of Nature*, Olympia OCD 714, 2002.

——, 'Rawsthorne's Recorder Suite', *The Recorder Magazine*, **13** (1), March 1993, 13–14.

——, 'The Rawsthorne Suite: a postscript', *The Recorder Magazine*, **17** (1), March 1997, 36 only.

Welch, Christopher, 'Literature relating to the recorder', *Proceedings of the Musical Association*, **24**, 1897–98, 145.

——, *Six Lectures on the Recorder and Other Flutes in Relation to Literature*, London: Henry Frowde [for the] Oxford University Press, 1911.

Whiting, B.C., 'The recorder music of Arnold Cooke', *Recorder & Music*, **5** (10), June 1977, 318–22; **5** (11), 355–58.

Winters, Ross, 'The Dolmetsch legacy: the recorder music composed for Carl Dolmetsch, 1939–1989', *The Recorder Education Journal*, **3**, 1996, 30–37.

List of Musical Works

Arnell, Richard, Quintet 'The Gambian', tr rec, str qt. Unpublished.
Bate, Stanley, Sonatina, tr rec, pn. London: Schott & Co. Ltd, 1950 (Edition 10040).
Bergmann, Walter, ('Anon. Master of the 20th century'), *Fuga à 3*, no instrumentation indicated. Unpublished: MS in Dolmetsch archive.
——, *Pastorella*, Soprano, sopranino rec. Sharon, Connecticut: Magnamusic Inc., 1972 (MM21).
Berkeley, Lennox, *Concertino*, Op. 49, rec, vn, vc, hpd. London: J & W Chester/Edition Wilhelm Hansen, 1961 (J.W.C. 279).
——, Sonatina, tr rec, pn. London: Schott & Co. Ltd, 1940 (Edition 10015; later OFB 1040).
——, *Una and the Lion*, cantata, Op. 98, Soprano, rec, hpd, gamba. London: J & W Chester/Edition Wilhelm Hansen, 1979.
Berkeley, Michael, *American Suite*, rec, bn. Oxford University Press, 1980.
Bernard, Anthony, Prelude and Scherzo, tr rec, hpd. Hebden Bridge: Peacock Press, 2001 (PD 02).
Bowen, York, Sonatina, Op. 121, rec, pn. Ampleforth: Emerson Edition, 1994 (Edition 113).
——, Two Pieces, des, tr, bass recs, kbd. London: Universal Edition Ltd, 1962 (UE 12638).
Butterley, Nigel, *The White-Throated Warbler*, sopranino rec, hpd. Sydney: Albert & Son, 1965. Repr. Armidale, Australia: Orpheus Music, 2001 (OMP 059).
Chagrin, Francis, *Preludes for Four*, tr rec, vn, vc. London: Novello & Co. Ltd, 1972.
Cooke, Arnold, Divertimento, des and tr recs, vn, vc, hpd. Unpublished: mechanically reproduced copy of MS score and MS parts in the Dolmetsch archive.
——, Divertimento, rec, str qt. Unpublished: MS score and parts in Dolmetsch archive.
——, Quartet (Sonata), tr rec, vn, vc, hpd. London: Schott & Co. Ltd, 1968 (Edition 10938).
——, Suite, des, tr and t recs, optional hpd. Celle: Moeck Verlag, 1974 (E.M. 1513).
Cooper, Elizabeth, Sonatina in G, Op. 8, des rec, pn. Unpublished: photocopy of MS score and rec part in Dolmetsch archive.
Crossley-Holland, Peter, *Albion*, des, tr and b recs, hpd. London: Universal Edition Ltd, 1960 (UE 12600).

Dalby, Martin: *Páginas*, tr rec, hpd. London: Novello & Co. Ltd, 1973.

Davison, Darrell, Introduction and Caprices, rec, str orch. Unpublished: MS score and rec part in Dolmetsch archive.

Dodgson, Stephen: *Warbeck Dances*, rec, hpd. Hebden Bridge: Peacock Press, (composer's 2001 revision, 2003).

Dolmetsch, Carl, Theme and Variations in A minor, des rec, hpd. Hebden Bridge: Peacock Press, 2001 (PD 01).

——, Two Dances, b rec, hpd. Unpublished: MS scores and rec parts in Dolmetsch archive.

Dorward, David, *Concert-Duo*, des rec, hpd. Wilhelmshaven: Heinrichsofen Verlag, 1977 (N1427).

Edmunds, Christopher, *Pastorale and Bourée*, des rec, pn. Hebden Bridge: Peacock Press, 2002 (PD 03).

Françaix, Jean, Quintet, rec, 2 vn, vc, hpd. Paris: Schott SARL, 1990 (ED 7644).

Fulton, Norman, *Scottish Suite*, tr rec, pn. London: Schott & Co. Ltd, 1955 (Edition 10466).

Gál, Hans, *Concertino*, Op. 82, tr rec, str qt. London: Universal Edition Ltd, 1963 (UE 12644).

——, Divertimento, Op. 98, rec trio. London: Schott & Co. Ltd, 1972 (OFB 120).

——, *Quartettino*, Op. 78, rec qt. London: Universal Edition Ltd, 1960 (UE 12622).

——, *Three Intermezzi*, Op. 103, tr rec, hpd. London: Schott & Co. Ltd, 1974 (OFB 134).

——, Trio Serenade, Op. 88, tr rec, vn, vc. London/Hamburg: N. Simrock, 1967 (Edition No. 3123).

Gardner, John, *Concerto da camera*, Op. 91, tr rec, vn, vc, hpd. Published by the composer.

——, *Little Suite* in C, Op. 60, tr rec, hpd. Oxford: Oxford University Press, 1965. Copyright assigned to Anglo-American Music Publishers 1984.

Glanville-Hicks, Peggy: Sonatina, tr rec, pn. London: Schott & Co. Ltd, 1941 (Edition 10029).

Godree, William, *A Birthday Present*, rec, pn. Unpublished: MS in Dolmetsch archive.

Godwin, Shelagh, Suite, rec qt. Unpublished: MS score in Dolmetsch archive.

Hand, Colin, *Concerto cantico*, Op. 112, tr rec, str qt. Unpublished: withdrawn by the composer. MS score and parts in Dolmetsch archive.

——, *Divertissement*, Op. 100, 2 recs, hpd. Unpublished: withdrawn by the composer. MS score and parts in Dolmetsch archive.

——, *Petite suite champêtre*, Op. 67, des rec, pn. London: Boosey and Hawkes Ltd, 1971 (19965).

——, *Plaint*, Op. 72, t rec, hpd. London: Schott & Co. Ltd, 1973 (Edition 11147).

——, *Sonata breve*, Op. 78, tr rec, pn. London: Schott & Co. Ltd, 1977 (Edition 11265).

——, *Sonata piccola*, Op. 63, tr rec, hpd. London: Boosey and Hawkes Ltd, 1968; n.p.: Lindis Edition, 1981; Hebden Bridge: Peacock Press, 2001.
Hoddinott, Alun, *Italian Suite*, rec, gui. London: Oxford University Press, 1983.
Hopkins, Antony, *Fifty-Fourth Festival Fanfare*, tr rec, pn. Unpublished: MS score and rec part in Dolmetsch archive.
——, Suite, des rec, pn. London: Schott & Co. Ltd, 1953 (Edition 10339).
Horovitz, Joseph, *Quartetto concertante*, tr rec, vn, vc, hpd. Unpublished, withdrawn by the composer. MS score and rec part only in Dolmetsch archive.
Hovhaness, Alan, Sextet, Op. 164, tr rec, str qt, hpd. New York: C.F. Peters, 1958. Copyright later assigned to Fujihara Music Co. Inc.
Jacob, Gordon, *A Consort of Recorders*, des, tr, t and b recs. Unpublished: MS score and parts in Dolmetsch archive.
——, *A 70-note Unfinished Tune for Carl's ...ieth Birthday*, solo rec. Unpublished: MS in Dolmetsch archive.
——, Suite, tr rec, str qt. Oxford: Oxford University Press, 1959. Republished under license, Hebden Bridge: Peacock Press, 2002 (PD 05).
——, *Trifles*, tr rec, vn, vc, hpd. Ampleforth: Emerson Edition, 2000 (Edition 355).
——, Variations, tr rec, hpd. London: Musica Rara, 1967 (MR 1110).
Johnson, Reginald, *Sonatina domestica*, des rec, pn. Unpublished: MS score and rec part in Dolmetsch archive.
Lambert, Cecily, *Aubade*, rec qt. London: Universal Edition, 1962 (UE 12639).
——, *Bergomask*, rec qt. Unpublished: MS score and parts in Dolmetsch archive.
——, *Eclogue*, tr rec, pn. Unpublished: MS score and rec part in Dolmetsch archive.
Leigh, Walter, Sonatina, tr rec, pn. London: Schott & Co. Ltd, 1944 (Edition 10030, later OFB 1041).
Lipkin, Malcolm, *Interplay*, tr rec, perc, gamba, hpd. Published by the composer, 1975.
Mathias, William, *Concertino*, Op. 65, tr rec, ob, bn, hpd. London: Oxford University Press, 1977.
Maw, Nicholas, *Discourse*, rec, hpd. Unpublished: MS of rec part only in Dolmetsch archive.
Migot, George, *Sonatine*, des rec, pn. Kassel: Bärenreiter-Verlag, 1958 (Edition 3224).
——, Suite, des, tr recs. Kassel: Bärenreiter-Verlag, 1958 (Edition 3225).
Milner, Arthur, Suite, tr rec, pn. Last mvt only published London: Novello & Co. Ltd, 1960. MS score and rec part of complete suite in Dolmetsch archive.
Murrill, Herbert, *Piece for my Friends*, 2 tr recs, hpd. London: Universal Edition Ltd, 1957 (UE 12575).
——, Sonata, tr rec, hpd. Oxford: Oxford University Press, 1951.
Nagan, Zvi Herbert, Trio, des rec, vn, va. Unpublished: mechanically reproduced copy of MS score in Dolmetsch archive.
Peter, H.A., *Präludium*, tr rec, pn. Unpublished: MS score and rec part in Dolmetsch archive.

Pitfield, Thomas, *Deva Suite*, rec trio. London: Boosey and Hawkes Ltd, 1956 (18228).
Pope, Peter, Sonatina, tr rec, pn. London: Schott & Co. Ltd, 1949 (Edition 10073).
Rawsthorne, Alan, Suite, tr rec, pn. Manchester: Forsyth Brothers Ltd, 1994.
Reizenstein, Franz, Partita, tr rec, pn. London: Schott & Co. Ltd, 1946 (Edition 10041, later OFB 1014).
Ridout, Alan, Chamber Concerto, rec, str qt. Unpublished: photocopy of MS score and MS parts in the Dolmetsch archive.
——, *Sequence*, rec, lute. Hebden Bridge: Peacock Press, 2003.
——, *Variants on a Tune of H.H.*, des rec, hpd. Hebden Bridge: Peacock Press, 2003.
Rubbra, Edmund, *Cantata pastorale*, Op. 92, high v, rec, hpd, vc. Croydon: Alfred Lengnick & Co. Ltd, 1962 (3980).
——, *Fantasia on a Chord*, Op. 154, rec, hpd, optional gamba. Croydon: Alfred Lengnick & Co. Ltd, 1979 (4554).
——, *Fantasia on a Theme of Machaut*, Op. 86, rec, str qt, hpd. Croydon: Alfred Lengnick & Co. Ltd, 1956 (3869).
——, *Meditazioni sopra 'Cœurs désolés'*, Op. 67, rec, hpd. Croydon: Alfred Lengnick & Co. Ltd, 1949 (3869).
——, *Notturno*, Op. 106, rec qt. Croydon: Alfred Lengnick & Co. Ltd, 1962 (4051).
——, *Passacaglia sopra 'Plusieurs regrets'*, Op. 113, rec, hpd. Croydon: Alfred Lengnick & Co. Ltd, 1964 (4144).
——, Sonatina, Op. 128, rec, hpd. Croydon: Alfred Lengnick & Co. Ltd, 1965 (4200).
Salter, Lionel, Air and Dance, tr rec, pn. Unpublished (in this form), MS piano score and rec part in the Dolmetsch archive.
Saux, Gaston, *Pour une églogue Virgilienne*, rec trio, Paris: Aug. Zurfluh, 1961 (A.1059 Z).
Saxby, Joseph, *Improvisation*, tr rec solo. Unpublished: MS in Dolmetsch archive.
Scott, Cyril, *Aubade*, tr rec, pn. London: Schott & Co. Ltd, 1953 (Edition 10330 (R.M.S. 512)).
Shaw, Martin: Sonata in E♭, rec, hpd. London: J.B. Cramer & Co., 1942 (15242).
Sherman, Elna, *Air de souvenir*, t rec, pn. MS score and rec part in Dolmetsch archive.
Short, Michael, *Giocata*, des rec, hpd. Unpublished: photocopy of MS score and rec part in Dolmetsch archive.
——, *Les quatre vingts: fantasie sur le nom 'C.D.'*, des rec solo, Unpublished: MS in Dolmetsch archive.
——, *Sinfonia*, tr rec, hpd, str qt. Unpublished: photocopy of MS score and parts in Dolmetsch archive.
——, Sonatina No. 1, tr rec, hpd. London: Studio Music Co., 1986.
Simar, León J., *Concerto 1741*, tr rec, hpd. Unpublished: mechanically reproduced copy of MS score in Dolmetsch archive.

Simpson, Robert: Variations and Fugue (*in memoriam* Horace Dann), rec, str qt. Unpublished: MS parts only in Dolmetsch archive

Swann, Donald, *Rhapsody from Within*, rec, pn. Hebden Bridge: Peacock Press, 2002 (PD 04).

Temprement, Jean, *Suite exotique*, des rec solo. Paris: Aug. Zurfluh, 1961 (A.1066 Z).

Velasco Llanos, Santiago, *Homenaje a J.S. Bach*, double fugue, rec qt. Unpublished: MS score and parts in Dolmetsch archive.

——, *Romanza*, tr rec, kbd/rec trio. Unpublished: MS score and rec parts in Dolmetsch archive.

Walsworth, Ivor, Sonata, tr rec, hpd. Unpublished: MS score and rec part in Dolmetsch archive.

Werder, Felix, *Gambit*, tr rec, hpd. Unpublished: MS score and rec part in Dolmetsch archive.

Wood, Christopher: *Concertante* in E, Op. 50, des rec, hpd. Unpublished: MS score and rec part in Dolmetsch archive.

——, *French Suite*, rec trio. Unpublished: MS score and parts in Dolmetsch archive.

——, *Sonata di* [sic] *camera*, Op. 18, rec, hpd. Unpublished: MS score and rec part in Dolmetsch archive.

Wordsworth, William: Theme and Variations, tr rec, hpd. Unpublished: MS score and rec part in Dolmetsch archive.

Selected Discography[1]

1. Commercial recordings

Compact discs

Shine and Shade. Includes: Fulton, *Scottish Suite*; Rubbra, *Meditazioni sopra 'Cœurs désolés'*; Bowen, Sonata; Lennox Berkeley, Sonatina; Swann, *Rhapsody from Within*. Piers Adams, rec; Julian Rhodes, pn. Tremula Records TREM 103-2 (1994). Re-issued by Upbeat Classics URCD 150.

John and Peter's Whistling Book (English music for recorder and piano). Includes: Rawsthorne, Suite; Leigh, Air. John Turner, rec; Peter Lawson, pn. Forsyth FS001/002 (1998) (two-CD set).

Fruit of a Different Vine. Includes: Lennox Berkeley, Sonatina; Hindemith, Trio for recorders; Leigh, Sonatina. Alison Melville, Natalie Michaud, Colin Savage, rec; Alayne Hall, pn. Atma ACD 2 2206 (1998).

Fluit Douceur (recorder music from the twentieth century). Includes: Hindemith, Trio for recorders; Leigh, Sonatina; Britten, Scherzo. Marina Klunder, rec; Gini Tamboer, pn. Marianne Englesman, Eva van den Eijnde, Carine Lacor, rec. BVHAAST CD 9804 (1998).

Alan Rawsthorne: Orchestral Works. Includes: Rawsthorne, Suite (orch. John McCabe). John Turner, rec, Northern Chamber Orchestra, conducted by David Lloyd-Jones. Naxos 8.553567 (1999).

English Recorder Music: the Dolmetsch Legacy. Includes: Jacob, Variations; Scott, Aubade; Rubbra, Sonatina, Passacaglia sopra 'Plusieurs regrets', *Meditazioni sopra 'Cœurs désolés'*; Hopkins, Suite; Gardner, *Little Suite* in C; Hand, *Sonata breve*; Reizenstein, Partita. Ross Winters, rec; Andrew Ball, pn. British Music Society BMS425CD (2000).

Thirteen Ways of Looking at a Blackbird (music for recorder and string quartet).

---

[1] The first section of this list of recordings includes only those cited in the text of the book. It is not intended to be comprehensive, but as a reference only. It should be stressed that some are no longer generally available. Non-commercial recordings of a number of works covered in the book have been identified. Because of their obvious importance and historic interest, details and locations of these are included in sections 2 and 3. In each section, recordings are listed in chronological order of release. The author would be grateful for any further information on recordings of the works discussed in this book.

Includes: Arnell, Quintet (The Gambian) and Simpson, Variations and Fugue. John Turner, rec; the Camerata Ensemble. Olympia OCD 710 (2001).

Aspects of Nature (English and Scottish recorder music). Includes: Britten (arr.), *I Wonder as I Wander*. John Turner, rec; Eleanor Maynell, soprano. Olympia OCD 714 (2002).

Cassettes

The Contemporary Recorder. Includes: Murrill, Sonata; Hopkins, Suite; Rubbra, *Meditazioni sopra 'Cœurs désolés'*; Edmunds, *Pastoral and Bourée*; Jacob, Variations; Hand, Plaint, *Petite Suite champêtre*; Butterley, *The White-Throated Warbler*. Carl Dolmetsch, rec; Joseph Saxby; hpd, pn. Orion Master Recordings OC 692 (1974).

The Dolmetsch–Schoenfeld Ensemble. Includes: Lennox Berkeley, *Concertino*; Cooke, Sonata (Quartet) *1964*. Carl Dolmetsch, rec; Alice Schoenfeld, vn; Eleonore Schoenfeld, cello, Joseph Saxby, hpd. Orion Master Recordings OC 9104 (1974).

Favourite Recorder Consorts. Includes: Jacob, *A Consort of Recorders*. Carl Dolmetsch, Jeanne Dolmetsch, Marguerite Dolmetsch, Brian Blood, rec. Arts Recordings ATD 8718 (1977).

Long-playing records

Music of Franz Reizenstein. Includes Partita. Carl Dolmetsch, rec; Joseph Saxby, pn. Editions L'Oiseau-Lyre SOL 344 (1975).

David Munrow: The Art of the Recorder. Includes: Hindemith, Trio for recorders; Britten, Scherzo; Butterley, *The White-Throated Warbler*. EMI two-record set FLS 5022 (1975).

2. Non-commercial recordings in the Dolmetsch archive

The following works are contained in recordings held in the Dolmetsch archives at Haslemere. These are on cassette or reel-to-reel tapes as indicated. Some have been referred to in the main text of the book.

Cassettes

Lennox Berkeley, *Una and the Lion* (Wigmore Hall,1979).
Ridout, Chamber Concerto (Wigmore Hall, 26 March 1981).
Jacob, *A Consort of Recorders* (Malvern Boys' College, 25 May 1981).
Swann, *Rhapsody from Within* (The Studio, 'Jesses', Haslemere, April 1982).
Jacob, Suite (with Utah Symphony Orchestra, 21 September 1982).

Jacob, Suite (*Trifles*) (rehearsal at Wigmore Hall, 24 March 1983).
Françaix, *Quintette* (first rehearsal, 29 March 1988).
Bernard, Prelude and Scherzo (with Nigel Foster, 1990).

Reel-to-reel

Bowen, Sonata; Cooke, Divertimento (1960), 3rd movement (recording location not noted, but dated 1960).
Murrill, Sonata; Jacob, *Tarantella* (from Suite); Rubbra, *Meditazioni sopra 'Cœurs désolés'* (Norfolk Society of Arts, Virginia, 16 October 1963).
Dodgson, *Warbeck Dances* (Wigmore Hall, 1971).
Maw, *Discourse*; Bergmann, *Pastorella* (Wigmore Hall?, 1972).
Gál, *Three Intermezzi* ('preliminary rehearsal tape', 19 February 1974).
Gál, *Trio Serenade*; Joseph Horovitz, *Quartet to concertante* (recording location not noted, but dated 1976). Another undated tape also contains a recording of Gál's *Trio Serenade*.
Rubbra, *Meditazioni sopra 'Cœurs désolés'*, Op. 67; *Fantasia on a Chord*, Op. 154 (location and date are not indicated, but the recording was probably made in 1978).

3. Non-commercial recordings in the National Sound Archive[2]

Rubbra, *Cantata pastoral*. NP3926R (4 February 1958).
Gál, *Concertino*. NP4479W (16 September 1962).
Cooke, Sonata (Quartet). M466W.
Rubbra, Sonatina. M412R.
Gál, *Trio Serenade*. M1674R (17 November 1969).
Horovitz, *Quartetto concertante*. M1721R.
Dodgson, *Warbeck Dances*. M4342R (2 March 1972).
Maw, *Discourse*. NP2315Y (8 July 1972).
Bergmann, *Pastorella*. M4825R (1 March 1972).
Ridout, *Sequence*. M5996BW.
Lennox Berkeley, *Una and the Lion*. M8109BW (8 August 1979).

---

[2] From enquiries made by the author, recordings of the following works are held in the National Sound Archive at the British Library, London. The NSA tape numbers and date of the recording, where known, are indicated. Where no date is given, the recordings have been listed as far as can be deduced in chronological order. It is evident from a number of Dolmetsch's letters that many more of the works premiered at the Wigmore Hall were also recorded by the BBC. Recordings may be extant in the National Sound Archive, but will only be identifiable by reference to other works performed in the same programmes.

Index

ABC (Australian Broadcasting Corporation) 103
Adams, Piers 180, 250, 286, 303, 309
   recordings and performances by 34, 35, 50, 179, 180n
Adler, Larry 59
Akbar Khan, Ali 57n
Albert & Son 103
Aldeburgh Music Club 280, 282, 283
aleatoric procedures 78, 308
Alexander, Joan 20, 56
alternative fingerings, *see* recorder
alternative techniques, *see* recorder
Alton, Edwin 242
Amici String Quartet, the 173
Ampleforth College Library 173n
Andriessen, Louis 307
Anglo-American Music Publishers 196
Arnell, Richard 41, 312
   Quintet (The Gambian) Op. 107 98–102, 310
      analysis of 101
      composer's programme note for 99
      correspondence in connection with 99–100
      first performance, reviews of 100
Arnold, Sir Malcolm 65, 284
ARS (American Recorder Society), (Boston chapter) 77
Arts Council of Great Britain, the 169, 172, 185, 186, 204
Arts Theatre Club, the 46
Ashby, Arnold 20, 54, 56
Ashdown (publishers) 230
Associated Board of the Royal Schools of Music, the 50
Attey, John 128
Augner 230
'authenticity' 299–305

Badings, Henk 307, 310
Baldwin, Alison 268n
Bartók, Béla 151, 171

bassoon 22, 147, 148, 171, 172
Bate, Stanley 13
   Concertino for piano and string orchestra 13
   Sonatina 7, 13, 17
Baur, Jürg 307
Bax, Sir Arnold 46, 278–80, 284
BBC 14, 120, 121, 206, 225, 242, 309
   Dolmetsch's contacts at 19–20, 39, 48, 64
   new works, recording and broadcast of 41, 61, 125, 126, 151, 153, 155, 195, 218
Beatty, Mary 218
Bedford, David 250, 286
bell key 34, 58, 151, 301, 302
Bender, Wilhelm 17
Benedictbeuern Monastery manuscript 55, 57
Benjamin, Arthur 8, 13
Bentley, Lionel 173, 184
Berger, Leon 179, 180n
Bergmann, Walter 12, 14, 16, 309
   Fuga á 3 214
   Hindemith, Paul, Trio, transposition of 2
   Hopkins, Antony, Suite, dedicatee of 46
   Pastorale 128, 237
   Pastorella 127–9
      composer's programme note for 128
      correspondence in connection with 127–8
   reviews by 68, 75, 76, 77, 286–7
   Sonata for tr rec and pn 295
Berio, Luciano 307
Berkeley, Sir Lennox 16n, 20
   Cantata 'Una and the Lion' Op. 98 169–71
      analysis of 169–70
      first performance, reviews of 170–71, 294
      programme note for 169
   Sonatina 7, 19, 26–30, 287, 291, 307

analysis of 29
correspondence in connection with 26–7, 28–9
first private performance, details of 26
first public performance, reviews of 26
harpsichord, use of in 28, 291
Concertino Op. 49 54–5, 107
alternative scoring for 293
correspondence in connection with 55
first performance, reviews of 54–5
programme note for 54
published edition, cuts in 55
Serenade for strings Op. 12 29
Six Preludes for Piano 28
Berkeley, Michael 21
American Suite 171–2
analysis of 172
composer's programme note for 171
first performance, review of 172
Berlin State Academy, the 10
Bernard, Anthony 218
Prelude and Scherzo 17, 217–19, 292
analysis of 219
United States, performance in 218n
Bialas, Antonina 189, 202
bitonality 308
Blades, James 157, 158, 158n
Bland, Dr 8
Blockflöten-Spiegel, Der 3
Blood, Dr Brian 134
du Bois, Rob 307
Boonin, Joseph, Inc 23n
Boosey and Hawkes Ltd 16, 242, 281
Boulanger, Nadia 12, 13
Bousted, Donald 285, 286, 287, 288, 289
Bowen, York 19, 23, 265, 273, 309
Sonatina Op. 121 31–6, 244, 275, 287, 292, 295
composer's programme note for 34
correspondence in connection with 31–3
ending, last movement, alternative for 35
first performance, reviews of 33
high notes for recorder in 34
manuscript score, annotation of different readings in 35
ornamentation in 305
title of 31
Two Pieces 273–5

composer's programme note for 274
published edition, review of 274
Bowen, Sylvia 31
Bressan, Pierre Jaillard 1
Bridge, Dr Joseph Cox 1
Bridges, Robert 258
Bristol University Madrigal Choir 3
British Institute of Recorded Sound, the, (BIRS) 11
British Music Information Centre, the, (BMIC) 11
British Music Society, the 309
Britten, Benjamin 7, 15–17, 280–84
Britten-Pears Library, the 16, 280, 280n, 281n
Brogue, Roslyn 105
Brüggen, Franz 307
Burgess, Christopher 184
Burgess, Martin 23
Bush, Alan 309
Bush, Geoffrey 82
Butterley, Nigel 20
Meditations of Thomas Traherne 105
Music for Sunrise 105
The White-Throated Warbler 103–5, 294, 305
birdcall used, identification of 103
programme note for 104
reviews of 103–4
serial technique, use of 104–5, 308

cadenza 41, 43, 73–5, 244, 304–5
Camden, Anthony 147
Camden, Kerry 147
Camerata Ensemble 69, 101
Cameron, Norman 128
Campbell, Margaret 146, 150
Carew, Anna 180
Casa d'Arte Studio 36
Chagrin, Francis 20
Preludes for Four 22, 113–19, 308
analysis of 116–18
correspondence in connection with 113–16, 118
first performance, review of 118
harpsichord, amplification, use of in 117, 117n
Chappell and Co. 113, 156
Chester, J W & Co. 54, 169
'Chester' recorders, 1
Chisholm, Alec H. 103
Clark, Paul 247
Collette, Joannes 12

Index 329

Committee for the Promotion of New
   Music 119
Concours National Union Française des
   Œuvres Laïques d'Education
   Artistique 231
Cooke, Arnold 20, 286–7, 312
   Concerto for recorder and strings 70
   Divertimento (1960) (rec, str qt) 70–75,
      287
      cadenza in second movement of
         73–5
      composer's programme note for 71
      correspondence in connection with
         70–71
      first performance, reviews of 75
   Divertimento (1974) (des and tr recs,
      vn, vc, hpd) 195–200
      alternatively scored version of 195,
         293
      composer's programme note for
         196–7
      correspondence in connection with
         195–6, 199
      first public performance, review of
         199–200
      serial technique, use in 196, 200,
         308
      tone rows, analysis of use in 197–8
   Little Suite No. 1 93, 286
   Quartet (Sonata) 89–94, 286, 294
      composer's programme note for 92
      correspondence in connection with
         90–92, 93–4
      first performance, reviews of 93
      Little Suite No. 1, thematic
         resemblance to 93
      title, composer's comments on 94
   Serial Theme and Variations 200
   Suite (three recs, optional hpd) 129–33
      composer's programme note for 132
      correspondence in connection with
         130, 132
      finale, composer's revisions of
         131–2
      first performance, reviews of 133
      published edition, review of 133
      trio version, first performance of
         132
      harpsichord, arrangement of trio
         version with 130
Cooper, Elizabeth 256–8
Couperin, François 103
Cramer, J.B. & Co. 220

Crossley-Holland, Peter 57n, 265, 273
   Albion 268–71
      composer's programme note for 270
      correspondence in connection with
         270–71
      fingered tremolos, use in 269
      published edition, review of 270
   Breton Tunes 265
   Invocation at Midsummer 271
   Irish Tunes 265, 268, 269
   Little Suite 265, 271

Dahl, Ingolf 23n
Daily Telegraph, the, reviews in 33, 41, 47,
   48, 53, 55, 60, 68, 75, 80, 83, 88, 93,
   97, 100, 104, 109, 111, 118, 121,
   141, 154, 170, 172
Dalby, Martin 277
   Commedia 138
   Páginas 136–42, 239, 294, 308
      composer's programme note for 140
      correspondence in connection with
         137–40
      first performance, reviews of 141–2
      Spanish tunes, work based on
         140–41
Dann, Horace 64, 65, 66
Darnton, Christian 7, 8
Davies, Joan 225
Davison, Arthur 259
Davison, Darrell 214, 259–60
Dawson, Michael 303
Deller, Alfred 128
Der getreue Musikmeister 286
Dodgson, Stephen 309, 312
   High Barbaree 120
   Shine and Shade 309
   Warbeck Dances 119–21, 294
      composer's programme note for 121
      correspondence in connection with
         119–20
      first performance, reviews of 121
      revisions, publication, ahead of 121
   Warbeck Trio 121n
Dolmetsch, Arnold 1, 2, 19, 202
Dolmetsch, Carl
   avant-garde recorder repertoire,
      comments on 139, 308
   Borey, see Two Dances
   Bressan recorder, loss of 1
   contemporary recorder repertoire,
      encouragement of 5, 19–20,
      312–13

form in new works, suggestions for 22, 122, 190
London Contemporary Music Centre, recital at 7
recorder, idiomatic writing for, comments on 287, 288, 289
Saxby, Joseph, first meeting and subsequent collaboration with 23
Tempo di gavotta, see Two Dances
Theme and variations in A minor 6, 24–6
    analysis of 25
    first performance, reviews of 24
    manuscript, discovery of 24–5
Two Dances 240–41
Wigmore Hall, first recital at 6, 19
see also bell key, cadenza, echo key, recorder, tone projector
Dolmetsch Consort, the 39
Dolmetsch Foundation, the 179, 195, 210, 214, 253, 270
Dolmetsch Foundation Bulletin, the 238
Dolmetsch, François 261, 262, 265, 266
    first performances, participation in 268, 271, 274
Dolmetsch, Greta (née Matthews) 24
    composers, correspondence with 95, 119, 122–3, 138, 149, 164, 173, 177, 187, 204–5
    information from 15, 23, 31, 89, 105, 173, 183n, 296, 308
Dolmetsch, Jeanne 40n, 122, 137, 156, 184, 197, 216, 246, 265, 266, 267
    first performances, participation in 21, 129, 134, 195, 268, 271, 274
    information from 25, 35, 75, 117n, 156, 181, 183, 219, 236, 241, 260, 273, 287, 290
Dolmetsch, Mabel 221
Dolmetsch, Marguerite 40n, 216, 246, 265, 266, 267
    first performances, participation in 21, 129, 134, 157, 163, 169, 268, 271, 274
    information from 117n, 165n, 169, 231, 236, 301n
Dolmetsch, Marie 43, 216
Dolmetsch, Natalie 216
Dolmetsch, Richard 231, 232, 236, 265, 266, 271
    first performances, participation in 268, 271, 274
Dolmetsch, Rudolph 2, 36, 308

Dolmetsch Summer School, the 189, 257
Dorward, David
    Concert-Duo 236–9
    analysis of 238
    correspondence in connection with 237
    first performance, review of 238–9
    published edition, review of 239
Dowding, Nicholas 173
Dickinson, Peter 29
Dinn, Freda 111
Division Flute, The 25
Dyson, Ruth 209

Eastbourne Festival, the 13
echo key 297, 301, 303
Edmunds, Christopher 17
    Pastorale and Bourée 243–4
Elcombe, Keith 107
Ellis, David 69
Emerson Edition 136, 184
Emerson, June 184
European Recorder Teachers Association (UK) (ERTA) 128, 180, 309
Evans, Carolyn, *see* Murrill
extended techniques, *see* recorder

Fairfield Halls, Croydon 147, 259
Farnham Herald, the, reviews in 159, 161, 177, 188
Faye, The Reverend John 99
Field-Hyde, Margaret 10
Finger, Godfrey 25
Flanders, Michael 180
Florizel String Quartet 184
flute 26, 148, 162, 221, 288
Ford, John 120, 121
Foreman, Lewis 98
form, in new works 22
Forsyth Brothers Ltd 13, 17, 93, 271
Foster, Nigel 218
Fox-Gál, Eva 106, 247, 273
Françaix, Jean 20, 146
    Quintette 202–8, 294
    analysis of 207–8
    composer's programme note for 206–7
    correspondence in connection with 202–6
    first performance, review of 207
Frances Ellis, Anne 254
Frank, Alan 60, 62
Franklin, Norman 10

Fricker, Peter Racine 65, 277–8
Fujihara Music Co. Inc. 77
Fuller, Ethel Romig 232
Fulton, Norman 19
  Scottish Suite 48–50, 287, 293
    analysis of 49
    first performance, reviews of 48
    score, performers' annotations in 48, 49–50

Gál, Hanna 146
Gál, Hans 20, 81, 288, 312
  Concertino Op. 82 81–4
    composer's programme note for 83
    correspondence in connection with 82
    first performance, reviews of 83
  Divertimento Op. 98 245–7
  influences on compositional style 83
  Quartettino Op. 78 265, 273
  Three Intermezzi Op. 103 142–7
    composer's programme note for 145
    correspondence in connection with 142–3, 144–5, 146
    first performance, reviews of 145, 146
  Trio Serenade Op. 88 21, 105–6
    composer's programme note for 106
    first UK performance, reviews of 106
gamba, *see* viola da gamba
Gardner, John 20, 287, 305, 312
  Concerto da camera 107–10
    analysis of 109
    correspondence in connection with 107, 108
    first performance, reviews of 108–9
  Little Suite in C Op. 60 87–9, 293
    analysis of 88–9
    first performance, reviews of 88
    published edition, review of 89
Genzmer, Harald 2, 17, 268, 307
Gilbert, Anthony 311
Glanville-Hicks, Peggy 8
  Sonatina 8, 9, 291
Goble, Robert 280n
Godfree, William 214
Godwin, Shelagh 182n, 258n
  Suite for recorders 213, 214
Gordon, David 28n, 292, 310
Gordon, Edgar 89
Gordon-Woodhouse, Violet 54n
Grainger, Eileen 50, 58, 64, 70, 77, 81

Gray-Fisk, Clinton 31
Greenfield, Edward 145, 150
Gregson, Edward 309
Grosvenor Museum, Chester 1
Guardian, The, reviews in 145, 150
guitar 22, 160, 163, 248n, 277, 311

Hand, Colin 312
  Concerto cantico Op. 112 184–9
    composer's programme note for 188
    correspondence in connection with 185–7, 188
    first performance, review of 188–9
    withdrawal of 189
  Divertissement Op. 100 185, 254–6
    composer's programme note for 255
    US performances, review of 255
    withdrawal of 256
  Petite suite champêtre Op. 67 185, 244–5
  Plaint Op. 72 185, 247–9, 294, 305
    published edition, review of 248
  Sonata alla Cadenza, *see Sonata breve*
  Sonata breve Op. 78 185, 249–51
    published edition, review of 251
  Sonata concisa 256
  Sonata No. 1 Op. 41 243
  Sonata piccola Op. 63 185, 242–3, 247
Handel, George Friderich 287
Harpsichord
  4' register on 294
  16' register on 207, 294, 301
  amplification of 117, 117n, 308
  construction, changes in 299
  Dolmetsch concert instrument, specification of 149, 300–301
  dynamic control device on 215, 292
  scarcity in late 1930s of 291
  sustaining device on 215, 216, 219, 292
  temperament, equal, use of 190; *see also* Short, Michael, Sinfonia
Harrison, Heather 184
Hart, Fritz 8
Harvey, Richard 309
Harwood, Elizabeth 124, 127, 129, 137, 169
Haslemere Festival, the 1, 5, 23, 185, 200, 237, 240, 251–2
Haslemere Hall 218
Haslemere Herald, reviews in 166, 170, 193
Haslemere Museum 179, 270
Haslemere Music Society, the 218, 259

Hawkins, Brian 98
Hell, Michael 310
Henning, Ervin 105
Henry, Jean 232, 233
Hersom, Herbert 248
Hindemith, Paul 2, 7, 10, 13, 70, 151, 237
Hirose, Ryohei 307
Hoddinott, Alun 312
　Italian Suite 160–63
　　composer's programme note for 161
　　correspondence in connection with 160–61, 162
　　first performance, review of 161–2
　　flute, alternative part for 162
　　manuscript, amendment of before publication 162
Holland, Ben 107
Holst, Imogen 281
Hope Simpson, Robert 173, 184
Hopkins, Antony
　Fifty-Fourth Festival Fanfare 251–2
　Four Dances 46
　Suite 12, 46–7, 293, 309
　　analysis of 47
　　Bergmann, Walter, dedication to 46
　　first performance, reviews of 47
　　programme note for 46–7
Horovitz, Joseph 20
　Quartetto Concertante 110–12
　　composer's programme note for 111
　　correspondence in connection with 110, 112
　　first performance, reviews of 111–12
　　withdrawal by composer of 112
Hovhaness, Alan 20
　Sextet Op. 164 76–8, 308
　　aleatoric procedures, use of in 78
　　ARS, Boston chapter, commission from 77
　　first performance, details of 77
　　first UK performance, reviews of 77–8
　　programme note for 77
Howells, Herbert 173, 209, 210, 211
Hunt, Edgar 1, 3, 5, 14, 24, 61, 76, 233n, 244
　Darnton, Christian, Suite, comments on 8
　Edmunds, Christopher, Sonatina, dedicatee of 17
　Jacobs, Manuel, encouragement of 6

London Contemporary Music Centre, recital at 7, 12
Reizenstein, Franz, Partita, comments on 12
Reviews by 6, 24, 80, 83, 86, 88, 93, 97, 166, 170, 211, 294
Rubbra, Edmund,
　first meeting with 36
　performance of *Meditazioni*... with 37, 39; *see also* Rubbra
Hyatt, Margaret, *see* Jacob, Margaret

Idyllwild Arts Foundation 20, 90
Incorporated Society of Musicians (ISM) 37, 39
Ireland, John 12, 218
Ishii, Maki 307

Jackson, Croft 41
Jackson, Sybil 26
Jacob, Gordon 13, 20, 173, 309, 312
　A Consort of Recorders 134–6
　　composer's programme note for 135
　　correspondence in connection with 134, 135
　　Dolmetsch Ensemble, recording by 136
　　wind quintet, composer's reworking of version for 136
　A 70-note unfinished tune for Carl's ...ieth birthday 214
　Suite (rec, str qt) 23, 58–64, 111, 287, 307
　　composer's programme note for 60
　　correspondence in connection with 58–60, 61–3
　　first performance, reviews of 60–61
　　manuscript, published edition, different readings between 63–4
　　piano reduction for 60
　　published edition, review of 63–4
　　sopranino recorder, use of in 60
　Suite (*Trifles*) 180–84, 195, 287, 296
　　analysis of 183–4
　　composer's programme note for 182
　　correspondence in connection with 181
　　first performance, review of 182
　　movements, French titles of 182
　　original title of 181, 183
　Variations for rec and hpd 84–7, 293
　　correspondence in connection with 84–5, 87

composer's programme note for
  85–6
 first performance reviews of 86
 published edition, review of 86
Jacob, (Hyatt), Margaret 184
Jacob, Sidney 62
Jacobs, Manuel 5, 9–10, 19, 31, 310
 contemporary composers,
  encouragement of 6, 7
 contemporary recorder repertoire,
  frustration at lack of 6
 Hunt, Edgar, early pupil of 5
 Musical Times, the, article in 5–6, 16
 Quatre Mouvements pour Voix & Piano
  10
 'Terpander', (pen name of) 5
Jersey College for Girls 175
'Jesses' (Dolmetsch family home) 95, 179n
'jet spinet' 300
Johnson, Reginald 258–9
Jones, Caroline 310
Josquin des Prez 38, 79

Kaine, Carmel 180
Kay, Garth 97
Kemp, M.J. 121
Keys of Canterbury, The 184
Keyte-Perry, Miss 31
Kirklees Music 258
Kisch, Eve 8
Klunder, Marina 310
Krone, Dr Max 90

Lambert, Cecily 213
 Aubade 235–6, 265, 275, 276
 Bergomask 236, 265, 275–6
 Eclogue 228
Lambert, Constant 8
Lavers, Marjorie 50, 58, 64, 70, 77, 81
Lawrence, Anne 209
Leaf, Walter 55, 57
Lee, Josephine 242
LeFanu, Nicola 137
Leigh, Walter 8
 Air 9, 310
 Sonatina 8–9, 287
  analysis of 9
  cadenza, Dolmetsch's, in third
   movement 304–5
  harpsichord, use of in 291
Leigh-Jacobs, Veronica 8
Leighton, Kenneth 82
Lengnick, Alfred & Co. 38, 80

Lewis, Lorna 124, 128
Limcuse, Charles 202
Linde, Hans-Martin 311
Lindis Edition 187, 188, 242, 254n
Linnel, Dorothy 156n
Lipkin, Malcolm
 Interplay 22, 157–60
  alternative scoring for 159–60, 294
  composer's programme note for 159
  correspondence in connection with
   157–8, 159
  first performance, reviews of 159
  percussion instruments used in 159
Lloyd, David 189
Loeb, Arthur 77
London Contemporary Music Centre, the
 7, 10, 12, 13, 26, 27
Loseley House 136
Lumsden, Sir David 23, 208
lute 22, 152
Lute Society, the 156

Macnaughton Concerts 237, 309
Macnaughten String Quartet, the 51
Maganamusic Inc 128
Martin, David 50, 51, 58, 59, 64, 70, 77,
 81, 85, 98, 99
Martin, Frank 303
Martin String Quartet, the 20, 50, 51, 58,
 59, 64, 70, 77, 81, 98, 173
Martlew, Zoe 202
Matesky, Ralph 147
Mathias, William 151
 Concertino Op. 65 147–51, 293
  composer's programme note for 150
  correspondence in connection with
   147–50
  first performance, review of 150
  sopranino recorder, use of in 148,
   149, 151
Matthews, Greta, *see* Dolmetsch, Greta
Matton-Painparé, Madame 36
Maw, Nicholas
 Discourse 122–7
  correspondence in connection with
   122–3, 124, 125
  Dolmetsch's comment on 138
  first performance, reviews of 124–5
  programme note for 123–4
Mayer, Robert 7
McCabe, John 14, 69, 277
McLeish, Kenneth 163
McLeish, Valerie 163

Melbourne Conservatorium, the 8
Mellers, Wilfrid 38, 44
Melville, Alison 309–10
Messiaen, Olivier 104
Meyer, Dr Ernst 3
Michels, Cécile 202
Migot, Georges 20
   Sonatine 75–6, 229
      correspondence in connection with 76
      first performance, reviews of 76
      programme note for 76
   Suite for Two Recorders 213, 228–9
Milford, Robin 2
Mills, John 160, 161, 277
Milner, Arthur 229–30
Monory, Michel 206
Morris, Christopher 149, 151
Morris, R(eginald) O(wen) 12, 13
Munrow, David 105, 120
Murrill, Carolyn Jane 39, 267n
Murrill, Herbert 19, 23, 42, 265, 287
   Piece for my Friends 267–8
   Sonata 39–44, 237, 293
      analysis of 43
      cadenza in second movement of 41, 43, 304
      correspondence in connection with 39–41, 43
      first performance, review of 43
Musgrave, Thea 277
Musica Rara 87
Musical Times, the 5, 6, 13, 16, 24

Nagan, Zvi Herbert 213, 234
Nallen, Evelyn 28n, 174, 175, 290, 300, 310
National Sound Archive, the 11n, 126
Novello & Co. Ltd 115, 142, 230

Oak Hall School (Haslemere) 31
Oboe 22, 39, 147, 148
Observer, The, reviews in 27
Oiseau-Lyre 11
Orford, John 171
Orga, Ates 86
ornamentation 37, 53, 80, 304–5
Orpheus Music (publishers) 105, 305
Otten, Kees 310
Oxford Playhouse, the 23
Oxford University Press (OUP) 60, 62, 135, 136, 148, 151, 162, 171n

Palme, Natalie 231n, 232
Panufnik, Roxanna 310
Partridge, Bernard 189, 195, 202
Payne, Anthony 124, 277
Peacock Press 121, 244, 258
Pears, Peter 16, 280
percussion 22, 157, 158, 159, 311
'Perkin Warbeck' 121
Peter, H.A. 235
Peters, C.F. 77
piano, or harpsichord, use of 28, 37, 45, 179, 221, 291–6
Pilkington, Vere 54n
Pinkham, Daniel 77
Pitfield, Thomas 312
   Concerto for recorder, strings and percussion 227
   Deva Suite 213, 227
   Three Nautical Sketches 227
Plato 55, 57
Pledge, Andrew 180, 202, 260n
Pognet, Jean 20, 54
Pope, Peter 12
   Sonatina 7, 12–13
Poston, Elizabeth 218
Potter, Mary 283
Powers, Ellen 77
Price, Jonathan 107
Prix de Rome 241
PRS (Performing Rights Society), the 187
Purcell, Daniel 25

quarter tones, *see* recorder

Ramsey, Basil 115
Rawsthorne, Alan 7
   Suite for tr rec and pn 9, 13–14, 17, 310
      disappearance and rediscovery of 14
      orchestration of 14
Rawsthorne Trust, the 14
recorder
   alternative fingerings on 290
   alternative techniques, use of 307; *see also* extended techniques
   comfortable keys for, Dolmetsch's advice on 110, 148
   compass of, Dolmetsch's advice on 148, 152
   earliest 20th-century compositions for 2–3
   extended techniques, use of 307, 308, 311; *see also* alternative techniques

high F#, treble, on 10–11, 30, 34,
    38–9, 43, 58, 151, 221, 224, 288,
    301
idiomatic and technical considerations
    of 285–90
quarter tones on 138, 311
sopranino, use of 50, 60, 66, 68, 93,
    121, 128, 130, 148, 186, 242
third tones on 138
windway, shape, differences in 299, 300
see also bell key, echo key, tone
    projector
Recorder in Education Summer School, the
    12
Recorder and Music Magazine, the,
    reviews in 86, 97, 100, 106, 111,
    121, 124, 128, 255
Recorder and Music Magazine, The,
    reviews in 86, 93, 97, 156n, 199,
    201, 207, 211, 274, 288
Recorder & Music, reviews in 159, 166n,
    176, 179, 182, 248, 251, 294
Recorder & Music Magazine, reviews in
    146, 150
Recorder Magazine, The 107, 180, 194
Recorder News 24
    reviews in 61, 63, 68, 75, 76, 78, 80,
    83, 270
Reizenstein, Franz 10, 82
    Partita 10–12, 46, 213, 244, 288, 291n
Reizenstein, Margaret 11–12
Revue moderne 232
Rhodes, Julian 179, 180n
Richards, Bernard 50, 58, 64, 70, 77, 81,
    85, 98, 173
Ridout, Alan 20, 310, 312
    Chamber Concerto (1956) 173, 174
    Chamber Concerto (1980) 173–7, 287
        analysis of 175
        composer's programme note for
            174
        correspondence in connection with
            174
        first performance, reviews of 176–7
        ornamentation in 305
    Concertante Music 175
    Concerto for treble recorder, strings and
        percussion 174
    Sequence 152–7
        composer's programme note for 154
        correspondence in connection with
            152–3, 154, 156
        first performance, review of 154

lute part, adaptation for keyboard of
    152, 156
sopranino recorder, use of in 156
Variants on a Tune of H.H. 208–12, 294
    analysis of 211
    composer's prefatory note on 209
    correspondence in connection with
        208, 209–10, 211
Rogers, Philip 70n, 242, 243, 247, 284
Rowher, Jens 307
Rowland-Jones, Anthony 63, 64
Royal Academy of Music, the 32
Royal Academy, Chamber Orchestra of the
    23
Royal College of Music (RCM), the 8, 12,
    13, 173
Royal Festival Hall Recital Room, the 268,
    271, 274
Royal Northern College of Music, the 69
Royaume de Musique 231
Rubbra, Edmund 19, 20, 82, 265, 287, 292,
    309
    Air and Variations Op. 70 272n
    Cantata Pastorale Op. 92 20, 55–8
        composer's programme note for 57
        correspondence in connection with
            56–7
        first performance, review of 57
    Fantasia on a Chord Op. 154 163–9,
        292
        composer's programme note for
            166
        correspondence in connection with
            163–4, 165–6, 167
        first performance, reviews of 166
        rhythmic structure, changes to
            167–8
        title, change of 164
    Fantasia on a Theme of Machaut Op. 86
        20, 50–53, 282, 292
        composer's programme note for
            52–3
        correspondence in connection with
            50–52
        first performance, reviews of 53
    Meditazioni sopra 'Cœurs désolés' Op.
        67 36–9, 50, 69, 237, 292, 304,
        307
        composer's performance of with
            Edgar Hunt 37
        composer's programme note for 38
        correspondence in connection with
            36, 37

first performance, reviews of 37–8
later performance, review of 38
Notturno Op. 106 265, 271–2
Passacaglia sopra 'Plusieurs regrets'
   Op. 113 78–81, 272, 292, 300
   composer's programme note for 79
   correspondence in connection with
      78–9, 80
   first performance, reviews of 80
Pezzo ostinato Op. 102 57n
Scott, Cyril, influence of 44
Sonatina Op. 128 94–8
   composer's programme note for 96
   correspondence in connection with
      94–5, 97
   first performance, reviews of 97
   published edition, review of 97–8
Rütti, Carl 310

St Andrews manuscript, *see* Wolfenbüttel manuscript
St Augustine manuscript, Canterbury 55, 57
Sala, Oskar 2
Salter, Lionel 23
   Air and Dance 22, 200–202, 293
   analysis of 201
   composer's programme note for 200
   first performance, review of 201
Sansom, Gillian 163
Sargent, Sir Malcolm 8
Saux, Gaston 146, 312
   Pour une églogue Virgilienne 213, 230–31
Saxby, Joseph 252, 259, 291
   ARP warden, service as 23, 28, 221
   Dolmetsch, Carl, first meeting and subsequent collaboration with 23
   first performances, participation in 24, 36, 44, 46, 48, 50, 54, 56, 75, 77, 78, 84, 87, 89, 94, 103, 107, 110, 113, 119, 122, 129, 136, 142, 147, 157, 163, 169, 177, 189, 195, 224, 236, 242, 247, 251, 252, 262
   'Improvisation' (for recorder solo) 225–6
   London Contemporary Music Centre, recital at 7
   performing scores, annotation of 25, 28, 48, 86, 92, 116, 177, 195, 223, 240, 291, 295
   public performance, virtual retirement from 211

Schoenfeld sisters, in ensemble with 20, 55, 91, 96, 110, 114, 182, 195
   Wigmore Hall, first recital at 19
Schoenfeld, Alice 20–21, 55, 85, 90, 95, 107, 114, 182, 195, 245
   first performances, participation in 89, 105–6, 107, 110, 113
Schoenfeld, Eleonore 20–21, 55, 85, 90, 95, 114, 182, 195, 245
   first performances, participation in 89, 105–6, 107, 110, 113
Schott & Co. Ltd 8, 10, 11, 17, 46, 94, 113, 146, 204–5, 247, 251
Schragenheim, Mrs 9, 14
scoring, new works of 20, 21–2, 213–14
Scotland, Tony 16n, 54n
Scott, Cyril 309
   Aubade 22, 44–6, 293, 295
   analysis of 45
   correspondence in connection with 45
   first performance, review of 45
Scott, Robert 174
Scottish Music Archive, the 224
Seiber, Mátyás 278
serialism 104, 105, 196, 197–8, 308
Serieninstrumente 301
Shaw, George Bernard 46
Shaw, Martin 292
   Sonata in E-flat 17, 219–22, 292
   analysis of 222
   correspondence in connection with 219–20, 221
   unpublished movement from 220
Sherman, Elna 231–2
Short, Michael 312
   Concert Music 190n
   Giocata 214, 262–3
   Les quatre vingts: fantasie sur le nom 'C.D.' 214
   Sinfonia 189–94
      composer's programme note for 191
      correspondence in connection with 189–91, 193, 194
      first performance, review of 193
      harpsichord, tuning, equal temperament, required for 190
      title, Dolmetsch's suggestion for 190
   Sonatina No. 1 252–4
   Sonatina No. 2 254
Shield, William 17n
Shinohara, Makoto 307
Sydney Morning Herald, the 103

Simar, León J. 241
Simpson, Angela 69
Simpson, Robert 19, 82, 137, 195, 277
   Variations and Fugue, 22, 64–70, 310
      analysis of 66–7
      composer's programme note for 66
      correspondence in connection with 65–6, 68
      first performance, reviews of 68
      manuscript parts, rediscovery of 69
      see also Horace Dann
Skeaping, Kenneth 61
Skene manuscript, the 269
Smith, Cyril 12
Smith, Fabienne 106
Smith, Martin 184
Smith, Melville 77
Society for the Promotion of New Music, the, see Committee for the Promotion of New Music
Society of Recorder Players (SRP), the 3, 81, 132, 202, 236, 261, 273, 300
Solomon, (Cutner, Solomon) 10
South East Arts 174
Southern Television 174
Spencer, Robert 152, 153, 160
Spenser, Edmund 169, 170
Stadlmair, Hans 311–12
Stainer and Bell 230
Star, The, review in 55
Steaps, Hans Ulrich 295, 307
Stevens, Dennis 269
Stilwell, John 189, 195
Stone, David 98
Strange, David 137
Strauss, Richard 83
Stravinsky, Igor 54
sustaining device, see harpsichord
Swain, Freda 12
Swann, Donald
   Rhapsody from Within 177–80
      composer's programme note for 178
      correspondence in connection with 177–8, 179
      first performance, review of 179, 294
      keyboard part, harpsichord or piano, for 179

Tarasov, Nikolaj 1
Taylor, Lily 270, 274
Telemann, Georg Philipp 286, 287, 289
Temprement, Jean 233n

Le charmeur de serpents 232
Suite exotique 213, 232–4
   analysis of 233–4
'Terpander', see Jacobs, Manuel
Times, The, reviews in 27–8, 33, 37–8, 43, 45, 47, 48, 53, 54–5, 57, 60, 68, 76, 80, 83, 86, 88, 97, 100, 104, 106, 108–9, 111, 141–2
Tippett, Sir Michael 173
Tomalin, Myles 3
tone projector 301, 303
Trifles, see Jacob, Gordon
Turmel, François 206
Turner, John 16, 17n, 69, 93, 100, 232, 240, 256, 271, 310, 313
   performances and recordings by 14, 69, 101, 107, 156n, 239, 310
twelve-tone technique, see serial technique
Tyson, John 78

United States, Dolmetsch tours of 19, 55, 73, 77, 90, 94–5, 105, 112, 114, 115, 118, 147, 218n, 243, 245, 248, 254
Universal Edition Ltd 246, 259, 265, 269, 273
Uppingham School 12

Valasco Llanos, Santiago
   Homenage a J.S. Bach (Fuga doble) 213, 261–2
   Romanza 213, 260–61
Vaughan Williams, Ralph 8, 10, 13
Vazquez, Juan 94n, 96
Vetter, Michael 307
vibrato 304
viol 156, 167, 233n
viola da gamba 22, 157, 159, 163, 164, 165, 166, 169, 254
viola d'amore 14
Vittet-Philippe, Patrick 206
Vivaldi, Antonio 241

Waddell, Helen 55, 57
Waldegrave Hall, the 132, 236
Walsworth, Ivor 224–5
Wandrausch, Mary 258n
'Warships Week' 218
Welch, Christopher 1
Welsh, Moray 106
Werder, Felix 239–40
West Midlands Arts 262
Westham (Adult Residential) College 210, 262

Westrup, Sir Jack 5, 7, 24
Wilson, Thomas 137
Winters, Leslie 236, 237, 238
Winters, Ross 39, 69, 180, 236, 239, 251, 307–8, 309
Wolf, Ilse 56
Wolfenbüttel manuscript 269
Wood, Christopher 26, 28, 215, 221, 291
   Concertante in E Op. 50 216
   French Suite 216–17
   Sonata di camera Op. 18 215, 292
Wordsworth, William 222–4
World War II 8, 28, 202

Zahnhausen, Markus 311
Zeitschrift für Spielmusik 3
Zurfluh, August 231